Reclaiming Democracy

Multicultural Educators' Journeys Toward Transformative Teaching

Jaime J. Romo
University of San Diego

Paula Bradfield
EDC, Inc.

Ramón Serrano
St. Cloud State University

PEARSON

Merrill
Prentice Hall

Upper Saddle River, New Jersey
Columbus, Ohio

Library of Congress Cataloging-in-Publication Data

Romo, Jaime J.
  Reclaiming democracy: multicultural educators' journeys toward transformative teaching/
Jaime J. Romo, Paula Bradfield, Ramón Serrano.—1st ed.
    p. cm.
  Includes bibliographical references.
  ISBN 0-13-094521-8
  1. Critical pedagogy—United States—Case studies. 2. Minorities—Education—United States—
Case studies. 3. Children with social disabilities—Education—United States—Case studies.
4. Multicultural education—United States—Case studies. I. Bradfield, Paula. II. Serrano, Ramón.
III. Title.
LC196.5. U6 R66 2003
370.11′5—dc21

2003009805

Vice President and Executive Publisher:
  Jeffrey W. Johnston
Executive Editor: Debra A. Stollenwerk
Editorial Assistant: Mary Morrill
Production Editor: Kris Robinson-Roach
Production Coordination: Karen Ettinger,
  The GTS Companies/York, PA Campus

Design Coordinator: Diane C. Lorenzo
Cover Designer: Mark Shumaker
Cover image: Superstock
Production Manager: Pamela D. Bennett
Director of Marketing: Ann Castel Davis
Marketing Manager: Darcy Betts Prybella
Marketing Coordinator: Tyra Poole

This book was set in Times Ten Roman by The GTS Companies/York, PA Campus. It was printed and
bound by R. R. Donnelley & Sons Company. The cover was printed by Coral Graphic Services, Inc.

Pearson Education Ltd.
Pearson Education Singapore Pte. Ltd.
Pearson Education Canada, Ltd.
Pearson Education—Japan

Pearson Education Australia Pty. Limited
Pearson Education North Asia Ltd.
Pearson Educación de Mexico, S.A. de C.V.
Pearson Education Malaysia Pte. Ltd.

10 9 8 7 6 5 4 3 2 1
ISBN: 0-13-094521-8

Contents

Foreword   vii

Jeannie Oakes and Martin Lipton, University of California, Los Angeles

Preface   x

Acknowledgments   xiv

Section

I

Immigration   1

INTRODUCTION
Themes of Immigrants Advancing Democracy   1

Paula Bradfield, EDC Inc., Chicago and Jaime J. Romo, University of San Diego, San Diego

CHAPTER 1
Voice of the Heart: Storytelling and the Journey of Advocacy   7

Juanita Santos Nacu, University of California, San Diego

CHAPTER 2
My Ethnography   22

Henry Trueba, University of Texas, Austin

CHAPTER 3
From Gangs to Teaching: Transforming My Past to Help Others   35

Ramón Serrano, St. Cloud State University, St. Cloud

Section

II

Social Class   45

INTRODUCTION
Themes of Social Class—Intersecting "Haves" and "Have-Nots"   45

Paula Bradfield, EDC Inc., Chicago and Jaime J. Romo, University of San Diego, San Diego

CHAPTER 4
Letting Go and Breaking Loose: Struggling Toward
Transformative Teaching 51

Paula Bradfield, EDC Inc., Chicago

CHAPTER 5
Embracing My Cultural, Intellectual, and Spiritual Identities on
My Journey to Become a Transformative Teacher 70

Ramona Maile Cutri, Brigham Young University, Provo

CHAPTER 6
Universal Human Rights Begin Close to Home 85

Nancy P. Gallavan, University of Nevada, Las Vegas

CHAPTER 7
On Becoming a Transformative Teacher: What Should I Do?
How Should I Do It? And Why? 101

Linda F. Quinn, University of Nevada, Las Vegas

Section III

Racial and Ethnic Identity 117

INTRODUCTION
Themes of Power, Privilege, Race, and Identity 117

Paula Bradfield, EDC Inc., Chicago and Jaime J. Romo, University of San Diego, San Diego

CHAPTER 8
Understand Them All: Identity and Advocacy 123

María G. Ramírez, University of Nevada, Las Vegas

CHAPTER 9
Safe and Growing Out of the Box: Immersion for Social Change 147

Jean Moule, Oregon State University, Corvallis

CHAPTER 10
Immersion and Rebellion: Growing Up and Out of South Carolina 172

Robin Hasslen, St. Cloud State University, St. Cloud

CHAPTER 11
My Personal Journey—In Part 186

Bruce Romanish, Washington State University, Vancouver

CHAPTER 12
The Miseducation, Reeducation, and Transformation of a "White" Male Educator Working for Social Justice   197

Paul Spies, Metropolitan State University, Minneapolis

Section
IV

The Praxis of Culturally Relevant Teaching   215

INTRODUCTION
Themes Reflecting Critical Thought and Action–Praxis   215

Paula Bradfield, EDC Inc., Chicago and Jaime J. Romo, University of San Diego, San Diego

CHAPTER 13
Something That Won't Compute: A Journey of Adult Literacy   219

Frank E. Kazemek, St. Cloud State University, St. Cloud

CHAPTER 14
Turning Points: A Teacher's Journey   233

Monica T. Rodriguez, Columbia College, Chicago

CHAPTER 15
Small Schools: A Metaphor for Caring   242

Steven Strull, Center for Collaborative Education, Boston

CHAPTER 16
Woman Warrior Liberating the Oppressed and the Oppressor: Cultural Relevancy Through Narrative   258

Suzanne SooHoo, Chapman University, Orange

CHAPTER 17
Hurting, Healing, Helping: A Pedagogy of Identity, Recovery, and Voice   281

Jaime J. Romo, University of San Diego, San Diego

AFTERWORD
Struggles for Recognition and Redistribution   301

Patrick Shannon, Pennsylvania State University, University Park

NOTE: Every effort has been made to provide accurate and current Internet information in this book. However, the Internet and information posted on it are constantly changing, it is inevitable that some of the Internet addresses listed in this textbook will change.

EDUCATOR LEARNING CENTER: AN INVALUABLE ONLINE RESOURCE

Merrill Education and the Association for Supervision and Curriculum Development (ASCD) invite you to take advantage of a new online resource, one that provides access to the top research and proven strategies associated with ASCD and Merrill—the Educator Learning Center. At **www.EducatorLearningCenter.com** you will find resources that will enhance your students' understanding of course topics and of current educational issues, in addition to being invaluable for further research.

How the Educator Learning Center will help your students become better teachers
With the combined resources of Merrill Education and ASCD, you and your students will find a wealth of tools and materials to better prepare them for the classroom.

Research

- More than 600 articles from the ASCD journal Educational Leadership discuss everyday issues faced by practicing teachers.
- A direct link on the site to Research Navigator™ gives students access to many of the leading education journals, as well as extensive content detailing the research process.
- Excerpts from Merrill Education texts give your students insights on important topics of instructional methods, diverse populations, assessment, classroom management, technology, and refining classroom practice.

Classroom Practice

- Hundreds of lesson plans and teaching strategies are categorized by content area and age range.
- Case studies and classroom video footage provide virtual field experience for student reflection.
- Computer simulations and other electronic tools keep your students abreast of today's classrooms and current technologies.

Look into the value of Educator Learning Center yourself
Preview the value of this educational environment by visiting **www.EducatorLearningCenter.com** and clicking on "Demo." For a free 4-month subscription to the Educator Learning Center in conjunction with this text, simply contact your Merrill/Prentice Hall sales representative.

Foreword

At the beginning of the 20th century, W. E. B. DuBois wrote, "The problem of the twentieth century is the problem of the color line." DuBois devoted his energy and intellect to the struggle for legal and political responses to racism. But DuBois also knew that addressing the educational and social needs of children of color requires something more than the political and technical arguments offered as school reform or, even more expansively, social change. In his 1935 article "Does the Negro Need Separate Schools?" DuBois offered a normative argument—a plea to those who have committed their lives to teaching. As much as children of color need desegregated schools, they also need relationships and understanding from teachers who can reach through the color line:

> The proper education of any people includes *sympathetic touch* between teacher and pupil; knowledge on the part of the teacher, not simply of the individual taught, but of his surroundings and background, and the history of his class and group; such contact between pupils, and between teacher and pupil, on the basis of perfect social equality, as will increase this sympathy and knowledge.[1]

(Emphasis added)

DuBois's idea of the *sympathetic touch* refers to the knowing, caring, and respectful learning relationships that multicultural schools and teachers must achieve. Educators must come to know those for whom they care, and they must build upon that understanding with actions that credibly demonstrate that they have understood. DuBois implored educators to embrace those for whom they care as growing persons with a future. It is not enough just to ask, "Who are we?" or "Where have we been?" We must also ask, "What will become of us in a future we share?"

At the beginning of the 21st century, the color line remains deeply etched across American culture and schools, even as a majority of American schoolchildren will soon be nonwhite. Multiculturalism is simply a demographic fact. Teaching only those students who share a teacher's or a community's background is neither desirable nor likely to happen. And teaching diverse groups of students only from a teacher's or a community's perspective (as if all shared the same past) is unacceptable. For American teachers, *multicultural* cannot be just a lesson, a curriculum, a teaching style, or a philosophy. In the 21st century, nonwhite and immigrant voices and languages will be heard or ignored, honored or derided, but they will not be silenced or assimilated out of existence.

---

[1] W. E. B. DuBois, 1935, "Does the Negro Need Separate Schools?" *The Journal of Negro Education,* 4(3), 328.

Teaching is a cultural activity, but not in the limited way that critics demean "cultural" by calling it political correctness. Most teachers of color and teachers for whom English is not their first language have had extensive experience with white, middle-class, mainstream culture as well as their own racial, ethnic, or language group. White teachers are more likely to be monocultural. But whether teachers are monocultural, bicultural, or multicultural, there are both generic and specific knowledge and skills they all must acquire. Unfortunately, teacher education that is dominated by modernist, enlightenment perspectives seeks to rip culture from skills, "background" from craft. A teacher's cultural assets too often are seen as "added value," somehow distinct from core classroom practices such as organizing a math lesson or designing writing experiences. When the great singer and actor Paul Robeson performed in *Othello,* he criticized the director for not coaching and guiding his acting—the director having believed that people of color could have talent but would not benefit from careful instruction.

Yet, today teacher education is changing—if not fast enough. Across the country, teacher education programs are seeking ways to bring history and knowledge, culture and craft, into a single core. Subject matter knowledge and subject-specific pedagogies are becoming infused with sociocultural and cultural historical learning theory, cultural and linguistic awareness, and methods for working in diverse classrooms. These are technical challenges—that is, challenges to "method" and program design—that are daunting but slowly being embraced by teacher education programs.

In our book *Teaching to Change the World,* we defined a social justice perspective on education as one that does three things:

1. It considers the values and politics that pervade education, as well as the more technical issues of teaching and organizing schools.
2. It asks critical questions about how conventional thinking and practice came to be and who in society benefits from them.
3. It pays particular attention to inequalities associated with race, social class, language, gender, and other social categories, and looks for alternatives to the inequalities.

We argued that a hopeful, democratic future depends on whether *all* students learn and experience academic rigor and social justice in school. If good teaching and rigorous academic achievement do not reach every student in every class, we lock out the possibility of both social justice and excellence, even for a few. If only a few students have such, there is no hope for our democracy. From this analysis, it is clear that enacting social justice in and through schools requires contentious political leveraging, careful technical innovation, and shifts in norms, beliefs, and values. Yet, social justice can easily remain a compelling theory—words upon words, ideas chasing ideas, colleagues scrutinizing colleagues. Social justice needs the flesh and blood of narrative: stories—demonstrations of lives and memories that reflect a living rather than a theoretical context for sympathetic touch. Without a sympathetic touch, teachers may be professionally competent and politically progressive, but they are not likely to be genuinely educative for diverse Americans.[2]

---

[2] Oakes, J., & Lipton, M. (2002). *Teaching to Change the World* (2nd ed.). New York: McGraw-Hill.

Making choices on behalf of children and social justice requires personal qualities of integrity, decency, and the capacity to work very hard. We find these qualities in abundance in people who choose to be teachers. Yet, without the deeply personal understandings such as those conveyed in the stories that follow, teachers are unlikely to connect in caring and sympathetic ways. By eliciting their students' transformative stories while sharing their own, teachers can act with knowledge and care in their lessons and relationships. Here is how a UCLA teacher graduate linked theory, action, and transformation:

> As a teacher, I must question everything I do. All my classroom practices must be open to a critical examination. How do issues of race, class, language, and gender influence what I do? How does my classroom resist and perpetuate the institutional, racism, classism, linguicism, and sexism of education and society? I must ask myself who benefits from the structure of my class. Yet with this awareness must also come action. I must commit myself to multiculturalism and a culturally relevant pedagogy that affirms and legitimizes the language and culture of my students. I must try to create a democratic classroom, where students actively construct their own knowledge. Finally, I must be a teacher who helps students discover their possibilities and urges them to claim their role as transformative members of society.

> Matthew Eide
> *First-year teacher, high school history*
> *Los Angeles, California*[3]

What better way to "[legitimize] the language and culture of . . . students" than through stories such as those that follow—stories that bring a sympathetic touch to life. These 17 often moving personal narratives expose in the most human terms, surroundings and background, and the "history of [their] class and group." Both the stories and the educators are at once exceptional and ordinary—exceptional in their unique telling, in their transformations, and in their underlying courage, but ordinary in that our classrooms and teacher education programs are filled with children and adults with comparable life experiences and who are undergoing comparable transformations. What those students and teacher candidates may lack is both their own and others' recognition of the deep moral and educative value of their stories. They may lack listeners with a sympathetic touch.

Jeannie Oakes and Martin Lipton
University of California, Los Angeles

---

[3] As quoted in *Teaching to Change the World* (2nd ed.).

Preface

Reclaiming Democracy: Multicultural Educators' Journeys Toward Transformative Teaching represents a break from the more traditional expository text on democratic teaching techniques or methods. Instead, it examines the lives of educators who have struggled *in the everyday* to advocate for *all* students in their ongoing efforts to provide more equitable access to meaningful, challenging educational opportunities. In doing so, they have become aware of their own identities, strengths, and biases, and have spent a lifetime reconstructing their own framework of teaching and learning toward these aims. This book will help preservice and in-service teachers answer the questions: What is a transformative teacher—one who is committed to advocating for all students? Where do I begin? What is the process?

The process of becoming democratic or transformative teachers is mystifying, and we do not generally help our students deconstruct the stories of others to identify the critical incidents and people who have guided their personal growth in a direction that is more socially just. This book does just that. It contains the narratives of teachers who have made a life commitment to advocating for all students. The narratives demystify the journeys—they are filled with barriers, biases that needed to be overcome, fears, and ongoing critical self-analysis pertaining to the development of their personal and professional identity. They help the reader understand how they have acknowledged and struggled to overcome their privilege, their prejudice, and their personal experiences either as perpetuators or recipients of the many "isms" that flourish in our society.

Reclaiming Democracy is unique because it parallels many of the major topics in multicultural education and teacher education through the voices of teachers who have lived the experiences—immigration, social class, racism, gender bias, and white privilege, to name a few. It makes these topics more than methods, more than theories. They become real for beginning teachers as they see how other teachers have experienced them.

Finally, this book is unique because it is based upon hope, that is, optimism with a memory. Every author has remained a *hopemonger,* one who persists in her or his dreams for all students and uses an eclectic array of strategies to continue to grow and to advocate for students.

RATIONALE

Upon examining the literature on teachers and change, we see two alarming facts. First, the overwhelming majority of teachers continue to be white or European American and tend to teach in the way that they learn. Consequently, they are least able or willing to teach students whose culture, gender, sexual orientation, first language, and social class are different from their own. This gives an advantage to the privileged European American students who are middle class and higher, and continues to marginalize the other students. A crisis is looming: While we have classrooms with diminishing numbers of students who are European American, the majority of teachers are still European American. Many teachers misunderstand, fear, mis-serve, or ignore the growing minority-majority population in many states and cities, as if all students are the same or are like the teacher. We urgently need more teachers who realize this crisis and will commit to the uncomfortable task of becoming aware of and then reconstructing their own identities to become more inclusive—that is, more socially just. We need teachers who are willing to move past guilt, blame, anger, apathy, and hopelessness to persist in their work in schools and to commit to building collaborations and networks with diverse others in both the school and community to create more equitable schools and classrooms.

Our extensive experiences in elementary, middle, and secondary schools and in higher education working with preservice and in-service teachers have made us realize that this type of book is critical if we expect our teachers and other school personnel to individually and collectively commit to and work toward a caring, safe, democratic school environment.

ORGANIZATION

Foreword

Nationally respected scholars Jeannie Oakes and Martin Lipton introduce the text with their discussion of how transformative teaching can change the world.

Preface

In a context of increasing standardization of curriculum and assessment, transformative teachers construct powerful learning and teaching opportunities. We encourage readers to take an active role in transformative educational practice and reform policy.

Section I: Immigration

We intentionally designated Immigration as Section I. So often, issues surrounding the plight of first- and second-generation immigrant families are ignored. The introduction, "Themes of Immigrants Advancing Democracy," addresses many of the issues immigrant students face and what some schools are doing to help make schools and classrooms more inviting and culturally validating for them. Juanita Santos Nacu, in "Voice of the Heart: Storytelling and the Journey of Advocacy," shares her transformative journey from advocacy for her own and her children's cultural identities to advocacy for other children's cultural identities. Henry Trueba, in his chapter entitled "My Ethnography," adds an intimate synthesis of personal narrative and research methodology. Finally, Ramón Serrano, in "From Gangs to Teaching: Transforming My Past to Help Others," relates his life in Brooklyn and Puerto Rico and the critical experiences that brought him to transformative teaching.

Section II: Social Class

In the introduction "Themes of Social Class—Intersecting 'Haves' and 'Have-Nots'," the authors explore broad issues dealing with social class, privilege, and poverty, illustrating what some schools and individuals are doing to overcome and transform the violence of poverty. In "Letting Go and Breaking Loose: Struggling Toward Transformative Teaching," Paula Bradfield relates her journey of being raised poor while acknowledging her white privilege. In "Embracing My Cultural, Intellectual, and Spiritual Identities on My Journey to Become a Transformative Teacher," Ramona Maile Cutri combines poverty and biracial identity with her spirituality as she narrates her growth toward transformative teaching. Both Nancy Gallavan in "Universal Human Rights Begin Close to Home" and Linda F. Quinn in "On Becoming a Transformative Teacher: What Should I Do? How Should I Do It? And Why?" reflect on how they became committed advocates for all children while being raised in middle- and upper-class neighborhoods.

Section III: Racial and Ethnic Identity

In the introduction "Themes of Power, Privilege, Race, and Identity," Paula Bradfield and Jaime J. Romo provide an overview of some of the educational issues surrounding these themes with illustrations of what seems to be working in some schools and classrooms. María Ramírez, in "Understand Them All: Identity and Advocacy," then speaks from her experience as a Chicana who has moved through the pain of personal and institutional racism in her commitment to advocate for all children. Jean Moule, in "Safe and Growing Out of the Box: Immersion for Social Change," speaks to readers from an African American female teacher's voice. In "Immersion and Rebellion: Growing Up and Out of South Carolina," Robin Hasslen engages in a frank discussion of her privilege and white racism and how she reconstructed her identity to one that is more caring, democratic, and inclusive. Bruce Romanish, in "My Personal Journey—In Part," narrates his story of working-class origins and articulates his struggles to overcome sexism in his journey as a democratic teacher. Finally, Paul Spies poignantly speaks from the voice of a white middle-class male who has owned and then disowned his own privilege and racism in "The Miseducation, Reeducation, and Transformation of a 'White' Male Educator Working for Social Justice."

Section IV: The Praxis of Culturally Relevant Teaching

In the introduction "Themes Reflecting Critical Thought and Action—Praxis," Paula Bradfield and Jaime J. Romo provide an overview of culturally relevant teaching—or teaching and advocating for all children in a culturally validating manner. Frank Kazemek, a poet and teacher, uses metaphor and prose in "Something That Won't Compute: A Journey of Adult Literacy" as he shares his successes and failures while teaching in Chicago schools. Monica T. Rodriguez writes about critical incidents in her experience in alternative schools and the small school movement in Chicago in her work, "Turning Points: A Teacher's Journey." Steven Strull, in "Small Schools: A Metaphor for Caring," speaks from the voice of a high school teacher in a reconstituted school in Chicago and describes his work in school reform. In "Woman

Warrior Liberating the Oppressed and the Oppressor: Cultural Relevancy Through Narrative," Suzanne SooHoo eloquently narrates her story as an Asian-American woman living and growing in a world dominated by white men. Jaime J. Romo concludes this section with his reflection on his recovery and development of personal and professional voice in "Hurting, Healing, Helping: A Pedagogy of Identity, Recovery, and Voice."

Afterword

In the concluding chapter, Patrick Shannon states that "reading these stories is like sitting around with good friends." He ties the themes together in "Struggles for Recognition and Redistribution."

FORMAT

Reclaiming Democracy provides readers with many helpful pedagogical features. The beginning of each section introduces the reader to some of the major theoretical issues that are alluded to in the narratives. In each chapter, focus questions pull out major themes for that section. At the end of each chapter, the reader will find chapter references, journal or reflection questions, activities for the college classroom and/or for the K–12 classroom, further reading, and chapter-related Web sites.

FEATURES

Reclaiming Democracy models the integration of theory and practice, concrete K–12 applications, and current/leading-edge research and resources. The authors provide narratives that combine theory with their own developmental experiences towards operationalizing teaching for social justice and multicultural competency development. Readers will be able to deconstruct the stories' topics such as immigration, social class, racism, gender, and white privilege as successful advocates have experienced them, so as to facilitate the reader's own personal growth in a direction that is more socially just.

Acknowledgments

First, we would like to thank the authors who have contributed to *Reclaiming Democracy.* Through their stories, we have been able to demystify the journeys of teachers who are committed to democratic teaching.

We also would like to thank our families and friends who have supported us, and our students who gave us many of the insights that inspired us to write this book. We would also like to thank Bill Ayers for encouraging us with the initial idea.

We are grateful to Debbie Stollenwerk, our executive editor at Merrill/Prentice Hall, whose advice and support have been invaluable, and others who have been involved in the production and development of this book. We would like to thank the reviewers who provided invaluable comments and suggestions. They are Violet Allain, James Madison University; Mary Lou Brotherson, Nova Southeastern University; Al R. Cade, Missouri Southern State College; Gail A. Cueto, Central Connecticut State University; Beatrice Fennimore, Indiana University of Pennsylvania; Bob Gustafson, Central Florida University; Susan Hahn, St. Mary's College of California; JoAnn Hohenbrink, Ohio Dominican University; and Ann Whitaker, Northeastern Illinois University.

 *Section* I

Immigration

Introduction:
Themes of Immigrants
Advancing Democracy

Paula Bradfield, EDC Inc., Chicago and Jaime J. Romo,
University of San Diego, San Diego

*Bob argued . . . I am still struggling with what you are telling
me about immigration. Why are immigrants nowadays sticking to themselves? Why can't they just blend in like everyone
else did? My grandfather came here from Europe, had to give
up his language and culture but he made it! Isn't that how
America came to be?*

*"Give me your tired, your poor,
Your huddled masses yearning to breathe free,
The wretched refuse of your teeming shores.*

Send these, the homeless, tempest-tossed, to me,
I lift my lamp beside the golden door."

(Written on the Statue of Liberty)
(Emma Lazarus, "The New Colossus," 1883)

Cha paused, gazed out the window at the falling snow and then quietly but resolutely
responded to his cooperating teacher with a sigh, "Yes, Bob, but you see, you are
white and I am brown. I can never 'lose' my culture. I wear it everyday—my culture
is my skin color."

America has power, but not justice.
In prison, we were victimized as if we were guilty.
Given no opportunity to explain, it was really brutal.
I bow my head in reflection but there is nothing I can do.

(Written by three high school students, Him Mark Lai, Genny Lim, and Judy Yung)

These quotes reflect the ongoing cacophony and contradiction of our collective understanding and valuation of immigrants. On one hand, we enshrine our immigrant roots, yet on the other, we reject current newcomers in covert ways reminiscent of our xenophobic heritage.

The United States, the ancestral home of American Indians, has been a nation of immigrants for centuries. Up to the 1940s, immigrants predominantly originated in Europe, using their fair skin as their passport for belonging. It allowed them the privilege of "losing their culture and first language" and "pulling themselves up by their bootstraps" (Nieto, 1999).

Over the past several decades, however, immigration patterns have changed dramatically. The wave of immigrants from Europe has diminished, and increasing numbers are coming from areas such as Korea, Vietnam, China, India, Philippines, Somalia, Laos, Mexico, and Central America, areas in which the dominant culture is more collective[1] and the immigrants are not able to "pass for white." According to the 2000 census, by the turn of the century, nearly 20% of all schoolchildren will be considered limited-English-proficient (LEP) and will be living in non-English-language homes. The United States has approximately 30 million Latinos, making it the fifth-largest Hispanic country in the world. At present, one out of every three people in the United States speaks Spanish as their first language. Teachers, the majority of whom have ancestral roots in Europe, are often surprised when they hear of discrimination and exclusionary issues facing recent immigrants (Nieto, 1999; Takaki, 1998). Due to education courses and the media, most teachers have been sensitized to issues facing marginalized U.S. groups such as Chicanos, Native

---

[1]Collective cultures generally put the family and community before the individual, are more cooperative than competitive, and have a stronger, more hierarchical social structure (e.g., Latino, American Indian, and Asian cultures). Individualistic cultures put the individual before family and community, are generally more competitive than cooperative, and have a more informal social structure.

Americans, Asian Americans and African Americans. Unfortunately, immigrant issues are virtually invisible to them, as can be seen by Bob's question: Why can't current immigrants just "become American" like we had to? They are not aware of changing immigration patterns nor the current movement of exclusionary immigration policies until they begin examining the question, Are current immigration laws and school policies structured in a way that favors those who can pass for white?

As immigration patterns shift, our federal and state laws regarding immigration also change. Until the early 1990s, federal aid and laws provided support for teacher training, books, study aids, and other instructional expenses for immigrant students. Since that time, congress has cut federal funding for immigrants' education by about 50% while the number of immigrant students has increased by nearly 50% and is still increasing. Recent laws such as the Illegal Immigration Reform and Immigrant Responsibility Act (P. L. 104–208), authorize rejection of due process protection for deportation, allow national registries to be created to track the employment of illegal immigrants, and authorize the summary rejection of arriving asylum seekers and international travelers.

A growing number of states are also passing legislation that impacts immigrants (Lacey, 1996; Rethinking Schools Online, 2000). In California, voters passed Proposition 187, denying illegal immigrants access to education. Fortunately, the federal district courts decreed that the proposition violates the U.S. Supreme Court decision in *Plyler v. Doe*—a case that allows undocumented children who are not legal residents of the United States the right to receive free public K–12 education.

The English-only movement is gaining momentum throughout the country. To illustrate, Oregon, California, Washington, and Arizona have recently passed a flurry of English-only laws. Newspapers and radio talk show programs frequently air public sentiment that equates patriotism and English-only use—the use of languages other than English is attacked as being divisive. Meanwhile, immigrants continue to spend years and thousands of dollars attempting to obtain entry to the United States or to procure their green card and master English.

Schools also maintain educational policies and practices that make successful educational experiences difficult to access for many immigrants (e.g., Miller & Tanners, 1995; Noguera, 1999b). School communities generally reinforce an assimilationist rather than a multicultural view of their role with immigrant students. Such environments frame current immigrants of color as outsiders in the European American school community. In addition, immigrants of color, who are often arbitrarily clumped into U.S. racial categories despite their nation of origin, often suffer the accompanying racism attached to that group (Commins, 1992). Consequently, students are ostracized by the European American community, and they often experience rejection by their own community members. Xiaojun (or Debbie, in her English-dominant classes; Takaki, 1998), illustrates this for us with her words:

> But of course I am not ABC, an American-born Chinese. The ABCs sometimes curse
> at us and call me and my friends FOB's, "fresh off the boat." I don't like that. I turn my
> eyes away. (p. 66)

Many scholars argue that we have a one-generation window of opportunity to meet the needs of the current population of immigrants (Ogbu, 1992; Trueba, 1993). They contend that involuntary minorities, those who were either born in the United States or who did not voluntarily migrate to the United States, have a different perspective of education in the United States. That perspective has fundamentally changed since the first generation of immigrants because of encountered racism, inequitable opportunity, and an apathetic or even hostile school environment.

Wittingly or unwittingly, schools act as transmitters and preservers of the dominant culture (European American), even in schools whose majority is not white (Books, 1994; Burkhart, 1997; Goode, 1997; Hickey, 1998). Schools become places requiring conformity to seemingly foreign ways, rather than places of opportunity and access. Many teachers, likewise, are likely to ask more complex questions, provide more praise, use a wider variety of strategies, provide more opportunities to learn, and positively evaluate students whose culture and first language are most like their own. Standardized tests reinforce on institutionalized levels the predictable misperceptions of what good students look or sound like. In short, immigrant students are generally "overlooked and underserved" (Ruiz-de-Velasco & Fix, 2000) both at the classroom and institutional level in pre-K–12 schools.

Few teacher education programs in the United States have changed their programs to adequately prepare teachers to accommodate their curriculum, instruction, and assessment to meet the needs of immigrant students from various backgrounds. Most programs require neither bilingual education nor English as a second language (ESL) course work of their teachers seeking licensure in mainstream classes. Consequently, many teachers are ill equipped to ensure that their limited-English-proficient (LEP) students will learn the content and be provided with a safe, challenging, and equitable learning environment. Rather than accept the blame for the LEP students' lack of success, many teachers tend to "blame the victim"—by assuming that the students are less intelligent or less motivated than dominant culture students, even though immigrant students may be fluent in several languages and quite capable of learning content in their own language (Crawford, 1999; Williams, 1997).

Despite the seemingly hostile climate for most immigrants of color, isolated pockets of effective educational programs do exist where children flourish (e.g., Burkhart & Sheppard, 2001; Trueba, 1993). In such programs, schools systematically attempt to bridge the gap between immigrant students' homes and the school so that the transition is smoother. Teachers in these schools recognize and acknowledge the immigrant student's native culture and linguistic background and design a curriculum that meets the needs of specific immigrant student populations at their school. They use progressive methods and strategies that are relevant to the immigrant students' experiences, such as cooperative learning, culturally relevant pedagogy, scaffolded instruction, and content-based ESL strategies (Burkhart & Sheppard, 2001; Goldfarb, 1998). Unfortunately, these schools remain isolated pockets of resistance while the majority of immigrant students face a daunting task: negotiating their identities while developing a sense of belonging in their new environments and gaining equitable access to a challenging, meaningful education.

In the poem "Becoming American," Khalilah Joseph[2] poignantly sums up the issues facing immigrant children of color today:

> *I looked into the eyes of my*
> *Japanese doll*
> *And knew I could not surrender her*
> *to the fury of the fire.*
> *My mother threw out the poetry*
> *she loved;*
> *my brother gave the fire his sword.*
> *We worked hours*
> *to vanish any traces of the Asian world*
> *from our home.*
> *Who could ask us*
> *to destroy*
> *gifts from a world that molded*
> *and shaped us?*
> *If I ate hamburgers*
> *and apple pies,*
> *if I wore jeans,*
> *then would I be American?*

The following authors offer us their insights into the hidden and overt dynamics that children and adults from immigrant families experience at societal and educational levels. Their experiences range from apparently benign lower performance expectations or stereotypes from educational gatekeepers to direct communication that they are unwelcome or subordinate visitors. Their support networks—socioeconomic status, parents, and individual academic prowess—helped them persevere in often hostile, assimilationist, or rejecting environments. By maintaining their connection to their backgrounds, and committing to transform the environments in which they suffered into arenas of support for others who may be seen as outsiders and thereby underserved, these educators transform their classrooms and schools.

Juanita Santos Nacu, a San Diego expert in Filipino language and culture, uses storytelling as a vehicle for teaching and helping readers value the multiple languages and dimensions that students from immigrant families bring to our schools and to society. Henry Trueba, one of the nation's most respected researchers of linguistic, cultural, and anthropological educational research issues, shares a distinctly personal reflection on his immigrant experiences and their relationship to democratizing the higher educational

---

[2]Many of the student poems used in this article are printed in a literary magazine, *Rites of Passage*. The magazine may be purchased through the NECA catalogue or by contacting Jefferson High School, 5210 N. Kerby St., Portland, OR 97217.

academy. Finally, Ramón Serrano, professor at St. Cloud State University, relates his life in Brooklyn and Puerto Rico and the critical experiences that brought him to transformative teaching. While all three authors are outstanding in their educational achievements and contributions, their experiences begin to give the reader an insight into the dynamics that many immigrant children do not overcome and what K–12 educators can do to advance democracy with those students.

REFERENCES

Books, S. (1994). Blaming villains: Stories of displacement and disengagement. *Educational Foundations, 8*(3), 5–16.

Burkhart, C. L. (1997). What happened to the golden door? *Rethinking Schools, 11,* 1.

Burkart, G. S., & Sheppard, K. (2001). A descriptive study of content-ESL practices. ERIC Clearinghouse on Urban Education, Institute for Urban and Minority Education.

Commins, N. L. (1992). Parents and public schools: The experiences of four Mexican immigrant families. *Equity and Choice, 8*(2), 40–45.

Crawford, J. (1999). Bilingual education: History, politics, theory and practice. Los Angeles: Bilingual Educational Services.

Goldfarb, K. P. (1998). Creating sanctuaries for Latino immigrant families. *The Journal for a Just and Caring Education, 4,* 454–466.

Goode, C. (1997). From our readers: The failure of education to deconstruct the American myth of success. *Equity & Excellence in Education, 30*(1), 82–84.

Hickey, M. G. (1998). "Back home, nobody'd do that": Immigrant Students and Cultural Models of Schooling. *Social Education, 62,* 442–447.

Him, M. L., Lim, G. & Yung, J. (1986). *Island: Poetry and history of Chinese immigrants on Angel Island 1910–1940.* San Francisco: HOC DOI.

Lacey, M. (1996, May 3). Senate approves broad assault on illegal immigration. *The Los Angeles Times,* pp. Al, A12.

Miller, L. P., & Tanners, L. A. (1995). Diversity and the new immigrants. *Teachers College Record, 96,* 671–680.

Nieto, S. (1999). *Affirming diversity: The sociopolitical context of multicultural education.* New York: Longman.

Noguera, P. (1999a). Confronting the challenge of diversity. *School Administrator, 56*(5), 16–18.

Noguera, P. A. (1999b). Crossing cultural borders: Education for immigrant families in America: Confronting the challenge of diversity. *School Administrator, 56*(5), 16–18.

Ogbu, J. (1992). Understanding cultural diversity. *Educational Researcher, 21*(8), 5–14.

Rethinking Schools Online. (2000). Bilingual education strike two: Arizona voters follow California's lead and mandate English-only programs. *Rethinking Schools,* (15), 2.

Ruiz-de-Velasco, J., & Fix, M. (2000). Overlooked & underserved: Immigrant students in U.S. secondary schools. Washington, DC: Urban Institute.

Takaki, R. (1998). *Strangers from a different shore: A history of Asian Americans.* New York: Viking Penguin.

Trueba, H. (1993). *Healing multicultural America: Mexican immigrants rise to power in rural California.* Washington, DC: Falmer.

Williams, G. M. (1997). *Challenging the political mirage of ESL and bilingual education: A study of public knowledge.* Paper presented at the annual meeting of the Teachers of English to Speakers of Other Languages, Orlando, FL.

Chapter 1

Voice of the Heart: Storytelling and the Journey of Advocacy

Juanita Santos Nacu, University of California, San Diego

Focus Questions

1. How do you think immigrants should treat or express their culture?

2. What would you do if you moved to another country and found that your prior training was not accepted? What can we learn from Juanita's story about her perseverance?

3. Since we all have our own stories, what is a story in your own family history that empowers you or helps you in your journey and identity development?

"What is more important than knowledge?" asked the mind.
"It is to come with your heart," said the soul.

Anonymous

STORYTELLING

According to Livo and Rietz (1986), storytelling is an art form, an ancient form, a ritualized and patterned act, an immediate experience, a negotiation, an entertainment, and a game. Storytelling is a means a person uses to express thoughts, feelings, and experiences in different ways—in oral form, gestures, songs, and literature—for the purpose of passing on traditions, preserving history, healing relationships, and building communities. Bellah, Madsen, Sullivan, Swidler, and Tipton (1985) coined the phrase "communities of memory," which calls for remembering and retelling stories of the past. It is a community that tells stories of success as well as failures, pains, and sufferings. Likewise, Rappaport (1993) saw narrative studies as a powerful analytical and methodological tool for those interested in the relationship between individual lives and the social processes of communities. The stories touch not only the past experiences, but also influence the present and link it to the future.

I will start with who I was, who I am, and who I am becoming. In telling my life story, I will explain the significance of the story for the reader, with the hope that it will provide insights for a learning experience and can be used for self-growth as well as for their students. I hope that the information that I will pass on to the reader can also help bridge the cultural gap that may exist with her or his Filipino American students and their parents.

The Storyteller

As the storyteller in this chapter, I bring my journey of becoming fully human. As I continually evolve into who I am, and as I grow, study, play, work, and acquire new relationships, different identities or roles come forth from my personhood, such as daughter, sister, friend, student, nurse, counselor, Catholic, wife, mother, and educator. I bring all these voices and lenses to this chapter and to my work as director of Project Heart to Heart, as a researcher, and as a teacher. The story develops as a potter molds the clay with nothing in mind to shape it into, but to allow it to take shape by itself. The clay needs someone or an event to help shape it again and again.

My story, the voice that comes from the heart, as it comes up to the surface from the depths of my inner being, groans in pain and agony of becoming; going through the darkness of the abyss like a fathomless depth of the ocean. So, I invite you to rise up to the surface of the vast ocean with my inner being, with the hope that in doing so, you will recognize a part of you, your own journey of becoming. I hope that in my story you will feel what I feel and understand what I am trying to say.

Finally, even though I manage, every now and then, to look at my life as a daily transformational experience, when asked to share specific transformative incidents that led me to "teaching to change the world" (Oakes & Lipton, 2002), I found it difficult to look back and select the appropriate incidents from more than half a century of life experiences, for I believe that becoming a transformative teacher starts way back at the time of conception.

I know it from experience. When my husband and I learned of my first pregnancy, after 7 years of waiting and hoping, we started to dream of what our child might become. We thought of what we could offer to our child, the best that we have. The same thing happened for our two other children, as we made a commitment to provide the best opportunities for them. Similarly, my journey started way back when I was conceived. However, I don't know when I consciously embraced the specific identity of a transformative teacher along my journey of becoming a whole person.

The Roots

When I came as an adult, professional immigrant to the United States, I left behind my family, people, and everything I grew up with. However, I took with me the roots of who I have become. My roots will forever be a part of me.

Significance: Students grow up with their immigrant parents, who pass on their values and way of life. Being informed of the students' cultural background will provide a better rounded individual approach in the classroom. Adult immigrants practice their cultural values more than their children born in the United States.

I came from the Republic of the Philippines, a country with less than 10% of the 7,000-odd islands inhabited. There are about 111 linguistic, cultural, and racial groups in the country. Besides Filipino as the national language, another 70 languages and dialects, all belonging to the Malayo-Polynesian family of tongues, are spoken in the country. Consequently, even though I speak two of the native languages, still I cannot understand those who communicate in the other languages, but I accept the limitation and condition, since it's a natural setting in my country of birth. This contributes also to acceptance of multiple cultural differences. It is not unusual to grow up in a town hearing different languages and witnessing, as well as participating in, different ethnic traditions.

At home, a harmonious family unit is a primary value. There is strong stress on interdependence and togetherness. Family is extended to relatives and trusted friends. In fact, it is not unusual to meet a relative wherever one goes. I have many memories of gathering with relatives, especially during fiestas, such as the birthday celebration of our patron saint, St. John the Baptist. The celebration starts a week before when fair rides, games, and street vendors set up in the plaza. On the actual feast day, we start with the mass, followed by a procession with the saint's statue. Two music bands lead practically the whole town, young and old with decorative hats and plant branches in their hands, dancing to the music. Along the route, others wait to douse the dancers with water, a practice signifying St. John as the baptizer of Jesus. Relatives arrive, days before the fiesta, from afar. It is just like an open house when anyone can come and partake in the feast.

Religion serves as a means to keep the Filipino family intact through their experience of religious traditions together. We celebrate religious traditions in such a way that it is often difficult to distinguish what is religious and what is social in major church celebrations. Our deep and personal faith is the very foundation of our values. Faith accompanied the Filipinos throughout our history, even before the Spaniards introduced the Christian religion in 1521. Pre-Hispanic Filipinos were animists: gods were worshipped through rituals, nature feasts, charms, and other symbols. Currently, the Philippines make up the only predominantly Christian nation in Asia. About 85% of the population is Roman Catholic, 3% is Protestant, 6% belong to indigenous Christian cults, and about 5% is Muslim (Chan, 1992, p. 266).

Filipinos are noted for their child-centeredness. Children are looked upon as blessings. Filipino families tend to be large, averaging five or more children. In my family, I am the fifth of nine children, five girls and four boys. My mother stayed home. Unlike other Asian groups, Filipino family authority is not patriarchal, but more egalitarian, where husband and wife share almost equally in financial and family decisions. I remember going to market in our town and traveling to nearby towns almost everyday with my mother, looking for the fresh catch of the day. Then she would cook several dishes at the same time. Our family dinner was like a daily celebration, a feast. The long dining table was filled with food and we, the children, had our assigned seats.

Besides making sure that we were all well fed, part of my mother's responsibility was to make sure that we went to church regularly. We were all baptized and confirmed in the Roman Catholic Church. At dusk, whatever my siblings and I were doing, we rushed home before Angelus (an evening devotion commemorating the Incarnation), when the church bells rung. Then, we prayed the rosary before our home altar, where we had the crucifix, a Blessed Mother statue, and icons. If we did not make it home, we stopped whatever we were doing and stood in silence with everyone else, including people in vehicles in the street, until the church bells stopped ringing.

I could not recall my late father being part of this particular family tradition. My father went to church only on Christmas day. His main responsibility was to support the family. He had his own medical practice. I tagged along on his numerous house calls. Most of his patients could not afford to pay, so they paid in kind with poultry and vegetables. Because he was the physician of the common people, they respected him and his family. I often witnessed his gentleness with his patients, his saving of lives, and his delivering of babies in homes where the whole neighborhood eagerly awaited the good news right at the doorstep.

When I was 5 years old, my father was kidnapped by guerillas to take care of their sick, including their commander. He lived their life in the mountains, always in danger of government army attacks, and moved constantly, lacking food, proper clothing, and shelter. After several months, he was one of the few released alive. After his release, my father's health was never the same. He died before his 52nd birthday.

I was 17 years old when my father died. His funeral had the largest attendance, with people from all walks of life. Even though he attended church only once a year, it did not matter. He lived his Christian life through his taking care of the medical needs of the poor. He touched many hearts and lives.

Later on, I found out that it wasn't his medical practice that provided for our needs but the acres of sugar plantation that he managed. However, after his death no one could manage the sugar plantation, the main source of income. My mother had to use the money my father established in individual savings accounts.

Fortunately for us, education is another important Filipino cultural value. Whether parents are rich or poor, their goal is to get the children to finish college. Education is considered an inheritance. Parents take pride in displaying school diplomas in their living rooms. Furthermore, offspring who finish college education are expected to support their brothers and sisters in return. This obligation is expected by the parents even when the offspring have their own families. Children are considered indebted to their parents for life because their parents gave life to them. As a result, my oldest sister took on the responsibility of getting me through college, fulfilling a promise she made to my father at his deathbed.

In his last days at the hospital, my father was moved to a private room. The hospital was located near my school, so I visited him everyday and sometimes would sleep in the chair in his room. On the day he died, when I woke up, I saw how he seemed to have been watching me for a while. Then, as the hours passed, he started getting restless and uttered words. In the presence of my oldest sister, my father called my name repeatedly. In tears, my sister assured my father not to worry, that she would take care of me. My father died before noon with me at his bedside.

Because of my father's example and my love for him, I thought of becoming a physician. But, knowing that I had a strong personality, I figured that I would end up an old maid or a missionary. In addition, in our culture, physicians are placed on pedestals. No man might dare to consider me as a spouse because of my profession.

So, I decided to earn a nursing degree and work in another service-oriented career. At least I would then have a chance of having my own family. This was the first of many decisions in which my family values affected my career path.

In my college freshman year, I made the women's volleyball varsity team. As a 16-year-old from a high school with less than 100 students in its graduating class, making it to the varsity team lessened my doubts about belonging to a prestigious university with over 1,000 students, representing the country's top 10%. I realized later on in life that being an athlete contributed to my philosophy of not giving up until I give it a try, however the odds against me may be. As underdogs in competitions, our team played against and beat better teams. In fact, in my first year with the team, our university won the regional championship for the first time.

It was not only athletics that helped me survive college life. As a little child, I began a practice of stopping by our church and saying a prayer on my way to and back from school. Somehow, the visits brought comfort to my young heart, a conviction that there was someone besides my family who loved me. In college, this practice turned into daily mass attendance and receiving Holy Eucharist in the campus chapel. In the physical absence of my family, spending time in the presence of a God I believe exists sustained my determination to finish college.

The Journey

Despite having some good foundations for survival, leaving my family and country for the United States to start a new life on my own in a different environment and culture really tested my determination to make it. The challenge continues today.

Significance: Longer stays in the adopted country of the United States provide opportunities for immigrants to change themselves for survival. However, changes need to take place in others, too. Living as a minority in a country with the need to start all over again puts tremendous stress on immigrant families. Parents with established jobs back home accept any work just to support their families. This causes instability in their families and affects their children's performance in school (e.g., failing to submit homework, which is usually a priority at home due to the cultural value of education).

For Filipino nurses, going to the United States is a common objective. On November 13, 1971, 2½ years after I finished my nursing degree, I arrived at the Los Angeles airport after a 16-hour flight from the Philippines. I was a 25-year-old, single, registered nurse without a job. I was excited but unsure of what awaited me in a foreign land. I left behind my country of birth, family, and friends, not knowing if I would ever go back again. I had $100, a loan from one of my classmates who worked on the East Coast, and all my belongings came in the largest luggage allowable for me to check on to the plane. They were all I had, plus the courage to start a new life so far away from home, across the ocean.

Right away, I found out that my professional nursing background did not qualify me to practice as a registered nurse. I had to pass the required nursing board exam, an exam which numerous foreign nurses had failed. Fortunately, I passed. It was the first awakening that I had to meet new standards and expectations before I could even practice my profession. In addition, being brown and Filipino made me stand out as someone different. Therefore, establishing trust and respect from my patients did not happen all the time. Sadly, this obstacle is not something I can erase or can make go away. On the other hand, I don't have any intention of giving up my Filipino culture. I continue to share it with pride in every opportunity I can. However, to this day, I am reminded daily where I belong as a member of a subordinate culture. But that's based on the dominant culture's definition of how different cultures are divided. For me, there is no division, only a normal existence of different cultures, none better than the other. The difference actually enhances what we can offer to further enrich the other culture. The more we are willing to know about and to adapt to each other's way of life, the better we can understand, appreciate, and live harmoniously together.

JOURNEY: FAMILY IDENTITY

Filipino strong family identity and love for children put an expectation on newly married couples of having children right away. Children are considered blessings from God. They bring pride and joy to the whole family. Taking care of the children is a high priority.

Opportunities to work and to provide for the family cause a dilemma for mothers, who assume the responsibility of caring for their children. Family comes first, but if you can earn money to provide for your children's future education, physical needs, and comfort, leaving the children to baby-sitters may not be a bad option.

Significance: Both parents often work multiple jobs, and are thus not available to supervise their children's homework and to participate in school activities. Providing for extended families here and back in the Philippines adds to financial need. Filipino family members are very interdependent; the higher you are in the family hierarchy, the more obligation there is to take care of the younger members, even at young ages, even extending to their family members.

As expected, upon arrival in Los Angeles, I stayed with my older sister, another nurse, who left for Canada when I was only 17 years old. I was so homesick that in 6 months after my arrival, I got married to Florentino, another Filipino professional immigrant and an engineer. As a couple, it took 7 years of waiting, praying (even drinking holy water), and medical procedures before we had our firstborn, John Joseph. Then, to our surprise, after 16 months, our son was followed by the birth of our daughter, Hannah Teresa. When they were ages 2 and 3, a baby born to a good friend fascinated them. This led to daily prayer on their knees in front of our home altar, a table with a picture of Jesus and lit candles, located in the living room. Every night they could not make up their minds whether to pray for a brother, a sister, or even twins.

On December 21, 1983, God answered their prayers. Our third child, Paul Nathan, was born. My husband read the name in the newspaper and liked it. Later on, I found out its meaning from the hospital's book of names—"little gift." On Christmas Eve, we came home with him inside a huge stocking, provided by the hospital staff. The "little gift" came home in time for Christmas for John Joseph, Hannah, Florentino, and myself.

Before I became a mother, I worked as an emergency room nurse. In 1978, we moved to San Diego due to a change of job for my husband. It was in San Diego, after 7 years as a couple, when my husband and I became the parents of three healthy children in 5 years. Within those years, I gradually gave up my working hours with the belief that I, as their mother and not a baby-sitter, am their primary caregiver. With my husband's blessing, I finally gave up my nursing career in 1984. Even though it had been my longtime dream of having my own family, I still went through agony in choosing between the professional and homemaker careers.

As a professional, I receive a paycheck for my work. As a homemaker, there is no paycheck. A homemaker's career does not have a monetary value. At a hospital, I make sure that my work is done before the next shift's arrival. There is a sense of closure, of accomplishment, witnessed by my coworkers. As a homemaker, I seem not to accomplish anything; tasks are unfinished all around the house. I have a degree in nursing, but not a degree in mothering children. As a mother, I learned unknown, unpredictable, mentally and physically demanding work on the job 24 hours a day, not on an 8-hour shift. On the job, I work and interact with other professionals and adults. At home, I interact with my young and growing children. I had to choose between two very different worlds.

It took over 2 years of on-and-off regrets and anguish over my decision to stay home before I finally realized that I had made the right choice: motherhood over professional career, priceless memories over money and financial stability. Nowhere can I buy the joy and love I felt those years: cuddling my babies, hearing their laughter, being needed and the center of their life, discovering, seeing, and experiencing a new world I could not recall as a child. I have watched them peacefully asleep and have stood in awe of how much love I am capable of giving. The older they grow, the more I appreciate the value of those limited early years of their lives, a time I could have missed if I had chosen to work instead of being there for my children in their formative years. Motherhood is a gift. Not every woman is called to be a mother. It is a calling. If I were not a mother, I would not be the person I am today, because, for every decision that I make, the first question I ask is, How will this benefit my children and family?

K–12 JOURNEY

Culturally, parents entrust their children to the teachers because everyone knows each other in the community. Growing up, I could not recall my parents helping in school.

Significance: I believe this is a major reason why parents don't volunteer at school or are less involved in school activities. Asking for help in classroom activities, especially sharing Filipino ways of life (cooking, regional festivals, native attire, and cottage industries) could encourage them and build their confidence to share what they have. Participation, in turn, will inform them of the need for active involvement in school.

Multiple opportunities of becoming and developing my potentials came with the privileges of being a full-time mother. Involvement in school, church, and the community came about for different reasons. My involvement in school began when I found out that someone had assigned my son to an English as a second language class without our permission. The reason we were given was that we filled out a questionnaire noting that our native Filipino language is spoken at home. He was pulled out of the class after we complained. However, it happened again with Hannah the following year. As a result of those experiences, I decided to become a PTA volunteer. I discovered how little many parents knew about each other's culture, especially those of the minority. Consequently, we developed and implemented the then-first annual Multicultural Fair at the elementary school level in our district. Being a parent volunteer, I informed others that even though I am a Filipino American who speaks a different language (Tagalog) and comes from another country, I am capable of doing what others can do and even effectively fulfilling the role of leadership.

My school involvement helped school administrators and staff learn about my culture and overcome some misconceptions about inequality in capabilities. Consequently, I saw expectation levels of what other parents could do raised, and increased interest in learning more about other cultures. In addition, the administrative staff implemented more approaches to personal communication, such as attempts to meet the parents in person and as a cultural group. There was a recognition and acceptance of differences in our way of life, which did not mean inferiority, just difference.

As of this writing, two of my children have already received their college degrees, and the youngest begins college this year. Because of my involvement in their schools, I got to know the students they interacted with and they got to know me. Equally important, I got to know the administrators and some of the staff, and we developed positive working relationships. Therefore, we established lines of communication necessary for dialogue on different issues and concerns of the past, present, and future. I continue as an active parent volunteer for, in doing so, I set a good example of parent involvement to my children. Also, my volunteerism and advocacy encompasses not only my children but also extends to other Filipino American students and parents who need representation, a voice, in our school district. One of the significant accomplishments or evidence of this advocacy has been the approval of Filipino as a district foreign language subject, a crucial move that can preserve the Filipino culture and build pride in being a Filipino.

RELIGIOUS JOURNEY

Underlying all their values is the Filipino deep and personal faith that sustains them through difficult times, strengthens them in critical moments, and gives them hope even when things and events seem impossible.

Significance: Excluding the religious practices, especially Roman Catholic religion, in discussing and understanding the Filipino and many other cultures is like listening to a song without the music.

As I reflect on my current career as an educator, I see that my training started in home-taught religion classes. I have been a catechist—a church volunteer teacher—for the last 22 years at different grade levels. In addition to being a full-time mother, I helped found a mothers' group that met weekly to share experiences based on our study of the women in the Bible. This support group led me to design an annual mothers' retreat and subsequently begin spending time with a spiritual director, a practice I still maintain.

It is in the church environment where I have the most opportunities to seek, to explore, and to know who I am and what I can do with my God-given gifts. It is there where I can confront my spiritual pride and get down on my knees, humble and grateful for everything that I have.

At one of our retreats, I rose up very early in the morning, bundled up with warm clothes, and hiked in the narrow pathway between the trees to the top of the hill, where I could barely see the fog-covered mountaintops. As I stood on a rock, the fog rushed toward me. I stretched my arms to meet the cool, refreshing breeze on my uncovered face and hands. I did not know how long I stood in that special time and place, where my soul and whole being sensed the indescribable presence of love and well-being. The immense "presence" was a humbling experience that brought tears of joy, a grateful heart, sadness for wrong things done in the past, and a love for other human beings. With it came the recognition of a call for service that we, as creations of God, may love one another regardless of any differences. Similar experiences occur in the presence of others, when I am able to listen to their stories.

ACADEMIC JOURNEY

Being a minority in race and gender can either work for or against me. In my lifetime, it has been more of the former, as I have constantly accepted the challenge of what I am capable of accomplishing, especially when the odds are against me.

Significance: Students of immigrant parents who take pride in their roots will likely accept more challenges and continue to explore their heritage in an attempt to establish a link with their American identity. Partnership between parents and teachers can make a difference in whether the students will pursue this quest or not for the rest of their lives.

After 10 years as a full-time mother and 24 years after I earned my undergraduate degree in the Philippines, I went back to the university setting for personal enrichment. Knowing that our standard of education is considered lower than what many here in the United States have, I felt insecure and unsure if I could succeed. Getting a grade of "A" in my first subject convinced me that, yes, I could do it. In 2 years, I eventually earned my master's degree in pastoral care and counseling at the University of San Diego. However, it was only after my second year as a graduate student that I bought a sweatshirt with the university insignia. By that time, I felt confident that I had proven to myself that I could wear it with pride.

But that's not the end. I thought of completing a master's degree in counseling, but my advisor convinced me to consider a doctorate in education instead. It blew my mind! Me, take up doctoral studies!? I shared this possibility with another professor, who discouraged me from pursuing it. His rationale was that he knew who had developed the program and how difficult it was. But for him to underestimate what I could do became the deciding factor for me to disregard my fear of failing and to prove that I could do it just like anyone else. And I did. In 1998, I earned my doctoral degree in education in leadership studies.

It took 5 years of long, challenging, intermittent moments of insanity and sanity, sleepless nights, doubts, and lost time with my family. In the end, I recognized how the process, my experiences, the relationships, situations, and interactions that I had to go through made the difference to me, and not the degree. The pursuit for the degree became the means to bring about an in-depth transformation because I had to draw strength from deep within me—my faith in a God, who I believe cares and never abandons me; my family who stood by me; and the friends I gained as we took the same journey. On graduation day, as I marched alongside my classmates, I remembered 5 years before when I watched the degree recipients, how in my mind I said, "Wow! I wonder how does it feel to be in their shoes." And on the stage sat the same professor who discouraged me from pursuing the degree. As I passed by him with my diploma, I gave him a big smile and raised my hand holding the degree. He knew what it meant: "See, you are wrong. I can do it!"

STORYTELLING AND ADVOCACY

As a mother, I tried to understand the expanding world of my children. Growing up in two different cultures made it more difficult. As I got more involved with youths the same age as my children or older, I began to better understand and adapt to my children's way of life. Hearing stories from others provided enlightenment about my children's world outside our home. This contributed to my recognizing storytelling as a tool for bridging generational gaps within immigrant families. I discovered a lack of knowledge among the younger generation about their Filipino heritage. This lack of knowledge contributed to a cultural gap, which aggravated a naturally existing generational gap. As I searched for resources, I found almost nothing in schools, government, or nonprofit agencies.

FILIPINO IMMIGRATION HISTORY

For our children's acquisition of global knowledge, we normally rely on our educational institutions. However, there is hardly any information about the Republic of the Philippines and the Filipino people in the books used in our schools. Current information relates mostly to other Southeast Asian countries.

Significance: Knowledge of the Filipino immigration history is critical in understanding the link between the Republic of the Philippines and the United States. This lack of knowledge has aggravated the generational and cultural gap among Filipino Americans and has contributed to a loss of cultural pride among Filipino students.

Asians started coming to the United States even before the first colony was established in Jamestown (Cordova, 1983; Kitano & Daniels, 1995). The Filipinos, in particular, settled in the United States as a result of the Manila-Acapulco Galleon Trade in the late 16th century. Filipinos had a permanent settlement in Louisiana even before The Philippines became part of the United States (Cordova, 1983; Kitano & Daniels, 1995; Macabenta, 1994), on December 10, 1898, after purchasing the archipelago for $20,000,000 from Spain under the Treaty of Paris (Guerrero, 1970; Philippines Department of Tourism, 1976; Saulo, 1987). In addition to paying money, the United States fought the Filipinos in order to establish sovereignty.

The history of Filipinos in the United States is, in one way, different from that of all other Asian ethnic groups in that it was a direct and unforeseen result of American imperialism. Because the Philippines were under the sovereignty of the United States, Filipino Americans enjoyed, for a time, a unique status among Asian immigrants. They were not "aliens," but enjoyed a "privileged" status as American nationals. In other ways, however, the early history of 20th-century Filipino immigrants bears a resemblance to that of other Asian migrations (Kitano & Daniels, 1995, p. 83).

Filipinos, like thousands of people from all over the world, come to make the United States, known as the land of the free, their new home. In their country of birth, they leave behind friends, relatives, and material possessions. However, what they don't leave behind is who they are and who they have become as a result of growing up in their place of birth and with their families. Everyone is born to specific parents in a certain locality within a specific culture or way of life. Cultural understanding in one's first culture occurs early and is typically established by the age of 5 (Lynch, 1992, p. 19). Therefore, when adults with their young children move to (or when immigrant parents have children in) another country, parents and children vary in their acculturation levels. The differences in culture of the family members aggravate intergenerational conflict. This situation is true for most immigrant families, including Filipino Americans (Baptiste, 1993; Heras & Revilla, 1994). Traub and Dodder (1988) studied how the use of established norms (structured) by adults caused conflict with the young, who used emerging norms (a here-and-now structure). This "great Gap" is a reality that the different generations have to deal with (Traub & Dodder, 1988).

For Filipino immigrant families, as ethnic families of color, familistic values are vital adaptive resources for survival (Cooper, Baker, Polichar, & Welsh, 1993). "As with most immigrant groups, Filipino children acculturate at a faster rate than their parents, whereas their parents continue to function using more traditional values brought with them from the Philippines" (Agbayani-Siewert & Revilla, 1995, p. 163). Intergenerational conflict for the Filipino American family is a day-to-day reality. Therefore, bridging the cultural and generational gaps is critical to maintain its family values in their new country.

PROJECT HEART TO HEART

In 1993, I organized a one-day field trip called Project Heart to Heart at the University of San Diego. It came about out of a desire to bring my children in junior high school together with other Filipino American students to experience a university setting. I wanted them to see beyond the level of grade school education. Because a university policy stated that such a trip had to be organization sponsored, we founded the Filipino Ugnayan Student Organization (FUSO). We were able to bring in two buses of students in two separate field trips.

Besides listening to admission officers and touring the campus, the young students watched role plays by the older students that showed what it was like to be a college student. It turned out that the most effective aspect of the event was this storytelling approach, which helped the younger students understand images of what college life was like and take them home with them.

A year later, I thought of inviting the FUSO group to do another Project Heart to Heart workshop, this time not only for the young but also for their parents. They were hesitant and wary because they thought that parents might not respond to individual storytelling and role-play based on real-life experiences with their families. To their surprise, the parents cried when stories in the role plays described student experiences. In the small group meetings, some parents even asked for advice from the college students. One student made the comment, "I was so surprised! Even my parents never asked me for advice!" As a result of the parents' response, I identified the need to continue with the Project Heart to Heart workshops. The one-time field trip evolved into a one-day conference for youths and parents.

In these conferences, the sharing of stories clarified the family members' intentions, feelings, and thoughts that were not understood in their own home environment. There were moving moments of realization of the hurt and damage done in the past because of an inability to understand oneself and family members. But there were also more moments of warmth, joy and relief when students realized that they were truly loved. The stories that I heard confirmed the growing gap between generations because of a cultural gap, mainly caused by the loss of heritage language. I felt a sense of urgency to respond to this crisis, so I decided to advocate for the inclusion of Filipino as a high school foreign language. I started at my son's school.

NATIVE LANGUAGE LOSS

Our children began to use English with the onset of schooling. They only heard their native language at home. Even other Filipino American students in their schools spoke only English. Growing up in that kind of environment made it difficult for us to encourage them to communicate with us in our native Filipino. We, as their parents, without support from the school, resorted to the use of English, even though we could not always fully and freely express our thoughts. As a result, our children could not fully appreciate the beauty and richness of our culture.

Significance: "Heritage languages, absent active intervention or new immigration, are lost over time both in the individuals who once spoke them and in the immigrant community, and typically die out within three generations" (Brecht & Ingold, 1998). With knowledge of the native language as an opening to full comprehension of the culture's beauty and richness, its loss is also the death of the culture.

It took 5 years before the district school board finally approved Filipino as a foreign language subject. In those years, due to the unavailability of qualified Filipino language teachers, I became the education specialist to teach it as an after school class, with a non-Filipino-speaking Filipino American English teacher. During those years, I shared stories of Filipino immigration and my immigration to the United States. I told stories of Filipino traditions, ways of life, colonization, war, heroes, and heroines. To sustain students' interest, we created and presented Philippine Culture Nights, based on their research. During those years, I witnessed a transformation among the students as they moved from curiosity to serious reflection and Filipino pride in their Filipino identity.

My mission to pass on the Filipino culture to my children extended to others, including college students. Perseverance and approaching the right people at the right time led to the approval of the Filipino foreign language curriculum that I developed and taught for 3 years in a multicultural studies class at Palomar Junior College. In the same year, I was hired to teach a similar language and culture class at San Diego Mesa College, where I actively participated in the expansion of the subject from the beginning to the intermediate level, both of which were included in the master schedule as morning classes so that more students could more readily enroll. In 2002, the University of California–San Diego Department of Linguistics introduced the first Heritage Tagalog class in the University of California system. I considered the opportunity to teach this subject as an acknowledgment of all my efforts to become a respected and qualified Filipino language educator. It is clear to me that all these developments came about because of my advocacy and perseverance for preserving our culture through the preservation of our native language across generations.

THE JOURNEY CONTINUES

The journey of advocacy for my own children that led to teaching Filipino at the high school, college, and university level brought about a lot of changes in my life and others. Staying with my roots helped me keep my self-respect and belief in what I have to offer as a Filipino and pursue changes for survival. There were times of giving up and walking away, but the call was to move forward and to open new doors for others and myself to enter for self-discovery.

I have been encouraged by the testimony from students who have reclaimed their native language. In reclaiming their language, they have redeemed their cultural identities with family members, as evidenced in a few excerpts of the many stories they have shared:

> "My grandmother talks more since I started speaking to her in Tagalog, and I could see how excited she is that I now speak Tagalog!"
>
> "Before [the class], I just repeated what I heard, but now I know what I am talking about. I have more self-confidence in conversing with my parents."
>
> "Our group project to translate Philippine/American folktales or short stories provided a rare opportunity to spend time with my parents and brother—especially my brother—and we had fun!"
>
> "Before [the class], I ignored my dad telling the same story. Now, I listen and ask more questions."

In addition, students reach out to others beyond family members with pride after developing ability in their native language:

> An old lady sells food in this little booth at the navy exchange. The first time I came to her booth, she asked what I wanted in a grumpy voice. When I answered "Dinuguan," she asked, "Are you a Filipino?" I said yes, and she smiled and became friendlier.

This student, who is half Filipino and half white, now intentionally seeks out Filipinos whenever he goes to the navy exchange in order to practice his Tagalog. As a result of the exchange, he asked the Filipino worker to talk to him in Tagalog whenever he comes to visit, which transforms and redeems their relationship and their identities. Another student reported a similar story: "I greeted in Tagalog a Filipino worker at the airport, and he asked, 'Are you a Filipino?' When I said 'yes,' he was really happy."

From my students, I continue to hear stories of joy, surprises and gratitude for their new found tool to communicate with their loved ones in a language that they can call their own. As they share their stories with others, they learn, as well as enrich and preserve, their Filipino culture.

REFERENCES

Agbayani-Siewert, P. (1994). Filipino American culture and family: Guidelines for practitioners. *Families in Society: The Journal of Contemporary Human Services, 75,* 429–434.

Agbayani-Siewert, P., & Revilla, L. (1995). Filipino Americans. In P. G. Min (Ed.), *Asian Americans: Contemporary trends and issues* (pp. 134–168). Thousand Oaks, CA: Sage.

Baptiste, D. A. (1993). Immigrant families, adolescents and acculturation: Insights for therapists. *Marriage and Family Review, 19,* 341–363.

Bellah, R., Madsen, R., Sullivan, W., Swidler, A., & Tipton, S. (1985). *Habits of the heart.* Los Angeles: University of California Press.

Brecht, R. D., & Ingold, C. W. (1998). *Tapping a national resource: Heritage languages in the United States* [On-line]. Available: ERIC Clearinghouse on Languages and Linguistics. Washington, D.C. ERIC Identifier: ED424791

Chan, S. (1992). Families with Filipino roots. In E. W. Lynch & M. J. Hanson (Eds.), Developing cross-cultural competence: A guide for working with children and their families (pp. 251–300). Baltimore: Brookes.

Cooper, C. R., Baker, H., Polichar, D., & Welsh, M. (1993). Values and communication of Chinese, Filipino, European, Mexican, and Vietnamese American adolescents with their families and friends. *New Directions For Child Development, 62,* 73–89.

Cordova, F. (1983). *Filipinos: Forgotten Asian Americans.* Dubuque, IA: Kendall/Hunt.

Guerrero, A. (1970). *Philippine society and revolution.* Hong Kong: Ta Kung Pao.

Heras, P., & Revilla, L. A. (1994). Acculturation, generational status, and family environment of Pilipino Americans: A study in cultural adaptation. *Family Therapy, 21,* 129–138.

Kitano, H. H. L., & Daniels, R. (1995). *Asian Americans: Emerging minorities* (pp. 1–37, 83–95). Upper Saddle River, NJ: Prentice Hall.

Livo, N., & Rietz, S. (1986). *Storytelling: Process and practice* (pp. 1–43). Littleton, CO: Libraries Unlimited.

Lynch, E. W. (1992). From cultural shock to cultural learning. In E. W. Lynch & M. J. Hanson (Eds.), *Developing cross-cultural competence: A guide for working with young children and their families* (pp. 19–33). Baltimore: Brookes.

Macabenta, G. (1994, October). Filipino historical footprints. *Filipinas Magazine,* 38–39.

Oakes, J., & Lipton, M. (2002). *Teaching to change the world* (2nd ed.). New York: McGraw-Hill.

Philippines Department of Tourism. (1976). *Philippines.* Manila: Author.

Rappaport, J. (1993). Narrative studies, personal stories, and identity transformation in the mutual help context. *The Journal of Applied Behavioral Science, 29*(2), 239–256.

Santos Nacu, J. (2002). *Storytelling in Project Heart to Heart: A means to bridge generational gap in post-1965 Filipino immigrant families.* Manila: Author.

Saulo, A. B. (1987). *The truth about Aguinaldo and other heroes.* Quezon City, the Philippines: Phoenix.

Traub, S. H., & Dodder, R. A. (1998). Intergenerational conflict of values and norms: A theoretical model. *Adolescence, 23,* 975–989.

Zaide, S. M. (1994). The Philippines: A unique nation. Quezon City, the Philippines: All-Nations.

Activities for the Classroom

Listening is a very important element of storytelling. In the following activities, the teacher does the listening while the students share their stories. In offering one-to-one regular appointments with the students, the teachers may find ways to improve their teaching methods to meet the needs of their students. The appointments may build a nonintimidating classroom atmosphere that may enhance students' performances. It may also help the teachers know more about their students' backgrounds, and therefore they can better understand their needs.

1. Schedule a 5- to 10-minute individual appointment with your students after class or break time at least once a year. Use any of the following as guideline questions:
   a. What do you enjoy most in our class? Why?
   b. Which class project did your parent/parents/guardian like most? Why?
   c. How can your classmates and I help you in class?

This activity is similar to the family tree activity but shorter. The assignment will encourage the sharing of stories at home and the gathering of unknown information about family members. The students may share immigrant stories, talk about their country of birth, how they got here, and why. The activity can be used for different class topics, such as the study of different countries and history.

2. Ask the students to bring a family picture to class to share. The picture may include relatives. The students need to prepare stories, funny or sad, about one or two of their family members. In the presentation, the students will share the following:
   a. Their relationships to the people in the picture
   b. Stories about one or two of the family members.

FURTHER READING

Hwang, P. (1995). *Other-esteem.* San Diego, CA: Black Forrest.

Lappe, F. M., & Du Bois, P. M. (1994). *The quickening of America: Rebuilding our nation, remaking our lives.* San Francisco: Jossey-Bass.

Street, R. S. (1992). *Organizing for our lives.* Portland, OR: New Sage.

WEB RESOURCE

www.seasite.niu.edu

Chapter 2

My Ethnography

Henry Trueba, University of Texas, Austin

Focus Questions

1. What experiences have you had when someone underestimated you? How does this connect with Henry's story?

2. How could you be an ally for someone like Henry and why would it be important to do so?

What lessons have I learned after 34 years of teaching (3 years in two Mexican Jesuit colleges and 31 years in American universities)? From my first job at Macomb, Illinois, in 1968, to my current position at Austin, Texas, I have learned that failure and successes are part of the same journey, and that I have a soft heart and many times cannot say no to requests for time and help.

I have learned that I have a very fragile ego with individuals with whom I become close, whose welfare is important to me, and that I can be a tough man with people who are distant or try to hurt those I love. For some things that I consider important and personal, I seem to have an unusual determination. I don't mind changes in diet, lack of material things, lack of comfort, physical mobility, or interaction with persons from very diverse socioeconomic, ethnic, and linguistic backgrounds.

I am also touchy about a few matters: expressions that convey lack of respect, disdain, or neglect in a context that reminds me of the degrading incidents I suffered when I first came to this country. I tend to become hypersensitive to questions about my accent, about my ability to think and write, about my honesty and integrity, or about basic fairness. I think we immigrants all have a measure of paranoia and feel defensive about some of these issues. If somebody asks me, "Where are you from?" I may answer,

"From California." If I read some disbelief, I may ask, "What do you want to know: (1) where I was born, or (2) where I last lived, or (3) what kind of accent I have?" I am defensive some times! If someone asks me loudly, enunciating his or her words, "Do you speak English?" I may answer, "As well as you do, and I certainly write it better than you do."

On a more serious note, my desire to make a difference in other people's lives, to help them improve their quality of life and their capacity to enjoy the dignity, peace, and prosperity other human beings seem to enjoy, came to me early in life. I often listened to the stories of missionaries who visited our middle school. In fact, I was so moved to help the missions that I began to save from my weekly allowance to donate money to missionaries, a group whose spirit I respected and embraced.

Many years later, I realized that despite leaving the institutional priesthood, I was still a priest, and that my commitment to students' intellectual growth was advocated in lieu of my previous vocation to proselytize and convert. In lieu of nurturing spiritually Christian souls, I would nurture the intellectual life of students. My life and my academic career are still a work in progress, and my journey continues to lead me in new directions.

SOCIAL JUSTICE AND CRITICAL THINKING: MY ETHNIC IDENTITY AND PERSONAL JOURNEY

I began my life as an ethnographer much before I began to study anthropology. Because life changes have taken me to so many settings—from a large and low-income home to the Jesuit seminary, from Mexico to the United States—I have learned to adapt to people and places. One major adaptation came when I changed my studies from philosophy and theology to anthropology. Another came when I changed my lifestyle from the life of a Jesuit priest to one of secular freedom and economic responsibility. Another change came when I went from single life to a marriage with an Anglo woman whose family never accepted me because I was "of different race." Change is inherent in my life.

I was born in an immigrant family and was the 10th child and youngest son in a family of 13 children (one of whom died at birth). When I was born in Mexico, in 1931, poverty was pervasive and affected my family in spite of the fact that my father was well educated. I left my home at the age of 10, when my mother took me to the Escuela Apostólica de San José (a Jesuit elementary boarding school for potential candidates). She expected me to enter the Jesuit Novitiate upon completion of high school. Although I didn't have much to say on the matter, I was certainly not opposed. Living in very crowded quarters with such a large family and not getting along with my older brothers at the time presented good reasons to go to the boarding school.

I had no idea of what was ahead of me, who I was, or what I wanted to do, much less how I wanted to spend the rest of my life as a Jesuit. In time, I tried everything to get out of the future priesthood: I often misbehaved, fleeing the boarding house overnight (escaping to my maternal aunt Nina's home). Once, when I was 11 and had saved enough money from doing odd jobs, I secretly left the boarding school by climbing the walls and crossing through the military academy next door. I did that even though I was really frightened by the black dog that guarded the grounds. I took a train from Mexico City to Guadalajara and walked from the station to my maternal cousins' home. I begged them to keep me there. Naturally, my mother soon found out where I was and came to see me. She kindly persuaded me to go back to school, behave, and be a good person by accepting my "vocation" to the priesthood.

In 1947, I entered the Jesuit order. Two years later, my father died of cancer, just as he began to do well financially as the chief executive officer of a large cement factory. His resistance against the cement black market and the efforts from corrupt government officials won him the town's respect. At his death in Cuernavaca, Morelos, thousands of workers came to pay their last respects to my father. We held a vigil in Mexico City with hundreds of bankers and politicians in attendance, and we buried my father in the Panteon Español, a cemetery reserved primarily for Spanish immigrants and their families. My father was originally from Navarra and my mother's family from a small village near Pamplona. However, they were raised in Mexico and we were always "Mexican" in our culture and lifestyle.

So I entered the Jesuit order and spent 18 years as a Jesuit, from December 31, 1947, to December 25, 1965. In my first years, I had plenty of time to meditate, as well as plan resistance strategies and try to get out of the order. It was a drastic change in lifestyle.

In time, I made peace with my life as a Jesuit—at least for several years. As I mentioned earlier, I had been always extremely enthusiastic about the missionaries working with Indian communities. During this turbulent period in my life, when I was to do my 3 years of teaching, an assignment at the Mission of Bachajón happened to become available. It was a dream for me. It was not unusual for young Jesuits to be permitted to work in a mission during the teaching years instead of teaching in a regular college. I had organized my life as a Jesuit in order to become a missionary.

When I discovered my true love, the life as a missionary among the Mayan Indians, I subsequently asked to be sent to Chiapas to work with the Tzeltals as a paramedical missionary in the Jesuit Mission of Bachajón. In order to prepare for my missionary work, I obtained special permission to reduce recreation and sleep time in order to study the Mayan languages and to get some basic training at the Cruz Roja (Red Cross) in Mexico City.

I saw myself as a lucky Jesuit who was allowed to join extraordinary people working with the Tzeltals. I had been searching for a meaningful life with the Jesuits, beyond the intellectual life of intense study (which I had already enjoyed when I went to Chiapas), and this newfound love helped me forget the fundamental problem of having lost my freedom and being in a place where I did not want to be. Furthermore, this assignment strengthened my ability to sacrifice and empathize with racially segregated, economically exploited, abused and neglected groups in Mexico. I took final vows of poverty, chastity, and obedience on January 1, 1950.

In the years that followed, I developed my disposition as a scholar. From 1950–1953, I studied the humanities, especially Greek and Latin literature. Between 1953 and 1954, I studied mathematics and natural sciences; between 1954 and 1957, I studied philosophy.

All my studies had prepared me for a teaching career, which began between 1957 and 1958 at the Jesuit colleges of El Instituto Patria in Mexico City and El Instituto Lux of Puebla. My experience in college was most rewarding: One year I was at El Instituto Patria in the Elementary grades as vice principal (in charge of transportation and discipline) and the second year at El Instituto Lux teaching psychology in a high school. In addition, between 1958 and 1959 (and later in brief periods of time) I managed to spend over a year in the Jesuit Mission of Bachajón, in Chiapas.

In the fall of 1959 I returned to Mexico City to begin my theology studies. I completed an abbreviated version of the first year of theology, took early examinations and, in the fall of 1960, left Mexico City to continue my theology studies at Woodstock College in Maryland.

My superiors felt that going to the United States would help me make up my mind to stay in the Jesuit order. They liked me, and although I was not a trouble maker, I was often troubled inside. I felt happy and free in the missions, but now I was being transplanted to the United States, where my anxiety over ordination was extraordinary. The phrase "Thou art a priest forever . . ." and the image of ordination took on an omnipresent life in my thoughts.

I wrestled with the thought of ordination: How, having gone for years and years as a Jesuit, could I walk away from this ritual? There were many pressures from all corners of the earth, and many expectations from my family. My mother had been making plans years in advance, and she was going to be there that day. Several of my brothers and sisters were coming from Mexico to attend the ceremony.

I was not the only one who struggled with ordination. The night before the ordination I could not help but notice how classmates dragged one of my peers, who was drunk, to his room. Another classmate disappeared the night before and was never heard from again. The rector of the theologate, who made our lives miserable with details and rules and regulations, ran away two months after the ordination.

My 2 short years at Woodstock were traumatic, related to struggles with language. In addition, it was there that I first experienced racism. I noticed that when there was going to be permission to speak at the table (on certain days), the U.S. Euro-American students would not sit next to any of the foreign students; the apparent jokes and clear disdain for the Mexican and Filipino students were evident. Minor errors, as we tried to learn to wait on tables and carry the food, resulted in abusive language or nasty remarks. At times, I would rather not eat than to come down to the dining room. Eventually I found some kind persons who began to teach me some English (I had read a little and studied some grammar, but could not communicate). Worse, the Latin I learned in Mexico was phonetically confusing to the American faculty at Woodstock. I felt totally stupid, although I knew a great deal more than I was ever given credit for.

I began to dream of getting out of Woodstock, as well as out of the Jesuit order. I began a campaign of letters and requests, arguing that I was not suitable for the priesthood. Although I was a priest only for a short time, I had the opportunity to work in parishes and became a special confessor for priests. During that time, I learned to recognize voices and sins confessed in the past. One thing came clear in my mind, "I do not want to be like these priests; I will leave the order with permission of the Church."

At that time, my return visit to Chiapas, Mexico, where I had been a missionary, had resulted in total disappointment; no matter how hard we worked baptizing and curing people, in the next visit to the village (2 to 6 months later) things were identical: chaotic, with a strange mixture of Catholic faith and a pagan religion, and an overwhelming series of problems in public health, nutrition, poverty, conflicts over land, and sheer abuse on the part of the Mexican people and authorities working with the Mayan Indians (Tzeltal and Tzotzil speakers).

One of my last visits to the hinterland ended with the death of small children who had been sick with diarrhea, malnutrition, and dehydration. I felt so guilty because I was unable to cure them! I flew back to Washington, DC, to ride to Woodstock, where the theological school was, and stopped for supper at Georgetown University. My images of the poverty and misery of the Indians contrasted with the many types of wines and the rich table for the priests. I felt nauseated and left the table.

As I contemplated the idea of leaving the priesthood during the fourth year of theology in Cleveland, I applied to Stanford University and was accepted to study anthropology with some of the scholars from Stanford I had met in Chiapas a few years before. During my last year at Woodstock, I also began to get some stipends from masses, baptisms, and other sources, and was happy to send some money to my mother. Eventually, I stopped asking for permission to have and send money, and began saving money. I saved enough to help me, at the end of the fourth year of theology, to buy a little car and drive to California (and eventually I shared this information with my superiors in Mexico).

I was accepted to Stanford through the help of anthropologists I had met in Chiapas. Then I arranged to come to the Newman Center in Palo Alto and attend classes at Stanford while earning some spending money. I was truly fortunate.

MY LIFE AT STANFORD

Changing from theology to anthropology, from being a seminarian to being a student, from being a practicing priest to preparing to leave the priesthood, were drastic changes in my life. After 3 years of correspondence, I wrote my superiors and told them that if their permission did not come by December 31, 1965, I would just leave the order without permission. Finally, in a letter that seemed abusive to me at the time, my permission came. However, I was denied the right to see anybody I had known as a priest, especially my religious brothers of the same cohort and friends in the Jesuit order. In addition, I had to report periodically to the local bishops as I traveled throughout the country. I was happy to leave, but I was very scared.

Part of my sense of liberation was based on the possibility of continuing a university career. My main reason to leave the order was the inconsistency between policies of piety, generosity, and a fully committed life to the welfare of others, and the observed practice of behind-the-scenes scandalous lives. My having been a confessor of priests taught me plenty.

On the other hand, the most redeeming value of Jesuit life was what I learned about intellectual discipline and commitment and the example of truly extraordinary minds (for example, my classmate who spoke, read, and wrote 12 languages, including Mandarin—he was a fellow with a photographic memory for speeches and the ability to read documents very quickly).

Nevertheless, my liberation from the Jesuit order did not do away with my inner self and my will to help others. I knew I had an enormous resiliency in the face of challenges and oppression. However, having worked in Chiapas and having outlived the profound crises of leaving the priesthood, also left me scarred and insecure. Furthermore, changing disciplines from philosophy and theology to anthropology was a huge leap.

MY PERSONAL EXPERIENCE AS ETHNOGRAPHER

I began my life as an ethnographer much before I began to study anthropology. I lived among the Mayan Indians of Chiapas, in the Bachajón and Chilón areas, not far from San Cristóbal las Casas (in the area now well-known because of the Zapatista rebellion) between 1958 and 1963, 4 or 5 months at a time. I was a Jesuit missionary and a priest after June 1962. Much of my time prior to my first visit to Chiapas was at home learning the Tzeltal and Tzotzil languages. My Jesuit brothers and superiors were my mentors in the language, and only through long trips alone with the native Tzeltals and Tzotzils did I learn to disregard my first interpretations, not only of the Christian dogma (sin, sacraments, prayer, etc.), but more importantly about people's unique use of both Mayan languages and local varieties of Spanish in order to convey subtle meanings (for example, in reference to sacred matters).

The expected discourse presenting the etic version of the truth, as seen by the Western reader, reminds me of the many efforts to translate into Tzeltal my partial truths and categories in order to convey a parallel thought and partial "truth" without breaking cultural norms, and my frustration when I found no equivalent in the Tzeltal or Tzotzil world. I also remember my ethnocentric stupidity when I was trying to make sense of the profound philosophical differences between the Mayas and us, the missionaries. For example, the division between the living and the dead, between the natural elements (often conceived as truly divine and personal entities), between the human and animal domains, and the human spirits and the animal spirits living in the underground and forming part of our self-identities.

In order to get at the emic, one needs to attempt to reconstruct the world around, to develop a new perception and interpretation of events. Often one goes through a cultural shock at first, and then gradually finds a personal identity that fits well into the local Mayan society. I came to love the Tzeltals as my own family. Of course, trying to explain the Mayan world to outsiders was most difficult and unpleasant.

For example, one time, Samuel Ruiz, then bishop of Chiapas, and I were called to a small town (Santa Rosa) to help some Stanford professors and students who were hiding in an old church, afraid for their lives. They had violated a sacred cultural norm when they took blood samples for a study; blood is the *xchulel* or "soul" of the people. This provided a good anthropological example of how unexpected responses are only a measure of our ethnocentrism and the misassumptions we bring to the field.

The same thing happened when I worked with other cultures, including the Nahuat in Mexico, and the Miao in China. When I had the opportunity to do field-work among the Nahuat Indians of Puebla, I found out how superficial acculturation to the Mexican lifestyle indeed camouflaged profound philosophical and cultural differences in worldview and daily behavior.

Because Nahuat Indians spoke to me in Spanish (I never learned Nahuat well enough to communicate in that language, but I could understand some), and because they dressed like other Mexicans, I assumed they were like other Mexican people. I learned the hard way when I violated their cultural expectations. I was once kicked out of Xalacapan, near Zacapoaxtla, and it took me 14 years to "mend fences" and belong there again. In the end, I discovered how wrong my early assumptions were.

For me, however, the cross-cultural journey within this continent was not nearly as frightening as going from Western societies to China. In a period of 5 years of traveling to China to collect and analyze data, with the continued help and support of Chinese graduate students who were with me in China, I finally began to realize how difficult it was to interpret firsthand Miao students' accounts of their educational experiences, collected in two different parts of China. I learned how different their own philosophical assumptions were about the world, about China, and the United States. When they finally placed us in the right category, we then began to collect significant data and ask the right questions. In the end, many of the old accounts we gathered were thrown away as misrepresentations of what Miao was all about. And some of the genuine accounts could not be published because they would have put in danger the persons interviewed.

My research projects and adventures in the United States, but especially in China, were linked to my work with Asian American students and their dissertations I directed. And my efforts to understand Chinese minority groups and their relationship to Indo-Chinese refugees in our country led me to new challenges about my own identity and lack of ability to make inferences across cultures. The most frustrating (at times traumatic) experiences in China were associated with massive crowds and the lack of control over my space, as well as my inability to communicate with people. Yet, gradually I began to understand the motivation behind the Miao students to pursue an academic career in Beijing, as they endured the ethnic hostility and disdain towards them on the part of mainstream persons.

Much of this experience would take years to be digested and eventually was reflected in my *Latinos Unidos: From Cultural Diversity to the Politics of Solidarity* (Trueba, 1999). Influenced by Paulo Freire and my colleagues associated with him (Donaldo Macedo, Moacir Gadotti, Peter McLaren, Henry Giroux, and many others) I began to deconstruct my previous experiences. I soon realized that I was still a priest, and that my commitment to students' intellectual growth was advocated in lieu of my previous vocation to proselytize and convert, and in lieu of nurturing spiritually Christian souls, I would nurture the intellectual life of students.

CRITICAL CONSCIOUSNESS AND CHALLENGES IN THE ACADEMY

My first personal encounter with Paulo Freire was in 1984, when I was teaching at the University of California in Santa Barbara. He was not able to speak English yet, and I had the privilege of taking him and his first wife out for supper and spending quality time with both of them. I have since admired his work and followed him for a short visit to Brazil in the early 1990s. Today, many young scholars who had read Paulo Freire's *Pedagogy of the Oppressed* (1970), and who were exposed to "critical theory" and the reactions against "hegemonic" structures in educational institutions, view racism, hostility, and ethno-phobias as the reason for perpetuating the neglect of students of color.

Today, the comparison between Freire and George Spindler, my two spiritual and intellectual leaders, continues to be a topic of personal interest for me. Freire's concept of "conscientization" comes across as parallel to Spindler's notion of cultural reflectivity, or reflective analysis via ethnographic research. There are, however, profound differences in philosophy and research method between Freire and Spindler. Freire views education as inherently and necessarily "political," and as an expression of power and a reflection of the social order. In other words, for Freire, literacy ("reading the word and reading the world") is the key instrument to under-stand oppression and to overcome it. Conscientization and the construction of "utopias" demand political awareness and the possession of knowledge that trans-lates into political power, and results in the final analysis in justice. Furthermore, Freire views "culture" in its context of class, power, and international relations of countries such as the United States with developing countries, such as in Latin America, Asia, or Africa. The role of culture in social, economic, and political oppression is central to Freire's concept of a "utopia" in which we liberate ourselves from cultural imperialism.

Spindler, however, views education as a socialization process that facilitates a person's active participation (true belonging) in a social group; that is, the acquisi-tion of the necessary cultural and social knowledge is essential in order to function effectively in that group. Thus, education is not necessarily political (dealing with conflict and distribution of power), but rather a mechanism within each society to prepare new members for life in their community. I share in the views of both Freire and Spindler, and I don't see any contradiction between the two approaches. But I feel that sheer knowledge does not give low-income immigrants and other disad-vantaged groups membership in mainstream societies. That knowledge must come with a clear vision of how the politics of participation work, what resources and mechanisms there are to open up closed institutions, and how to break up racist poli-cies and practices, dismantle unfair economic policies, and establish a basis of equal respect for all groups in society.

My transfer of religious values and cognitive categories to academic values and domains confronted me with several questions. I questioned ranks, academic purity, and ethnic aspirations of some and rejection by others. Tenure or promotion deci-sions by a committee convinced me that rejection of ethnic candidates meant reten-tion of the purity of science and protection of the academy. In other words, faculty would not openly use derogatory language to refer to persons of color; committees would simply go by the rules and apply them to define scholarly work, quality of teaching, and the relevance of research and excellence in ways that reinforced their own power and curtailed the incorporation of Latino, African-American, Asian-American, and Native American faculty.

At times, euphemistic expressions would call into question the character of a minority candidate by referring to his or her cultural values and a possible conflict re-sulting from his or her coming on board. I learned that survival in academia required a great deal more than simple intellectual excellence; it demanded political know-how and an instinct to adopt survival strategies. Indeed, resiliency was a mix of prac-tical talent, emotional strength, and political know-how that assisted my colleagues crossing the color line. Their profound confidence in their skills and capabilities was tempered by a cautious affiliation with groups across ethnic boundaries.

Success, whatever that means to different academicians, required survival and resiliency. Success in the face of predicted failure was a cause for quiet celebration even if success was only a small event in the larger context (the publication of a pa-per, support for tenure recommendation, nomination to important committees, or collaborative research efforts with well-known scholars). Certainly, success was never a steady climb to the peak of recognition and admiration by peers. It was always up and down. But failure was never terminal either; it was a learning lesson for the next challenge, a means of discovery, a test of will, an opportunity to show gratitude to others, an answer to prayers, and most of all, a chance for conscientization, reflection, and planning.

During my final year of doctoral studies, my personal and academic reflection and discovery coincided in a surprising way. When I was deciding to settle down and marry during the last year of my doctorate, I also had to confront decisions on a dissertation research site, and I picked the Nahuat Indians from Zacapoaxtla and Xalacapan, in Puebla, Mexico. The most serious crisis I faced there (which was totally unexpected) was one of self-identity. I was considered "*a gringo protestante y comunista*" and consequently hated by many Catholics. Some Indians close to the local priest put a price on my head. (The previous year they had already killed a European researcher.) I had built rapport fast enough that the local teachers warned me about the danger and accompanied me continuously. Eventually, however, the man in charge of killing me came and apologized (he was so drunk!) and gave me 10 pesos, the money he had received for taking care of me. All in all, my fieldwork promoted friendships among Spanish- and Nahuatl-speaking persons from Zacapoaxtla, and we have remained close friends for decades.

Back in the United States, however, I was again confronting different identities. People trying to be complementary would say, "But you are not really Mexican, are you? You don't look Mexican," meaning you are not as dark as the Mexicans I know from movies and personal encounters. Thus, by confronting normative expectations on a personal level, I could expand my work in the arena of higher education.

TRANSFORMATIVE RESEARCH

One way that I see my transformative teaching is through research, an area rich in ethnocentrism and inaccuracies. The "armchair search for the truth" is intrinsically arrogant; it demands that natives of other cultures tell me in my own semantically appropriate categories something I consider credible. For example, if I feel inclined to reject the obvious analysis of testimonies given by a native Indian without examining possible misinterpretation across cultures and languages, primarily on the grounds that some scholars disagree with an Indian, I show prejudice. I should question the ethnohistorical evidence presented by the scholars who reject the Indian's testimony, and then confront them with possible alternatives to interpret the Indian account in culturally and linguistically appropriate ways before rejecting the account. Because of my experiences with the Tzeltals and my identification with being seen as less intelligent than others because of ethnocentrism, I ask questions and raise questions in the "academy" that others do not.

For example, I find much of the discourse on this armchair search for truth biased and irrelevant to the central issues. Indeed, it looks to me highly suspicious of an implied commitment to exonerate groups of individuals who were involved in serious human rights violations in Guatemala. We need to learn from our experiences in Argentina, Brazil, Mexico, and other Latin American countries. But even in the United States, the protection of "informants" who had been involved in the Holocaust and whose records remained secret fostered a pro-Nazi movement that attempted to deny the "truth" of the Holocaust. In Mexico, the killings in Tlaltelolco in the late 1960s were historically disguised as a student revolt stopped by the central government.

Likewise, we cannot ignore the words of a young Chinese woman who investigated the massacre of 300,000 Chinese in Nanking by the Japanese between 1937 and 1938:

> An event that sixty years ago made front-page news in American newspapers appears to have vanished, almost without a trace . . . I became terrified that the history of three hundred thousand murdered Chinese might disappear just as they themselves had disappeared under Japanese occupation and the world might actually one day believe the Japanese politicians who have insisted that the Rape of Nanking was a hoax and a fabrication—the massacre never happened at all.   (Chang, 1997, p. 200)

What motivated Iris Chang is precisely what has motivated Rigoberta Menchú to tell the truth as she recalls it and to express it in a foreign language the best she could. The fact that a "Truth Commission" questioned Rigoberta's account should not surprise many of the scholars who have been studying the Zapatista movement in Mexico. The duplicity of the government in searching for the truth is a *sine qua non* of the politics of oppression in Latin America. DeVillar cites Cecilia Rodríguez (the U.S. coordinator of the National Commission for Democracy in Mexico), alluding to the duplicity of the Mexican government in dealing with the Zapatistas:

> People have to realize the dual face of the Mexican government. [It first sent] the head of the Justice Department to dialogue with the EZLN [Zapatista National Liberation Front]. In that way, they gave sort of a *de facto* legitimacy to the EZLN. However . . . [later on] labeling the Zapatistas as terrorists and criminals, the government has essentially shown the other side of their face, the real side; their intent was never to deal with the EZLN in good faith.
>
> (cited in DeVillar, 1998, pp. 200–201, emphasis in original)

The Mexican government was pressed to deal with the peso crisis and to demonstrate to the rest of the world that it could eliminate the rebellious Indians from Chiapas. Indeed, under presidential order the soldiers rolled and descended with an impressive array of weapons and machinery into Chiapas to crack down on the rebels and arrest them as criminals (DeVillar, 1998, p. 203).

As in Guatemala, Chiapas Indians had to use the media in order to have their voices heard. They represented their movement as an uprising in the name of democracy, liberty, and defense of human rights, as well as a genuinely indigenous movement. In fact, most recently, Mayan Indians from Chiapas toured all the Mexican states, speaking with everyone who would listen to them, and very frequently were welcomed as heroes. Parades were organized on their behalf, and a genuine democratic spirit guided the public support for the Mayans in Mexico. Using the media, the Zapatistas recounted the facts: over 15,000 fatalities per year in the last few years due to hunger, lack of medical services, poverty, and military oppression (DeVillar & Franco, 1998, p. 229). In the end, as the Chiapas Indians stated, and the peace commissioner, Manuel Camacho, expressed it:

> I think that the road to peace in Chiapas will be in new responses for the State, not only for them [the Zapatista army] but for all society . . . in a new treatment of the indigenous communities throughout the country . . . in a commitment to democracy in Mexico.   (cited by DeVillar & Franco, 1998, p. 231)

What lessons have we learned from the oppression of native indigenous groups in the Americas? As researchers, we are aware that Eurocentric arrogance justified rape, killings, military oppression, slavery, and other abuses to human dignity on the basis of religion and truth. Indeed, the presumed "lower level" of spirit ("soul") possessed by the Indians gave license to "good" Christians to rape and kill those semi-humans who opposed their glorious divine destiny to progress and "civilization" in the Americas.

Some may not believe that much of the colonialist underpinnings of American and European scholarship are still alive and well. The justification for the anti-Semitism of German social anthropologists during the Nazi regime is now being restudied and has come to light. Modern anthropology essentially discards "race" as an operational concept because there is an infinite number of combinations and permutations of human characteristics beyond eye and skin color, bone structure, weight and stature, distribution of fat, and overall appearance. Today's anthropologists regret the "crimes of anthropology" and the role of European anthropologists in the Nazi regime, in which they became "race experts" and decided the lives of thousands of villagers in Poland and contributed to the crimes of the Third Reich. Anthropologists regret their role in developing the "theory" of a Europe "racially pure." Their files in Berlin, Koblenz, and Krakow, albeit cleansing efforts, clearly show how Nazi anthropologists were the instrument of a racist regime (Schafft, 1999, p. 56).

I see that miscegenation between European, Meso-American Indians, and between mestizos from Mexico and European North Americans, is of such proportions that we all need to go beyond genetic research, and beyond the chemical and physiological structure of internal organs, blood types, and genes, to understand the biological foundations of race. What we do know, however, is that racism continues to play a primary role in the exploitation and mistreatment of people of color, and continues to attract the support of some scholars. We need to be on guard and protect the voices of the few Indians who have had the courage to speak out. And, in my opinion, it is not too late to conduct genuine, systematic, firsthand research on the oppression and cruelty suffered by the Mayans in Guatemala and Mexico.

Many refugees from Guatemala who survived by fleeing to Chiapas under the protection of the Zapatistas against the federales are still alive and eager to talk—in a number of Mayan languages and in Spanish. There is no substitute for systematic, long-term ethnographic research. My hope is that such research takes into consideration the advice from the great scholars who established the methodological foundations of sound educational ethnography, ethnoscience, and sociolinguistics. And these giants are still alive: George Spindler, Dell Hymes, Roy D'Andrade, Charles Frake, and William Sturtevant, among others. Any theory about how to search for the "truth" is contingent on the linguistic and cultural interpretations of behavior, and the political contexts of the people involved in the present human conflict surrounding us.

These are questions that higher education scholars must face, and in doing so, be transformed by their questions. This is what Dell Hymes meant when he said that "the practice of linguistics itself," the study of meaning through language use, cannot be cultivated without "coming to grips with questions of philosophical, psychological and ethnographic order."

The prevailing disregard that Eurocentric searchers for the truth display is, fundamentally, a residue of a colonialist anachronic approach to support existing political powers, not a genuine effort to make sense of the life as experienced by Indians and other low-esteem people who now refuse to serve their masters. The anachronism is a basic contradiction: We want to come across as truly democratic, but we want to retain (as researchers) the quintessential lie of European exploitation of the Indians as if it were humane and good for the Indians.

As long as Indians and migrants of color continue to be used as slaves or cheap labor because they seem to us to be of an inferior order—some racist people still think Indians do not have a human soul of the same quality as that of the Europeans—we will not be able to find the "truth." We will certainly not from our comfortable chairs. The old excuse, It is fine to exploit the Indians if in the end we can acculturate them and give them a superior culture with Western values, is no longer acceptable on many grounds, not even by those who have been acculturated and never achieved equity in Eurocentric societies (not only in Europe and the United States, but in a South American metropolis). The assumptions that the Indians lie, that they are stupid or morally inferior, is part of the philosophical infrastructure accepted by some scholars who cannot cross ethnic barriers in order to understand the philosophical and psychological world of Indian cultures.

NOTES FOR TEACHERS

At the end of my career in academia, I feel that the ability to make a difference in students is contingent upon the nature of our relationship with them. If we truly care, if we are willing to sacrifice in order to become a mentor, a friend, a guide, the relationship with students is transformed into a very rich and personal experience. University teaching can be genuinely directed to assist others in becoming caring and reflective teachers in their daily lives. This is not an effort to sugarcoat the very difficult challenges facing teachers in public schools and universities. However, in describing the most significant experiences that affect our roles as teachers, our attitude towards others and our values are at the center of this book.

REFERENCES

Chang, I. (1997). *The rape of Nanking: The forgotten holocaust of World War II.* New York: Basic Books.

DeVillar, R. (1998). Indigenous images and identity in pluricultural Mexico: Media as official apologist and catalyst for democratic action. In Y. Zou & H. Trueba (Eds.), *Ethnic identity and power: Cultural context of political action in school and society* (pp. 221–257). New York: State University of New York Press.

DeVillar, R., & Franco, V. (1998). The role of media in armed and peaceful struggles for identity: Indigenous self-expression in Mexico. In Y. Zou & H. Trueba (Eds.), *Ethnic identity and power: Cultural context of political action in school and society* (pp. 187–219). New York: State University of New York Press.

Frake, C. O. (1964). Notes on queries in ethnography. [Special issue: Transcultural Studies in Cognition]. *American Anthropologist, 66(3, 2),* 132–145.

Freire, P. (1970). *Pedagogy of the oppressed.* New York: Continuum.

Hymes, D. (1964). Directions in (ethno-) linguistic theory. [Special issue: Transcultural Studies in Cognition]. *American Anthropologist, 66(3, 2),* 6–56.

Lincoln, Y. S. (1999, June). Courage, Vulnerability and Truth. Unpublished paper prepared for the Reclaiming Voice II Conference, University of California–Irvine.

Menchú, R. (1996). *I, Rigoberta Menchú: An Indian Woman in Guatemala.* London, New York: Verso. (Original work published in 1983 as *Me Llamo Rigoberta Menchú Y Así me Nació la Conciencia*).

Romney, A. K., & D'Andrade, R. G. (Eds.). (1964). *Transcultural Studies in Cognition* [Special issue]. *American Anthropologist, 66(3, 2).*

Schafft, G. (1999). Commentary: Professional Denial. *Anthropology Newsletter,* January 1999: 54–56.

Spindler, G. (2000). Fifty years of anthropology and education, 1956–2000: A Spindler anthology. Mahwah, NJ: Erlbaum.

Spindler, G. (Ed.). (1955). *Anthropology and education.* Stanford, CA: Stanford University Press.

Spindler, G. (Ed.). (1987). *Education and cultural process: Anthropological approaches* (2nd ed.). Prospect Heights, IL: Waveland.

Spindler, G., & Spindler, L., (Eds.). (1987a). *The interpretive ethnography of education: At home and abroad.* Hillsdale, NJ: Erlbaum.

Spindler, G., & Spindler, L. (Eds.). (1994). *Pathways to cultural awareness: Cultural therapy with teachers and students.* Newbury Park, CA: Corwin.

Sturtevant. W. C. (1964). Studies in ethnoscience. [Special issue: Transcultural Studies in Cognition]. *American Anthropologist, 66(3, 2),* 99–131.

Trueba, H. T. (1999). *Latinos unidos: From cultural diversity to the politics of solidarity.* New York: Rowman & Littlefield.

chapter 3

From Gangs to Teaching: Transforming My Past to Help Others

Ramón Serrano, St. Cloud State University, St. Cloud

Focus Questions

1. What marked differences did Ramón find in Puerto Rico versus New York? How did that promote transformation in him?

2. Ramón's culture shock was evidenced in the attitudes he saw in his peers in Puerto Rico versus New York. What were they? How did this impact his life?

3. What do gangs provide that schools do not? What can we learn from this?

4. Given that there are forces that are aggressively recruiting for gang membership, to what degree can schools continue to be neutral and silent? How does this neutrality impact students?

As I recall, as a student in the New York Public School system, I was always considered a good student. When the school year began I would usually start off in one group and then be transferred to a more advanced group. While this may sound like something good to many, it was not until I reached ninth grade that it really became a problem. That was the year when all my problems began. At the school I attended there were several ninth-grade groups, and they were ranked from the best to the worst. The higher the group number, the more you were considered at risk. The students in the higher ninth-grade groups were often referred to as the losers and the retards, and they were usually treated as such by many students, teachers, and administrators. This tracking process in my school was "heavily mediated by teacher expectations" (Darder, 1991, p. 17), expectations that included the personal characteristics as well as the social context of students, the teachers' own pedagogical theories (which were based on a "deficit orientation"), and the teachers' personal understandings and experiences with the community around them (Darder, 1991).

I started my ninth-grade experience in group nine-five, and after being there a couple of months I was transferred to nine-two, a "better" group. It was never discussed with me, but I can remember that my first day of class was a nightmare. That following Monday I reported to the counselor's office, and he escorted me to my new classroom, which immediately turned out to be my own living hell. I can still remember with pain the first thing that happened—an argument broke out between my new teacher and my counselor. It started because my teacher could not accept that a Puerto Rican would be placed in his class. He argued that someone must have made a mistake because the "Puerto Ricans in this school did not have the brains it took to be placed so far ahead." In my defense, my counselor replied that "maybe he is different and we should give him a chance." This was a clear example of deficit orientation at work. Through his statement, my counselor was in reality reinforcing deficit orientation, which supported tracking by skin color and ethnicity, and explaining "exceptions." Deficit orientation not only produces such practices; it also leads to a pedagogy of exclusion that limits and silences the voices of students (Macedo, 1994).

After a couple of minutes, my new teacher agreed to the situation and told me where to sit down. That day, as I recall, I was asked to solve a math problem on the board, which I was unable to solve. As I told him I did not know the answer, he looked at me then turned to the class and said, "It looks like someone did not eat their Goya beans this morning" (Goya is a brand name which is very popular among Puerto Ricans in New York). With this comment the class (which happened to be all Anglos) began to laugh. I felt really bad and wished he would have dropped dead on the spot. This was the start of my problem, and shortly after that I ended up suspended for 2 weeks because I threw a chair at him. This act of violence came about because of a confrontation in which he called me stupid, and I replied that I knew two languages and he only knew one. At that point he turned and made a remark about my mother, which in my culture is something you do not do unless you are willing to go all the way. Upon hearing this remark I picked up a chair and tossed it in his direction, giving him the opportunity he had been waiting for—to finally get me out of his class.

During my suspension (of which my parents knew nothing about), I hung out in the hallways of the school. It was during this time that I had my first encounter with members of a local gang. I shared with them what had happened, and in their eyes I had done the right thing because the teacher should never have said anything about my mother. As I continued to share my story, about rejecting that teacher's authority and the "decorum" of the classroom, I gained acceptance into a culture that would later embrace me as one of their own. I felt like one of them because I was treated like one of them, and this lead me to believe that I had found my place. During my 2-week suspension, I learned ways of getting in and out of the school building without ever getting caught. It was a fascinating time, which created in me a sense of power and control that I had never experienced before.

When my suspension was up I reported to the office and waited until someone came for me. I remember thinking it would be good to get back into my old classroom, where I knew everyone and everyone knew me. After sitting for a while I was told to follow the counselor, who would escort me to the classroom. As we started down the hall, in front of the stairs, I was immediately surprised to see that instead of going up to the second floor, we headed down to the basement. I told him that my classroom was upstairs, thinking that there was a mistake, but he just looked at me and said that my new classroom was downstairs. When we finally arrived I looked around and found that many of the faces surrounding me were familiar; they were my friends from the halls. My new teacher had a sort of noncaring look on his face, and I later found out that he really did not care about anything. We could do whatever we wanted, and he just went about his own business.

I adapted quickly to the environment, as my new friends taught me the ropes while assuring me that the teacher did not care if we were there or not. One of the first things that shocked me was my friends' disrespect towards their teachers. It was like the teachers did not care about what was said to them or who said it, they just went through their lessons and if you learned fine and if you did not learn it was also fine too. I remember one day asking why nobody cared about what happened in class, and the response was, "No one cared because we are all considered kind of crazy and hopeless," and that the only teachers who were there were the ones who "sucked and did not give a damn about us." I later found this to be true: The teachers who taught us were in fact the worst in the school.

Their idea of teaching us was just to lecture and never allow us to ask the questions that we felt were important. The most common answer I remember receiving was "That's the way it is." Classes were usually boring and full of disruptions. It was clear that we were there to listen and not ask questions, especially questions to start discussions that were meaningful to our lives. In other words, we were being schooled to become semiliterate in the sense that while we could read the words around us we were not taught to read the world (Macedo, 1994). There were no connections made between what we learned in our textbooks and the social and political realities in which we lived. We were experiencing a situation similar to that found in a study on silencing by Michelle Fine (1987). In her study, Fine (1987) referred to silencing as a process in which schools avoid discussions that name social and other tensions relevant to students' lives. One example of silencing, or what Fine (1987) refers to as "not naming," happened frequently in my school, especially when problems between gangs surfaced. Teachers never wanted to discuss these problems because they felt that it would make things worse. Their attitude was that if they ignored the problems, the problems would go away by themselves. This was truly a problem in itself, because in reality, the problem was not discussing gangs—it was not discussing gangs that made things worse.

During high school things got worse. Throughout high school I continued to get involved in gang activities. I tried to change, but the environment I was in would not allow me to make changes in my life. I was at a point when I felt that my own sense of power and possibilities were spiraling downward; I knew that I had to do something, but the harder I tried the harder it became. On several occasions I attempted to go to class only to be met by my teachers' refusal to accept that I was there to participate. In their eyes I was already labeled a troublemaker who was there to disrupt the class and make life miserable for them. This rejection frustrated me and pushed me deeper into a world that seemed hopeless and full of violence.

On other occasions my attempts to change were met by peer pressure that reminded me that I was one of them and that the school administration had it in for me. Because of my failures to change, I found myself no longer contemplating the idea of going to college, but rather finishing up and going to work in a factory somewhere. What made matters worse was a conversation I had with one of the school counselors in which she told me that my best alternative was to learn a trade, such as repairing cars. According to her, there were a lot of Puerto Ricans that were very good mechanics, because "It runs in your blood."

There was only one teacher throughout my high school experience who made a difference. He was young, from the ghettos, and was not well liked by some of the senior teachers. He was a teacher who talked with us and not just to us. His openness to share many of his personal experiences, which happened to be very similar to ours, showed us that we could make it if we tried. He pushed us hard and was not afraid of "telling it as it is." He got me to a point where I began questioning my actions, my involvement with gangs, and finally my lack of personal confidence. The first thing he helped me realize was that I had to decide whether it was worth being in a gang and how I was going to get out. It was hard, but finally my break came through.

FREEDOM'S TRAIL

One day the opportunity to get out of gangs arrived. My parents had been talking about returning to Puerto Rico in about a year, and I saw this as an opportunity to change my life completely. My sister and her husband had left first to buy a piece of land and build a house. Once I heard this I managed to convince my parents that I should be sent ahead because I could finish my last year of high school there and learn how to read and write Spanish.

Going to school in Puerto Rico was a real cultural shock. The biggest difference I saw was the attitudes of my new peers. In New York, all we talked about was graduating and getting a job in a factory, but in Puerto Rico all I heard was talk about graduating and going on to college. At first, this was a real shock, but over time I began to embrace that goal myself and found myself working hard to learn to read and write Spanish so that I could join many of my new peers in their dreams of a better life.

In my new high school, my attitude towards school changed completely. I credit this to my new teachers and the way they taught. They were open and had us participating in a lot of discussions. They also helped me personally by being willing to listen to my stories and to talk about them with me. They took the time to sit down and help me with my Spanish, which in turn helped my perceptions of teachers to change. The caring environment that was provided was very different from the environment I had experienced in New York. And it was in Puerto Rico that I finally began to see hope again and the opportunity to become someone. It was there that I discovered that I had always had the potential to get to where I am today and to help others see that they also have the potential to succeed in life.

CHOOSING A BUMPY ROAD

After finishing high school, I decided I wanted to become a teacher, and soon after I enrolled in college and became an elementary school teacher for 12 years. As a teacher, I quickly learned that there were still inequalities in schools. I struggled hard to help kids who I knew had the potential but never really had the opportunity to show it. And along the way I made many enemies who, rather than being kids or gang members, were actually my own colleagues. Life as a teacher was not easy for me. I had to face the harsh reality that even though I cared there were many out there who did not. Finally, I decided that I needed to do more and that those who did not care were not going to change overnight. I felt that the best way to create any change was to help prepare new teachers with a vision of hope for kids. I realized that in order to prepare teachers with this vision I needed to go back to college and become a college professor. Today, as college professor, my goal is to help prepare teachers who will not ruin the lives of their students. Rather than working alone in a classroom, I decided that I could help others work with so-called at risk kids by sharing my own experiences and struggles.

SHARING MY EXPERIENCES TO HELP OTHERS

As I look back on my life, I think about how many of my peers in New York really could have been able to make it. We all had something in common back then—that schooling was not preparing us to live a productive life. Today I work preparing future teachers at a midsized university in the Midwest. The challenge I face here is helping my students understand the culture of poverty, gangs, and urban schools. Through my experiences, I also hope to help my students understand that many so-called at risk students have potential, but sometimes the environment they find themselves in does not provide the conditions and support needed to succeed.

Today I work with teenagers in a local group home to develop the skills needed to help them get their lives back on track. I have implemented a program I call Daring to Share, which targets youths who are at high risk and who are currently residents at a county boy's home. The home residents are racially composed of Caucasian, Latino, and Native American youth. One of the program's goals is to use the experiences of these youths to help schools, the community, and the College of Education at St. Cloud State University understand the culture, problems, lives, and needs of at risk youth. I also seek to involve parents in the process of healing so that they, along with their children, can participate in an open dialogue that will encourage growth and respect.

Currently, intervention that focuses on at risk youth comes at a time when damage to their self-esteem has been done. I feel that this program has helped raise the self-esteem of these youths by having them share their experiences with other youths, teachers, members of the community, and future teachers. My goal is that they will become resources to agencies on how we can effectively deal with at risk students by pointing out what conditions encouraged them to get in trouble. One of the things I found in working with these youths, who share common experiences with me, such as being isolated and often rejected by society, was that they had very few options available to them in which a sense of hope is present. Because of this hopeless feeling, the goals of the program are to

- Encourage youth to share their stories
- Engage them in public speaking
- Develop their communication skills

- Develop competent writing skills
- Develop conflict and anger management skills
- Develop in them a high sense of self-esteem and regard for peers
- Develop a strong sense of responsibility
- Develop a sense of community involvement and action
- Help them understand the dynamics of peer pressure
- Serve as a resource to the community and other institutional communities.

In order to accomplish these goals, I developed seven activities aimed at engaging youth and adults in an open and constructive dialogue. These activities follow.

DISCUSSION PANEL

Members of this panel consist of colleagues and students from the university who at one point were "at risk" themselves. The primary function of this panel is to help develop an open dialogue, explore what students feel about their situation, and, most important, allow them to see that they could change and succeed in life. The panel also gives students the opportunity to ask questions and listen to the different stories panel members share.

COMMUNITY INVOLVEMENT

At a later stage and with help from the community, I get students involved in community activities. These include helping in shelters, at school, and working with different organizations around the community. The goal here is not only to get them involved with the community, but also to get the community involved with them and even employing some of these youths.

GUEST SPEAKER FORUM

I have started a guest speaker forum at my university. This is known as the Institute of Critical Pedagogy and Children's Rights. The objective of this institute is to develop a forum that will serve the university, the community, and other higher education institutions in the area. The institute has presented national speakers addressing issues in critical pedagogy and children's rights, and the presentations and misrepresentations found in the media and popular films. The issues presented and discussed are aimed at enticing the general public and students to attend and participate in the institute. Within the program, the youth I am working with attend activities sponsored by it. The local speakers include people from social organizations, ex-gang members, convicts from prisons, and possible employers from the community interested in helping.

MEDIATION COUNCIL

This council is composed of students, faculty, and members of the community. It provides a forum to discuss conflicts among youth in a healthy environment. The aim is to help the council become a self-governing body sponsored by different youth organizations. It is also a forum in which youths can vent problems affecting their school or community.

SUPPORT GROUP

A support group is in the process of being developed, similar to other twelve-step groups. Its purpose will be to support youth as they are trying to change their lives. This group will become a forum for youths to share what is going on in their lives with others who are able to understand their problems.

FILM CRITIQUE CLUB

This club allows students to view and critique popular films and the ways they (mis)represent youth. The club's format gives youth an opportunity to discuss stereotypes, racism, sexism, and the glorification of negative behaviors in the media. Along with their own critiques, members will also read critiques by other viewers and writers. Films such as *Pulp Fiction, Kids, Dangerous Minds,* and *Born to Kill* are just a few that will be discussed from a critical perspective. These discussions allow members to see the injustice that the media can do to different social groups and how these (mis)representations have affected their own lives because of who they are and where they came from.

TEACHER WORKSHOPS

With the help of youth from a local group home I am working with, I am planning to deliver a series of workshops to help teachers understand the importance of showing that they care about their students. The workshops will also help teachers understand the importance of students' voices in the learning process. Youth from the group home are involved in these workshops through presentations and open question activities. Basically, the workshops will be planned and delivered by youth who are currently in the group home I work with. I have teachers participate in the workshops. My undergraduate students also benefit from the opportunity to talk with kids who have been labeled as at risk and learn that a negative label about students does not represent reality.

CONCLUSION

While my experiences growing up were not the best, I did learn from them. I learned how to survive and live in a world full of injustice, and I also learned that to create change you have to get up and do something about it. Just talking is not enough, becoming active and helping others become active is the only way we can create changes that will benefit all.

   While schools are getting more violent, the answer to eliminating a school's contribution to increasing gang membership may be as simple as caring about and respecting our students, their families, and their lives. We also need to turn to those we haven't usually respected in the past (gang members and former gang members) for expertise in just how to carry out such a humane agenda. The issue then is plain and simple: Either we critically examine our own practices or we will continue to reproduce injustice again and again. It is time we stop blaming others and ask ourselves how we have contributed to the formations of gangs. We need to ask questions and challenge injustice when we see it. We need to prepare our students and future teachers well so that they may become agents of change and promoters of social justice.

REFERENCES

Darder, A. (1991). *Culture and power in the classroom: A critical foundation for bicultural education.* New York: Bergin & Garvey.

Fine, M. (1987). Silencing in public schools. *Language Arts, 64*(2), 157–174.

Macedo, D. (1994). *Literacies of power: What Americans are not allowed to know.* San Francisco: Westview.

Activities for the Classroom

1. Log on to the Web sites listed and examine the different gang prevention programs around the nation. Discuss what they all have in common.

2. Interview local law enforcement officers in regards to how they handle gang activities.

3. Compare and contrast gang prevention programs with that of law enforcement intervention programs.

4. Talk to youth centers about their views on how to deal with gang prevention.

5. Explore and discuss the negatives of gang membership.

6. Discuss how peer pressure can contribute and/or discourage gang involvement.

FURTHER READING

Canada, G. (1995). *Fist stick knife gun.* Boston: Beacon.

Cohen, A. K. (1955). *Delinquent boys: The culture of the gang.* New York: Macmillan.

Goldstien, A. P., & Kodluboy, D. W. (1998). *Gangs in schools: Signs, symbols, and solutions.* Champaign, IL: Research Press.

Hernandez, A. (1998). *Peace in the streets: Breaking the cycle of gang violence.* Washington, DC: Child Welfare League of America.

Jackson, L. (1998). *Gangbusters: Strategies for prevention and intervention.* Lanham, MD: American Correctional Association.

Joosse, B. (2002). *Stars in the darkness.* Vancouver, BC: Chronicle.

Knox, M. (1995). *Gansta in the house: Understanding gang culture.* Royal Oak, MI: Momentum.

Sánchez–Jankowski, M. (1991). *Islands in the street: Gangs and urban society.* Oxford, England: University of California Press.

WEB SITES

http://www.streetgangs.com

http://www.iir.com/nygc

http://www.mgia.org

http://www.nagia.org

http://eric-Web.tc.columbia.edu/monographs/uds107index.html

http://www.gangwar.com/

http://www.aywnpublications.com

 *section* **II**

Social Class

Introduction: Themes of Social Class—Intersecting "Haves" and "Have-Nots"

Paula Bradfield, EDC Inc., Chicago and Jaime J. Romo, University of San Diego, San Diego

Dream Deferred

What happens to a dream deferred?
Does it dry up
Like a raisin in the sun?
Or fester like a sore–
And then run?
Does it stink like rotten meat?
Or crust and sugar over–
like a syrupy sweet?
Maybe it just sags
like a heavy load.
Or does it explode?

—Langston Hughes

Across the nation, a growing number of children are born into poverty. They enter kindergarten with hopes and dreams of opportunity, progress, and dreams fulfilled. Unfortunately, by the time most leave school, many of their hopes have withered—dried up like raisins in the sun. Within our society, education is about social class. It cuts across gendered, racial, and ethnic groups. The social class of the poor, or underclass, consists of "black, Hispanic, and Asian class fractions, together with the white aged, the unemployed and underemployed, large sections of women, the handicapped, and other marginalized economic groups" (McLaren, 1994, p. 180). In the United States, the underclass continues to increase as access to the privileges held by the middle and upper class diminishes. And, despite the "myth of meritocracy," which maintains that a solid work ethic is all one needs to pull oneself up "by the bootstraps," the U.S. middle class is diminishing, the upper class remains relatively static, and the underclass is growing. About 25% of U.S. children live in poverty, and that percentage continues to increase.

Schools in rural or urban poverty-stricken neighborhoods have a particularly significant opportunity to make or break underclass children. If such schools are not proactive in mitigating the negative impact poverty can have on children who grow up poor, they can negatively impact children's lives (e.g., Books, 1997; Duncan & Brooks-Gunn, 1997; McDermott & Rothenberg, 1999, 2000; Payne, 1998). For example, schools with large populations of poor children often have policies and practices that reinforce compliance, obedience, and passive intake of knowledge (e.g., Anyon, 1980a, 1980b; Anyon & Wilson, 1997). They generally have at least three tracks of classes and overplace poor students in academic tracks beneath their actual ability level (e.g., tracking) due to preconceived notions of performance. Teachers in these schools generally use worksheets, basic skill drills, and other teacher-directed activities. Students are expected to do the work on their own with minimal interaction with peers or the teacher. The schoolwork requires only the most basic thinking skills—recall and comprehension. Consequently, social class becomes a powerful filter that practically defines who succeeds and who does not. Students' self-esteem is often permanently affected as perceptions of their academic abilities and future possibilities dry up over time.

Fortunately, not all schools negatively impact the lives of students who grow up poor. Over the last few decades, several researchers have discovered several common characteristics of successful schools at both the institutional level and in individual classrooms. Several of these characteristics are described in the next sections.

The Building

Successful schools have reexamined how power is expressed to determine if they are treating "some groups as privileged while disconfirming others" (Giroux, 1988, pp. 130–131). These schools resist simplistic discipline policies and practices such as zero tolerance (e.g., Ayers & Dohrn, 1999). They persist in a variety of school-wide efforts to link with the community and empower community members and families from a variety of social strata and cultural backgrounds to have a voice in school decisions (Levin, 1995; Weiner, 1993). They often restructure into small caring communities called small schools, or schools within schools (e.g., Howley, Bickel, & Strange, 2000; Meier, 1995; Small Schools Workshop, 2001) with the belief that schools must take all of the child's life experiences into account (Weiner, 1999) and must connect personally and meaningfully with each child.

Such schools reinforce practices and policies that exemplify their belief that all children can successfully learn meaningful, challenging content. Consequently, they have restructured inequitable policies such as tracking and single-score entrance policies to certain classes and programs (Lee & Smith, 1994; Oakes, Quartz, Ryan, & Lipton, 1999). They make systematic efforts to

1. Systematically integrate state standards in curriculum design, instruction, and assessment
2. Increase instructional time in both reading and mathematics
3. Devote a larger percentage of district and school funds for teacher professional development focused on changing instructional practice based on current research and best practices
4. Implement comprehensive systems to follow individual student achievement and provide extra support as soon as it is needed rather than penalizing the student for poor performance
5. Involve parents in helping students succeed on high-stakes assessments
6. Have state and district accountability systems in place that have real consequences for staff in the schools (Barth et al., 1998)

THE STAFF

Even when systematic policies and practices that affirm students of poverty have not been endorsed on a building-wide basis, counselors, teachers, and other building staff can make a difference in a child who has grown up poor. Similar to Kohl (1994), they spend their lives helping children resist the institutional and societal educational inertia that face the underclass in a variety of ways (e.g., Haberman, 1995; Haberman & Post, 1998; Knapp et al., 1995; McDermott & Rothenberg, 1999, 2000; Weiner, 1993, 1999). Among other activities, these school workers

- Resist "drill and kill" strategies and expectations of passive compliance from children—they consider themselves coaches
- Become adept at navigating school bureaucracies as they advocate for students
- Remain resilient when faced with complications and setbacks caused by school and district inertia
- Are passionate about continued learning and teaching

- Demonstrate an ethic of caring
- Are eager to teach children from poverty
- Believe it is critical to know the children in a cultural context
- Collaborate with other teachers and persist in situations wrought with violence and/or death
- Maintain high standards for all children—they never blame the children (blaming the victim) or their families

In short, they truly believe they can make a difference and spend their lives doing so (Knapp et al., 1995).

Under the influence of adults such as these, children learn to be resilient (e.g., Wang, Haertel, & Walberg, 1998)—they thwart statistical odds and succeed, both in and out of school. They believe they add value to the world—and they do.

In the following section, we read about the impact of poverty and privilege on several current advocates. Paula Bradfield-Kreider, associate professor at St. Cloud State University in Minnesota in the Department of Teacher Development, explores the early impact of exclusion through socioeconomic status and the power of white privilege. Ramona Maile Cutri, assistant professor at Brigham Young University in the Department of Teacher Education, examines the complexities of biracial, spiritual, and economic identity development. Nancy Gallavan, associate professor of teacher educator, social studies, and multicultural education at the University of Nevada, Las Vegas, offers a perspective of privilege and her work as an advocate for justice. Similarly, Linda F. Quinn, associate dean at the University of Nevada at Las Vegas, College of Education, examines "diversity hiding behind a mask of sameness." Each relates the psychic and physical violence that poverty engenders. Each offers readers insights into the ways teachers can help students be successful.

REFERENCES

Anyon, J. (1980a). Elementary schooling and the distinctions of social class. *Interchange, 12,* 118–132.

Anyon, J. (1980b). Social class and the hidden curriculum of work. *Journal of Social Education, 16*(2), 1.

Anyon, J., & Wilson, W. J. (1997). Ghetto schooling: A political economy of urban educational reform. New York: Teachers College Press.

Barth, P., Haycock, K., Jackson, H., Mora, K., Ruiz, P., Robinson, S., & Wilkins, A. (Eds.). (1998). Dispelling the myth: High poverty schools exceeding expectations. Washington, DC: U.S. Department of Education.

Bickel, R., Howley, C. B., & Strange, M. (2000). Research about school size and school performance in impoverished communities. ERIC Digest EDO-RC-00-10. Las Cruces, NM: Clearinghouse on Rural Education and Small Schools, Appalachian Educational Laboratory.

Books, S. (1997). The other poor: Rural poverty and education. *Educational Foundations, 11*(1), 73–85.

Duncan, G. J., & Brooks-Gunn, J. (Eds.). (1997). Consequences of growing up poor. New York: Russell Sage Foundation.

Giroux, H. (1988). Teachers as intellectuals: Toward a critical pedagogy of learning. South Hadly, MA: Bergin & Garvey.

Haberman, M. (1995). Selecting "star" teachers for children and youth in urban poverty. *Phi Delta Kappan, 76,* 777–781.

Haberman, M., & Post, L. (1998). Teachers for multicultural schools: The power of selection. *Theory Into Practice, 37*(2), 96–104.

Howley, C. B., Bickel, R., & Strange, M. (1999). *The Matthew Project: National report.* Randolf, VT: Ohio State University, Columbus.

Kohl, H. (1994). I won't learn from you! New York: New Press.

Knapp, M. S., Shields, P. M., Zucker, A. A., Needels, M. C., Turnbul, B. J., Adelman, N. E., & McCollum, H. (1995). Teaching for meaning in high-poverty classrooms. New York: Teachers College Press.

Lee, V. E., & Smith, J. B. (1994). *High school restructuring and student achievement: A new study finds strong links: Issue report #7.* Madison, WI: Center on Organization and Restructuring of Schools.

Levin, B. (1995). Poverty and education. *Education Canada, 35*(2), 28–35.

McDermott, P. C., & Rothenberg, J. J. (1999). *Teaching in high poverty, urban schools—Learning from practitioners and students.* Paper presented at the annual meeting of the American Educational Research Association, Montreal, Quebec, Canada.

McDermott, P., & Rothenberg, J. (1999). *The characteristics of effective teachers in high poverty schools— Triangulating our data.* New Orleans, LA: Educational Document Reproduction Service.

Meier, D. (1995). *The power of their ideas: Lessons from a small school in Harlem.* Boston: Beacon.

Oakes, J., Quartz, K. H., Ryan, S., & Lipton, M. (1999). *Becoming good American schools: The struggle for civic virtue in educational reform.* San Francisco: Jossey-Bass.

Payne, R. K. (1998). *A framework for understanding poverty.* Highlands, TX: aha! Process

Small Schools Workshop, (2001). [on-line]. Available: http://www.smallschools.com/index.html.

Wang, M. C., Haertel, G. D., & Walberg, H. J. (1998). *Building educational resilience. Fastback 430.* Bloomington, IN: Phi Delta Kappa Foundation.

Weiner, L. (1993). *Preparing teachers for urban schools: Lessons from thirty years of school reform.* New York: Teachers College Press.

Chapter 4

Letting Go and Breaking Loose: Struggling Toward Transformative Teaching

Paula Bradfield, EDC Inc., Chicago

Focus Questions

1. How do school communities perpetuate in-groups and out-groups? How do these compound personal and family shame?

2. To what extremes would you go to hide shame or a family secret?

3. What were critical experiences that enabled Paula to be a border crosser?

4. As you read, examine how we absorb messages of material wealth, strength, maleness, and the myth of meritocracy.

5. The power of a teacher is tremendous. What can you learn from the teachers in Paula's story—both the positive and negative lessons?

(A small town in Wyoming, 1975). Five minutes. Ralph steadies Thunder for her first ride this season. The horse is huge, over 15 hands, tense, and covered with a fine film of sweat. Can I do this again? The familiar fear of the unknown surges through my body, slamming into my fingertips and toes. The horse shifts, sensing my fear.

Four minutes. I remember my first horse, 5 years ago. Callie was a chestnut—short, stocky, fiery eyed, and frothing with energy. I had no doubts about my ability to train her. Cocky, young, and sure the universe centered on me, I strutted over to the gate that held her. What more did I have to know about her besides the fact that she was an unbroken horse? I had seen it done a thousand times and practiced in my backyard on an old barrel held up with ropes. This was the way my neighbor Elmer trained horses: "You have to dominate the horse, show him who's boss. You do that and you will break his spirit. Then he is yours. The rest is easy."

Three minutes. How wrong I was about training and Callie. The instant I settled into the saddle, I knew I was in trouble. Elmer let go of the harness, and I was alone with the horse. She bucked and twisted in opposition to my position on her. She paid close attention to what I was doing, anticipated every shift in the saddle, and used that knowledge to throw me. I, on the other hand, ignored her. I held on tighter, closed my eyes and held my breath, knowing that I could hold out. Surely she was beginning to sense that she was boss. Two seconds later, I was in the air, plummeting towards the ground. Callie stopped, turned, and watched me spit dirt out of my mouth and limp back to the corral fence. Eye to eye, I realized that I was no more than a fleeting irritant to her. She had been in charge the entire time.

Two minutes. For the next year, I was afraid to get back on an untrained horse. I didn't want to talk about it, especially to Uncle Elmer. I felt weak and not in charge. One day Karen Blackwell, a woman who had been training horses for years in Big Piney, stopped by the stables to see if I wanted a job. "Doing what?" "Assistant trainer. I heard from your neighbor that you might want to work with horses." "Naw, I don't have the knack. I'm not strong enough." She looked at me for a few seconds then smiled. "You don't have to be strong. You leave that up to the horse."

One minute. I worked with Karen for two years. Before she would even consider allowing me on a horse, she wanted me to become one. I slept with horses, fed and groomed them, talked and sang to them, and, most important, I listened to them. "Karen, when can I begin training again?" She chuckled and retorted, "You already are." "Yeah, but when can I get on again?" "You will know when you are ready. The horse will tell you."

Goose told me. He was a stocky, muscled gelding 2-year-old that had been treated roughly by his previous owners, who had attempted to break him—Goose wouldn't break. A family then bought him for $25 for their children and hoped that we could gentle him. Karen said, "He's yours. It's time." Goose and I lived in the same space for a month. Each day, he allowed me to get to know him a little better. Trust was forming between the two of us.

Ten seconds. The first ride was terrifying, exhilarating, a blur with a few lucid moments. Over the next several days, Goose and I worked out a deal. It was simple. When I ignored him or assumed too much, I ended up in the dirt. When I paid full attention, we learned.

It was time. Ralph held Thunder's harness. She craned her neck around so I could see her eye. She was afraid too. Was I ready for this ride? Have we learned enough about each other? What mistakes would I make? Would I ever get it right? No. I would make mistakes. Thunder and I would work together. I would get bucked off at least once. I was ready. "Okay, Ralph, let go of the harness."

Letting go of the harness—trusting others enough to reveal secrets, to be wrong, to care, and to grow. Trusting myself enough to become stronger—to feel comfortable with my own background, gender, and heritage. Breaking loose from the harnesses of a male-dominated, conservative, middle-class Wyoming community and trusting strong women friends to help me become another strong woman. My journey is filled with stories of letting go and breaking loose and is never ending.

I have been progressing slowly towards transformative teaching and engaging in praxis related to social justice for a lifetime—at times moving forward, at times stalled, and at times slipping backwards. Until I acknowledged and then let go of childhood stories steeped with parental sexual abuse, marital violence, alcoholism, prison, situational poverty, and the unearned power and privilege of my own whiteness, I seemed to be alternately drowning or floating rather than progressing. I then had to begin to learn to recognize and then break loose from heterosexism, sexism, classism, and the gravitational force of Eurocentrism. I am still engaged in this process. My story is written from the perspective of a lower class, white girl-child struggling for identity in a middle-class male-dominated, cowboy way of life in Wyoming. Still a beginner—a newly transformed antiracist and cultural worker—my story is filled with mistakes, false smugness, and small victories. During my narrative, I will first detail the events and people who have been instrumental in my journey and accompanying emotions that were the catalysts for the radical changes in my perceptions of race, power, privilege, dominance, and oppression in schools and society.

EARLY INFLUENCES

From the beginning, women have nourished me. I was raised by my mother, aunt, and grandmother in a small Wyoming "cow town" in the foothills of the Rocky Mountains. Although all three women had been married for part of their lives, the men had been alcoholics and either drunk or absent. Each of the three women took on a unique role in our family; my aunt provided leadership and made the decisions, my grandmother provided nurturing and moral guidance, and my mother was the peacemaker. Soon after she graduated from high school, my mother married my father, an oil field worker from Texas who had a reputation for drinking and "womanizing." She divorced my father after being the primary breadwinner for 7 years of marriage and then married her second husband, also an alcoholic.

Again, alcohol created a turbulent and financially unstable home life. My stepfather was in and out of our lives as he moved from jail to involuntary commitments at the state hospital. When he was at home and drinking, he and my mother had emotionally and physically violent fights. We knew the drill—flee the house, go to the neighbors, and call the police. Fred's comings and leavings during that time rendered my mother emotionally bereft and financially unable to maintain our way of life. I was lonely much of the time at home—often seeking solace with my grandmother, a wonderful, loving woman who always had time for her only granddaughter.

Soon after I began school, my mother and new stepfather were forced to move to the only neighborhood they could afford—Southside, "across the tracks" (Payne, 1998). My grandmother remained supportive but mourned our descent into poverty. My aunt, angry at our disgrace to the family, fumed silently and kept her distance. Family gatherings during those years were tense—long silences with sudden eruptions of anger and name calling among the three women I loved.

I remember my first day in Southside's Washington Elementary. The smells were different than my first 3 years in a suburban school—there was a lingering smell of varnish, mildew, and chalk. The red brick building was three stories with wooden floors, noisy stairs, and big windows. The playground only had one swing set, one small slide, and a field where the boys played sports. Huge cottonwood trees and older homes surrounded the school. I grew to love that school. The surrounding neighborhood was the only diverse neighborhood in the city, consisting primarily of Latinos, African Americans, American Indians, and second-generation families from Eastern Europe.

Since my mother had to work long hours, the boys went to day care and, as the oldest, I was allowed to return home after school. I spent most of my time outside on my porch or at the school playground. My two neighborhood friends were Carlos, a Mexican American, and Clarence, an African American. I became a regular in their homes. I saw no color at that age and either did not hear or suppressed the inevitable racist comments of my family. Since neither of their mothers worked, Clarence's and Carlos' homes were continually filled with children and family, noise, smells of cooking, and activity. I didn't notice that Carlos and Clarence did not come into my home but only yelled down the stairs when they wanted me to come out to play. At the time, I never questioned their absence in my home. The years passed with friends and my grandmother providing me with a sense of belonging.

MIDDLE GRADES INFLUENCES

Upper Elementary School

I lost my Southside community of friends and family near the end of fifth grade. Under pressure from my relatives and with a better paying job, my mother rented a house in a white middle-class neighborhood. I was devastated with the news and dreaded the impending move.

As soon as we settled into our new house, I began scouting the neighborhood for other children. I was dismayed at the quiet, sterile streets. Nobody was sitting on porches ready to offer a friendly word. Nobody had open doors with smells of cooking and the tumultuous sounds of children wafting outward. The neighborhood appeared deserted. And the few children I did see outside playing were white. Without the influence of a television, I was not prepared for what I saw or for the emotional reaction it would cause—fear and loneliness. I was an outsider.

I began school the next day and was again faced with only white children who already had their groups of friends. After a few weeks of loneliness, a few of the neighborhood boys invited me to play. In my matriarchal family, I never had a father around enough to socialize me in the role of a woman-child, and my mother, aunt, and grandmother did not mind the fact that my favorite friends had always been boys. Soon thereafter, Donna, a sister of one of the neighborhood boys, began to befriend me. Unlike me, Donna had been socialized in a large, patriarchal family. She had been acculturated in "appropriate" girl-play and was unwilling to play "boy games" or do "boy things." Over the next year, she taught me how to play "girl games" and do "girl things." This was my induction into gender-specific rules for childhood play. Although I missed the embrace of the families of my Southside friends, my new social arrangement soon became "good enough." I began to accept a white world as normal and that young women had set gender roles. I never questioned why culturally or linguistically distinct families did not populate the neighborhood.

Several months later, however, I was forced to confront race and white privilege for the first time. In the span of one week, I learned about social class and became aware of overt racism. Edna, a lonely older woman with time on her hands who had been spending time at our house chatting with my mother and lending a helping hand with us, initiated the first incident. With each visit, the neighbor woman made it her duty to bestow at least one pearl of wisdom upon me—woman to girl-child. One day she discovered we had lived in Southside. She asked me about my neighbors and friends, something all other adults had been silent about. I told her about my school, about Carlos and Clarence, and about their homes and families. She was dismayed when she learned how much time I had spent in their homes. She then took it upon herself to enlighten me. She spent hours making sure I knew that Southside was not a safe place to live and that I had been brainwashed by "those people" who lived "across the track." What did she mean? It made no sense to me. A few days later, I began to ask questions. I quizzed her about her knowledge of Southside and asked her what she meant by "those people." She retorted, "Why, poor white trash, niggers and spics—those people who don't care about our American way of life."

My early conceptions of race, family, and community were rocked. Everything she said contradicted years of personal experience. In an attempt to make sense of her comments, I asked my mother what *nigger* and *spic* meant. "Well, a nigger is a black person and a spic is a light brown person who speaks Mexican." Unwittingly, my mother attested to the veracity of Edna's remarks. How could Carlos and Clarence be "niggers" and "spics"—un-American without my knowing it? I felt betrayed.

Several days later, another component of Edna's diatribe resurfaced to haunt me—the phrase "poor white trash." My aunt made a comment that she was glad we were not acting like poor white trash anymore. Later that night, I asked my mother if we were poor white trash. She cried, "Don't you ever say that again! It's not my fault that we *had* to live in Southside. I am sick of being blamed for everything!" What did she mean by that? I then asked my aunt about "poor white trash," "niggers" and "spics." She whispered, "Your mother should be ashamed of herself for what she put you through in Southside. I was worried sick about you every night. No, you are not white trash anymore." Anymore?

White trash. Un-American. Those people. I was ashamed. Terrified that someone would learn my secret, I buried memories of Southside, never mentioning my friends to anyone. I decided that I was lucky to be white because it allowed me to live in our neighborhood. Looking back, I realize that this decision was a major turning point in my life. Carlos, Clarence, and their families had become the "Other." I was a passive racist. I had come to believe that whiteness had something to do with class and privilege, that is, choice of neighborhood. I was part of the problem of white American racism.

Secondary School

I maintained my newly formed racist and classist beliefs until my senior year in high school, separating myself from my early memories and friends of Southside. I occasionally thought of Carlos and Clarence when I encountered them in the halls. When we parted, we were children, oblivious to race and gender. As young adolescents, we had lost our easy camaraderie and resorted to stilted and shy interactions, exchanged smiles, quiet hellos, and half waves. I was always worried about who would see me acknowledging them, so I made sure my hellos were discreet. We never had a class together. They were in the basement, taking classes my friends and I called "bonehead" classes. Similar to most secondary schools, our heavily tracked curriculum sorted the students into "haves" and "have-nots," perpetuating Eurocentric dominance and the myth of meritocracy. Both Clarence and Carlos were placed in the lower tracked classes along with almost all of the Southside students of color and poor whites. New to the neighborhood, I was mislabeled. Nobody knew I had lived in Southside, and I told no one.

Over my middle and high school years, I spent a great deal of time and energy learning the middle-class social structure, doggedly maintaining my place in the hierarchy, and looking for opportunities to increase my status. I had to learn the hidden rules of the middle class without revealing my secrets of Southside. Afraid that my family might still be considered white trash, I attempted to hide my family from my friends. I abandoned all that was good about my prior life and had nothing left except the shallow label of groupie. I expressed no independent thoughts and no values of my own. Basking in the heat of membership, I did not rock the boat of power and privilege until my senior year.

Similar to other white Americans who do not have a strong sense of belonging, I was sucked into belonging to groups committed to pathological behavior, similar to that exhibited by hate groups. We did a thorough job rejecting and ridiculing other students who either desired entrance or who were "on their way out," something none of us would ever have done on our own. In my particular group of white friends, race was never actually mentioned. It was as if Southside students did not exist in our school—rendered invisible by the dominant culture.

Fortunately, before and during my years as a groupie, seeds of discontent were being sown. Four outside influences—a counselor, a teacher, a library full of books, and Clarence planted those seeds. Mr. Bidden, my eighth-grade math teacher and high school counselor, sowed seeds of breaking loose. He sparked my interest in life after high school as a woman professional. Aware of my fragile psyche, he spent time nurturing my love for mathematics, convincing me that I was bright and could have any career I wanted. He nagged at me to keep my sights set on the future rather than the present. Where there was only pessimism, Mr. Bidden nurtured hope. When I became a groupie, he did not abandon me but continued his mission, encouraging the personal qualities I kept hidden from others. At a moment critical to my development, Mr. Bidden showed me my IQ score—an illegal act at the time. He did what it took to convince me to let go of my narrow aspirations of secretary or store clerk and to be more than a shallow groupie.

My second influence came from Miss Tiway, my Latin teacher for 4 years. Her life was her students and the Latin language. Because of her, I began to develop a lifelong passion for culture, language, and travel. Miss Tiway was also the first woman I had met who stood fiercely and overtly by her ideals, advocated publicly for her students, and demanded that her students set goals, work toward them, and "live their talk." Each time she caught me floundering in hypocrisy or laxness or class-related self-doubt, she called me on it. Because of her, I began to examine my own life. Over time, I began to see the inconsistency between what I thought I believed and my actions. I began to be torn between the enjoyment of clique membership and the enjoyment of learning about other languages, cultures, and ideas. I began to give myself permission to realize virtues outside of clique membership.

Library books were my third influence. I had been an avid reader since my days of self-selected isolation at home as a child in Southside—books were my alternate world. In middle and high school, I read widely from an eclectic genre of literature, including fantasy, science fiction, and books written by authors whose worldview was not Western European. Literature provided me with options, constructs, and multiple ways of learning to know my world. The worldview that began to emerge from my reading began looking quite different than that which I espoused. The disequilibrium continued to increase.

Clarence was the last and most powerful influence during that time of introspection and analysis. My racism was subtle, virtually unnoticeable to the majority of white Americans in the school, including myself. Since I was unaware of it, I had no need to overcome it—until Clarence got shot. In the middle of my senior year, I noticed an article in the paper about a gunfight in Southside. One of the shooters was in the hospital. It was Clarence. Without thinking, I immediately drove to the hospital. After a few uncomfortable moments, I began to babble, nervous and afraid he would not remember me. He did. We began to talk, not like when we were children, but as young adults who are looking forward and looking back at the same time. As we talked, I became more aware of my intentional abandonment of Clarence. I tried to convince myself that he had not noticed it after all. He had. Finally, Clarence began teasing me about not acknowledging him in school. I was terrified and too mortified to speak: What do I tell him? The moment had come in our relationship for me to be honest. I was ready to confess but I couldn't—I retreated into white silence by avoiding the issue (Ladson-Billings, 1996). I only apologized, hoping he would not challenge my cowardice. He chose not to push me. I wasn't strong enough to stand beside him and he drifted away, losing interest. I wanted Clarence to like me again, trying to recapture the sense of belonging I remembered from Southside, but I lost my final chance.

Although Clarence never said the words, he knew that my withdrawal from him and Carlos was a racist act, as I know now. While no groupie mentioned white skin as criteria for membership, I leapt to the assumption that it was. No one had pressured me into my actions. I could only blame myself. At the time of the incident, I became vaguely ashamed and intuitively knew that it was time to slowly extricate myself from the clique. I was ready to begin again. I began inventing excuses to stay home on weekends to spend time reading. The confines of clique membership began to lose its addictive powers.

COLLEGE YEARS

Because of lack of money, I spent my first two years in a local junior college. Since I still lived at home, I was bound by my mother's and stepfather's insistence that I attend the junior college and major in secretarial science, a woman's job with a steady income. I agreed about the school but not about the major. Since neither parent had attended college, it was quite easy to lie. I convinced them that my major was secretarial science. Thanks to Mr. Bidden, I had enrolled in a strong academic course load. During my first semester I inserted business management into my schedule, laden with science, math, and literature courses so that I could at least develop the terminology to keep my parents fooled. After that first semester, however, I took out a student loan and moved into the dormitory, eliminating the need for lies about majors and course work.

College became a time for me to rebuild. I avoided preestablished cliques, peers who exhibited racist behaviors, and students who were not taking their studies seriously. I took difficult courses, enjoying the power of choosing what I wanted to take, relishing in being able to meet the mental challenges. Since most of the professors were not from my hometown, I began to let go of some of my fear of being labeled by my past as they began to know me as a good student.

Midway through my second semester, Margaret Demorest, one of my favorite professors, introduced me to another of her students, Grace Demitrius. Although we had attended the same high school, Grace and I had been in completely different social worlds. She surrounded herself with academics and artists while I, in an attempt to deny my lower class beginnings, spent my time and energy gaining entry into the clique of the social "elite." Grace and I became the best of friends and, since she lived in town, we spent a great deal of time at her home. The Demitrius family maintained strong Greek and Basque familial ties—with dozens of first-generation relatives who had recently moved to this area from the Pyrenees Mountains or Greece. Until I left for the university, I spent most of my free time with them, basking again in the warmth of extended family. I mused about familial relationships, belonging, and responsibility. I struggled to extract myself from my prior habits of isolation and Eurocentric notions of individualism—a source of contention with the Demitrius family.

ADULTHOOD

Upon graduation from the University of Wyoming with a degree in biology, I began looking for a career. In my junior and senior year, I was most interested in either veterinary medicine or psychology. I had held two part-time jobs, one in a veterinary laboratory and the other as a houseparent in a small home for runaway teens from all cultural backgrounds.

When I was given a group of 18 students to teach, I had to step outside of "self" for the first time. I had no prior experience with children other than my brothers and began working with the students under the assumption that "children are children"; they were the same regardless of culture or race. Although my personal perception of races was slightly more sophisticated, my teaching worldview with accompanying pedagogy was color and culture blind.

I fell into the equality trap, fearing that differential treatment or approaches would lead to labeling and discrimination. Within a month, my charges revolted. Some students took advantage of my naiveté, while others either became apathetic and withdrawn or aggressive and overtly angry. I was forced to discard the naive perception that children are all the same and my simplistic, one-dimensional strategies. I spent the next several months using a trial-and-error approach to reconstruct my perceptions of children in a cultural and racial context. By the time I left that job, my perceptions were radically different. I had switched from a flat, static view of "children are children" to an "individual differences" paradigm in which each child is unique. Because of my experiences, teaching suddenly became intriguing—a way to teach and help each child.

I returned to the university for a second bachelor's degree in K–12 education. As a teacher, I actualized my passion for advocacy by striving to create successful learning environments for each child. Because of my wanderlust and interest in cultures other than my own, I sought many teaching opportunities in different regions and with different populations of children. I taught in suburban schools, small town schools, rural schools, city schools, and international schools. I taught poor students, rich students, middle-class students, students who lived in cars, students whose families were migrant orchard workers, and students whose parents earned their living by collecting mussels along the shoreline of the Pacific Ocean. To illustrate, I will elaborate on three schools that most profoundly influenced my continually evolving beliefs on racism, power, and privilege.

NEW ZEALAND

Shortly after we married, my partner Thomas and I decided to seek teaching posts in New Zealand for a year. We had difficulty finding positions, because of the perception that schools and teachers in the United States were similar to the television series *Welcome Back Kotter*, with no discipline and little academic work. After dozens of rejected applications, one administrator hired me who knew U.S. teachers from his exchange in an Idaho school. A friend of his hired Thomas. I taught 6th through 10th grades for 1 year in a small town outside Auckland, in the north island, where the majority of the native Maoris lived.

In New Zealand secondary schools (6th through 11th grades), all students were ranked according to scores on grade-level school exams and are then placed in classes with others of similar ranking. At the end of their sophomore year, students had to pass a national exam in order to continue school. The curriculum and teaching strategies were almost exclusively British, favoring the children of European descent. At Taranapoa High School, however, over 60% of the students and a third of the teachers were Maori. Many of the Maori students fell victim to the institutionalized racism that landed them in the lower tracked classes, making it almost impossible to pass the national exams at the end of their sophomore year.

I began teaching high school after only having experience in elementary school. I was in a heavily tracked school system and in a country that I knew little about. As the "new kid on the block," four out of my six classes were in the lowest tracks and almost exclusively Maori. I was the only woman in the mathematics department and the only "Yank" in the school. I remained naively optimistic, maintaining the belief that all children were the same, which implied that I could use strategies that had worked in the past. And my students, not yet biased against U.S. teachers, were proud to have the "Yank" and gave me the benefit of the doubt.

After the first week, I discovered that all my conceptions of teaching Maori students in a British, heavily tracked secondary school were misconceptions. First, I knew nothing about teaching and learning in a cultural context different from my own. My Maori students, disenfranchised from the school system, had no trust in the system or hopes that school would provide opportunities for them. They were waiting until they could legally leave school and begin a trade. Since I had never taught culturally or linguistically distinct children, their apathy about their future and behaviors that did not help them succeed in school surprised me. I doubled my efforts to teach them without considering their learning.

Unfortunately, despite my efforts, my students were still not achieving. When the scores were posted for each class, all of mine remained on the bottom. My Eurocentric teaching framework was completely inadequate. I had no construct to accommodate my teaching to a group of students who were primarily relational, verbal, strong willed, proud, collective and high energy. I knew nothing about the Maori culture, social norms, and proud traditions.

Embarrassed by our poor ranking and passive acceptance of failure by my students, I attempted to begin again. For the next month, I tried at least a dozen different strategies to increase the learning of each child, most of which failed. I spent hours each day reworking my lessons and searching for new ideas. Finally, I joined the Maori table at "tea," a tea and cookie break given to the staff at midmorning. I queried Margaret, a Maori English teacher who had offered her help earlier in the year. Over time, Margaret, Don, Tooi, and Sammy helped me understand "their students," as they called them. Near the end of that month, I attempted to use what I learned from my Maori colleagues. I attempted to nurture a learning environment that fostered a sense of community and used techniques that allowed students to work together, to debate and solve problems together in manners that were supportive of their cultural expectations. In twos and threes, my students began preparing for grade-level exams, given monthly, using these new strategies—a great deal of partner tutoring and short, intense periods of partner oral quizzing. We developed a bantering, humorous style of interaction interspersed with periods of intense concentration and hard work. Scores began to increase, to my students' astonishment and delight.

The day after their second monthly exam, I found a container of mussels, olive oil, vinegar, and onions on my desk. From that day on, I had fresh mussels on my desk each morning that the students or their families collected from the beach. By the end of the year, our class ranking had gone from lowest to second highest. My students and their families were elated. My department chair was stunned. I was recommitted.

Because of the year with the students in New Zealand, my worldview began to broaden—experience added substance to my books. I had a glimmer of a new belief—that all children were not alike and could be successful if I put in the effort to learn from them. Although the Maori children suffered from educational inequities similar to our American Indian children, I still refused to acknowledge that racism was part of the reason their national performance rates were so low. I had yet to acknowledge the role that racism and other forms of oppression had on access to challenging and meaningful teaching and learning.

CENTRAL FLORIDA

When I returned from New Zealand, I believed that I could learn to teach anyone if I worked hard enough to figure out how they learned. After deciding to try living nearer one of my younger brothers, Thomas and I obtained teaching positions in Florida. I accepted a post teaching basic competency mathematics at a high school in which over half of the students were African American. Over 73% of the students in the high school were on free and reduced lunch, and over 60% of the students did not graduate from high school. With a false sense of invincibility, I was ready to begin teaching. As the only female in the department, I had accepted the fact that my teaching load consisted of all six competency math classes, a required course for students who had failed the state mathematics exam.

I had no idea who my students would be but assumed that I would have a mix similar to the demographics of the school. My first period class, however, was all African American. By the end of my six-period day, I discovered that 154 of my 160 students were African American and six were white. I was stunned. Undaunted, I arrived the second day, believing I could find a way to teach my students. I came fully prepared—lesson plans, overheads, and a quiz. Between the headphones, boom boxes, bantering exchange of insults, profanities, and quips, the classroom noise was deafening—impossible for me to teach in the manner that I had prepared. That day ended up being a continual competition to be heard; my students were the uncontested champions. To my new group of students, I was just another "snowflake," disinterested in them and waiting until I could be reassigned to higher level math classes. I was terrified of my own students and fear turned to depression and withdrawal. After 3 weeks of one disaster after another with no learning occurring, my students' prediction about my performance had come true. Nothing I tried worked, including the strategies that I used for the Maori students. None of my colleagues were African American, so I had no one to ask. I had not thought of asking the students or their parents. I hated my job. I began calling in sick. I either had to quit teaching or change.

That Friday, I was slated to chaperone a football game and dance. At the game, I sat next to Taniesha, a student in my first-period class who often attempted to quiet the students down for me. We chatted throughout the game about our lives, our class, and the school. A mother of a 2-year-old, she talked about how hard it was to work, go to school, and raise her daughter, but she would not let her grandmother down. She asked me why I had such "attitude" about them. I mulled over our conversation and her question all weekend. Was I even *trying* to learn from them, or had I retreated into old habits out of fear? I was not yet ready to give up on either them or myself.

Monday, when my students arrived, I had my own boom box with music playing in the background. I had a note on the board: "No math today—let's talk." Taniesha and a few of the more vocal African American female students noticed and got the others to listen. We spent the next 2 days talking about their frustrations with the class. Everyone hated math, hated the text (many of them had used this text before and some since the seventh grade). But they knew that this class could be their ticket to graduation—they wanted to pass the state exam. We had a class goal.

I re-collected the texts, studied the state exam, and created an individualized course. Some students worked independently, but most preferred to work in small groups. They promised to tone down their profanities if I would try to have less "attitude" about their language and bantering. After a few weeks of this working arrangement, my tunnel vision began to broaden. I began to notice inequities centered on language. Many of my students were bidialectical and could not easily "code-switch" between their own use of the language and that used by European American test makers. They were frustrated when they understood the mathematics but could not pass the sample test questions. When Taniesha began asking me to help her with meaning during lunch and after school, I attempted to work on what I now know is code switching to make explicit the hidden rules and formal language of the school and state test. We had Post-it notes and "cheat sheets" all over the room. It began to help other students.

By the end of the first semester, almost all of my students were working, if not for me, for each other or family members who hoped they would pass the test. The only five students who were not working included one African American male and all four white male students. My African American male student remained unengaged despite efforts by his classmates and me. He began the year angry, verbally abusive to all. Eventually, we formed a begrudging pact. He would watch his treatment of the others and me and make an attempt at learning. The uneasy truce lasted throughout the year, but without much academic progress. My four white male students were also not working. They quietly insulted me and the other students with jokes and other racial and sexual innuendos. They became overtly hostile towards me when I rejected their sexual bantering and racial jokes. During class, they quietly made sexual and racial comments to me as I passed their desks: "Nigger lover." And they alluded to what happens to "nigger-loving women" in this state. I was terrified but furious at them. I was unwilling to work with them, to attempt to teach them. An administrator that I had been working with put them in an academic chokehold—if any of the four did anything remotely resembling disrespect of me, they would be removed from class immediately and automatically suspended the next day—no due process and no questioning my judgment. For about a month, they were in school one day and out the next, getting hopelessly behind. For the rest of the year, they succumbed to the system, but we rarely spoke. They sat sullenly and counted the minutes until class was out. I know I failed them. I was less tolerant of them than the rest of my students. I never considered their lives, growing up poor, and seeing their white privilege threatened by African Americans who were suddenly doing better than they were. I only drove them deeper into their racism, sexism, and apathy towards education.

Despite my five failures, over 92% of my students passed the state mathematics exam at the end of that year. They were able to move out of that class. At the end of that year, however, my beliefs in my ability to single-handedly teach each child had been shaken. I had begun to acknowledge the impact that institutional racism and social class biases had on student performance. I began to realize that meritocracy was a myth. I was fortunate only because I was white and was new to my middle school—nobody knew where I had lived. I spent a great deal of time trying to understand the institutional inequities that ensured the maintenance of power and privilege. My image in the American Dream, "equality," and the power of the individual began to tarnish.

HIGHER EDUCATION

For the next 6 years, I attended graduate school part-time in a small, Florida university and taught full-time in another large, urban high school. With two small children, graduate school, and a full-time job, I survived day to day in my attempts to do three full-time jobs well. Upon completion of my Ph.D., I obtained a teacher education post in a small, private, northwestern liberal arts college. As in most small colleges, I had to wear many hats and frequently taught outside my area of expertise, science education. I spent the majority of my time with a team who created an authentic, field-based, integrated cohort program for preservice teachers in a postgraduate teacher preparation program. I had to learn to conceptualize more broadly than before and to work outside my area of expertise on a daily basis. I taught and team-taught qualitative research, educational technology, general methods, and multicultural education with an attached month-long immersion in another culture. I spent thousands of hours filling in gaps in my conceptual framework, especially in multicultural and intercultural education, my weakest area.

My growth during those 4 years was exponential—I learned to be comfortable outside my own area of expertise. My previous smugness about teacher education and my content area was shattered as I continued to encounter perceptual and conceptual gaps about teaching, learning, and culture. I also began to realize that neither learning nor change occurs in isolation, that it occurs in intercultural teams, in which each member brings culture- and gender-rich meaning and depth.

Our students were all teamed and so were we. Mike Shitaki, a faculty member with a Ph.D. in intercultural education, was the most instrumental in our growth as an intercultural team and a critical contributor to my development as an intercultural collaborator and networker. My remaining European American vestiges of lone-wolf mentality were again challenged as it interfered with our collective progress. I was able to release another piece of the ethnocentric cocoon I had used in the past—to render myself invisible and to avoid conflict—when I realized that I now used it as a convenience and a white privilege to either get my way or to disagree (Ladson-Billings, 1995). Fortunately, the power of our collective work and strong sense of belonging provided the catalyst to begin reconstructing a more public transformative teaching personage. The only permanent changes in our 4 years occurred when we worked collectively in critical teams. None of us was able to overcome the inertia of our status quo schools alone; we could only avoid conflict.

At this institution, I discovered my research passion and a vehicle to effect change in preservice teachers about their willingness and ability to teach students who are different from themselves. An opportunity to lead a group of students for a month-long immersion in Latin America surfaced at the last minute. I located a site in central Mexico and developed a program with the help of other committed colleagues that allowed preservice teachers to experience living with, learning from, and depending on a family in a community whose dominant culture was Mexican. In our first site immersion, I witnessed the beginnings of changes in most of my students after about 2 weeks of immersion (Bradfield-Kreider, 1998), but nothing permanent. I had made hundreds of errors due to my tendency to act in isolation before I began listening to and learning from my Mexican and other Latino and Latina colleagues. In the second year, thanks to the help of colleagues and scholars in the field of immersion research, my students began to develop a more sound, broad, committed approach to learning to teach all children. They discontinued using the term *color-blind* and the phrase "All children are the same." They began to realize the richness and depth other cultures bring to the classroom and that they were not prepared to teach children different from themselves. "I feel like I need to start starting all over again. There is so much I need to learn" (Journal entry #34, 1994). All but one of the seven students decided to continue their language studies when they returned, and over half began work on their bilingual education endorsement. Would these results have happened in the United States? Would the students have been able to escape their immersion? Would they have experienced life in a region in which the culture in power was European American? In an urban neighborhood? On tribal lands? How do these immersions affect Latino and Latina students? I only know that the two who went both felt reaffirmed in an area where they did not stand out as the "Other." However, they both spoke Spanish fluently—where other students had names like theirs. Would this change if their Spanish were similar to our other students? What about other preservice teachers? What prompts the changes?

We were in the last two weeks of our month-long immersion in Aguascalientes, Mexico. Hannah, one of my students, was in tears—again. She sat with her face covered on the bench in the *zócalo* (town square) in Leon, Mexico, with tears dripping onto her flowered dress. Raised on a farm in the northwest, Hannah was not afraid of hard work. She worked all summer on the crops and worked all winter finishing her elementary education degree. She wanted to get a job near home, teach kids, and have a little adventure in Mexico before she settled down. "It is so black in here. I cannot even see past my own prejudices and fear. I am so lonely," Hannah wailed as onlookers graciously gave us some distance. She noticed and snuggled closer, and lowered her voice in the hope that she could retain some of her dashed dignity.

When she agreed to come on an immersion experience in Mexico, Hannah had three aspirations: speaking a little Spanish, serving the poor children, and having a vacation. Despite my warnings, she blithely entered the experience with high hopes and no fear. When the seven students and I arrived in Mexico, her host family immediately whisked her away for 3 days to immerse her in the family, language, and culture. I saw her large brown eyes get even larger as their car headed out. The family spoke very little English, and Hannah already was in for more than she bargained for. Three days later, when we all reconnected for the first day of language school and school practicum experience, Hannah looked haggard and irritable. "Why couldn't they offer me something to eat that was American? I would have done that for them. I am the guest, don't you think they could try to use English?" She snapped at the rest of us and at her language teacher for the rest of the day.

Each day grew worse. Hannah came to class withdrawn, complaining that her cooperating teacher at the local school was too lenient, her language teacher was too hard, the food her family cooked was too hot, and the family rules were too strict. The family was concerned by her withdrawal at home. She would go to bed soon after *comida* (supper) and not emerge until the next day before class. "This is the longest month of my life. I am so lonely, so tired, and so frustrated." I moved towards her, but she flinched. "Hannah, can you put your finger on the core of this?" She thought, a scowl on her face, and then replied, "Yeah, kind of. I was a straight-A student and prided myself on that. I thought I knew what I wanted and where I was going. Now, no one seems to understand me and I cannot follow most of what is being said. I feel so white—I stick out like a neon light. Now, I feel out of control and not in charge of my life."

One day, the head language instructor and I decided to hold class in a nearby city of Leon, famous for its leather products, especially shoes. Spirits were high as we embarked on the 40-km journey on a second-class bus. Six of the immersion students were babbling away with each other and their Spanish instructors while residents looked on discreetly at these female students whose exuberance emanated from their entire bodies. All except Hannah. Since she refused to attempt to speak, both in class and on the bus, she again sat alone, above our mistakes and continual state of being humbled by the richness and complexity of the language.

As the students tumbled out of the bus, Hannah slithered, hoping to avoid notice. "We have to talk, Hannah. I am losing you and won't settle for that." We found a bench in the *zócalo* and began to talk. "Hannah, help me. Knowing you like I do, you must be intensely lonely." The tears began, and Hannah replied hesitantly,

"Yeah, I guess." I shared my previous experience in Mexico, in which I experienced a transformation in my worldview. I began to talk, to find a way in. "Hannah, I don't know how you feel, but I don't think I have ever been so humbled. I can't communicate without errors, I am frequently left out of conversations because the group around me assumes I cannot speak Spanish, and everything I thought I knew about people, families, teaching, and learning have been blown out of the water."

I began asking bigger questions after the immersions: Can these experiences, if mediated by an insider to the dominant culture of the student (Paley, 1979), increase monocultural teachers' awareness of their own power and privilege and how cultural lenses can obscure vision? Will the experiences, if mediated by host families and community members, change their perceptions of bicultural children? Will mediated experiences merged with theory and best practice, along with culturally relevant teaching, provide the catalyst for them to desire to become advocates for all their children and to reconstruct their classes accordingly? What about my own growth? What effect does this type of cultural work have on the mediator? These questions have become the driving energy behind my work in teacher education.

The changes for me have been profound, promoting a deeper awareness of race, gender, sexual orientation, and class inequities, a passion for reconstructing teacher education to enable teachers to be reconstructioneers of culture (Delpit, 1995; Sikula, 1996), and a more overt commitment to both urban and global education. I began to see the need for challenging authority and social stratification, for detecting class or group oppression, and for taking an active role in restructuring unequal relationships (Sleeter & Grant, 1993).

Because of my renewed efforts, hours of reading and writing, ongoing construction of my sociocultural framework, and a position in a larger, more liberal public institution, I am making progress and am recommitted (Chávez Chávez, 1995). Work is slowly getting done. Colleagues are being identified and networks are forming. I am continually stretched beyond my comfort zone as I try different strategies to give voice to my convictions when the moments occur, without alienating myself completely. Colleagues find me a little pricklier, perhaps. I find myself irritated many times throughout the day at student and colleague comments, decisions, or bantering that reinforces racism. I have already burned a few political bridges, especially with the "old guard." I am now learning how to watch my back, pick my political fights. I occasionally offend well-intended colleagues and put others in a defensive stance. I still have moments of sheer terror when I am forced to take action or speak in the face of injustice. I have moments of despair when I fall back in cowardice and let the moment pass. I have moments of blindness when my culture has clouded my vision. Fortunately, I now have a small group of colleagues and friends who will gently hand me a mirror so I can revisit who I am, then nudge me towards a window so I regain a sense of direction. Slowly I am beginning to let go of childhood secrets and fears so I can break loose from personal and societal constraints that hobble my personal and collective work as we teach to change the world (Oakes & Lipton, 2000).

I will continue to work steadily with committed colleagues to change preservice teachers' perceptions of race, gender, sexual preference, first language, and how they interact with their own perceptions of power and privilege (hooks, 1993). Kerry Hume (1983), a Maori author who writes of New Zealand life in her book *The Bone People*, best describes my renewed commitment to collective change:

[We] were nothing more than people, by [ourselves].
Even paired, any pairing,
[we] would have been nothing more than people by [ourselves].
But all together, [we] have become the heart and muscles and mind
of something perilous and new something strange and growing and great.
Together, all together, [we] are the instruments of change.
(p. 5)

I am continually learning to differentiate between battles and skirmishes, and to keep focused on our common goal, a quality school and community-based partnership teacher education program committed to social justice. I am learning to steadily work together with colleagues to readjust the power structure so that individual and institutional oppression—the "dream killers"—will not continue to feed upon the hope and idealism of our children. I will do this because "Some of the most important means to create a society in which there is peace, harmony, respect for cultural differences, and cooperation towards common goals are developed in the school years through the influence of teachers with vision and commitment to the democratic principles of American society" (Trueba, 1993, p. 137).

REFERENCES

Anyon, J., & Wilson, W. J. (1997). *Ghetto schooling: A political economy of urban educational reform.* New York: Teachers College Press.

Bradfield-Kreider, P. (1998). Mediated cultural immersion and antiracism: An opportunity for monocultural preservice teachers to begin the dialogue. In C. Grant (Ed.), *1998 National Association of Multicultural Education Conference Proceedings* (pp. 117–148). New York: Caddo.

Bronfenbrenner, J. (1974). The origins of alienation. *Scientific American, 127,* 882–887.

Chávez Chávez, R. (1995). *Multicultural education for the everyday: A renaissance for the recommitted.* Washington, DC: American Association for Colleges for Teacher Education.

Dauber, S. L., & Epstein, J. L. (1993). Parents' attitudes and practices of involvement in inner-city elementary and middle schools. In N. F. Chawkin (Ed.), *Families and schools in a pluralistic society.* Albany: State University of New York Press.

Delpit, L. (1995). *Other people's children: Cultural conflict in the classroom.* New York: New York Press.

Haberman, M. (1991). The pedagogy of poverty versus good teaching. *Phi Delta Kappan, 73,* 290–294.

Haberman, M. (1995). Selecting "star" teachers for children and youth in urban poverty. *Phi Delta Kappan, 76,* 777–781.

hooks, b. (1993). Transformative pedagogy and multiculturalism. In T. P. J. Fraser (Ed.), *Freedom's plow* (pp. 91–98). New York: Routledge.

Ladson-Billings, G. (1995). Toward theory of culturally relevant pedagogy. *American Educational Research Journal, 32,* 465–491.

Ladson-Billings, G. (1996). Silences as weapons: Challenges of a black professor teaching white students. *Theory Into Practice, 35*(2), 79–85.

Lee, V. & Croninger, R. (1994, May). The relative importance of home and school in the development of literary skills for middle grade students. *American Journal of Education, 102*(3), 286–329.

Paley, V. (1979). *White teacher.* Cambridge, MA: Harvard University Press.

Payne, R. K. (1998). *A framework for understanding poverty.* Baytown, TX: RFT.

Radin, P. (1972). *The trickster: A study in American Indian mythology.* (With commentaries by Kerenyl, K. and Jung, C. G.). New York: Schocken Books.

Sikula, J. (1996, February). *Be an ARC: An American reconstructioneer of culture.* Paper presented at the 76th annual meeting of the Association for Teacher Educators, St. Louis, MO.

Sleeter, C., & Grant, C. (1993). *Making choices for multicultural education.* New York: Merrill.

Trueba, H. (1993). *Healing multicultural America: Mexican immigrants rise to power in rural California.* Washington, DC: Falmer.

Reflective Questions

1. Poor white trash. What personal and societal messages do we send to children in poverty in our classrooms? How can we move past this?

2. Ruby Payne has differentiated between situational poverty, which arises from circumstances such as divorce or the incarceration of a wage earner in one generation only, and generational poverty, which occurs when the children are not able to work their way out of poverty. What do you think are differences for students from each poverty group?

3. Often, the bootstrap theory of recovering from situational poverty is touted rather than looking at more systemic reasons, such as personal and institutional racism. How do you think that being white impacted Paula's ability to recover from the situational poverty she experienced?

4. Envision your ideal classroom. Now share that vision with two others, creating a web of things you would see and experience. Students whose families live in poverty in middle-class schools often find themselves in the lower tracks of reading and math groups. Why do you think that is? When school is in a poor community, the teaching becomes noticeably different than in schools in middle-class or upper class neighborhoods (Anyon & Wilson, 1997; Haberman, 1991, 1995). Students in schools in urban and other poverty-stricken areas see and experience teachers engaged in the following: giving information, asking questions, giving directions, making assignments, monitoring seat work, reviewing assignments, giving tests, reviewing tests, assigning homework, reviewing homework, settling disputes, punishing noncompliance, marking papers, and giving grades (Haberman, 1991).

   How does this differ from what you envisioned? What is the message to the children regarding what counts? What are they being trained to do? Read Martin Haberman's article, "The Pedagogy of Poverty versus Good Teaching," located on the Eisenhower National Clearing House Equity Section at http://www.enc.org/topics/equity/articles/documents/ 0, 1946, ACQ-111376-1376, 00. shtm, and discuss it in small groups.

5. Project: Michael Klonsky, director of the small schools workshop in Chicago, Illinois, once stated that education is a class issue that cuts across racial lines. He mentioned that teachers needed political savvy to create change. The teachers should know the history and present state of the communities where they teach, which includes (1) union politics, networking, and organizing; (2) district and building budget policies and practices; (3) high-stakes testing history and local implementation; (4) school reform history and current efforts; and (5) small-schools research.

   (Note: According to many teachers in the small-schools workshop, two "must read" authors are bell hooks and Lisa Delpit). Navigate the Small Schools Workshop Web site at http://www.smallschools.com/ and build a case for small schools in your community or school.

6. Ruby Payne (1998) has a variety of activities in her book, *A Framework for Understanding Poverty.*

7. *The Simulation Star Power* (1993), by Simulation Training Systems, does a good job with power and social class—including the "haves" and "have-nots." Available at http://www.stsintl.com/schools/star_power.html.

Activities for the Classroom

Suggestions for use: Set up an emotionally charged scenario—one in which the teens can identify with. Either have a skit or a vignette to work from. Then have three students or three adults role-play the voices. Discuss the voices and how they are different. Then, put the participants into pairs with a new scenario and let them practice each voice. Debrief afterward, clarifying and differentiating the concepts and feelings of all three. Finally, set up groups of three and assign roles, with each participant taking a voice. Debrief. Afterward, help the participants requalify their conversations in these tones and understand the benefit of doing so. Many variations of this will work.

Middle and High School

Three voices: This activity will help students realize which voice they are using. Many children raised in poverty speak from the child's voice. Role-playing from different voices can impact their awareness and subsequent growth in the use of their voice. Taken from Payne (1998).

Adult Voice: Nonjudgmental, free of negative statements or nonverbals, factual, focused on behavior and not the person, often couched in question format, has an attitude of win–win.

>   **Examples:** In what ways could this be resolved? What factors will be used to determine the quality, effectiveness, outcome, etc.? I would like to recommend_____. What are the choices in this situation? I am (un)comfortable with_____. Options that could be considered are_____. For me to be comfortable, I need the following to occur_____. These are the consequences of that choice or action. We agree to disagree.

Child Voice: Defensive, victimized, emotional, whining, losing attitude, strongly negative, negative nonverbals, powerless, helpless.

>   **Examples:** Quit picking on me. You don't like me. You want me to leave. Nobody likes me. I hate you. You're ugly, stupid, or boring. You make me sick. It's your fault. Don't blame me. She or he did it. You make me mad. You made me do it. Can be playful, spontaneous, curious, etc. (occurs in conflictual or manipulative situations).

Parent Voice: Authoritative, directive, judgmental, evaluative, win–lose mentality, demanding, punitive, sometimes threatening. Can create shame or guilt in others. Can be very loving and supportive.

>   **Examples:** You should (shouldn't) do that. It is wrong (right) to . . . That is stupid, immature, out of line, or ridiculous. Life is not fair. Get busy. You are good, bad, lazy, thoughtless, or beautiful (any judgmental word). You do as I say. If you weren't so . . . this would not happen. Why can't you be like . . .

Parent Participation

Actively encourage parents to get involved in the school or class.
http://eric-web.tc.columbia.edu/families/strong/key research.html

1. Finding a variety of ways to encourage parents to participate in their children's education is more important than parental educational level, family size, marital status, socioeconomic level, or student grade level in determining whether parents get involved (Dauber & Epstein, 1993). Because low-income parents generally wait for the school to approach them, we need to make ongoing, systematic efforts to help such families become involved. We need strategies that will help them help their children, because they may also have increasing difficulty in helping children with schoolwork as children enter the higher grades (Lee & Croninger, 1994). Children from low-income families who are at risk of failing or falling behind can succeed academically if their parents are taught home teaching techniques (Bronfenbrenner, 1974; Radin, 1969, 1972).

2. School practices to encourage parents to participate in their children's education are more important than family characteristics such as parental education, family size, marital status, socioeconomic level, or student grade level in determining whether parents get involved (Dauber & Epstein, 1993). At the same time, schools need to make a concerted effort to help low-income families become involved, because they often wait for an approach from the school. Such families may also have increasing difficulty in helping children with their academics as children advance in age and in grade (Lee & Croninger, 1994). Children from low-income families who are at risk of failing or falling behind can succeed academically if their parents are taught home teaching techniques (Bronfenbrenner, 1974; Radin, 1969, 1972; Scott & Davis, 1979).

WEB SITES

http://www.enc.org/topics/equity/articles/documents/0, 1946, ACQ-111376-1376, 00.shtm
http://www.smallschools.com/
http://www.stsintl.com/schools/star_power.html

Chapter 5

Embracing My Cultural, Intellectual, and Spiritual Identities on My Journey to Become a Transformative Teacher

Ramona Maile Cutri, Brigham Young University, Provo

Focus Questions

1. How has socioeconomic status impacted our sense of identity?

2. What were some of the critical experiences that helped Ramona develop a strong sense of self?

3. In what ways have you identified with other groups to gain a sense of belonging or identity?

4. What causes us to reach out to others? How do we get beyond ourselves to connect with someone else who is different? How does the discovery of self influence relationships? What tensions could surface?

TRANSFORMATIVE INCIDENTS THAT CHANGED MY WORLD

It is early in my first year of graduate school. Dolores, Lisa, and I are sitting in Ackerman Student Union. They are asking me: "Who are you? Why do you want to do this type of work?" I'm not sure who I am. I want to work for the rights of poor students and students of color and be with the two of them because I feel, for the first time in my life, that I can be honest about my background—my secrets about food stamps and jail. I've never told anyone in my life about these "secrets." (What a delusion I maintained that others didn't know—a memory of Jodie Wingate's mother saying that Jodie couldn't play with me because of who my dad was.) Dolores, Lisa, and I sit around the table as the night grows late. They keep pushing me.

I had no verbal answers that night, only tears and a beginning revelation about how much energy I was spending keeping my secrets. For 27 years of my life before graduate school, I considered my family's poverty and involvement with drug addiction and other illegal activities as secrets. I kept these secrets from my friends because life circumstances made me different from them and, I believed, would make me unacceptable in their eyes. My pattern of keeping secrets had rarely been challenged. In graduate school, though, the stress and pressure I experienced strained my ability to devote so much emotional and psychological energy to keeping my secrets. In addition, the people that I was meeting and the issues that I was studying suggested to me that perhaps my secrets were not so horribly unique. I began to consider that, at that point in my life and in the work that I wanted to do, maybe it was better not to keep secrets, but to tell and share.

I started a process of asking myself *why* I had decided to keep my secrets, and then began to ask *how* I had been able to do it. Through these processes, I came to recognize the social pressures of the trajectory I had set for myself. My goal was to become a legitimate person through education. I also began to identify the privileges afforded me by my physical appearance. "So, what are you?" I am so often asked. But perhaps, just as often, if not more so, people don't ask and assume that I am the white, middle-class, well-educated, *legitimate* girl that I had been killing myself to be.

In graduate school, my name became important to me—all three of them—Ramona Maile Barreto.[1] Instead of wishing to be named Stacy Pope, I valued the origins of each of my names. (I have a vivid memory of sitting on the floor of my bedroom as a little girl crying and wishing that I was Stacy Pope. I wanted her name, her house, and her family.) That first year of graduate school also brought a lot of stress. Who was "radical" enough to be in the favored group with the "radical" professors? Who was smart enough to be in the favored group with the established professors? I didn't know who I was politically, culturally, or intellectually.

I remember going to Student Psychological Services that first year of graduate school when I was at the end of my rope. The counselor listened to me and supported me. Before I left, she gave me a brochure about an organization for people of mixed ethnicities called Multiracial Americans of Southern California (M.A.S.C.) and a one-page handout from a keynote address given by Maria P. P. Root at the organization's 1993 conference. The handout was titled "Bill of Rights for Persons of Racially Mixed Ancestry." As I read it, I was shocked at how the sentences resonated with me. They described some of the conflicts, shames, and frustrations that I had experienced but had never articulated. For example, my cousins and I have very different perceptions of who we are despite the fact that we are all half white, one fourth Korean, and one fourth Puerto Rican. These differences stemmed, in part, from the fact that their parents were not the black sheep of the family—*that* was my dad. But also, their very names made them different. The cousins that I most often compared myself to were the daughters of my father's sister. My aunt had married a white man, and they had given each of their girls traditional names—pretty names that could

---

[1] I have since married and decided to take my husband's family name—Cutri. I can't promise that I would have taken his name if it had been something like Smith or Jones. But, for whatever reason, I felt that Ramona Maile Cutri still reflected who I am.

easily be found on key chains and little bicycle license plates at Disneyland. (I could never find my name preprinted on such items. My only hope was having my name specially embroidered on the Mickey Mouse ears hat.) The bill of rights document that the student psychological counselor gave me said that I had every right to feel different than my cousins and identify myself differently from them, even though we shared the same ethnic mix. The counselor must have seen how these issues of identity affected me. I, at the time, was only just beginning to recognize their complexities and influence in my life.

After reading the "Bill of Rights for Persons of Racially Mixed Ancestry," I found myself not wanting to just check the "white" box on forms. I started checking the "other" box and writing in all three of my ethnicities—white, Korean, and Puerto Rican. This felt right and false all at the same time. We never even knew that we were part Puerto Rican until my grandfather died when I was 20 years old. We had grown up believing that we were Italian, and that my grandfather had left Italy and come to America never to speak to his family again. After he died, my Aunt and I were looking through some of his papers and discovered that he was born in Puerto Rico, not Italy. No wonder there were so many Puerto Ricans that spelled their last name just like ours—two *r*'s and one *t*—Barreto. From this event, it seemed like I was not the only one in our family who turned to keeping secrets as a way to deal with our ethnic identity. Because this discovery happened after my grandfather was dead, there was no way of getting to know why he lied, and there was no way of bringing the Puerto Rican culture into our lives through our grandfather. Aside from genealogy research and studying about Puerto Rican culture, this part of our family culture has, in a sense, died.

My Korean cultural roots have always been present in our family through food—a persisting cultural tradition long after language and other traditions fall to the wayside. Traditional Thanksgiving and Christmas dinners at my aunt's house consisted of turkey, stuffing, a layered salad, and a Jell-O salad, and then a big bowl of white rice and a bowl of kimchee. My oldest aunt still remembers how to make *mandoo* for New Year's Day and even taught me and some of my cousins how. But language and other Korean customs have dwindled in our family. My father and his brother and sisters came from Hawaii with their parents to California right after Pearl Harbor was bombed. At that time, it was not smart to continue any traditions associated with being Asian or anything remotely related to Japan. What was it like to look Asian and be from Hawaii in Long Beach, California, at the height of World War II and the Japanese internment camps? Because my own father died before I began to explore my own identity and its impact on our lives, I never got to ask him. His brother and sisters just avoid the topic or gloss over it when I ask them. But I can't help but wonder how my father's own experiences with prejudice may have influenced his turn toward drugs and crime. So, even though it felt new and strange to check the "other" box rather than the "white" box on forms, it also felt right because I was acknowledging a part of our family history that, though not talked about, certainly has influenced us.

Technically, I have never fit each of the characteristics of the majority culture—white, middle class, English speaking, Christian. I did fit some of them (English speaking and Christian) and often passed for others (white and middle class). Scholars studying white racial identity development speak of the "contact" phase, in which an encounter with the "other" occurs that sparks whites to recognize their whiteness rather than continue to let this part of their identity remain invisible to them or just not significant (Helms, 1990). I never went through an initial "contact" incident with the "other" because, to a certain extent, I always have been the "other" even though I didn't look like it. My father was not white and did not look white. We were poor, and our house looked poor. Therefore, I was always aware that I was different than other people, especially those from the majority culture. I knew this even though it was not until years later that I gained the vocabulary to describe the norm against which I compared myself as "the majority culture."

As I look back on my own racial identity development through the lens of white racial identity development, I see similarities with the process scholars describe, but I also see how my mixed ethnicities have influenced my own racial identity process. In the disintegration stage, scholars describe whites as feeling "anxiety, guilt, or shame" upon recognizing how minorities are treated in society (Howard, 1999, p. 90). I felt anxiety, guilt, and shame regarding my own identity and my family throughout my childhood and into my adult years. Like whites who have to gain an awareness of their racial identity and racial inequalities, I had to gain a vocabulary to describe my feelings and explain why I felt the way I did. My study of critical theory, my experience with the counselor at Student Psychological Services, and my friendship with my Chicana friends gave me the experiences and vocabulary to begin to articulate my racial identity and gain strength from it.

I wasn't a Chicana, but I wanted to be with my new Chicana friends in graduate school because I felt an affinity with them—with certain aspects of their lives that I hadn't felt with others before. I had nothing to prove—no badges to flash saying I was a Chicana, or a person who had felt oppression, or a person that they could trust. The only thing that I could say was that the experiences they shared with me rang true. I remember being shocked at how readily and without apparent shame they talked about their family being poor or their uncle who was in jail. Were they so much braver than I was to be able to share these things publicly? Or was it that they had never had the privilege of being able to hide these things like I had. Growing up with brown skin and growing up with white-looking skin is different. I didn't have, nor have I ever had, brown skin, but I shared so many other things in common with these women. It felt good to reveal my "secrets" to them.

I was starting to sort out years of wanting to fit into the white middle-class community. My physical appearance allowed and allows me to do so, as does my education. But, because of my secrets, I didn't allow myself to feel that I fit in. I went to Europe in high school like the rest of my friends, but only *I* knew that the money my parents had worked so hard and lovingly to obtain to finance the trip had probably come from gambling and selling drugs. My awareness of my ethnic and socioeconomic background prevented me from lapsing into the reintegration stage of white racial identity development, when whites are described as accepting "the belief in White racial superiority" (Helms, 1990, p. 60). I was not gaining fear or anxiety toward minority cultures, but rather finding a home among them that I had never known about before.

I wasn't a white, middle-class woman, but I did feel affinity with my new white friend Anne, too. For the majority of my life, I had passed as a white middle-class woman. I could very much relate to many of Anne's experiences. I didn't feel that I had to hide my affiliation with or affinity toward Anne as a white woman or toward Dolores and Lisa as Chicanas. In the past, Anne would have represented all that

I wanted to be—middle class, secure, and from a "legitimate" family. How ironic it was that when I met her, she was in the process of critiquing some of those very characteristics of her life.

Through my friendship with Anne and my continuing study of critical theory and pedagogy, I was passing through the white racial identity development stage called pseudo-independence (Helms, 1990). I was beginning to acknowledge that, as Howard (1999) describes it, "White people have intentionally or unintentionally benefited from [racism]" (p. 92). However, I did not assume the "missionary" attitude of saving minorities that is often associated with the pseudo-independence stage of white racial identity development. Rather, the intellectual and emotional energies that I poured into my graduate studies and my friendships with diverse people were toward the project of saving myself by acknowledging and embracing my mixed ethnicities and socioeconomic background.

As Anne listened to my stories and to Dolores' and Lisa's, she shared her own. She did not judge or reject me, as I had always thought my other white middle-class friends would have. She showed me that I had probably underestimated my friends of the past, and that my keeping secrets had just as much, or more, to do with my own judgments of myself and family than others'. I am not saying that all members of the dominant culture are ready and willing to accept others into their company, only that I, along with pressure from the dominant culture, contributed to my own shame regarding my family and, by association, myself.

I still buy into certain aspects of this shame even though my father has passed away and my mother has achieved, with God's help, a remarkable recovery from her addictions. The labels that we give ourselves are the hardest to shake, I believe. Legitimate accomplishments can fill our curriculum vitas, but years of self-doubt and shame regarding one's background do not easily dissipate.

Anne, Dolores, Lisa, and I got to know each other more socially and academically. We formed a study group to prepare for our qualifying examinations. We were four women of diverse cultural and economic backgrounds with different levels of prior experience critiquing society and ourselves. However, within our graduate program, we shared similar feelings of marginalization and academic insecurity. In our associations with one another, I did not feel that I had to hide my feelings and insecurities. Yet, I also knew that these women would not let me just wallow in my feelings or insecurities. Because of our collective and individual experiences and the critical pedagogy we were studying in graduate school, I was encouraged to analyze my feelings of marginalization and academic insecurities. I began to ask myself what contributed to them and what I could do about them. This process of analyzing and asking questions differed greatly from my previous pattern of keeping secrets.

Through our friendship and academic work together, we redefined our marginalization from a place of isolation into a place of resistance and power. From what hooks (1984) describes as the "special vantage point that our marginality gives us" (p. 15), Anne, Dolores, Lisa, and I developed a critical ethic of care that guided and sustained us. We came to define a critical ethic of care as "the practice of critiquing without negating as we attempt to reconceptualize our differences and critically examine and transform ourselves and society" (Cutri, Delgado Bernal, Powell, & Ramirez Wiedeman, 1998, p. 108). As I lived a critical ethic of care, I broke my pattern of keeping secrets and denying parts of myself to exist. Free of this cycle,

I was able to make connections between my "private concerns and the public space" (Greene, 1998, p. xxxiv). In an article we wrote about our study group, I reflected:

> I look back now and see how my friendships with these three women encouraged and guided my process of locating my cultural identity. As I participated in this friendship, and as I proceeded with my studies and research, I had to make sure that my ethics were firmly in place (Nakashima, 1996). This was because as an outsider really to both groups—the White middle-class community and the Chicano/a community—I wasn't an automatic insider who could be trusted. I felt this and am grateful for it because I want to live in integrity. Two things have allowed me to more fully live in integrity. First, freeing myself from keeping "my class and cultural secrets." Second, establishing myself—my identity, my credibility, and my motives for doing multicultural/bilingual education research—has forced me to refine my thoughts and actions even more than if I had automatically been accepted based on one "pure" cultural identity—whether or not it was from the dominant or a minority culture.
>
> (Cutri et al., 1998, pp. 107–108)

I now deeply value my mixed and multiple ethnicity and culture. I want others to have to deal with the complexity and dynamics of my identity. I am a Korean, Puerto Rican, white girl (in alphabetical order), with a Ph.D., from a low socioeconomic background married to a very "American" man whose parents are immigrants from Argentina, and I am a Latter-day Saint (Mormon). I do not fit many stereotypes, but, perhaps, that is one of my best qualities.

Helms (1990) describes people in one of the latter stages of white racial identity development, immersion/emersion, as searching for the answers to the questions, Who am I racially? Who do I want to be? and Who are you really? (p. 62). I look back on the transformative incidents in my life and see how I have pursued these questions. Though some of the stages of white racial identity development do not reflect my experiences as a woman of mixed ethnicity, this stage, represented by these questions, best captures the focus of my own racial identity development. Helms (1990) goes on to elaborate that people in the immersion/emersion stage take upon themselves "the goal of changing White people" by helping them to acknowledge a white racial identity and make "tackl[ing] racism and oppression in its various forms" a personal goal (p. 62). This was the stage of my racial identity development as I left graduate school.

My enriched understanding of and belief about myself allows me to articulate why I want to work for the rights of poor children and children of color. The pain and destructive patterns of keeping secrets and denying parts of myself to exist that dominated so much of my life cannot be allowed to destroy another generation of kids who find themselves on the outside looking in, or on the inside thinking that they do not belong there. My own transformative journey has been a balance of identifying the external forces that contributed to my shame and pain and recognizing my own contributions to these feelings. Because I worked collaboratively with others to transform my own world, I knew that others could carve out their own transformative journeys, and I wanted to be there to help.

Now, as I am in my third year as an assistant professor, by Helms's (1990) stages of white racial identity development, I could be classified as having entered the autonomous stage. Helms (1990) defines this as a stage in which a person actively learns from other cultural groups and recognizes and fights against personal and institutionalized racism. Yet, I argue that my path to the autonomous stage has differed from a white person's journey. The lived experiences of underprivileged students resonate with my own experiences. I fight to improve their lives, but in a sense I am also fighting to make up for my own experiences as a child ashamed and confused about her own racial identity as a mixed-blood poor kid who could pass for white. The experiences, frustrations, and special vantage points of underprivileged students, including myself, inspire and inform my efforts to teach to change the world. I will now describe some of the work that currently comprises my struggle for social justice and how I pursue it with my cultures, intellect, politics, and spirituality.

CURRENT CULTURAL WORK

I am now an assistant professor of multicultural and bilingual and English as a second language education at a religiously affiliated university. In this setting, I have been drawing upon the lessons that I have learned in the past and seeking to embrace my intellect, politics, and spirituality. These three forces have always motivated and informed my work. Yet, in the past I had considered spirituality to be rather taboo in the realms of academia. I remember raising the topic of spirituality in a critical pedagogy class that I had in graduate school. The professor referred me to a book he thought might interest me and then proceeded with the class. I quickly gathered that the topic was not one he deemed appropriate or important enough to take up class time. Though in graduate school I did not keep my spirituality necessarily a "secret," I did not publicly draw upon it as a source of strength and insight in my work. (Old habits of compartmentalizing myself and keeping secrets die hard.)

Initially, my decision to accept a position as a professor of multicultural and bilingual teacher education at a religious university had little to do with wanting to incorporate spirituality into my work. I felt that the university and department needed my perspectives and solid knowledge base to enrich their program. However, after arriving, I began to realize the freedom that I had at a religious university to pursue my academic work with public acknowledgment of my spiritual interests and commitments. I am of the same faith tradition that officially sponsors the university and the same faith tradition that the majority of students belong to—that of Latter-day Saint.

I began to explore where spirituality figures into social reconstructionist multicultural education, what the spiritual components of social justice are, and what a teacher education program that focuses on the social, moral, and spiritual dimensions of multicultural and bilingual education would look like. At first, I thought that I was relatively alone in these interests, and I hesitated to share them with many people. However, because of the courage and confidence that I gained through the transformative incidents in my life, I resolved to approach my new faculty responsibilities as a whole person consisting of multiple cultures and an intellectual, political, and spiritual self, and not to keep secrets. As I have explored the literature and attended sessions at different national conferences, I have found others from various faiths exploring the connections between spirituality and the social sciences, spirituality and education, and spirituality and their own personal commitment to teaching to change the world.[2] My professional identity as a scholar, motivated and informed by intellect, politics, and spirituality, allows me to acknowledge how the principles and goals of "fairness, equality, freedom, peace, and respect of each human's dignity" (Greene, 1998, p. xxxiv) coalesce and resonate with my cultural, intellectual, political, and spiritual beliefs. These private concerns and public commitments enrich my work as a transformative teacher.

My goals as a transformative teacher are threefold. First, I strive to open students' minds to knowledge and perspectives they have previously been unaware of or have not recognized. Second, in my opinion a transformative teacher is able to pierce the heart of the students by connecting the knowledge and perspectives taught to the students' prior spiritual beliefs. Third, a transformative teacher in my mind must remain teachable herself. Unless one is able to learn, I do not think that she or he can teach. Recognizing that I am still learning to be a transformative teacher helps me identify patterns in my learning journey toward becoming a transformative teacher. I will now describe how I pursue each of these goals in my current cultural work.

OPENING STUDENTS' MINDS TO NEW KNOWLEDGE AND PERSPECTIVES

Before writing this chapter, I had not consciously analyzed how my own transformative experiences and racial identity development impact the work I now do as an assistant professor of multicultural education. Examining specifically how my experiences facilitate my teaching will hopefully encourage others to put their own experiences to work as teaching tools. To illustrate the impact my own transformative development has on my teaching and my students, I will provide a vignette based on my multicultural education course. I structure this vignette around three key teaching points that I focus on in my course: (1) a definition of culture, (2) recognizing everyday privileges and how these privileges translate into power to learn and succeed in school, and (3) the myth of meritocracy. My course includes more than just these three teaching points, but I have found that my own transformative experiences are particularly powerful when teaching these issues.

My experiences as a poor kid with mixed blood who could pass for white lend me acceptance and credibility in my students' eyes. Because I look like most of my majority culture students, I am easily accepted as an insider to their culture. My students do not consider me as an outsider seeking to "fix" them by making them more multiculturally aware. Because they *see* me as an insider, I am able to deliver content and messages that perhaps they would resist if coming from a different messenger. However, it is not long before I reveal to my students that I am not quite the "majority culture insider" that I might at first appear to be.

In my current teaching, I have made the journey from keeping my personal background a secret to using my ethnic and socioeconomic background as teaching tools. Ironically, I am still hesitant to share my background with acquaintances, but I do not feel fear or hesitation to share it with my students. I believe that this is

---

[2]I have found the work of the following individuals to be particularly insightful and motivating: Wexler (1996), West (1990), Mayes (in press), Palmer (1993, 1998), and Capper and Keyes (1999).

because I have come to see the great teaching value that sharing my experiences can have.

On the first day of my course, I define culture as more than just the color of one's skin or the customs and traditions a person enjoys. The definition of culture I present includes people's ethnic backgrounds, socioeconomic backgrounds, religious beliefs, gender, familial roles, education, political opinions, geographic origins, and more. I explain that these cultural components foster shared beliefs, values, traits, and traditions that people use to make sense of the world around them. This definition allows my students to recognize that they have culture (a point that we explore the impact of throughout the rest of the course). This definition of culture also allows me to share my own background. I explain to my students that I am a woman of mixed ethnicities—white, Korean, and Puerto Rican; that I grew up as a poor kid who got free breakfast and lunch at school; that my mom didn't even graduate from high school, but I now have a Ph.D.; that my father was in and out of jail, and I am a law abiding citizen; that I am a working mother; that I am a Democrat; that I am Mormon; and so much more.

I remember one of the first times that I shared my cultural background with a class; I received an e-mail from a student. She thanked me for my honesty and told me that she thought it took courage to share my experiences, especially about my family's involvement with drugs and jail. She then reassured me that she and other students thought that it was okay for me to share these experiences. I was grateful for her support, but also annoyed that somehow there was an assumption that if it wasn't okay with the students, I would not go on sharing about myself. Multicultural students do not have the luxury of choosing whether or not to share their backgrounds. Their backgrounds are known through the color of their skin, their clothing, their accents, their reputations, and other qualities. The experience reaffirmed to me how being able to pass for a member of the majority culture is a privilege that not all multicultural students can count on. This notion of privilege that majority culture members take for granted leads to the next teaching point with which I use my own experiences as teaching tools.

As part of my students' own cultural identity exploration, I teach them Bourdieu's (1984) concept of cultural capital. I define cultural capital as a set of cultural traits that help individuals know how to "play the game" and win in different cultural settings. I explain that, though everyone has cultural capital, because everyone has culture, different cultural capital has different status in society. I also explain that the cultural capital from the majority culture has the highest status in school and society. The students then make a "quick list" of their cultural capital—their ethnic background, linguistic background, and socioeconomic background—and compare their lists to the cultural capital of the teachers and administrators they had when going to school. The students then reflect on how having cultural capital that matched the cultural capital most valued in school translated into everyday privileges they took for granted in school. If their cultural capital did not match that of their teachers and administrators, the students reflect on what everyday privileges they did not enjoy in school. The students come up with powerful examples of everyday privileges, such as trusting the teacher, having the teacher assume that you can learn, feeling comfortable and safe at home and in the classroom, and not worrying about your parents. As a class, we then identify how these everyday privileges translate into power to learn and succeed in school. For example, trusting the teacher could translate into the power to ask questions when you need help; a teacher assuming that you can learn could translate into the power to receive a challenging curriculum and support through it; feeling safe and comfortable could translate into the power to devote your energy to learning rather than worrying. I share how lack of certain everyday privileges in my own life impacted my schooling experiences. I obviously succeeded in school well enough to complete my graduate studies, so some of my students have a hard time seeing exactly how my education was impacted. I relate stories of my childhood—when I remember not being able to concentrate on my schoolwork because of some issue at home, whether it was the electricity being turned off that morning or my dad being arrested the day before. Students in the class whose cultural capital also does not match the majority culture share their own school experiences too. These discussions illustrate that multicultural education issues are not just "touchy feeling fluff." Rather, through these discussions, as a class we try to trace specifically how issues of culture can impact the power to learn and succeed in school.

We also discuss how differences in privileges impact not just individuals but whole schools. In their textbook, the students read about Kozol's (1991) study *Savage Inequalities: Children in America's Schools*. One group of students expressed amazement that more people did not know about such inequalities and were not taking specific steps to rectify them. One student asked why we do not have a system in this country to address the disparity of funding to rich and poor communities. I explained that property and income taxation are systems in our country designed to distribute funding to various communities. I went on to explain that most people, however, when they are choosing which candidate to vote for, are not asking themselves which candidate will collect tax dollars and use them to more equitably fund school and social services for underprivileged communities. Most voters are asking themselves which candidate will save them the most money in taxes. The student didn't verbally respond to my comment, but from the look on her face I believe she and others were making a connection between politicians' policy decisions and real people's everyday lives. (Incidentally, our university is located in a state that is a Republican stronghold.)

I remind the students that much of my meals and education were paid for with someone else's tax dollars (free breakfast and lunch programs, welfare, financial aid, etc.). The students have to struggle with the fact that from my example they can see the value of federal assistance programs, but for the most part they, or their families, have probably always voted to cut taxes and decrease such programs. My example and issues raised in their textbook cause the students to ponder the discontinuity between the moral stance that all children deserve everyday privileges and the power to learn and succeed in school, and the political stance that federal assistance programs are "bad" big government.

My experiences as a student who did not have everyday privileges also relates to another teaching point I focus on in my multicultural education course—the myth of meritocracy. I define meritocracy as the belief that anyone, if they work hard enough, can become anything that they want to be. I explain that critiques of meritocracy assert that at times hard work alone is still not enough to overcome obstacles like racism and poverty, which limit a person's opportunities. I emphasize that these critiques do not mean to convey hopelessness, but rather highlight that if a person isn't traditionally "successful," it may not be simply because they have not worked hard enough or do not have merit as a person.

If I were to allow my students to simply hear my story of educational and social "success," it is likely that most of them would conclude that I had made it because of my individual hard work and merit as a person. Or, in other words, they are quick to conclude that I am the "poster child" for meritocracy. As illustrated in the previous example about tax dollars, the students, on their own, do not tend to realize how interventions like federal assistance are appropriate in light of obstacles like poverty in a child's life. This tendency is understandable, since for most of their lives they have not realized how the everyday privileges that they took for granted actually helped them to be what they are today—successful college students.

It is my goal to have my students analyze my own journey toward educational and social success so that they recognize that hard work alone did not get me to where I am. I teach my students about factors in multicultural students' lives that they cannot immediately control, such as poverty and racism, and I label these "macro factors." I also teach my students that there are factors they can control, such as their responses to different situations and their use of available resources, and I label these as "micro factors." I try to illustrate how in my own life I have dealt with both macro and micro factors. It is crucial for students to analyze my own life experiences by identifying which factors in my life I had no control over and which factors I did have control over. If they do not learn to make this distinction in the lives of multicultural students, they will end up either pitying them as mere victims of circumstances or dismissing them as not working or trying hard enough. Multicultural students' lives are a dynamic mix of both factors they can control and those that they cannot.

I try to stress to my students that the teacher's role is to help students learn to distinguish between these factors. Multicultural education is not about encouraging minority students to have chips on their shoulders because of the many macro factors beyond their control. Rather, I teach my students that multicultural education helps alert teachers to the impact that macro factors can have on a students' school performance and behavior. In addition, I stress that teachers must teach multicultural students about the agency or capacity they have to make life-changing decisions.

Connecting New Knowledge and Perspectives to Students' Spiritual Beliefs

The connection between agency and multicultural education may seem vague to the reader, but to my students the mention of agency immediately connects to their spiritual beliefs. As I mentioned before, almost all of my students share the same faith—they are members of the Church of Jesus Christ of Latter-day Saints, as am I. The notion of individuals having free agency to choose between right and wrong and influence the outcomes of their lives is a central tenet of our faith. This belief in free agency lends hope to the struggles of life and gives strength to individuals. However, this belief can also lead to the assumption that anyone can overcome anything if they just work hard enough and have enough faith. When applied in this form to multicultural students, a belief in agency may disregard the daily impact that macro factors (poverty, racism, lack of access to the school curriculum, etc.) can have on their school performance and behavior.

I remind my students that though we all do have our agency in this earthly life, there are always factors beyond our control. I stress that it is our role as teachers to teach our students about their individual free agency and help them apply it to the micro factors they can identify in their lives. In addition, I emphasize that teachers must teach multicultural students coping strategies to help them deal with the influence of macro factors in their lives that are currently beyond their control. Through this process, students are able to connect the multicultural education concepts that they are learning in my course to spiritual beliefs that they already have.

I believe that the success of multicultural education is tied to the process of connecting the goals and project of multicultural education to beliefs that students already hold. The influence of teacher candidates' prior beliefs on the way that they make sense of information taught to them in teacher education programs cannot be discounted (Bullough & Gitlin, 1995). In my multicultural education course, I draw upon the shared faith beliefs that my students and I hold and connect these beliefs to the goal of working toward social justice through education.

Early in my course, I explain that different types of multicultural education can be thought of along a continuum. At one end is multicultural education that focuses on celebrating food and holidays from different cultures. At the other end of the continuum is multicultural education that seeks to make the world a better place. Our religious beliefs teach us that, in essence, if we are not striving to make the world a better place, then we are helping it to become worse. One primary source of doctrine in our faith is the Book of Mormon. These scriptures tell the accounts of people who lived on the American continent centuries before the birth of Christ, but we believe that the lessons taught here are specifically meant to apply to our day. A central theme in this scripture is that when a civilization becomes prosperous, it becomes prideful, and then begins to treat its members inequitably. One specific scriptural reference describes how a wealthy sect of people began to discriminate against other people based on their riches and opportunities for learning. This leads to the prosperous people's ultimate spiritual and societal destruction. I require my students to make specific connections between the account given in the Book of Mormon and our situation in society today. I thus situate multicultural education in the context of preventing the social and spiritual destruction of our society. My students, from their belief in the Book of Mormon, recognize the destructive pattern of discriminating against people based on their lack of riches and lack of opportunity to learn. What I help them to do in my course is to recognize how this pattern is being fulfilled in the majority of our schools and larger society today and how they can alter it.

This approach to multicultural education draws strength from spiritual motivation and commitment. This acknowledgment of the power of spirituality and religion as forces of social action does not mean that one must necessarily join organized religion. Yet, I do acknowledge that many organized religions have strong doctrines of working toward social justice. In teacher education programs associated with religious universities, such as my own, I believe that these doctrines should be explicitly connected to students' motivation and commitment to teaching social justice. In nonreligiously affiliated teacher education programs, the spiritual moral dimensions of teaching can also be a very important element in how preservice teachers reflect on their calling and practice.

Teaching to transform the world involves difficult, prolonged struggling. An exclusively intellectual and political commitment to social justice may initiate this struggle, but I argue that it is not always enough to continually motivate and sustain people. People must be nurtured and inspired at an intellectual, political, and fundamentally spiritual level to sustain their struggle for social justice. A commitment to multicultural education rooted in an overarching spiritual morality includes and energizes a critical awareness of the various factors that impact multicultural students' school experiences and performance.

REMAINING TEACHABLE MYSELF

I specifically identify "fairness, equality, freedom, peace, and respect of each human's dignity" as both ideal principles and obtainable goals. These ideal societal conditions serve me as "north stars" to guide my work (Fenstermacher, 1999). Fenstermacher (1999) describes how such north stars can orient our daily travels and long-term journeys. Yet he stresses that we must acknowledge that individuals probably do not ever expect to actually arrive at the "North Star."

I combine this North Star notion with the sociocultural conception of mastery. The journey toward mastery is an ongoing process in which one assumes multiple roles of novice, active observer, and expert (Lave & Wenger, 1991). When just starting out on my journey of self-awareness and social critique, I was a novice supported and pushed by more experienced others such as my friends Dolores and Lisa. At times in my journey I have been scared of the pain involved in confronting my self-doubt and shame. At other times, for example, when finishing my dissertation or in my first trimester of pregnancy, I've found myself simply physically exhausted. During these times of fear and exhaustion, I observed my friends, professors, and colleagues engaging in transformative work. Thus, though I may have only been observing transformative work at these times rather than doing it myself, mine was not a passive observation. As I observed others' efforts, I learned from them.

As an assistant professor, I have found myself lacking the expertise that others expect I should have. My first year as a professor, I was asked to codevelop one course on second language acquisition and one on assessment issues with language minority students. I agreed and worked hard to do my best. However, neither of these are areas that I had previously studied. I was a novice regarding these topics, but my job title implied that I should be an expert. Would the role of professor allow me to pursue the journey toward mastery as an ongoing process in which one assumes multiple roles of novice, active observer, and expert? Through my willingness to admit my lack of expertise and my colleagues' willingness to share theirs, I have proceeded through the stages of novice and active observer and am gaining expertise in these areas and sharing my own expertise.

Others also regularly expect me, as a professor, to be an expert at "teaching to change the world" (Oakes & Lipton, 2000). Though I do know more about this topic than I did about second-language acquisition and assessment, I still do not consider myself an expert. Yet, mastery of this process is one that I do not believe is ever attainable or even desirable. As a teacher struggling to change the world, I may help realize the goals of fairness, equality, freedom, peace, and respect of each human's dignity in one situation at a given moment. Yet, in another instance, I may unintentionally frustrate these goals. I must continually critique my efforts, strive for humility, and learn from others in my daily efforts. This process of trying, succeeding, falling short, reflecting, and learning is one of humility and faith for me. Oakes and Lipton (2000) described their own efforts and others as a "hopeful struggle" (p. xxiii). They further defined struggle as "the directing of one's unflinching commitment, endurance, and hope in order to achieve social justice" (Oakes & Lipton, 2000, pp. xx–xxi). For me, this indicates and implicates a spiritual, not just an intellectual, engagement with social justice.

When teaching preservice teachers, I stress that learning to teach is an ongoing struggle. This notion often frustrates preservice teachers, who often expect their teacher education professors to provide a complete list of "things to do to be successful" or teach them everything they need to know in order to be politically correct. I try to stress that, especially as new teachers, they do not have to be experts. I emphasize that they are going to make mistakes. For example, they are probably going to offend someone by calling them the wrong name—Latino versus Hispanic, Native American versus Indian—or misinterpret a student's behavior, or make an assumption about a parent. I stress to my students the main things that they must be concerned about are (1) sincerely and compassionately caring about their students, (2) remaining accountable for the scholastic well-being of their students, and (3) knowing where to get help from various sources (administrative, community, spiritual, etc.). I cannot ask my students to strive for these three goals unless I myself am striving for them in my own teaching.

CONCLUSION

My own transformative journey has involved women and men who have pushed, supported, and critiqued me with love and diligence. Through my teaching, I am now working to help others on their journeys and their efforts to transform the world through teaching. Learning as I go, I make mistakes, learn from others and myself, and try again. I have found the margins from which we work to be sources of intellectual, political, and spiritual strength that sustain my struggle.

REFERENCES

Banks, J. A. (1991). Teaching multicultural literacy to teachers. *Teaching Education, 4*, 135–144.

Bourdieu, P. (1984). *Distinction: A social critique of the judgment of taste.* Cambridge, MA: Harvard University Press.

Bullough, R., & Gitlin, A. (1995). *Becoming a student of teaching: Methodologies for exploring self and school context.* New York: Garland.

Capper, C. A., & Keyes, M. W. (1999, April). *The role of spirituality in educational leaders leading for social justice.* Paper presented at the annual meeting of the American Educational Research Association, Montreal, Canada.

Casanova, U. (1995). Bilingual education: Politics or pedagogy? In O. García & C. Baker (Eds.), *Policy and practice in bilingual education: Extending the foundations* (pp. 15–24). Clevedon, England: Multilingual Matters.

Cummins, J. (1995). Power and pedagogy in the education of culturally diverse students. In J. Frederickson (Ed.), *Reclaiming our voices: Bilingual education, critical pedagogy, and praxis* (pp. 139–162). Ontario, CA: California Association for Bilingual Education.

Cutri, R. M., Delgado Bernal, D., Powell, A., & Ramirez Wiedeman, C. (1998). An honorable sisterhood: Four diverse women identify a critical ethic of care. *Transformations: A Resource for Curriculum Transformation and Scholarship, 9*(2), 100–117.

Darder, A. (1991). *Culture and power in the classroom: A critical foundation for bilingual education.* Westport, CT: Bergin & Garvey.

Fenstermacher, G. (1999, April). Keynote address at the annual associates group conference of the Center for the Improvement of Teacher Education and Schooling (CITES), Provo, UT.

Frederickson, J. (1995). *Reclaiming our voices: Bilingual education critical pedagogy and praxis.* Ontario, CA: California Association for Bilingual Education.

Goodlad, J. I. (1990). The occupation of teaching in schools. In J. I. Goodlad, R. Soder, & K. A. Sirotnik (Eds.), *The moral dimensions of teaching* (pp. 3–34). San Francisco: Jossey-Bass.

Greene, M. (1998). Introduction: Teaching for social justice. In W. Ayers, J. A. Hunt, & T. Quinn (Eds.), *Teaching for social justice* (pp. xxvii–xlvi). New York: Teachers College Press.

Helms, J. E. (1990). *Black and white racial identity: Theory, research, and practice.* New York: Greenwood.

hooks, b. (1984). *Feminist theory: From margin to center.* Boston: South End.

hooks, b. (1994). Eros, eroticism, and the pedagogical process. In H. A. Giroux & P. McLaren (Eds.), *Between borders: Pedagogy and the politics of cultural studies* (pp. 113–118). New York: Routledge.

Howard, G. R. (1999). *We can't teach what we don't know: White teachers, multiracial schools.* New York: Teachers College Press.

Kozol, J. (1991). *Savage inequalities: Children in America's schools.* New York: Harper Perennial.

Lave, J., & Wenger, E. (1991). *Situated learning: Legitimate peripheral participation.* New York: Cambridge University Press.

Mayes, C. (1998). *An approach to spiritual reflectivity in teacher education.* Unpublished manuscript, Brigham Young University.

Mayes, C. (2001). A transpersonal developmental model for teacher reflectivity. *Journal of Curriculum Studies, 33*(4), 477–493.

McKay School of Education. (1997). *A conceptual framework for teacher education in the David O. McKay School of Education.* Provo, UT: Brigham Young University.

Oakes, J., & Lipton, M. (2000). *Teaching to change the world.* Boston: McGraw-Hill College.

O'Keefe, J. M. (1999, April). *The teaching for spiritual growth institute: How it influences the lives of professional educators.* Paper presented at the annual meeting of the American Educational Research Association, Montreal, Canada.

Palmer, P. J. (1993). *To know as we are known: Education as a spiritual journey* (2nd ed.). San Francisco: HarperCollins.

Palmer, P. J. (1998). *The courage to teach: Exploring the inner landscape of a teacher's life.* San Francisco: Jossey-Bass.

Root, M. P. P. (1993, March). *Bill of rights for persons of racially mixed ancestry.* Keynote address at the annual Kaleidoscope conference of the Multiracial Americans of Southern California, Long Beach, CA.

Teemant, A., Cutri, R. M., Gibb, G. & Squires, D. (1998). *Developing inclusive pedagogy for special populations: Meeting the challenge in pre-service teacher education.* Unpublished manuscript, Brigham Young University.

Teemant, A., Cutri, R. M., & Harris, M. (1998). *Bilingual/ESL endorsement through distance education project treatment document.* Unpublished manuscript, Brigham Young University.

West, C. (1990). The limits of neopragmatism. *Southern California Law Review, 63,* 1747–1751.

Wexler, P. (1996). *Holy sparks: Social theory, education, and religion.* New York: St. Martin's.

Zeichner, K. M. (1993). *Educating teachers for cultural diversity* (National Center for Research on Teacher Learning Special Rep.). East Lansing, MI: National Center for Research on Teacher Learning.

Activities for the Classroom

Reflective writing

1. Think about your town and a neighborhood that you think of as poor. What comes to your mind when you think of someone from that neighborhood competing against you, your child, or sibling for a scholarship? Let your mind struggle with the emotions and images for a while and then write about what you imagined. Did words like *lazy, work ethic,* and *educated* come to mind? In what context?

Chapter 6

Universal Human Rights Begin Close to Home

Nancy P. Gallavan, University of Nevada, Las Vegas

Focus Questions

1. Describe a time when you realized that people around you knew valuable information that you did not know and that you needed to know in order to function successfully. How did you feel to not have this information? Why did you not have it? How did you acquire it?

2. Focus on a time when you were trying to acquire information, function in a system, participate in a group, or join an organization, and you were denied access. Why were you denied access? How did this experience make you feel? What did you do about it then? How has this experience affected you over time?

3. Consider a time when you anticipated or expected to be accepted and treated like everyone else, and this opportunity did not occur. Describe the events and your reactions. How did you feel at the time? How did this experience affect you over time?

4. As you read, consider how Nancy moved from nonawareness to awareness, to sensitivity, to internalization and transformation, to advocacy.

> *Where, after all, do universal human rights begin? In small places, close to home—so close and so small that they cannot be seen on any map of the world. Yet they are the world of the individual person: the neighborhood, school, college, factory, farm, office. Such are the places where every man, woman, and child seek equal justice, equal opportunity, equal dignity without discrimination. Unless these rights have meaning there, they have little meaning anywhere. Without concerted citizen action to uphold them close to home, we shall look in vain for progress in the larger world.*
> —Eleanor Roosevelt, 1958

This visionary quote describing our individual roots and personal responsibilities for valuing cultural diversity and promoting social justice has served as a guiding light throughout my life's journey in becoming an elementary school teacher and a transformative multicultural educator. I discovered Mrs. Roosevelt's powerful message while I was a teenager in the late 1960s. At that time, outside of my immediate family, I seemed to be in the midst of people whose singular intent was to speak cruelly about everyone around them, especially anyone who was different from them in any way.

Everyday I would hear insensitive, harsh, and unrepeatable words to describe people throughout our society. Then, during the evening news, I watched with horror as our nation seemed determined to destroy itself. On the television screen I would view the actual events that provided evidence supporting the defamatory comments the local townspeople around me used to denigrate our neighbors, the people of our own community. Sadly, I have heard these same statements from elementary school students, their families, and their teachers, as well as viewed the same events on the nightly news for the last 30 years.

Concepts like equal opportunity and civil rights seemed like natural conditions to me as a child; I felt that all people should be treated the same, regardless of their race, ethnicity, gender, social class, sexual orientation, religion, place of birth, language, abilities, size, along with any and all personal affiliations. As a child and as an elementary school teacher (and still today), it seemed unfathomable that some people were considered less than other people simply due to their physical appearance, amount of money, or belief system. Our individual characteristics constitute the natural assumptions of our personal ideologies (Apple, 1993), creating a world of similarities and differences. We thrive from our differences; they offer us limitless opportunities to think, grow, and develop—to experience life through many different and exciting avenues of expression. In many ways we have come to believe that "different is good"; however, that premise frequently does not always apply to people's physical appearances or personal behaviors.

Beginning in my youth and guiding me well into my teacher education program and teaching careers, I found it increasingly difficult to accept the notions that unequal rules and disparate expectations would apply to various members of our society. Why did *I* understand Mrs. Roosevelt's words with such simplicity and clarity? How could it possibly be that we are not all the same, with each one of us entitled to the same privileges and opportunities? It pained me severely to see the sights and hear the sounds that surrounded me on television and throughout my daily life, especially those displayed by people I knew, loved, and respected. Even as a teenager I seemed aware that I should and *would* help change the map of the world. I was anxious for a time when I could speak up, do something, and make the world a better place. I soon discovered that becoming an elementary school teacher would offer me the ideal opportunity to help transform the future.

RETURNING TO SOUTHERN MISSOURI IN THE 1960S

I was raised in a small town in southern Missouri during the 1960s and 1970s. My parents moved our family to the "heart of the Ozarks" when I was in first grade so we could be near my father's relatives due to my grandfather's failing health. Ironically, neither my father nor his father had lived in this town for decades, although there was a century-old family business awaiting us and a multitude of relatives on both sides of my father's family still living there. My parents and grandparents had moved away many years earlier, attended college, traveled, and lived in a variety of places across the United States. Now I can only imagine how returning to this small town was a culture shock for each one of us in our various stages of life. Through my lifelong teaching and reflection, especially as a transformative multicultural educator, I have come to realize that there remains much for me to learn about my childhood years in this small Missouri town—elements that continue to shape the person and teacher I am and am yet to become.

On the surface, the town appeared to be an idyllic place to live and for a young family to raise its children. But my parents were different in that they both were fairly well established financially, they were college educated (my father having earned an advanced degree), and they openly practiced their beliefs of equity. During the 1960s, the people of the Ozarks had been declared the second most poverty-stricken population in the United States; we ranked only one step higher socioeconomically than the people living in the Appalachian Mountains. My family had relocated to an area in the Ozarks where many homes were heated with wood stoves and families used outhouses regularly. My friends' parents did not have college degrees; some of them left school at the end of eighth grade. People did not travel far; the next biggest town offering more goods and services was more than 100 miles away, and going there was a major event. Our town operated within its own parameters; we were isolated physically, intellectually, and socially.

EXPERIENCING MY FIRST TRANSFORMATION

In 1964, I was in fourth grade and a member of the popular girls' group that played together at every recess; we belonged to the same Girl Scout troop and socialized exclusively with one another after school and on weekends. Our worlds seemed inseparable, and I'm sure we believed that we were all the same as one another and always would be. One day we were talking about our future goals and aspirations—what we wanted to be when we grew up. This was a fascinating topic for me as most working women we knew in the 1960s were teachers, nurses, or office personnel. At that time, more ideas about women pursuing other careers had entered the popular press and our everyday conversations both in and out of classrooms. I must have framed my answer about my future aspirations by imagining aloud what college I would attend, what sorority I might pledge, and what exciting city I would go to live in—much like my mother had done before me. Only I envisioned how I would be starting some intriguing career, unlike my mother, who had never worked outside of the home. I did not answer my friends' questions in terms of working for a living or supporting a family; I dreamed of unlimited future opportunities I might explore and enjoy.

Suddenly, one outspoken girl in our group confronted me, interjecting with hostility that not everyone's parents, and especially their mothers, wanted to attend college or could even afford to go to school beyond 12th grade! My friend carried on vehemently that most of us girls would need to get jobs as soon as we graduated from high school to help make money for our families. She informed me, conclusively, that we would be getting married and raising our own children before we got too old. I quickly and clearly recognized that most 1960s families in the Ozarks did not look like the sitcom families portrayed on television, just as Coontz (1992) describes in *The Way We Never Were.* I also realized that I did not think, act, or believe like my young friends in the fourth grade. This first encounter began my life-long transformative process of understanding others and myself, ideals that have provided the conceptual framework of my work as an elementary school teacher and teacher educator.

I was jolted that my future dreams were not only totally unaligned with my friends' ways of thinking, but that I had obviously offended them with my outspoken assumptions about families and futures. This revealing episode opened my eyes and brought me resoundingly into their world, a construct I suddenly realized was more unlike than like mine. But, more important, it was a world understood and shared among most of my friends. Unbeknownst to them, my enthusiastic innocence for visualizing my own future threatened their current existence in ways that brought me pain and discomfort throughout my public school experience. Rarely again did I speak with them about my future hopes and dreams, which were based upon the realities shaped by my parents' experiences and expectations. As many youngsters at this age, I had started to define my sense of "normal," and I began to realize it was not a shared definition among my peers. Cuzort and King (1995) wrote about the invisible social world and how social relationships are learned only by participating in them. Each of us brings our individual interpretations of the social world based upon what we see and hear; that which we do not experience for ourselves may remain invisible to our way of thinking and knowing. This episode with my young fourth-grade friends awakened my senses and allowed me to see that I did not match the world around me, and that my world would remain invisible to them.

My parents raised my siblings and me in an open-minded, accepting manner. We did not discuss differences between our family and other families often, nor was there any direct instruction regarding our behavior. Wertsch, del Río, and Alvarez (1995) refer to two themes of sociocultural behavior: human action and mediation, and I witnessed each of these frequently in my parents' behaviors. My family tended to interact with other people in an equitable manner, and my parents were generous with their time and money, assisting others throughout the community as they could. I learned much from their modeling, and I innocently thought this was how everyone believed and behaved. It was not until I attended college to become an elementary school teacher and began my own teaching career that I fully understood and appreciated the messages and models that I had acquired from my parents. Later, as a young adult, I also began to realize the range of human actions and their influences upon our society and young people. Becoming an elementary school teacher with a deeply held passion for infusing human rights and social justice strengthened my opportunities to transform human action and mediation.

DISCOVERING DISCOMFORT IN MANY PLACES

When I was a young child in the Ozarks, I also did not realize that other children's parents were not like my parents. I was totally oblivious to the fact that not all people earned college degrees, traveled, or volunteered to help others. Many people could not afford these privileges, they did not value these experiences, nor did they know how to make these things happen easily in their lives. In addition, my family attended the Episcopal Church, where I learned many of the beliefs that have guided my equitable attitudes about societies near and far, much as Palmer (1993) notes in his works. As an elementary school teacher, I began to explore the power of that observation and how strongly each of us is molded by our early role models.

Here, too, I was naively misled in assuming that all religious groups celebrated life and living the way that we did. My small Missouri town was dominated by one large Protestant religious group and its beliefs. Conversations at school and among my peers related to church and religion were based on this particular denomination's viewpoints, many of which did not match my own beliefs and practices. Likewise, their religious functions influenced the scheduling of various school and social events. We rarely were assigned homework on Wednesday nights, as it was "church night"; there was no homework during the week of the church "revival." The occasional school dances were closely chaperoned, and some movies were not allowed to be shown at the public movie theater.

If I had been interviewed during the fourth or fifth grade, I would have reported that children could grow up to be anything they wanted to be; gender, race, money— nothing could get in the way. Little did I genuinely understand about social immobility in the United States, here in the "land of opportunity" (MacLeod, 1987). Many lessons about reality still awaited me. However, even as a young child, I was not always comfortable with comments made in school by teachers and peers, and I began to notice that the people around me were not like my family; my friends' homes were not like my home.

As I grew older during the turbulent 1960s, I was gaining much insight in both local and global awareness; how I had come to understand the world did not match how many people around me felt, spoke, and acted. The world outside my home often reflected the hatred playing out on the nightly news. I will always appreciate the messages I learned from my family, from my religious beliefs, and from some of my teachers, who both directly and indirectly established the foundations of my life's work, first as an elementary school teacher and then as a teacher educator. Long before I read Mrs. Roosevelt's quote, I understood the depth of her perceptive words; universal human rights do begin close to home.

Racism was evident in my small southern Missouri town. There were few African American families living in our community, and most of these people worked as domestic help in private homes or as after hours custodians in a few businesses. Although the black population was not noticeably visible in the community, the white people used racist language freely to disparage people of color or to marginalize them. I heard racist words from my earliest days in elementary school, but I clearly remember my mother stating quietly and simply that those words were not "home language." Racist language (along with other degrading or foul language) was never spoken in our home by us or our friends. My mother's subtle modeling regarding our language influenced our thinking and our behaviors, including our choice of friends and activities. This one lesson about life has served me quite well both as a teacher of young learners and now as a teacher educator. I have perpetuated my mother's attitudes and behaviors in my elementary school classrooms and share these stories proudly with my preservice teachers.

Early on I knew that all of the black students in my town attended the same elementary school on "the hill." Most of the poorest people lived on "the hill" too.

Of the three elementary schools that fed into our junior high school, we had been led to believe what kind of students came from "the hill," although there were no justifications for these statements. I cannot recall specific conversations or incidents to validate how I learned the attitudes that I acquired about African Americans; I know that these sentiments were shared in words and behaviors without reason. Sadly, I realize that I must have heard a multitude of racial jokes and outlandish stories at school about cultural groups, most of whom I had never met. I can only attribute these stories to the white people's lack of knowledge and perceived threats to their accepted ways of living. As an elementary school teacher, I continued to encounter these beliefs and behaviors not only in the elementary school children, but in their families and with some of my professional colleagues as well. Lessons related to racial identity and racist behaviors, along with lessons on biased and prejudicial interactions, substantiated a major focus of both my elementary school teaching and now my work as a multicultural educator instituting transformation and cultural competency into preservice and practicing teachers. Current research on why practicing teachers do not use effective multicultural education reflects the same resistance I experienced as an elementary school student of the 1960s and as an elementary school teacher in the 1970s, 1980s, and 1990s (Gallavan, 1998).

When I was in elementary school, I also started realizing that there were different rules in our town for people of different races. There was a movie theater where many children went on Saturday afternoons to watch the matinees. The restrooms were located on the main floor, but next to the door of the women's restroom hung a sign that read, "Colored Women's Restroom Upstairs." As a young child, I was fascinated and frightened by the idea that I would need to be separated from someone else based on the color of my skin, to be granted the same privilege that we all needed. At that time in my childhood, I didn't fully understand this accepted condition, and it was not something that I discussed with my friends or family. Unceremoniously, the bathroom sign in the movie theater disappeared before I graduated from high school, during the early 1970s.

No other posted signs were evident in my hometown, although most of the residents would not socialize with the black population publicly or privately. I also knew there was a "Sundown Law." I had learned that blacks, especially black people unknown to our community, should not be seen in town after the sun went down. In public, the black residents were treated rudely or simply ignored. Occasionally, I traveled to the nearby city with my friends and their families. If a black person worked in the store or restaurant where we stopped, my friends' families would leave mumbling racially oriented derogatory statements. These experiences taught me to see the world through various cultural lenses and to understand my friends' perspectives, especially how they were being raised. I also learned to appreciate my own family.

Gender bias also was clearly evident throughout my elementary and secondary school experiences. Repeatedly, teachers asked us to line up with girls in one line and boys in another. Boys participated far more often in classroom discussions and activities, particularly sports; boys dominated opportunities to try out new things and share their discoveries. Some high school courses were not open to girls. Although my aptitude testing proved my strength for understanding spatial relations and that I should pursue a career in architecture, the drafting class was for boys only. In general, the impersonal *he* referred mysteriously to boys and girls; the word *mankind* strangely included all humans in words but not actions (much as it still does today).

As an elementary school teacher, I worked hard to be gender neutral and gender fair, going as far as pointing this out to my young learners and asking them to give me feedback if they felt I was not treating each group equally. One day as we finished singing a patriotic song to start our school day, a mindful female fourth grader observed that we needed to change the words in the song. The song, "America," contains the line "crown thy good with brotherhood," and she felt it was not a gender fair phrase. The class voted to change the word to *peoplehood*. To this day when I sing "America," I proudly sing out the word *peoplehood* while thinking fondly of those transformed students who I hope have become transformed young adults.

During my high school (and college) years, as my friends and I began socializing and dating, I became attuned to many more new observations about society. My parents appeared open-minded about my choice of friends. There was no discussion related to the kinds of people with whom my siblings and I should be associated as friends or date. Yet my girlfriends talked about this subject incessantly, as their parents had established strict guidelines and carefully delineated expectations. However, these rules were never topics of conversation in our home, even when one sister dated outside of our race, one sister dated outside our religion, and one sister dated outside of our economic status. My parents welcomed all of our friends into our home as long as they were kind and respectful. Ironically, it was my girlfriends who questioned the various relationships that my sisters and I established; I rarely responded to my friends' inquiries and maintained my invisible social world like the lessons learned much earlier. Again, I grew in my understanding that my family and I were different. Now I realize that our freedom of choice must have threatened my friends' beliefs about their families, people they respected, and the world around them.

During my junior year of high school, in 1971, I was serving on the student council when we were planning the junior–senior prom. A senior girl, the vice president of our student council, asked if students could bring dates to the prom who were not juniors or seniors enrolled in our school. This question was raised annually, and repeatedly the administration told the students no based on an assortment of unreasonable explanations. However, this particular year the question posed new concerns; the student council vice president was black, and there were no other black students in our school. This girl was dating a boy who attended a school in a neighboring county. The student council unanimously supported the girl's request and submitted the question once more to the administration. That year the policy (and history) was changed. Whether this occurred to avoid an uncomfortable student scene or it truly was a beginning of social justice will remain unknown. The student council vice president brought her black date, and our world began to improve. It would be the first of many similar conversations that I would hear over time, and events that would change the map of my world.

With this change in policy, students were allowed to bring dates who were not juniors or seniors attending our school. I was intrigued as I watched how this policy changed, probably due to issues related to race, yet the outcome benefited everyone in many different ways. Students of all colors could participate fully in the prom, and the event was more student-centered, as all students were allowed to bring their invited dates. Shortly thereafter, students were even bringing dates of different races. It amazes me to think that more than 25 years after this decision, there are high school students in the United States who still cannot bring dates of different races to their high school prom.

EXPANDING MY HORIZONS

After high school, few of my high school friends and classmates continued on to college. This was a major fork in my life's road. From a graduating class of almost 250 seniors, approximately 10 of us packed up and went away to college. During our senior year of high school, discussions related to college were rare. Most of my friends assumed that they would find jobs in the few local factories, marry, and start families right away, or join the armed forces. For many of my fellow students, simply completing high school was a major accomplishment, and in some families they would be the first to earn a high school diploma. Understandably, much earlier in my life, I had stopped talking about the days when my parents attended college, much less went to graduate school. The conversations and role modeling for my future did not match the world around me beyond the safety of my home, and I had known this fully well since that revealing conversation in the fourth grade.

I decided to attend college in southern Missouri and to become an elementary school teacher. It is interesting that I chose teaching not because it was what women were limited to pursuing at that time, but it was what I truly wanted to do. I wanted to make a difference in our young people; I wanted them to know and understand what I had come to appreciate and believe. I had volunteered to be a Girl Scout troop leader during my senior year of high school, and I understood the powerful impact of effective guidance on young people to experience and understand themselves and the world around us. Becoming an elementary school teacher afforded me the ideal opportunities to pursue a career to fulfill these same ideals and expectations while preparing young people for lifelong learning and success.

Going away to college was exciting and I naively expected to be among people just like me. However, shortly after I arrived at the university, I realized that I had been labeled a country kid or a farm girl. Granted, since I came from a small farming community 100 miles down the road, I certainly was not one of the "city kids." But to be called a farm girl sounded ugly and stupid. Most of us university students who came from small farming towns spoke with a southern drawl or were unexposed to some of the more sophisticated ways our new peers exhibited. But it did not take us "country" or "farm kids" long to acquire the behaviors of the "city kids." We wanted to blend in, to assimilate as quickly as possible. However, we "country kids" also quickly found one another and often ate together in the student union and socialized together outside of our classes. I began to understand the need to be with my own people, although I had never felt like one of the people from my hometown before going away to college. Some of the "city kids" would mock us for our self-segregation when we ate or studied together. This condition perplexed me, and I experienced confusion regarding my own identity.

Tatum's book, *"Why Are All the Black Kids Sitting Together in the Cafeteria?"* (1997), stirred vivid memories of my own college years. Now that we "country kids" were grouped together for a different reason, I could see that sometimes I was like the people from my hometown, and sometimes I was not. My cultural identification reflected what others knew or expected from me, as well as what I understood about myself.

The university student population was primarily white and Christian; there were few students of color. However, it was during the 1960s that groups such as the Black Student Union were being formed. With only 50 black students on a campus of 12,000, it was impressive to watch the Black Student Union operate, select a black homecoming queen, and organize its members. It was equally fascinating to watch the white students mediate their discomfort with this small group, having been given their newfound equal opportunities and privileges. Many student conversations were focused on what the black students were doing and why. I was openly supportive of all groups participating equally and voicing their needs for recognition, privilege, and power.

The reflections in Tatum's book were clearly evident when I was a university undergraduate in the early 1970s. The white students attending this university in southern Missouri had not been raised with black students attending their schools or having a voice in student affairs; the formation of the Black Student Union challenged the white students' sense of power and privilege. In my own way, I understood this dilemma, as we students from the country also were disenfranchised from the dominant culture.

During my college years, the Vietnam conflict came to an end. The United States had committed itself to helping the South Vietnamese by bringing some of them to the United States. One relocation camp was only 100 miles from my college. From the camp, the South Vietnamese often moved to my university town to reconstitute their lives. The new immigrants were people from all strata of life; some were even doctors, lawyers, and college professors, yet they were forced to begin again with nothing in a strange and distant land.

I was enrolled in a series of literacy graduate courses during the summer immediately following my college graduation. Our task was to teach the South Vietnamese to read, write, and learn the ways of their new country. This was my first formal adventure into cross-cultural education, and I was drawn excitedly into the experience. During the summer semester we not only taught the new immigrants how to communicate through structured, direct classroom reading and writing lessons, we decided that we would simply go out into the community with them and help them to understand their new world. This was the most meaningful part of the summer school experience for me. We practiced making telephone calls, shopping at the grocery store, going to the bank, and visiting many other places of importance. Initially, all of the learning occurred at the university and was controlled by the university students. Then we expanded the learning by going places for fun and entertainment.

By midsemester several of the university students voiced the concern that this experience seemed limited or one-way. It was decided that we could go into the immigrants' homes, enter their worlds as they had redefined themselves in the United States. This was one of the most eye-opening transformations early in my journey of valuing cultural diversity. The immigrants' homes looked nothing like our homes, as many immigrant families lived under one roof. Often they did not cook in their kitchens; they had habachis on their patios. Their homes were spotlessly clean, but the smells were bold and different. I was in awe of how we young university students from south Missouri had presumed to know what these families from South Vietnam would want and need. I know I learned as much about myself and the new immigrants as they did about the United States. Now, more than 25 years later, I wonder how much help we actually provided them at that time. I wonder where their roads have taken them and if we made a difference. They certainly changed my map of the world.

I probably learned more about the teaching–learning process and our interdependent global society during this summer school experience than all of my preservice teaching courses combined. These events built upon my childhood knowledge and beliefs of helping others and established a vital and essential foundation of human rights and social justice that would guide me as an elementary school teacher. I learned to value similarities and differences and the need to participate fully and equitably in the human experience. I quickly appreciated that cultural competency meant much more than learning about other groups of people; it meant transforming oneself and doing something. My career in elementary school teaching and as a teacher educator, as well as my personal life, benefited immensely from these 3 short months of learning and service.

BECOMING A TEACHER

My brief summer school cross-cultural experience served as a precursor for a teaching career that I never could have predicted, nor one for which I was fully prepared. I moved from south Missouri to northern Colorado and began teaching in a large elementary school on the prairie. The school's population was distributed into several major sociocultural groups: one third of the students were Anglo with parents ranging from CEOs and highly skilled engineers working at a major technological center to some of the poorest families I had ever encountered. One third of the students were Hispanic—some of whom spoke English fluently and some who spoke no English at all, ranging from families who had been in Colorado for multiple generations to migrant working families we would see every fall and spring. And one third of the students were first-generation Italian children whose families had moved as an intact community from a small town in Italy to this particular area of Colorado. Our school was not only bilingual with Spanish and English, we had translators to assist us with the Italian speakers. Likewise, we teachers received guidance to meet the needs of our migrant students and students of poverty.

During my early years of teaching I experienced culturally related confrontation and gang-related fights for the first time. Each of the three ethnic groups (Italians, Hispanics, and Anglos) needed to establish superiority and territory between both the boys and the girls. This redefinition of self-identity began openly in the mid-1970s, when many cultural groups across the United States were establishing themselves more vocally and politically within the dominant society. The young students reflected the concerns and conversations they heard among the adults around them much as Delpit describes in her text, *Other People's Children* (1995). It was evident to me which adults were open to celebrating diversity and which were attached to the melting pot analogy.

As a young teacher I witnessed biased, stereotypical, and prejudicial behaviors from the community, as well as among my "educated" peers. Another huge transformation began as I started understanding my colleagues through their self-selected cultural lenses, much as Paley describes in *White Teacher* (1989). I soon realized that not all teachers come from the same belief system as I had naively wanted to believe they came from. My awareness about teachers expanded to include how they bring their own personal backgrounds and values about people with them into the classroom. Their choices regarding curriculum design and instructional practices, as well as their ability to interact supportively with a variety of people, reflected who they are and what they believe about the world. I was in awe not only about the diversity of young learners and the families with whom I worked, but the diversity of adults who looked like me on the surface but behaved quite differently with their students. I quickly learned that I must pick and choose my way carefully, reinforcing the notion that teaching is also a sociopolitical arena. I wanted to change everyone's map of the world.

During my first 6 years of teaching, I earned a master's degree at a large state university. I studied gifted and talented education as I wanted to capitalize on the strengths each student brings into the learning process. I soon realized that building on these gifts, later associated with learning styles and multiple intelligences, was another avenue for celebrating individuality, personal qualities, and cultural diversity. It was becoming more difficult for me to differentiate between the questions of how we learn and who we are. One topic seemed to overlap with the other, and my transformation escalated through more reading, writing, and research.

During my master's degree, I was enrolled in one course that examined the global connections related to teaching and learning. The professor prompted us to consider how we were engaging our young students actively in their own learning processes. We were asked to investigate how our young students viewed the world and where they perceived they fit into the greater scheme. Fortunately, this professor modeled the need for each of us to do this for ourselves. This was my introductory experience to reflect on my own personal influences, educational preparation, and professional background when designing curriculum and implementing instruction. No professor had ever clarified the connections between who I am and what I bring into the classroom regarding what children are learning and how they learn it. I was overwhelmed by the links that forged during this course in discovering the power of an effective and accepting teaching and learning environment. These lessons transformed not only who I am personally, they transformed my views of curriculum and instruction and what I value in education.

The professor arranged for us to visit the Center for Teaching International Relations (CTIR) at the University of Denver. CTIR instructors offered a variety of classes for students, most of whom were practicing teachers located throughout the Denver metropolitan region; the courses explored how classroom curriculum and instruction fit into the global scene and how to share that understanding more efficiently with students of all ages and developmental levels, students from all over the world, and individuals working from a variety of cultural contexts. Most of the classes were taught through strategies such as simulations, role play, and other engaging and challenging interactions that I had not experienced. This brief introduction was the start of my knowledge of multicultural education, self-empowerment, and social reconstruction for me as a person and as an educator (Spring, 1995).

During our session, we participated in some of the simulations and explored how teachers can motivate students to learn more about themselves and others through teaching strategies other than direct instruction. Not only was I mesmerized by the introduction of these teaching and learning strategies, I was thoroughly impressed with learning about our international relations and the importance of each person on a global scale. The map of my cultural transformation was expanded as I started to view all children as equal players within the international community, and the importance for all teachers to have this information to do their best for all students in their classrooms. Some of the lessons I learned remain in my repertoire as a teacher educator promoting equity issues and social justice.

In the mid-1980s, I moved into southwest Denver and changed school districts. I began teaching in an inner-city school that provided for the children of new immigrants, many of whom worked in their family businesses each afternoon after school and lived with their families in the spaces above their stores. This environment differed radically from the children living on the prairies of northern Colorado. These new immigrant families were keenly aware that education correlated strongly with social and financial success in the United States. The parents of these children pushed and supported the teachers and school. The focus on achievement, as demonstrated on test scores, acceptance to universities, as well as comfort in U. S. society was evident early during this phase of my career. I was ready for this new challenge, as I found novel and rewarding ways to celebrate both the academics and cultures (Branch, 1994).

Fortunately in this school I had more in common with my professional peers, too. In all of my 20 years in the elementary and middle school classrooms, my 3 years at this school were the ones that celebrated cultures most authentically. This time in my career gave me the assurance that cultural awareness and global knowledge are closely intertwined with one's self-esteem and understanding of others—all essential elements for social and academic success. I had just discovered the importance of these facets of education and had arrived in a place that valued them as much as I did. My career had provided me with a wealth of rich and powerful environments to learn, change, and grow personally and professionally. I transformed my beliefs about children, teachers, pedagogy, and social justice. I also came to understand and appreciate that throughout a teaching career, one is always changing and growing. Both preservice and practicing teachers must remain open to new ideas and multiple perspectives about themselves and the world around them.

However, the remainder of my K–12 teaching career was spent at two different schools: a middle school and an elementary school—two schools with similar student and faculty populations. The focus at each school was on raising test scores and maintaining student safety. Both schools seemed uncomfortably narrow in thinking and embodied primarily negative learning climates. As I continued to mature in my own teaching, I learned to create my own positive and rewarding learning environments while celebrating the global nature of our existence for my own students. In many ways, I felt that I had grown in directions that were different from most of my colleagues, and it simply was easier to do the right thing with my own students than to try to readjust the entire school, which was following a different, more negative, administrative-compliant attitude. I could not change their maps of the world, so I concentrated on my own. Obviously my approaches were successful, as my students liked school and their test scores consistently were high. Now, more than 10 years later, many of those students continue to stay in touch with me and thank me for helping them understand and appreciate the world as young children preparing to interact successfully in their futures.

But my separation from my peers (at all ages and stages) was neither easy nor safe—issues that continue to influence my work today as a transformative multicultural educator. Although I was fully aware of the need to integrate culture and celebrations authentically, the schools where I was teaching advocated isolated events such as multicultural fairs and singular days commemorating some historical significance. Repeatedly, I was challenged by my discomfort at these events as token, international festivals showcasing food and fashions, instead of finding ways to integrate cultural diversity authentically. I had discovered Banks's levels of cultural integration (1994) and Díaz's (1992) notions of cultural infusion; neither the middle school nor the elementary school reflected these ideals. Likewise, I became more reluctant to voice my concerns as popular white students were selected for the gifted and talented classes and rowdy black students (usually boys) and second-language students were placed in reading, learning disability, and special education classes supporting research conducted by Ladson-Billings (1994). The teaching cultures in these schools focused on keeping the wealthier, vocal parents pacified.

TRANSFORMING INTO A MULTICULTURAL EDUCATOR

My own multicultural transformation became clearer and stronger as I refined my ability to distinguish between behaviors that I did not want to support or perpetuate and behaviors that needed to be incorporated into curriculum design and instructional practices. As I grew, I attempted to express my pedagogical observations and concerns. On several occasions I participated in curricular writing projects, and I addressed the need to be culturally inclusive with our terminology and examples. Frequently, the responses from my peers centered on defensiveness and indignation at my suggestions. Remarks regarding my role as "language police" or the "cultural customs agent" would bring their humor and spitefulness toward my interventions. These reactions have continued in my work with teachers. To this day, I continue to be amazed at the resistance many teachers exhibit if they are encouraged to expand authentic educational opportunities to everyone. Mrs. Roosevelt's words regarding universal human rights are so true: They do begin in small places, close to home—they cannot be seen on any map of the world. And many teachers need desperately to put equal opportunity and social justice on their pedagogical maps (Liston & Zeichner, 1996).

During my last few years teaching public school I earned a doctorate at the University of Denver. My cognate focused on multicultural education. I was inspired by taking a course in the sociology of education with Dr. Edith King. Finally, I found what I had been seeking for 20 years of teaching and attending college. Over the years I had learned what to teach, how to teach, when to teach, where to teach, and why to teach; no class had addressed the questions related to *who: who* are the students, *who* are the teachers, *who* are we as a society—locally and globally. I had pondered these questions repeatedly in my professional work and through various connections during my college courses. Now I could focus entirely on the questions of "who." I could bring all of myself together through my personal and professional experiences to enhance my growth and development, my own cultural identity as learner and teacher (Freire, 1998). My path toward becoming a transformative multicultural educator, by focusing on who we are as students, teachers, and a society and the need for social justice (Ayers, 1998), was about to begin full force, and I welcomed this opportunity heartily. After all of these years, I knew what questions I wanted to pursue; I had experienced some of the changes that needed to be made, and I was sure that many more unforeseeable ideas would be shared with me.

My studies at the University of Denver allowed me to explore our society locally, nationally, and globally. Opportunities were afforded me to research relationships at schools comparing and contrasting believed perceptions and actual events occurring within our society. I was able to step back and look at the inequities in our schools, among classrooms, for teachers, and among students, validating for myself the work of researchers such as Kozol documents in *Savage Inequalities* (1991). My research and studies transformed me from teacher to multicultural teacher educator as I began a career in higher education. My desire to change the map of the world and to make a difference had been granted; this work is my life and my life is this work. I am still transforming and becoming multicultural as the map of the world continues to change and evolve around us.

Like Smith (1999), I have many friends and colleagues who are not mainstream white nor "American." I am comfortable in my own skin and in voicing concerns related to cultural diversity, even if I am viewed as a representative of the dominant culture. My work in higher education allows me to interact with both preservice and practicing teachers, most of whom are just beginning their need to care for children, understand the learning process beyond academic achievement (Noddings, 1998), and develop their individual stages of transformation (Boyer & Baptiste, 1996) both personally and professionally.

From these revealing episodes, I have grown to value and understand my own elementary school students' and preservice teachers' attitudes resulting from the ingrained, multigenerational influences they have received from their families, schools, religious institutions, and childhood communities. Early in my teaching career, it became natural for me to infuse cultural competency (Gallavan, 2002) passionately into my own elementary school teaching, as well as my courses in teacher education, to help transform all my students' beliefs and behaviors.

Howard (1999) writes in *We Can't Teach What We Don't Know* that accepting diversity is not a choice. However, in my work I continue to encounter teachers, administrators, families, university faculty, and community members who, unfortunately, have made resisting diversity their choice. Sleeter and McLaren (1995) write of the mounting evidence that shows how disparities within our society exist and are supported by various sociocultural groups in the name of justice and democracy. Much as Giroux (1997) encourages us to "rethink the boundaries of education discourse" as teachers and teacher educators, I am energized to carry on my efforts in becoming a transformative teacher and multicultural educator, to model changing the map of the world, and to prompt educators to experience and understand how universal rights do indeed begin close to home.

REFERENCES

Apple, M. W. (1993). Constructing the "other": Rightist reconstructions of common sense. In C. McCarthy & W. Crichlow (Eds.), *Race identity and representation in education* (pp. 24–39). New York: Routledge.

Ayers, W. (1998). Forward: Popular education: Teaching for social justice. In W. Ayers, J. A. Hunt, & T. Quinn (Eds.), *Teaching for social justice* (pp. xvii–xxv). New York: Teachers College Press.

Banks, J. (1994). *An introduction to multicultural education.* Boston: Allyn & Bacon.

Boyer, J. B., & Baptiste, Jr., H. P. (1996). *Transforming the curriculum for multicultural understandings: A practitioner's handbook.* San Francisco: Caddo Gap.

Branch, C. W. (1994). Ethnic identity as a variable in the learning equation. In E. R. Hollins, J. E. King, & W. D. Hayman (Eds.), *Teaching diverse populations: Formulating a knowledge base* (pp. 207–224). Albany, NY: State University of New York Press.

Coontz, S. (1992). *The way we never were: American families and the nostalgia trap.* New York: Basic Books.

Cuzort, R. P., & King, E. (1995). *Twentieth-century social thought* (5th ed.). Fort Worth, TX: Harcourt Brace College.

Delpit, L. (1995). *Other people's children: Cultural conflict in the classroom.* New York: New Press.

Díaz, C. F. (1992). *The next millennium: A multicultural imperative for education.* In C. F. Díaz (Ed.), *Multicultural education for the 21st century* (pp. 12–22). Washington, DC: National Education Association.

Freire, P. (1998). *Teachers as cultural workers: Letters to those who dare teach.* Boulder, CO: Westview.

Gallavan, N. P. (1998). "Why aren't teachers using effective multicultural education practices?" Five major insights from experienced teachers. *Equity and Excellence in Education, 31*(2), 20–27.

Gallavan, N. P. (2002). Cultural competency for transformative education. In J. Wink and L. G. Wink (Eds.), *Visions of Vygotsky* (pp. 157–175). Boston: Allyn & Bacon.

Giroux, H. A. (1997). *Pedagogy and the politics of hope: Theory, culture, and schooling.* Boulder, CO: Westview.

Howard, G. R. (1999). *We can't teach what we don't know: White teachers, multiracial schools.* New York: Teachers College Press.

Kozol, J. (1991). *Savage inequalities: Children in American's schools.* New York: Crown Publishers.

Ladson-Billings, G. (1994). *The dreamkeepers: Successful teachers of African-American children.* San Francisco: Jossey-Bass.

Liston, D. P., & Zeichner, K. M. (1999). *Culture and teaching.* Mahwah, NJ: Erlbaum.

MacLeod, J. (1987). *Ain't no makin' it: Aspirations and attainment in a low-income neighborhood.* Boulder, CO: Westview.

Noddings, N. (1998). Teaching themes of care. In K. Ryan & J. M. Cooper (Eds.), *Kaleidoscope: Readings in Education* (8th ed., pp. 185–192). New York: Houghton Mifflin.

Paley, V. G. (1989). *White teacher.* Cambridge, MA: Harvard University Press.

Palmer, P. J. (1993). *To know as we are known: Education as a spiritual journey.* San Francisco: HarperCollins.

Sleeter, C. E., & McLaren, P. L. (Eds.). (1995). Introduction: Exploring connections to build a critical multiculturalism. In C. E. Slater & P. L. McLaren (Eds.), *Multicultural education, critical pedagogy, and the politics of difference* (pp. 1–5). Albany: State University of New York Press.

Smith, G. P. (1999). If you're not standing in this line, you're standing in the wrong line. In C. Clark & J. O'Donnell (Eds.), *Becoming and unbecoming white: Owning and disowning a racial identity* (pp. 160–177). Westport, CT: Bergin & Garvey.

Spring, J. (1995). *The intersection of cultures: Multicultural education in the United States.* New York: McGraw-Hill.

Tatum, B. D. (1997). *"Why are all the black kids sitting together in the cafeteria?" and other conversations about race.* New York: Basic Books.

Wertsch, J. V., del Río, P., & Alvarez, A. (1995). Sociocultural studies: History, action, and mediation. In J. V. Wertsch, P. del Río, & A. Alvarez (Eds.), *Sociocultural studies of mind* (pp. 1–36). New York: Cambridge University Press.

Reflective Questions

1. Think about a time when you initiated a journey (physical, mental, and/or emotional) that changed your assumptions, values, and beliefs about yourself, others, and the world. Write about the journey, identifying the outstanding events that have stayed with you over time and why those events have remained important to you.

2. Reflect on a time when someone close to you—such as a family member, friend, or colleague—mentored you with information and support that provided you unanticipated and/or requisite access and opportunity. What opportunities were you provided that led to additional opportunities that you could not have created on your own? How have these events changed your personal and professional development?

3. Describe a time when you were "in the right place at the right time." By chance or serendipity, you met someone, acquired valuable information, or were invited to join a group that changed your life positively. Specify the events and how they have influenced you today.

Activities for the Classroom

1. Interview a close family member such as your mother or father or sibling and share your different perspectives on events that occurred and shaped your thoughts, words, and behaviors during your childhood and teenage years.

2. Interview someone who grew up at the same time you did but in a different part of the country in different circumstances. Compare and contrast your personal experiences.

3. Visit a part of your current city or town that you do not know well. Consider how children in this part of your community live compared with where and how you were raised.

FURTHER READINGS

McBride, J. (1996). *The color of water: A black man's tribute to his white mother.* New York: Riverhead.

Nieto, S. (2000). *Affirming diversity: The sociopolitical context of multicultural education* (3rd ed.). New York: Addison Wesley Longman.

Oakes, J., & Tipton, M. (1999). *Teaching to change the world.* Boston: McGraw-Hill.

Smith, G. P. (1994). *Common sense about uncommon knowledge: The knowledge bases for diversity.* Washington, DC: American Association of College for Teacher Education.

Wink, J., & Putney, L. (2001). *A vision of Vygotsky.* New York: Allyn, Bacon, & Longman.

CHILDREN'S LITERATURE

Ackerman, K. (1992). *I know a place.* Boston: Houghton Mifflin.

Baylor, B. (1995). *I'm in charge of celebrations.* New York: Aladdin.

Bouchard, D. (1995). *If you're not from the prairie . . .* Hong Kong: Simon & Schuster.

Bridges, R. (1999). *Through my eyes.* New York: Scholastic.

Cohn, J. (1995). *The Christmas menorahs: How a town fought hate.* Morton Grove, IL: Whitman & Company.

Freedman, R. (1993). *Eleanor Roosevelt: A life of discovery.* New York: Clarion.

Gray, L. M. (1993). *Dear Willie Rudd.* New York: Simon & Schuster.

Taylor, M. D. (1976). *Roll of thunder, hear my cry.* New York: Dial.

WEB SITES

Center for Research on Education, Diversity and Excellence (CREDE):
www.crede.ucsc.edu

U.S. Bureau of the Census:
www.census.gov

Multicultural Pavilion:
curry.edschool.virginia.edu/go/multicultural/

Rethinking Schools:
www.rethinkingschools.org

Teaching Tolerance:
www.splcenter.org

UCLA Center X:
www.centerx.gseis.ucla.edu/

U.S. Committee for UNICEF:
www.webmaster@unicefusa.org

Chapter 7

On Becoming a Transformative Teacher: What Should I Do? How Should I Do It? And Why?

Linda F. Quinn, University of Nevada, Las Vegas

Focus Questions

1. In what ways did Linda's life experiences mold her social identity as a teacher and her relationships with her students?

2. In what ways did the world change her as she learned to teach in it?

3. What stages of professional development do you see in Linda's journey?

Life is always full of more questions than answers. When we're young, in our first attempts to understand the world, we utter each question we have, sometimes again and again. In the beginning, the words *why* or *what* are as numerous as raindrops in Seattle. As we grow older and more experienced we learn to dismiss most of our questions as "not now" or "not important," and focus on those that can be easily answered, that seem to fit the occasion, or that won't bring frowns or reprimands. Teachers often lament this sparseness of questions in older students, imagining a loss of interest in learning.

It seems that my entire life has been taken up with questions about teaching. The more I think I know about teaching the more questions I have. How does an education major learn to teach? How long does it take? Is it possible for someone who has never been a good student to become a good teacher? What does a student need to know to become a teacher? How does one learn to teach to change the world? In what ways does the world change us as we learn to teach in it? And, since we all can't be born into the same set of circumstances, how do we learn to appreciate the diversity each person's place in the universe creates?

I have come to realize that there are as many ways to learn *how* to teach as there are teachers. But when I think about *what* someone needs to know to become a teacher, there are fewer options. Both experience (learning how) and knowledge (learning about) are necessary in learning to teach. I can memorize a set of guidelines from a text for preparing a classroom or a lesson to maximize student success, but until I've interacted with actual students in what Doyle (1986) calls the "multidimensionality" of the classroom, my "book learning" knowledge does not fully prepare me for the task at hand.

Experience has always been a formidable molder of behavior. Yet experience by itself, such as an accident or a natural disaster, can leave one dazed and confused. Transformative teaching requires both experience and knowledge, and the combination can take many forms. More important than the balance or any special mix are the meaningful ways that our formative experiences are connected with well-structured, larger bodies of knowledge that help us learn "how" in ways that help us help others. The connection between experience and knowledge is like a magnet that pulls pieces into the puzzle of teaching for us, that pushes us into new places and gives us the courage to attempt the untried, to step into the unknown.

Journeys of experience and knowledge that lead to becoming a transformative teacher may vary as much as the individuals who embark on them. The success of these journeys depends, to a great extent, on the opportunities that present themselves and on the people who are there to articulate the opportunities. To reflect on what might have influenced my own transformation as a teacher I examined some of the times, people, places, and events that were pivotal to the attainment of my present status as a teacher educator. Often, I am at a loss to pinpoint where and when I even became aware of myself as a teacher, let alone a transformative one! My professional journey certainly has not followed a straight line. There have been peaks more precipitous than the Matterhorn and dips more daunting than the Grand Canyon. At times I have traveled down paths that were cul-de-sacs, and more often than I care to admit, I have had to backtrack. As you learn about teaching and how to teach, certitude battles with uncertainty while assumptions are confirmed or challenged. Balance and clear direction can only be achieved through a constant, critical process of reflection on experiences and a continued exploration of one's beliefs. My journey has been a series of opportunities (frequently unanticipated), discoveries, practice, reflection, and renewal.

FIRST STEPS

Does learning to teach begin with understanding what it feels like to be a learner? I am not a "born" educator. When my sister and I played school with the kids in the "defense house" neighborhood where we grew up, I never asked to be the teacher. I was, instead, the problem student who carelessly finished the exercises my sister ran us through, got bored, and wanted to go outside. Even in real school, I was seldom the brightest or best-behaved student. I often thought of skipping. So why, you might ask, did I chose a career that would require me to go to school every day?

Once in fourth grade, after my parents had moved us to the country, I went home with a friend for lunch and we decided it was too nice a day to go back, so we played hooky along the creek out behind her house until the farmer next door yelled at us, "Get back to school!" We picked scotch broom for our teacher, Mrs. Snyder, as an offering of apology. She was understandably upset when we were an hour late coming back from lunch.

What I remember, though, is that Mrs. Snyder seemed more upset with me than with my friend, Bernadine. Bernadine got to go home after school, but I had to stay behind and sit in the silent classroom watching Mrs. Snyder work at her desk, waiting for her to speak. When I could sit quietly no longer, I asked her what had happened in the story she had read to the class after lunch. She wouldn't tell me that, but she did tell me how she was surprised that I would play hooky, how worried she had been about me, and how she had always felt that she could depend on me doing what was right. I was confused about the feelings of regret and remorse that mingled with my pleasure from knowing that the teacher thought me special in some way. Her concern and attention gave rise to a silent promise on my part to "be better" and "try harder." To this day, I wonder if Bernadine also would have benefited from the same thought-provoking encounter that I was subjected to, and why she wasn't. That single event and Mrs. Snyder's approach to it was surely an early marker at the beginning of my journey in learning to teach.

Are there specific people who point the way toward teaching? Are there signposts along that way that they notice when inexperienced heads are too full of gathering information to see for themselves? Joane McKay (1990) found through her dissertation research that teacher of the year recipients often identified family members as being highly influential in and supportive of their career choice. What was it during my senior year in high school that pointed me toward the state teacher's college in Monmouth, Oregon? Up until that time I had wanted to be a veterinarian like my friend, Dallas, and take care of the farm animals in and around my hometown of Boring, Oregon (yes, *Boring,* believe it or not!). Certainly, my family had a strong influence on my choice of teaching as a career. Uncle Linden and Aunt Hazel, and Uncle Kenny and Aunt Betty all had been teachers. My sister was going to be a teacher.

Growing up in a small rural community in Oregon surrounded by fields of every berry imaginable, I worked alongside locals, young and old day workers bussed out from nearby Portland, Oregon, and migrant workers living in temporary housing on large Japanese-owned farms. We moved from farm to farm as a troop to harvest the next ripening crop and ended the season picking beans on the Latter-day Saints' farm near Blue Lake. To my young eyes we were the same at the end of each long, back-breaking day, and it never entered my mind that my intent to go to college set me apart in any way from my summertime colleagues. But when I went off to college to become a teacher, they didn't start college with me. At that time I didn't give much thought to the circumstances that set us off on different courses, but later, observing my own students, I was reminded of the opportunities that come so easily for some and not at all for others.

At the state teacher's college my roommate, Virginia Hopkins, was one of only two black students in the freshman class. When we asked to be roommates, the housemother was concerned that we wouldn't get along, being of different "color," but we assured her that we would get along just fine since we had both come from the same neighborhood in Portland. I learned as much from Virginia that first year as I did in my classes. The grace with which she "handled" her part in a nearly all-white college would also be a model and a sense of strength for me in my role as *gaijin* (alien) many years later.

How does one stay the course of teaching? What choices have the greatest potential for success? Is there a pattern to the choices one makes? Or to the opportunities that present themselves? Are there certain teaching experiences that lead more directly to becoming a transformative teacher than others? Is variety of experience a benefit or a hindrance?

My own growth as a teacher was haphazard—not *mis*guided, but *un*guided—a series of instinctive responses to the unanticipated circumstances of 20 years of classroom teaching under a bewildering variety of conditions. Don't get me wrong, random isn't necessarily bad. I did so many different things in so many different ways that I was never bored or tempted to look for any other way to live my life. In putting the pieces of my career together into a coherent philosophical overview, I can look back and see that I was passing through all the classic stages of professional growth. But it is still the journey—the names and places and dates and faces—that is most important, and not the theory that would explain it. It is, after all, the lived life that education is all about. You will discover this as you build your own memories of students, parents, and schools. And these memories will guide you in times of indecision.

STAYING THE COURSE THROUGH EXPERIENCE AND PRACTICE

During my first 10 years as a teacher in elementary classrooms in Beaverton, Oregon, I taught third, fourth, fifth, and sixth grades and coordinated the "new" Scott Foresman language-based reading program. My attitudes toward students and their parents, and my ideas about teaching and learning, went through some pretty heady transformations during that time. I traveled from Paul Burden's (1986) "survival" stage to what McDonald (1982) terms "exploring" and what Gregorc (1973) calls "growing." Roz Summers, an ex-flight-attendant-cum-first-grade-teacher, taught me to laugh and take it easy, Claire Wagoner took me under her wing, gave me helpful advice and materials to use with my third-grade students, and Rod Kvistad taught me the value of planning and that principals are human beings too. The students, mostly white and middle class, taught me that diversity often hides behind a mask of sameness, and it is a teacher's job to uncover differences, to celebrate them, and help students recognize the value in themselves.

It was also "the sixties," so I took part in school-wide sensitivity training, learning how to make decisions by consensus and became vividly aware of the ways in which the margins and centers of "power" underlie all group decisions. In the classroom, I experienced firsthand the theories of John Dewey (1916), Jerome Bruner (1962), and William Glasser (1969), and began to make practical meaning of the knowledge I had been exposed to in college classes.

More importantly, I learned through a fifth-grade production of Macbeth that when students choose what they will learn and how they will learn it, the end result is mighty and memorable. I saw students free to discover knowledge, working as a group in ways I had never noticed before and in which I had no part other than to provide resources and settle the rare conflict of claim on space and time. I learned that including parents in the design of curriculum can produce materials and expertise far beyond the scope of any single teacher or school. A pioneer unit in the fourth grade produced a wealth of artifacts, from a butter churn, to an appaloosa pony, to a rare antique oil lamp, all accompanied by facts and personal stories from the owners, and all absorbed and handled with extreme care by the students. And I learned that all students should have the opportunity to touch and talk about things both familiar and unknown.

The sixties were also a time of "inclusion," and I worked in tandem with special education teachers as they determined individual programs for students in my classroom. Sally, from the county education office, helped me with strategies for helping a deaf student and gave me a new perspective on teachers' lives as she told stories of climbing El Capitan in Yosemite National Park. I was cooperating teacher for two student teachers, and as I watched them practice their newly acquired skills, I began to question my own practices and to modify some of them to fit the challenging ideas coming along with these neophytes from the university.

Then, recently divorced, I fell in love with a poet and left Oregon to travel to Europe and the Middle East with my new husband and two small sons. Travel became my teacher as I learned in ways quite new to me. I had never noticed before how much going and coming there is among people of the world, from village to village, from town to town, city to city, and country to country. It seems a common human characteristic to explore new places and to learn about the people who inhabit them. I had inadvertently joined this pilgrimage, having no idea of the impact that it would have on my future teaching.

We quickly got busy learning to travel as a family—from Oregon to Boston to New York and England, and then from England to Ireland, and to Germany. We rode undergrounds and metros, taxis, trains, boats, and planes until the fateful day we bought our own car and headed for Italy. On a whim, I had applied for a teaching job with the Department of Defense Dependent Schools in Karlsruh, Germany. I was notified of a job 2 days later. To my surprise, it was in Avellino, Italy, and I had to report in 3 days. All the way to Naples I wondered what my students would be like, what the school would be like, and how I would teach them. I had no idea what surprises were in store (or that coffee in Italian really meant espresso), or the path my seemingly random travels were taking me down.

In Avellino I taught grades four, five, six, seven, and eight in a two-room school in the warehouse district. Tom Masucci, the Italian school secretary who drove a yellow Alfa Romeo, handled his American charges with panache and made certain we had fresh water daily. There was a chain link fence around the playground, and the workers from the shoe factory next-door would watch the students play soccer at recess. They would yell and clap and offer advice in a language we didn't know while their smiles dissolved whatever dread or fear the lack of understanding caused in us. Over time, the students and workers became familiar partners in this recess ritual, and we were all enriched as we learned about one another while yelling and kicking our way around the enclosure.

I had 19 students. I was teaching in a multiage, multicultural classroom with no previous knowledge or theoretical frameworks to support me. My only frames of reference were what I knew about the ungraded primary system, which was scant, and my own experience of being a student in a very large third- and fourth-grade classroom in a four-room schoolhouse back in Boring.

In Boring, Mrs. TenEyck had placed all the third-grade students on one side of the room and the fourth-grade students on the other, with the brightest third-grade students and the poorest fourth-grade students in the middle. It seemed to work for her, but I was at a loss as to how that could work with 19 students across five grades. So we improvised. I established peer tutoring groups and implemented "whole language" in Avellino before it became popular in Arizona. Projects and centers became the organizational framework of our classroom. We shared work and stories. We became a learning family and helped one another. We protected one another. The students helped me learn the protocols of the military, and I helped them learn to read, write, solve problems and wonder.

We lived and worked in a global village in Avellino. Most of the permanent military personnel at the Avellino radar site were African American. Sergeant Pugh's wife, a Muslim from Jamica, had a son the same age as my youngest, and we quickly became part of her "tribe" as she welcomed us into her home, explained the shopping norms in Italy and getting around on the Autostrada. Sunday afternoons at the Pugh's, surrounded by children and their folks from around the world, became a ritual of rich conversation, and learning about the differences that we shared. There were no racial lines or class barriers in our companionship. We needed one another.[1]

LEARNING THROUGH REFLECTION

My greatest epiphany regarding the students in Italy came when my principal (she taught first, second, and third grades) and I took the students on a field trip to Pompeii. Here was a place I had long dreamed of seeing. Listening with my students as the guide related the story of the rise and fall of Pompeii, I saw these learners in a new light. I had always thought of military children as being somewhat disadvantaged, having to frequently change schools, moving from country to country as fathers were transferred from base to base. But at Pompeii these students suddenly became the "advantaged." Their perspective was global. How differently they must see the world from the way my students back in Beaverton would see it. In that instant, my role as their teacher came to be to nurture and encourage that global perspective and to help them recognize the true value of their experience. This realization, standing in the dust of Pompeii, had a profound influence on my relationships with future students in elementary, secondary and university classrooms in Beaverton, Damascus, and Japan, and in teacher education programs in Texas, Nevada, and Iowa.

Jerome Kagen (1998) suggests that all of us, students too, have the potential to grow beyond our present circumstances. Becoming aware of one's potential and the worth of individual lives within unique contexts transforms the ways we teach and the ways we view learners and content. Less Schulman (1998) says the stories our teaching experiences create are just stories until we learn from them, until we look inside our experiences and reflect on them through questions and wonder.

From Avellino we journeyed to Ahwaz, Iran, where my poet–husband had preceded us, to be a visiting professor in a new university in the oil province of Khuzestan. Once we were settled in Ahwaz, I also began teaching at Jundi Shapur University. I was asked by the College of Education to design a second language program for the

---

[1]Teachers and students also need one another. You need your students as much as they need you. Learn as much about them as quickly as possible. Recognize and honor the attraction that brings you together in a meaningful exchange of experiences.

elementary students at the new college laboratory school. I taught English classes to first and second graders, while education majors observed and took notes.

In the morning before my classes began, I would often stand at the window and watch the workmen who had come to plant grass and bougainvillea around the school roll out their prayer carpets and offer their praises to Allah. I wondered at the ways this ritual seemed consistent with that of the 6-year-olds across the hall, sitting on wooden benches at long narrow tables writing a single stroke over and over as their teacher chanted, "ah."[2]

Good teachers are constantly engaged in a sort of mental research they accept as a second conscience, forever reminding them that they could do better if they just had another piece of information. This mental research often leads to a broader involvement in the school or in local, state, and national organizations, where conversations with fellow educators lead to new research and implementation of more effective teaching strategies. This healthy cycle of professional development creates the energy that renews a teacher's life, and it is central in the journey to becoming a teacher. A recluse cannot become a transformative teacher. For teachers to grow and to help others to grow, they must play an active role in a community of teachers and learners. They must work in the company of others seeking answers to similar questions.

Formulating questions about my own practice, about what I see taking place in classrooms, and about what I read and hear about schools and teachers has always been second nature to me. I developed the habit of questioning from my father. We would drive the country roads around Boring, Oregon, and my father would pose questions about the weather, the crops, the news, songs, and peoples' actions. My sense of wonder was tempered by "rules" and carefully plotted conundrums designed to "trip me up," as I tried to answer his questions and pose new ones for his amusement.

From Iran, we came back, once again, to Oregon, where I learned that culture shock works both ways. I also became aware of the provincialism of the place I had left 2 years before. "Home" is never like you've left it once you've been out in the world, and learning can cause discomfort when we grow in ways not understood by our "home" group. How often do classrooms resemble foreign worlds to children who must navigate an unnatural cultural gap on a daily basis? What beacons can teachers provide to help these students make this daily transition with competence and confidence?

PRACTICE, PRACTICE, AND MORE PRACTICE

Back in Beaverton School District, I was asked to join the faculty of a new open-concept school. In-service training was provided for the new faculty, and we re-learned communication skills and how to share learning space and opportunities. Our new building was supposed to be ready in September. It wasn't. As a result, two elementary student bodies had to be housed in one of the district's older school buildings for the first 4 months of the school year.

The other fourth-grade teacher and I didn't want to be separated because we had decided to team-teach our 60 students, and we wanted to start the school year as a team. In order to accommodate our wishes, we were relegated to the gymnasium.

---

[2]Sometimes as a teacher you will find yourself in a culture so distant from anything you can understand that it will be necessary to stand very still and listen for meaning in the silences between acts.

We had half of the gym; gym classes had the other half. We were separated from the P.E. classes by moveable partitions. Each of us was given a student teacher, and we were assigned an aide because of the large number of fourth-grade students. It was a horrendous autumn. By the time we moved into our new, open school building, we had not one complaint about noise or distractions. While the rest of the faculty struggled with the reality of the open-space concept, we welcomed the quietness of our new open space. I was apparently entering the "mature" stage, as Burden (1986) suggests: learning how to accept what "is" and make the best of it.

My next significant learning experience in my journey as a teacher was in a year-round school in Damascus, Oregon—closer to Boring, where my husband and I had settled on the family's homestead—right back where I'd grown up. I was hired as a sixth-grade teacher and was getting ready to start the year in an outdoor camp with my sixth graders when the principal called and asked me if I would please take a first-grade position instead. One of his teachers had just quit, and he had someone else who would take the sixth grade but not the first. I was terrified. I had tried to teach my 6-year-old son, Max, to read in Iran and it had been a disaster. How could I possibly teach first grade? Betty Cramer, a former colleague in Beaverton, who had been a first-grade teacher for 10 years, gave me encouragement and enough materials to get started, and the children and the other first-grade teachers at the school kept me going for the next 3 years.

Year-round school was great. That first year my 29 first graders and I came back from each 3-week break a little further along than where we had left off and raring to go forward. At the end of 3 years, I switched tracks and grade levels and so was able to spend the summer months in Alaska, where my poet–husband had gone to build highways and prospect for poems. Since there are no idle hours in the land of the midnight sun, I wound up working as a teamster, weighing trucks that carried gravel to finish the Valdez terminal for the Alaskan oil pipeline. I saw and learned a lot that summer out of the classroom. Alone in the weigh shack waiting for trucks to arrive, I also had a lot of time to think. I learned to carry a gun to work because the weigh shack on the edge of the glacial gravel pit was frequented by bears searching for the nests of arctic terns, birds so out of touch with the learning curve that they repeatedly build their nests in the middle of a haul road and then dive-bomb the dump trucks and bears that kill their babies. I learned to be on the side of the stubborn terns. And I saw the aurora borealis light up the northern sky. And I brought home stories and artifacts for my students back in Damascus.

After 5 years in Damascus, I followed my husband to Nagoya, Japan, where he reentered the academic world as a professor of English. In Nagoya, I taught English at a catholic university, at a women's college, for Encyclopaedia Britannica, to a group of bank managers, and to a private group that included a world renowned cancer surgeon, an industrialist, and Japan's leading mystery novelist. It seems that all foreigners in Japan, regardless of nationality, training, or fluency, teach English, and that all Japanese study it. I was merely lending my teaching skills to the national effort.

DISCOVERIES, DISAPPOINTMENTS, AND MORE REFLECTION

When we first arrived in Japan, I had hoped to place my sons in the local schools, but I soon discovered that this would not be possible. In Nagoya, in those days, having a foreign student in the classroom was seen as an unnecessary disruption of the education of the Japanese students. This attitude on the part of the Japanese public school system was the first time I experienced being the object of discrimination. There was no getting around it, so I enrolled my sons in the Nagoya International School and worked part-time at the library to defray a portion of their substantial tuition until we moved so far from the school that it became impractical for them to go there. My boys continued their schooling through Calvert School in Maryland and the University of Nebraska's correspondence high school, and I became a homeschooling mama. I learned the value of alternative forms of education and realized that the choice to homeschool one's children does not always stem from disapproval of the public school system. From and with my sons, I learned that there is more than one way to accomplish educational goals. But that's not all I learned in Nagoya.

There are all sorts of teachers, and there are just as many different ways that they develop professionally, but until a teacher becomes intentional about teaching, professional growth is something that just happens. It takes place even when your job is just a job, but it doesn't take real shape or form until it becomes intentional. It is intent that makes a teacher transformative.

When we bought our first Japanese vehicle, a used Yamaha motorcycle, my husband and I had to travel across the city to pick it up. Since there were few street signs and since we couldn't read them anyway, I watched out the back window of our friend's car for landmarks that would guide us back home on the motorcycle later that night. This act of looking back to remember which way we'd come so we could find our way home is a device that has been used by learners and travelers for centuries. I remember feeling part explorer, part fool, as we wended our way home, but I never forgot that route or the huge billboard advertisements that were landmarks as formidable as mountain ranges and rivers had been for my pioneering ancestors. I learned to tell where I was and where I was headed, as well as where I had been, by looking back with a critical eye. Now, from time to time, I revisit my journey as an educator in much the same way, to check where I've come from so I never forget where I'm headed. As a new teacher, you need to establish your own guideposts, and sometimes the ones that are the most helpful will be the ones that you weren't looking for.

In time, my eldest son graduated from correspondence high school and left for college. Life is not always fair for teachers or students. (He had originally been accepted at the California University of Technology and then politely rejected because he hadn't attended a "regular" school and could not produce a letter of recommendation from a high school counselor.) Teachers should always be alert to the ways rules and routines block learners from opportunities while providing others free reign. To paraphrase Doris Lessing (1987), people at the top should know what goes on underneath them.

So we moved back across the city, and I took a teaching position at the international school so our youngest could have friends and play basketball. At Nagoya International School (NIS) I taught high school English, fifth grade, and middle school math, and served administratively as middle school coordinator. I had become, by this time, an "old Japan hand," and the international school setting provided a link with "home"—an American style of education that I missed. White students were in the minority at NIS. The students in my fifth-grade classroom represented 15 nations, some with learning disabilities. Students with disabilities did not have an easy time in Japanese public schools, and some of this cultural racism spilled over into the international school. Not everyone was always comfortable with the multiracial community that existed in the classroom, but John Jordan, from Tyler, Texas, did learn to treat his classmate, Hiroyasu, with respect and to help his autistic friend learn to joke.

In the 4 years I had been away from the elementary school classroom changes had taken place, and I spent some time catching up on things. I started to think about all I had seen and done. Reading day after day in *The Japan Times, The Pacific Stars and Stripes* and *Newsweek* of the many crises in American education, I began thinking about passing the torch to a new generation of educators. I began to wonder how what I had learned about teaching and the world might help other educators. I had never seriously considered going back to school. A teacher's place was in the classroom. All the rest was egos, budgets, and buzzwords as far as I was concerned. But then, who would show the newcomers all the neat stuff that I had learned about the schoolroom and the world outside it, if not me?

RENEWAL THROUGH KNOWLEDGE AND REFLECTION

That was the point at which my development as a teacher became "professional" in my own mind. I had discovered an intention that was larger than personal desire, more purposeful than the whims of fate. Maybe it would even turn out to be bigger than my skills, but there was only one way to find out.

My dread of going back to school was shortly circumvented by a U.S. Department of State International Fellowship offered to teachers in American overseas schools. In 1988 I left Japan for Texas, another foreign country, to pursue a doctoral degree in curriculum and instruction. For 3 years I studied and read and watched and wrote and revised and developed a deep new pride in the profession I had chosen rather haphazardly so many years before. I worked with Dr. Jane Stallings in research in instructional strategies and management in inner city schools. I taught seminars in supervision to cooperating teachers and university supervisors. I conducted research in on-site math methods curriculum. I was a graduate assistant to Dr. Robert Houston while he was editing the first edition of the *Handbook on Research on Teacher Education* (Houston, 1990) and had the enlightening opportunity to read the chapters as they came in from the authors. I took a curriculum class from Laurel Tanner. I had my own carrel in the library, and I spent long quiet afternoons reading and thinking.

They finally made me leave. I would have stayed forever, but my mentors at the University of Houston said it was time for me to get back to teaching and launch others on professional journeys. So I did—and I loved it. It felt a lot like coming into port on a quiet summer evening after long, adventuresome months at sea.

While I was at the University of Northern Iowa, I taught a class in human relations. The summer section is for students who will be doing their student teaching out of state or in international settings, for instructors at Black Hawk Community College who are seeking recertification, and for speech pathologists who must have this course on their transcripts to be licensed in Iowa. It is often an odd mix of students who walk through the door on the first day of class, yet, as Iowans, they are still mostly white, young, and middle class. It was always a challenge for me to find the types of experiences that would help them to become aware of and, better yet, to understand the richness hiding in the multicultural situations they would encounter once they began working and teaching in other places. It naturally pleases me when my efforts as a teacher are influential in changing or challenging students' assumptions and ways of thinking.

This excerpt from a letter I received from one of my students at the end of that class serves to remind me of the responsibility teachers have to their students. The student had been laid off during a "downsizing" in the school district, and though he had never lost his desire to teach he had stayed away from the classroom for many years thinking that he just wasn't cut out to be a teacher. Finally, the desire to return to the classroom became so strong he couldn't ignore it, so he enrolled in the human relations course in an attempt to become recertified:

> This course woke me up regarding how insulated I had become to multicultural issues. I had considered myself still somewhat hip. I really entered this course with the idea of not getting much out of it because it was a state mandate probably conjured up by someone on a do-gooder mission who had never spent a day in a K–12 teaching situation. I was going to be the older person among all the rookie young people. I just wanted to complete the course and get out. I distinctly remember telling Ken while in the hall the first day before class that it would take a stick of dynamite to get me to say anything in this class. I had never really anticipated ever being in a situation requiring me to deal with the issues we discussed in this class. I guess I was wrong.

The transformation that this student underwent seems to me to be what we should always hope for as teachers as we continually strive to change and heal the world. Transformative teachers must assume this responsibility toward their students with courage. They must never forget that it is the students for whom they struggle, not for themselves, not for the institution, and not for the content. It is the students they teach who will do the healing. Transformative teachers simply point the way. Abraham Lincoln knew the value of teaching our children well:

> A child is a person who is going to carry on what you have started. He is going to sit where you are sitting and when you are gone, attend to those things which you think are important. You may adopt all the policies you please, but how they are carried out depends on him. He will assume control of your cities, states, and nations. He is going to move in and take over your churches, schools and corporations . . . The fate of humanity is in his hands.

FULFILLMENT, GRATITUDE, AND HOPE

It seems I have been a teacher forever. I have taught first graders how to read, seventh graders how to dance, fourth graders how to conjugate verbs, and I have discussed the not so subtle meaning of *The Crucible* with high school juniors. Nothing, however, in my career has been as challenging and as rewarding as teaching education majors what it means to teach and to call oneself a teacher. A graduate student once told me that teaching was not a career, "It's a way of life." It is. It is a way of becoming who you were meant to be.

I have spent a lot of time overseas on my journey, and each new place I visit awakens more potential within, a deeper understanding of the human enterprise, and a greater desire to help others to find and build those places where they can discover who they are to become. I tell every experienced teacher I meet to go back to school. The path to professional fulfillment passes that way. They have the background to make everything they learn relevant, and each time another abstract chunk of information falls into place, they will just shake their heads and say, sure—of course, I knew that.

I also know that my learning as a teacher is not complete, but it *is* mature. As an educator, I know what I'm doing (most of the time!) and why I'm doing it. As a person, I am satisfied, as the Japanese would say, that I have done my best. It has been a marvelous journey, and what makes it even more rewarding is that I have never undertaken any part of it alone. I've shared the journey with friends, colleagues, teachers, and students all over America and the world. We meet often—our paths *do* cross—and we exchange looks, gestures, and stories. We are *compadres* in learning and teaching.

Time lines and textbooks are straightforward. They're tidy, going from one year, one event to the next—but textbooks are not curricula, and time lines are not careers. And becoming a teacher is not always so neatly arranged, either. There are indeed as many ways teachers develop as there are teachers. As John Dewey (who else?) put it:

> If education is growth, it must progressively realize present possibilities, and thus make individuals better fitted to cope with later requirements. Growing is not something which is complete in odd moments; it is a continuous leading into the future.
>
> (1959, p. 51)

The world is focused on changes in work and lifestyles. Changes we have seen in the past decade fire the imagination while public education seems trapped in a time warp, leaning toward tests and norm-referenced measures of accountability the same as it did in the fifties and seventies. This approach seems to leave little opportunity for thinking beyond what we have already experienced. It leaves me believing that education is missing or misinterpreting present possibilities that could prepare us more adequately than standardized testing for the amazing possibilities of the 21st century.

An important step toward becoming an effective teacher is to first understand your own attitudes and assumptions about children, teachers, schools, teaching, and learning. The next step is to challenge these assumptions, to recognize how inflexible they are, to identify and assess the basis for them, and to continually reevaluate them through new experiences. This is not an easy task, and it is not something that becomes easier with age, though it does become easier with practice. Max Stirner, a 19th-century school teacher and philosopher (yes, you can be both) refers to any thought that an individual cannot give up as a "wheel in the head" (Spring, 1999, p. 40). Stirner believed a "wheel in the head" used the individual, rather than being used by the individual. An idea or belief that is a wheel in the head owns the individual, as opposed to the thoughts that individuals own and can use for their own benefit.

Education is about the teacher who holds hands and hearts and hope and knows the difference between cohesion and adhesion and how to teach these concepts to 6-, 7-, and 8-year-olds so the next time they see raindrops on a window they see them in a new light. It's about the teacher who talks about mathematics like music and gets the students to sing along and to keep track of numbers and things that add up to something more than problems in a book. It's about the teacher who thinks children are worth listening to and knows that when children grow up they should know how to listen to ideas and sounds that are uncommon, and that this takes practice and patience and paying attention.

Transformative teaching means taking risks, from time to time breaking the mold, and sometimes even fixing something that may not appear to be broken. Nothing in my life's experience has remained as fundamentally consistent as the schools and classrooms where I have taught (even as varied as they have seemed outwardly), but I never cease to hope for those transformative epiphanies that enable educators to move resolutely to the forefront of cultural progress where they belong.

REFERENCES

Bruner, J. (1962). *On knowing: Essays for the left hand*. Cambridge, MA: Harvard University Press.

Burden, P. R. (1986). Teacher development: Implications for teacher education. In L. Katz & J. Raths (Eds.), *Advances in teacher education* (Vol. 2, pp. 185–219). Norwood, NJ: Ablex.

Dewey, J. (1916). *Democracy and education*. New York: Macmillan.

Doyle, W. (1986). Classroom organization and management. In M. Witrock (Ed.), *Handbook of research on teaching* (3rd ed., pp. 392–431). New York: Macmillan.

Glasser, W. (1969). *Schools without failure*. New York: Harper & Row.

Gregorc, A. F. (1973). Developing plans for professional growth. *NASSP Bulletin, 57,* 1–8.

Houston, W. R. (Ed.). (1990). *Handbook of research on teacher education*. New York: Macmillan.

Kagan, J. (1998). *Three seductive ideas*. Cambridge, MA: Harvard University Press.

Lessing, D. (1987). *Prisons we choose to live inside: Switching off to see "Dallas."* New York: Harper & Row.

McDonald, F. J. (1982, April). *A theory of the professional development of teachers*. Paper presented at the annual meeting of the American Educational Research Association, New York.

McKay, J. W. (1990). *Iowa teachers of the year: A case study*. Unpublished doctoral dissertation, Iowa State University, Ames.

Shulman, L. (1998, February). *Teaching and teacher education among the professions*. Charles W. Hunt Lecture at the annual meeting of the American Association of Colleges of Teacher Education, New Orleans, LA.

Spring, J. (1999). *Wheels in the head.* Dubuque, IA: McGraw-Hill.

Winn, R. B. (1959). *John Dewey: Dictionary of education.* New York: Philosophical Library.

Reflective Activities

Students examine their own assumptions and beliefs regarding their social identity in terms of their ethnic and racial heritage by answering the following questions. Who or what has had the most influence in the formation of your attitudes and opinions about people of different cultural groups? What influences in your experiences have led to the development of positive or negative feelings about your own cultural heritage and background? What changes, if any, would you like to make in your attitudes or experiences in relation to people of other ethnic or cultural groups?

Look Who's Coming to School Interview

Have students work with an elementary or secondary school student to create a collage of the student's background, attitudes, and assumptions about teachers and schools, opinions about the school curriculum, and relationships with the other students in the school. Require a paper that reports salient points of the interview and considers ways a teacher might promote this particular student's academic achievement.

Activities for the Classroom

Have students document ways that schooling and elementary and secondary school students are portrayed through film or in literature. Through class discussions of personal experience and required course readings, have students determine the accuracy of this portrayal. Have them create a data retrieval chart to illustrate examples of possible trends or issues perceived as detrimental to equity in education (i.e., stereotypes, teachers' assumptions, testing, and expectations).

Require students to research the backgrounds of their local school board members and to attend a local school board meeting. They should make note of the relationship between board membership and the demographics of a particular geographical area. At the meeting, students should keep a record of who talks and for how long. Subsequent class discussion of these meetings will help students recognize where and with whom the power in their community resides.

Community Action Activity

Have students visit a nursing home, ride along with a law enforcement officer or social case worker or a county health nurse, visit the Goodwill Industries Office, ride a bus that picks up people in wheelchairs, visit a hospital, look at special summer programs for students with special needs, visit a church of a denomination different from their own, find some of the most unusual jobs in the area, investigate the number of languages spoken in the area, or look at citizenship data over the past 10 years. Make students responsible for arranging their own activity, and have them give a brief oral report to the class and submit a written report.

Have students complete a Venn diagram with a fellow student, illustrating membership in social groups they have in common and those that are different. Have them reflect on ways memberships in various social groups might determine teaching practice and relationships with students.

FURTHER READING

Apple, M. W., & Beane, J. A. (Eds.). (1995). *Democratic schools*. Alexandria, VA: Association for Supervision and Curriculum Development

Banks, J. A. (1997). *Educating citizens in a multicultural society*. New York: Teachers College Press.

Clark, C. M. (1995). *Thoughtful teaching*. New York: Teachers College Press.

Goodlad, S. J. (2001). *The last best hope: A democracy reader*. San Francisco: Jossey-Bass.

McEwan, B. (2000). *The art of classroom management: Effective practices for building equitable learning communities*. Upper Saddle River, NJ: Prentice Hall.

Merryfield, M. M., Jarchow, E., & Pickert, S. (1997). *Preparing teachers to teach global perspectives: A handbook for teacher educators*. Thousand Oaks, CA: Corwin.

Shimarhara, N. K., & Sakai, A. (1995). *Learning to teach in two cultures: Japan and the United States*. New York: Garland.

Spring, J. (1994). *Deculturalization and the struggle for equality*. New York: McGraw-Hill.

Winn, R. B. (1959). *John Dewey: Dictionary of education*. New York: Philosophical Library.

WEB SITES

The Global Schoolhouse:
http://www.gsh.org. Search projects posted by teachers according to grade level, topic, or time.

Intercultural E-mail Classroom Connections (IECC):
http://www.stolaf.edu/network/iecc. This is a good source, especially for linking with partners from different countries. The IECC is a mailing list for K–12 teachers who are looking for partner classrooms.

China the Beautiful:
http://www.chinapage.com/china.html

Africa Online Kids Only:
http://www.africaonline.com/AfricaOnline/kidsonly.html

Section III

Racial and Ethnic Identity

Introduction:
Themes of Power, Privilege, Race, and Identity

Paula Bradfield, EDC, Inc., Chicago and Jaime J. Romo, University of San Diego, San Diego

> Those with power are frequently least aware of—or least willing to acknowledge—its existence. Those with less power are often most aware of its existence.   (Delpit, 1995, p. 26)

I Am Who I Am Because of a White Man

Mother divorces my father and marries a White man.
We move from a house above the tunnel near Chinatown
to a brick and wrought iron house in San Francisco's
posh Marina district.
The other two Chinese families that live in this area
are also part white.

This was the only way Chinese could live in this part
of town.
My formative adolescent years are newly rooted in the
white part of town, away from Chinatown's little dark
alleys, smells of roast duck and garbage, clicking
Cantonese tongues.

Mother has new friends—white friends.
She quickly forgets the language she spoke to her
parents with.
She only speaks Cantonese when she swears at the cooks
in her restaurants.
Although I am a Chinese-American, I don't speak
Chinese.
I understand only a little.
The word behind the hyphen was emphasized more in my
household
Even as she prepares for her death, mother told her
daughters,
She didn't want to be buried on the side of the
cemetery with all those "Chinamen."
Not until I am an adult do I mourn the loss of my
Chinese identity.

I am who I am because of a White man.
It's my pre-tenure year at the university.
Will I make it or am I merely ethnic window dressing?
I have traversed many boundaries to get here.
While I know it is I who I must not disappoint, I also
respect what the community thinks of me.
I want to be a part of shaping this institution's
future not be a temporary house guest.
My destiny lies in the hands primarily of white men.

I am who I am because of a White man and so are you.
I am who I am because I am an Asian woman.
Grandmother lived with us and took care of me the
first five years of my life before she died.
I remember her gray streaked hair, her broad smile,
and her frail walk; the crippling results of early
foot binding.
She would soak them in a large tin pan each night.
I would help towel dry her broken feet.
What kind of life did she want for me?

I am who I am because I am both the White man and the
Asian woman.
The strong, silent woman warrior
Who stretches her unbound feet and boldly crosses
borders
Whose influence like burning incense perfumes the air
to stir social consciousness.

Suzanne Soo Hoo

As can be seen by excerpts from Suzanne Soo Hoo's poem, power and privilege are unequivocably intertwined with race in U.S. society. Power, inequitably distributed, is represented by time, territory and task—who gets the most time and attention. Who sets the schedule? Whose schedule counts? Who dominates or lives in positions and organization? Who is an insider? Who determines what's important for us to do, value, and compare to as a measure of our worth? Power and privilege intersect race and gender, the balance of which falls into the hands of white males. Teachers must understand this intersection to provide a more equitable education for students outside the circle of power. One way to do so is to examine the school performance of students who do not have access to the power or privilege of the white U.S. dominant culture.

To illustrate, the dropout rates across the nation for Hispanics/Latinos, African Americans, and American Indians are particularly high (Kitchen, Velasquez, & Myers, 2000) when compared to European American students. In the United States, dropout rates for Latinos and American Indians hover between 40% and 50%, almost double that for African Americans and triple that for whites. Higher than average dropout rates occur among students with similar abilities, socioeconomic class, immigrant status, and home languages. The only difference is ethnicity and race. Students of color report that white, ethnically encapsulated teachers (a) did not know them nor did they care to, (b) were biased against students' cultures, and (c) were insensitive to issues they faced at home (Kitchen, Velasquez, & Myers, 2000). Schools often felt like prisons, and students faced cultural discontinuities and personal and institutional racism on a daily basis (e.g., Chávez Chávez, 1995, 1997; Delpit, 1995; Kitchen, Velasquez, & Myers, 2000).

The problem becomes more dramatic upon examining the racial mix of teachers to students. The teaching force is approximately 93% white, whereas over 30% of the students are of color. The latest census had indicated that currently, in some states such as Arizona, Florida, California, and Texas, people of color comprise more than 50% of the population. By the year 2010, the European American white population will be the minority—an estimated 35% (National Education Association, 1992). Unfortunately, teachers have the most success with students who are most like themselves (Stanton-Salazar, 1997). If European American teachers remain encapsulated, or monocultural, they will be unwilling or unable to successfully teach and advocate for students different from themselves.

Fortunately, teachers can and do move beyond their own cultural lenses to reach out to all students. Multicultural scholars refer to them as culturally responsive (Ladson-Billings, 1995) or culturally relevant (Davidman & Davidman, 2001) and report several characteristics they appear to have in common, many of which will be described in the introduction to the last section in the book. They have a strong sense of their own ethnic identity and affirm the ethnic and racial identity development of their students (Cummins, 1996). Since healthy ethnic identity development is critical as an essential characteristic in culturally relevant teachers, an overview of identity development follows.

Frameworks of racial and ethnic identity development generally work from a lower to higher level, whether they relate to dominant culture members (Hardiman, 1982; Helms, 1990; Howard, 1999), people of color who claim one identity (Atkinson, Morten, & Sue, 1989; Cross, 1991; Kim, 1981; Solis, 1981) or biracial individuals (Poston, 1990; Stonequist, 1937/1961). Similar to other developmental models, growth varies based on context and experiences. In the case of racial and ethnic identity development, sociopolitical and contextual factors create conditions which could prevent normal development and, at times, arrest normal progression. We are complex people and often are either unwilling or unable to examine our own racial and ethnic identity development, access or lack thereof to power, and the role our families, communities, media, schools, and other organizations have in our growth.

In short, identity development models first move from unconsciousness—not seeing difference—to discomfort—the moment when difference confronts us. We may remain in the discomfort or guilt stage for months or years. From discomfort we grow towards an "us against them" phase, blaming them and sticking with others most like us. This stage is filled with anger at the "other" and a beginning understanding of the richness of who we are. A phrase that epitomizes this stage is the "Pain Olympics." The next stage is often one of awe—finding oneself and one's people. The anger diminishes and is replaced with the fullness of one's own cultural, racial, and gendered uniqueness. We tend to choose to be with others like ourselves in celebration. The last two stages generally begin in early adolescence and continue into adulthood. This often occurs during the middle and high school age. As Beverly Tatum reminds us in her book *Why are all the black kids sitting together in the cafeteria?* (1997), students of color who are in a healthy developmental stage often strike fear into the heart of European American teachers; images of gangs color their perceptions and cause many to create rules in schools to keep youths apart. The final stage is one of action. Here, we join arms across identities, redistribute access to power, and work for civic virtue—the common public good (Oakes, Quartz, Ryan, & Lipton, 1999).

The authors in the following section unpack their identity development as it relates to their work as teachers struggling in the everyday as advocates for their students. One striking commonality is that their identity development seems to relate to a metaphoric literacy. Once they learn to read (their identity as it relates to the world), they can no longer look at words as mere meaningless symbols. When this identity literacy happens, we can see the circles of power that exist in our society and how the various identities of ourselves and the children we teach are placed in the power hierarchy. The metaphor of parking garage spikes speaks clearly to this, at both the interpersonal and institutional level. For those closer to the vortex of power, those who enjoy the privilege of being in society's dominant group (not necessarily the majority), the garage spikes lay down—and they proceed unhampered. For the rest, the spikes present levels of barriers that can become almost insurmountable.

Socrates reminds us that the unexamined life is not worth living. This also ties in with our identity development—a centerpiece of our lived experiences. Unfortunately, examining our place in the power structure of U.S. society is intimately bound to the examination of our identities and those of our students. It is easier to render the garage spikes as invisible and blame the drivers of the cars for their carelessness: "If those people would just tone it down and get to work, we would go further. I know oppression too" (Howard, 1999; McIntosh, 1989; Romo & Salerno, 2000).

Maria G. Ramirez, associate professor in the Department of Curriculum and Instruction at the University of Nevada, Las Vegas, reflects upon her life experience related to language, identity and critical consciousness. In "Understand Them All: Identity and Advocacy" she speaks from her experience as a Chicana who has moved through the pain of personal and institutional racism in her commitment to advocate for all children. Jean Moule, a member of the School of Education faculty at Oregon State University, guides the reader through the nuances of racial identity development. In "Safe and Growing Out of the Box: Immersion for Social Change," she speaks to the readers from an African American female teacher's voice. In "Immersion and Rebellion: Growing Up and Out of South Carolina," Robin Hasslen, associate professor at St. Cloud State University, engages in a frank discussion of her privilege and white racism and how she reconstructed her identity to one that is more caring, democratic, and inclusive. Bruce Romanish, associate dean at Washington State University, in "My Personal Journey—In Part" narrates his story from working class origins and articulates his struggles to overcome sexism in his journey as a democratic teacher. Finally, Paul Spies poignantly speaks from the voice of a white middle-class male who has owned and then disowned his own privilege and racism.

The authors of this book are committed to examining their lives, to breaking through constraints imposed by themselves and society, and moving past their own lives to that of the youth with whom they work. They recognize both the reality of their own and the privilege of others and their identity in the context of marginalized groups; they maintain one foot in and one foot out of their areas of influence to be authentic and effective as advocates for all children.

REFERENCES

Atkinson, D. R., Morten, G., & Sue, D. W. (Eds.). (1989). *Counseling American minorities: A cross-cultural perspective* (3rd ed.). Dubuque, IA: Brown.

Chávez Chávez, R. (1995). *Multicultural education for the everyday: A renaissance for the recommitted.* Washington, DC: American Association for Colleges of Teacher Education.

Chávez Chávez, R. (1997). *A curriculum discourse for achieving equity: Implications for teachers when engaged with Latina and Latino students.* Unpublished manuscript, New Mexico State University.

Cross, W. E. (1991). *Shades of black: Diversity in African-American identity.* Philadelphia, PA: Temple University Press.

Cummins, J. (1996). *Negotiating identities: Education for empowerment in a diverse society* (1st ed.). Ontario, CA: California Association for Bilingual Education.

Davidman, L., Davidman, P. (2000). *Teaching with a multicultural perspective: A practical guide.* New York: Longman.

Delpit, L. (1995). *Other people's children: Cultural conflict in the classroom.* New York: New York Press.

Gay, G. (2000). *Culturally responsive teaching: Theory, research and practice.* New York: Teachers College Press.

Hardiman, R. (1982). *White identity development: A process oriented model for describing the racial consciousness of white Americans.* Unpublished doctoral dissertation, University of Massachusetts, Amherst.

Helms, J. E. (1990). *Black and white racial identity: Theory, research and practice.* Westport, CT: Greenwood.

Howard, G. R. (1999). *We can't teach what we don't know.* New York: Teachers College Press.

Kim, J. (1981). *Process of Asian-American identity development: A study of Japanese American women's perceptions of their struggle to achieve positive identities.* Ann Arbor, MI: Microfilms International.

Kitchen, R. S., Velasquez, D. T., Myers, J. (2000, April). *Dropouts in New Mexico: Native American and Hispanic students speak out.* Paper presented at the annual meeting of the American Educational Research Association, New Orleans, LA.

Ladson-Billings, G. (1994). *The dreamkeepers: Successful teachers of African American children.* San Francisco: Jossey-Bass.

Ladson-Billings, G. (1995). Toward theory of culturally relevant pedagogy. *American Educational Research Journal, 32,* 465–491.

McGown, K., & Hart, L. (1990). Still different after all these years: Gender differences in professional identity formation. *Professional Psychology Research and Practice, 21* (2), ll8.

McIntosh, P. (1989). White privilege: Unpacking the invisible knapsack. *Peace and Freedom, 49* (4), 10–12.

National Education Association. (1992). *The status of the American School Teacher, 1991–1992.* Washington, DC: Author.

Oakes, J., Quartz, K. H., Ryan, S., & Lipton, M. (1999). *Becoming good American schools: The struggle for civic virtue in educational reform.* San Francisco: Jossey-Bass.

Poston, W. S. C. (1990). The biracial identity development model: A needed addition. *Journal of Counseling and Development, 69,* 152–155.

Romo, J., & Salerno, C. (2000). *Toward cultural democracy: The journey from knowledge to action in diverse classrooms.* Boston: Houghton Mifflin.

Solis, A. (1981). Theory of biculturality. *Calmecac de Aztlan en Los, 2,* 36–41.

Stanton-Salazar, R. D. (1997, Spring). A social capital framework for understanding the socialization of racial minority children and youths. *Harvard Educational Review, 67* (1), 1–41.

Stonequist, E. V. (1961). *The marginal man: A study in personality and culture conflict.* New York: Russell & Russell. (Original work published 1937)

Tatum, B. (1998). *Why are all the black kids sitting together in the cafeteria?* New York: Perseus.

Zeichner, K. M., & Hoeft, K. (1996). Teacher socialization for cultural diversity. In J. Sikula (Ed.), *Handbook of research on teacher education* (pp. 525–547). New York: Macmillan.

Chapter 8

Understand Them All: Identity and Advocacy

María G. Ramírez, University of Nevada, Las Vegas

Focus Questions

1. How do your roots help you to overcome adversity?

2. When do you feel most American? Why?

3. When do you feel the least American? Why?

VISTAS OF UNDERSTANDING

Most people thought Howard Street was a deadend. It was just one block long, with two sets of railroad tracks running north and south at the end of the street. Those who lived there, as well as those who drove to the end of the block, knew the street actually looped around and came out on the street that ran parallel to it, Commanche. Our house was situated toward the end of the block, sometimes painted white with yellow window frames, and at other times the colors were reversed. The yellow painted house was neither gaudy nor tacky appearing, but a soft, muted, soothing yellow that Dad chose to paint it. The wooden-framed house always looked grand, one of the nicest houses on the block, commonly acknowledged by family, friends, and passersby.

The yard, although small, was always beautifully adorned with seasonal flowers. The four large clay pots, neatly resting across the inverted T-shaped front sidewalk of our house, consistently had colorful outdoor plants, at times ferns, and when the season permitted, morning glories. Dad took great care to mount three ceramic squirrels on the huge pecan tree that stood at the front of the yard. The mother squirrel was positioned at the top of the branch that arched across the front gate of the hurricane fence. Two baby squirrels were spaced along the vertical base of the tree, as if scurrying up to reach the mother. Dad was careful to secure the squirrels, so the wires holding them in place could not be easily seen. Young children in the neighborhood enjoyed stopping by to pick up the ripe pecans fallen to the ground. Even when pecans were not in season, children would stop to look at and point to the squirrels, many times counting them, as if to note any additions to the family of squirrels.

Our house was a comfortable blend of old and new. When Mom and Dad bought it, it had only three rooms. Through the years, with house additions and renovations, it became a three-bedroom house, including a kitchen, living room, bath, and laundry room. The laundry room was always referred to as the wash room, a label not commonly used by members other than our family, but laundry room conveys a middle-class status absent from wash room.

The expansion to the house created what is now considered a split-level house. Actually, the older section of the house was a lower elevation than the newer portion, not for aesthetic purposes but for practical, financial reasons. The older section did not rest on a foundation that could be raised, while the newer section conformed to building codes governing foundations. The new section was therefore higher, and three steps were added to connect the old section with the new.

Our house was unique for another peculiar reason. It was impossible to walk from one room to the next without going from the front of the house to the back, or vice versa, in almost a straight line. The I-shaped house provided little privacy but also fostered close intimacy, as each member of the family had to walk from one room through the next to get to another room. The bathroom and wash room were at the end of the linear series of rooms.

Our house was not like anyone else's, but it was nonetheless special and our treasured sanctuary. The three steps connecting our parents' bedroom to the kitchen became a place for young and old to sit and talk as Mom prepared a meal, cleaned the kitchen, or the elderly sat at the kitchen table and enjoyed their afternoon *merienda* of coffee with *pan dulce*—Mexican pastry. The convenience of sitting on the steps and seeing past the bedroom to the front door of the living room did not seem unusual, since it afforded us a vista to the activities in our home and in the neighborhood from a relatively obscure and safe place. The north–south built house also made the sunrise and sunset bearable during the long summer months. It really didn't matter that we had no air conditioning, even though the summer season seemed to last for most of the year in southern Texas.

UNCONSCIOUS AND CONSCIOUS CONNECTIONS

That house lives only in my memories now, as do my beloved parents. Our current house, my husband's and mine, has three steps connecting the kitchen to a sunken family room, an original design, not part of renovations or additions. I still enjoy sitting on the steps, as I did in my parent's home, particularly when my older siblings visit us. I have no younger siblings, an unfortunate consequence, and at times a blessing, of being the youngest.

The decision to purchase our house was not based on a conscious connection to my childhood home. In fact, when I first saw the house, I disliked the steps leading down to the family room. The thought of constantly walking up and down just to get from the family room to the kitchen seemed unnecessary and impractical. What was the builder thinking of when designing the house? Was it really necessary? The steps were not initially appealing at all. The house had so many other attractive features that I soon chose to ignore the inconvenience created by the three steps. It wasn't until we had moved in and had time to adjust that I realized, as I described the house over the phone to my brother, René, the similarity to my childhood home. Suddenly, the three steps weren't peculiar or inconvenient; they were a connection to my past. An unconscious association became a conscious connection. The three steps have a special place in my heart, and the moments I sit at the top of the stairs transform our current home to my childhood home, a home filled with love, feelings of security and acceptance, but most of all, a home fostering a strong sense of belonging.

The Foundations of Transformations

Transformations result from a conscious decision to change, but long before the change occurs, events and experiences are at play, laying the foundation for making the decision to change and, ultimately, the subsequent change to follow. The events and experiences reside at an unconscious level and aren't transformed to conscious awareness until cognizant connections are made, linking the old and new experiences and events. While some individuals initially set out to transform themselves, they often attempt to transform someone else, an impossible task to effect. A transformation is an individual change that can only be undertaken by the person wanting to make a change. No one can transform another person. A transformation can only be achieved through individual, personal commitment to change, but the person wanting to change may not always be successful. A transformation is an awakening of self through critical self-examination and an equally critical examination of events and interactions with others. Each transformation is unique, since each person is unique. For the transformation to reach completion, the person must embrace the change, but that is not as simple as it sounds. The temptation to return to the old, no matter how dysfunctional or destructive it might prove, stems from a security through familiarity that the new does not yet furnish.

Transformations are the culmination of an arduous process, involving multiple and varied conscious and unconscious acts and experiences, extending over a prolonged period of time. Initially, the experiences appear discrete and isolated incidents or events, but with time and reflection, a pattern emerges that links the experiences and makes their significance apparent. Imagine one piece of a puzzle. While the one piece can be recognized as belonging to a puzzle, it is impossible to picture the puzzle itself. Even when puzzles have been solved previously, since discrete pieces offer few clues, a singular piece remains a separate piece offering no meaning and serving no particular significance. One piece does not a puzzle make. Generally, one experience, no matter how powerful or dynamic, does not result in a transformation. Only when the one experience is linked to others can the possibility for comprehending their significance result.

Everyone has transformative experiences, but not all experiences lead to a transformation. Why do some individuals reach an epiphany and others not? Do the experiences have to be the same for all individuals in order for a transformation to occur? The common element is not the experience but recognizing and connecting the experiences in a conscious manner. Some choose not to make the connections. It is safer not to recognize and acknowledge the relatedness of certain experiences. A marriage partner might not want to see a repeated pattern of infidelity. It is safer not to recognize and acknowledge it. To do so might require action that the reluctant spouse does not want to take, since acknowledgment might mean having to deal with a change in marital status. The same can be said for patterns of discrimination. It is not that some never experience discrimination; rather, they choose not to recognize or acknowledge it. Some can encapsulate themselves so well from the reality of racism that they convince themselves that others are exaggerating or fabricating their occurrence. Can the person in denial be made to see by having others relate experiences, provide anecdotes, or offer reading material? Probably not.

ORIGINS OF A TRANSFORMATIVE JOURNEY

The transformative journey is not always taken voluntarily. Growing up in southern Texas, in a predominantly Hispanic neighborhood, was a safe, comfortable experience. Most everyone spoke both Spanish and English, and code-switching between the two languages was as natural and common as the humidity. Little thought was given to cultural issues; after all, we were basically one cluster of Americans who happen to speak two languages. We didn't always eat Mexican food, but neither did other Americans. We didn't always speak Spanish, although our parents and grandparents tended to speak it more often and routinely. We preferred to listen to American music on the radio, even when our parents felt more comfortable listening to Mexican music. The generational differences did not appear any different from those of other American families. We knew we were Hispanic, but we identified ourselves as Americans.

The elementary school in our neighborhood was almost exclusively Hispanic, except for the teachers, most of whom were Anglos. *European American* was not a term in vogue at that time. Then, they were Anglos or, of course, *gringos,* not intended as a pejorative ethnophaulism, but merely serving as a descriptor, the way gender, age, or the color of one's hair or eyes are used. The distinctions made between the teachers and us, the characteristic "them versus us," were not based on ethnicity but more the typical teacher–student differentiations, not unlike those between parents and their offspring. There were some teachers who had Hispanic last names, Mr. Garza, Mr. Hernandez, Miss Martinez, and Miss Bosquez. The only male Anglo teachers were the shop teacher and the principal, Mr. Brennan. In the final analysis, we were all Americans.

If we had problems in school, we attributed them to the hegemonic relationship between the teacher and the students. It was not uncommon to hear complaints about how mean the teacher was to have given us such a difficult test or how unfair for the teacher to punish the entire class for the misbehavior of a few students. Other times, the concerns dealt with school-wide or state-supported policies.

Students were prohibited from speaking Spanish at any time on school grounds (Anderson & Boyer, 1970; Ortega, 1972; Stoddard, 1973), except when Spanish was taught as part of the Foreign Language in the Elementary School (FLES) program. Someone decided it was a good idea to teach a foreign language in the elementary school, and the foreign language chosen was Spanish. The conundrum centered on the teaching of Spanish to students who were fluent Spanish speakers by teachers who were not, as well as the choice of Spanish as a foreign language for a group of students who spoke it as their native language. Nonetheless, we learned to count in Spanish, the names for the color words, and other basic discrete vocabulary, even though we could communicate in connected discourse in Spanish long before the fifth grade. We didn't complain about the FLES program, nor the no-Spanish-speaking rule. We did speak Spanish, at times in the restroom, on the playground, or in the school cafeteria, and we were swiftly and, sometimes, harshly punished for doing so. We complained about the punishment but not the rule. It was similar to chewing gum in school, being caught, and having to write a hundred times, "I will not chew gum in school." We didn't like having to write the sentences, but we knew the rule, and violation meant punishment. It was the same with the no-Spanish-speaking rule. We didn't question the rule.

There were other more perplexing experiences in school, but some are too painful and personal to share. One that I suspect still occurs is too important not to discuss. It occurred in the fifth grade, when Mrs. Smith, a former beauty pageant winner, was our teacher. She made no secret of competing in and winning a beauty pageant title. It was still one of the first things she would share with each new group of fifth-grade students. She was very proud of the title she earned in her youth, but now she was a fifth-grade teacher in a predominantly Hispanic part of town, and she had a job to do—teach. The incident concerned Mrs. Smith and a student new to our school but, more important, to our classroom.

We didn't often get new students at our school, and almost never students from Mexico. Our neighborhood was old and established, with not much upward mobility. But we did get a student that year in the fifth grade who had grown up in Mexico. The student's name and gender are not important, but Mrs. Smith's words to another fifth-grade teacher are, as they are etched in my mind and tear at my heart, at the center of my being, even now. Mrs. Smith was explaining the difference between Mexicans born in the United States and those born in Mexico. The conversation centered on how much smarter Mexicans born in Mexico were than U.S.-born Mexicans— her referential words, not mine. She based her conclusion on how quickly the Mexican student, not knowing any English upon arrival, had mastered the English language. She continued the comparison by stating that while some U.S.-born Mexicans spoke English and others did not, none performed academically at grade level. This was long before the resurrection of bilingual education or the introduction of English as a second language programs to the elementary school's curriculum. This was also at a time when U.S.-born Mexican children were disproportionately placed in special education classes for failing a test administered in English, years before *Diana* v. *California State Board of Education* (1970), which prohibited testing children in a language they didn't know.

"Mexicans born in Mexico are smarter than U.S.-born Mexicans." For years I internalized my respected teacher's word of wisdom, not intended or meant as sarcasm, since teachers were respected and revered then. I, of course, was U.S. born, as were my parents, my grandparents, and all of my ancestors. We had always lived in that part of the United States that once was Mexico, but we didn't think of ourselves as Mexicans; we were Americans. To this day, we have no family in Mexico, and when asked where in Mexico I or my parents were born, I say, "Texas." "I or my parents," the phrase from the previous sentence, obviously grammatically incorrect, was written deliberately because inquiries are first made about my birthplace. When told Texas, the inquirers' bewilderment leads them to assume it was my parents who were born in Mexico, so the question migrates to them. The inquiry ends abruptly, with everyone embarrassed, when they hear that we were all born in Texas, once known as Mexico. The ceaseless inquiries begin anew each semester as students in different classes, at some point, ask, "Where in Mexico were you born?" The sequence of inquiry is always the same, progressing from me, to my parents, to my grandparents, until I attempt to explain the incomprehensible; I am an American, born in the United States, as were my parents, grandparents, and so forth. The irony is lost to them, but so familiar to me because in each class each semester, there is invariably a student who is not an American or one who is a first-generation American who goes unnoticed or detected by them. It's not just my name or caramel-colored skin that distinguishes me, but their rigid schema of the archetypal American. It hasn't mattered which state I've lived in: Texas, Kansas, Alabama, Washington, or Nevada, what age I was, what last name I've had. The inquiry is always the same.

Another common misconception is to think that Mexican Americans uniformly and traditionally celebrate Cinco de Mayo or Diez y Seis de Septiembre, when some actually never do. We knew what they were and represented, but we didn't celebrate them, any more than Mexico celebrates America's Fourth of July. We were Americans after all, for many, many generations. To further think that Mexican Americans retain a loyalty to Mexico makes as much sense as saying that Americans maintain a loyalty to England because they speak English, often referring to American English as the king's English. The twofold irony, of course, is that Americans don't speak the king's English and that American English is as much a linguistic melange of words from other languages (Lederer, 1991), as Americans are an ethnic aggregate. The danger in sharing these thoughts and experiences is being labeled as a spokesperson for all Mexican Americans, which I'm not, or having someone generalize my experiences to all Mexican Americans. I suspect that some Mexican Americans will be able to relate to and understand what I'm saying, but just as many will not. The intent is not to incur the ire of those who can't understand these statements or relate to these experiences but to reach out to those who feel the same as I have felt—isolated and alone for so long. Our experiences are not all the same, but we need to try to understand them all if we are truly to be tolerant and transformative teachers.

UNDERSTANDING TRANSFORMATIVE JOURNEYS

The pieces of the racist puzzle began to come together for me when I was 25 years old in graduate school, working on my doctorate. I had always believed that if I worked hard and excelled, I would succeed, be evaluated fairly and honestly on the merit of my work, and never need or have to affiliate with any ethnic group or minority association. I didn't fully comprehend the racism directed at me in my formative years until sometime later, when I was told by a nun at a Catholic university, "Go home and have your beans and tortillas." Having always seen myself as an American, I couldn't understand why others were having trouble seeing who I was, particularly since in Mexico they saw me only as an American, never as a Mexican.

I worked hard because I had learned to enjoy the love of doing something well, no matter what it was, from both my Mom and Dad. I was respectful to others because Dad had always said, *"A nadie se le niega un saludo."* The literal translation,

"To no one deny him a greeting," a common mistake made by novice speakers of Spanish when they merely translate words, was not the sentiment conveyed by my father's words. His message was one of respect and dignity that should be extended to everyone. The lessons from childhood, modeled rather than preached, were those of love, respect, hard work, fairness, and tolerance. They had always served me well. What was I doing to warrant the kind of treatment I was receiving?

The individualism my parents nurtured in us, while encouraging and permitting us to think for ourselves, to be who we were, without fear of comparison, allowed me to look beyond myself and begin to question the words and deeds of others. That is when I began to see myself as a Mexican American and later as a Chicana. With each instance of racism directed at me, the essence of my ethnicity became my source of strength. It's not that instances of racism hadn't occurred when I was young, but that I failed to recognize and understand them for what they were. Choosing to believe that education and hard work would open doors, and not having passed through the final portal, I maintained a deaf ear to the racist statements and acts directed at me or others like me. Racism was directed at African Americans, not Hispanics, since Hispanics were Caucasians and African Americans were not.

To realize that racism existed in the academy and among the ecclesiastic was difficult to accept or comprehend. How could educated people and members of the church be racist? Wasn't education supposed to open people's minds, making them more tolerant and accepting of others, and weren't members of the church supposed to be loving, charitable people? Why was this happening to me? Did it happen to others with the frequency and regularity that I came to expect? Even my sister didn't believe or understand some of the stories I shared with her, often thinking I was either overreacting or exaggerating, until she witnessed firsthand how differently I was treated compared to her. Her British last name, Anglo looks, and accent-free voice made her an American, my antithesis.

The nun who made the racist statement was also the dean of the school of education at the university where I was employed. It was the first summer of my employment at that university, having just finished the fall and spring semesters, on a Friday afternoon when she said, "Go home and have your beans and tortillas." We taught no classes on Friday, but I had been at work all day, and it was approaching 4 o'clock as I walked into the main office to check my mail before going home. I saw the Dean, another nun, and the secretary, and announced I would be going home shortly, to avoid the 5 o'clock traffic. As I turned to leave, I said, "Hope you all have a good weekend," when she uttered her reply. The words were not said in jest but reflected a contempt and disdain echoed by the nun sitting next to her who added, "Yes, María, just go home and have your beans and tortillas." I don't know if it was shame, shock, or disbelief that made me say, "With fajitas?" but I suspect I was trying, once again, to be the good American. I stayed at that university for four additional years but gave up when the discrimination evolved to a trilogy of racism, gender, and age discrimination, and it became abundantly evident that I couldn't make them see me.

I had always known I was Hispanic, even as a young child when I tried drinking milk in the hope that it would make my skin lighter or when I scrubbed my elbows and knees raw trying to make them less dark. I attributed those acts to childhood desires, typical of other children, to be different than I was. As I advanced through school, I consistently and deliberately directed my attention to excelling academically, an achievable, attainable goal. With each success, I felt more like an American.

Unfortunately, there are still pieces of the racist puzzle being added. The picture is clearly one of racism, and the instances haven't diminished. I try hard to belong, but I seldom feel that I do. Is it easier now? Not necessarily. Do I ignore them as I once did? Not always. Have I learned to deal with them any better? Not consistently. As painful as these are to share, they must be told.

There was a time when I saw a book about Hispanics and said, "What can it tell me that I haven't lived?" There was a time when I wouldn't take any courses dealing with Hispanic issues because they couldn't teach me what I already knew. There was a time in my youth when I was smarter than I am now.

The transformative journey takes time, self-examination, and reflection. Others could not make me see what I was not ready for or capable of understanding. The transformative teacher needs to recognize and understand that students are at different points in their journeys. We can't make students see or understand what they are not ready for, but we can provide additional experiences through anecdotes, exercises, and readings that might assist them in their journey, but ultimately, the journey is theirs.

THE TRANSFORMATIVE TEACHER

The transformative teacher subscribes to critical pedagogy—instruction which recognizes how different forces affect and influence educational policies and practices. The transformative teacher embraces the central tenet of critical pedagogy: that power, politics, history, culture, and language determine and shape how reality and meaning, within and outside the classroom, are defined and understood. Central to critical pedagogy is understanding that those defining the educational contexts, as well as those most adversely affected, are often not aware of how influential these seemingly noneducational forces are. Most believe that decisions are based on objective, logical thought, but thought is not objective, and the logic one uses is tainted by it. Thought is highly subjective, personal, and based on experiences, however unique or incomplete they might be. By failing to acknowledge that educational decisions are made based on ideologies not grounded in educational theory, but rather on beliefs influenced by politics, history, culture, language, and above all power, we are all, ultimately, affected adversely. The interrelated nature of these influences is so pervasive that traditional education does not acknowledge them (Corson, 1993; Cummins, 1995; Darder, 1995; Elsasser & John-Steiner, 1987; Finlay & Faith, 1987; Greene, 1998; Shor, 1987; Wallerstein, 1987; Walsh, 1995; Wink & Almanzo, 1995).

The transformative teacher understands that critical pedagogy is about understanding and responding to social injustice and political incoherence. It asks us to right the wrongs by understanding the difference between symbolic politics and pragmatic politics. It challenges us to think, analyze, and understand not only what we think and what we do but also to understand why others think and act differently from us (Darder, 1995; Walsh, 1995; Wink & Almanzo, 1995). The transformative teacher recognizes and embraces the centrality of language and culture to the essence of who the person is (Walsh, 1995). Critical pedagogy is about developing a critical social consciousness, resulting in a collective responsibility necessary for transforming ourselves and society (Reddy, 1998).

The transformative teacher strives to understand the complex and dynamic relationship between education and society, all the while cognizant of the difference between education which strives to open students' minds to the full range of possibilities and schooling that forces them to conform, comply, and obey (Ayers, 1998). My rigid, dogmatic schooling did not permit me to question what teachers said or did to me or to others. But the education I received from my parents liberated me from those constraints imposed by school and society, enabling my transformation from object (student) to subject (teacher) (Elsasser & John-Steiner, 1987).

What did my fifth-grade teacher lack that permitted her to stereotype and label (Mexican) students so contemptuously? Ironically, she failed to understand a basic principle of education that my father understood so well, even though he was illiterate. Dad's understanding of language and cognition became evident about the same time Mrs. Smith made her comparison of (Mexican) students, the autumn of my elementary school years, when we happened to be in Matamoros, Mexico, to buy sugar, cigarettes, and other items that were considerably cheaper there than in the United States. The conversation between my Mom and Dad occurred entirely in Spanish, but I'll share it in English. As we walked down one of the streets, Dad turned to Mom and said, "Tiburcia (not her name but a nickname he often called her), let me have a couple of dollars." "Why do you need the money?" Mom asked. "To buy a ruler," Dad replied. With a look of disbelief and slight restraint in her voice, she answered, "A ruler, but you have a ruler at home," the syntactic form clearly declarative but with the illocutionary force of a question. Dad, very cleverly and smugly answered, "The ruler I have at home has the numbers in English and I want to buy one with the numbers in Spanish." Mom stopped walking, grimaced slightly, looked him directly in the eye, and said, "You silly old man, I know what you want. You merely want money to buy beer." We all burst out laughing, and the more we thought about it (the numbers in English, the numbers in Spanish), the more we laughed. We continued on our shopping excursion, as Dad walked off to buy his beer.

It's easy to laugh with people you love and respect. Unfortunately, Mrs. Smith's judgments about the (Mexican) students revealed not only contempt and disdain but also a naive consciousness lacking in reflective thinking and replete with unqualified generalizations. What did Dad, a construction worker who never finished first grade, know that she, a teacher, failed to comprehend? Dad's tacit understanding of people and language, through the values he modeled and lived by, defined social consciousness for us in real and concrete terms. In Matamoros, Dad demonstrated understanding the transferability of literacy from one language to another by the joke he made. He realized that having a number concept in one language meant not having to relearn it in another language. In other words, literacy is like money in the bank. If you have money in the bank, you can transfer it from one account to another, but without any money, no transfer is possible. The student from Mexico had what most U.S.-born Hispanics lacked—literacy in his native language, tantamount to money in the bank. Because the schools provided no bilingual education or English as a second language instruction, Hispanic students were left on their own to "sink or swim," with 80% failing first grade, most spending 1 to 3 years in the first grade learning English, and usually dropping out by the fifth grade, but, sometimes, not before being labeled special education students (Anderson & Boyer, 1970; Ortega, 1972).

The student from Mexico (I often circumlocute the word *Mexican,* because I've heard it used disparagingly for so long that it's difficult for me to hear, say, or write it without it having an extremely negative connotation) had developed cognitive academic language proficiency (CALP), otherwise known as academic language, or literacy (Cummins, 1995). He had developed literacy in Spanish prior to coming to our school, and once in the United States, his task was to develop basic interpersonal communicative skills (BICS), or social language, also referred to as pragmatic language or conversational language (Cummins, 1995). He had to learn to speak English, but he came with money in the bank, with literacy in his first language (Collier, 1992; Cummins, 1991; Thomas & Collier, 1997; Walsh, 1995), something U.S.-born Hispanic students lacked, not due to any cognitive deficiencies, but to never having been instructed in their primary language. Thence, the teacher thought Mexican-born students were smarter than U.S.-born Hispanic students. If English language acquisition is a prerequisite for academic success, why do so many Anglo students lack CALP—after all, they are being taught in a language they know, understand, and speak? Did Mrs. Smith also feel that British students were smarter than American students?

It's not uncommon for students, consistently told they are dumb and worthless, to begin to doubt themselves, question their ability to succeed, and eventually internalize feeling of worthlessness. The desire to belong and be accepted is so central and critical to those who feel disenfranchised that conformity and obedience seem but a small price to pay (Ortega, 1972; Rios, 1972). Hispanics, in schools across the United States, in their place of work and in business establishments (Anderson & Boyer, 1970; Ortega, 1970; Stoddard, 1973), are routinely told they can't speak Spanish, a message with a dual meaning. Some, at a very young age, internalize the message and refuse to speak Spanish, developing only a receptive understanding of the language even when their parents or grandparents speak little or no English. They tacitly comply, regretting and realizing only as adults what they've lost in their efforts to belong and conform. The second message is equally debilitating, and an equal number or more embrace the belief that the Spanish which they speak is inferior or substandard, not really Spanish at all but Spanglish—a mixture of Spanish and English (Crawford, 1992; Crystal, 1992; Nobel, 1982). Both messages emotionally desensitize Hispanics to their language and culture, alienating them from their family and the Hispanic community and permanently robbing them of their cultural foundation (Cummins, 1996; Ogbu, 1978).

Both messages convey a worthlessness aimed at oppression and domination by reducing the people to empty, hollow shells, devoid of the essence that defines them and their existence (Rodriguez, 1982). In eradicating or restricting the bilingualism of Hispanics, schools and society destroy the centrality of language and culture to our being, the essence that defines us and our existence. As long as Hispanics look Hispanic and have a Spanish last name, they will never be thought of as real Americans. The price for pseudo acceptance is too high, since language and culture define how we think, feel, and behave, what makes us who we are (Anderson & Boyer, 1970; Hollins, 1996; Stoddard, 1973). When did being bilingual come to mean being un-American or less educated? The injury is exacerbated, and the shame is felt anew when an Anglo American monolingual English speaker says to a Hispanic, "You don't speak Spanish, but you're Hispanic. Why don't you speak Spanish?"

FACILITATING THE CONNECTIONS

To effect the change that will change the world, teachers, at all levels with all students, will need to alter their ways of teaching. They will need to engage students in a dialogic process for facilitating a personal transformation that will ultimately lead to a social transformation (Darder, 1995; Shor, 1987; Wallerstein, 1987; Walsh, 1995). The classroom will need to be transformed from a teacher-centered environment where the teacher controls the content, method of instruction, and students, to a problem-posing community of learners centering on issues and concerns identified by the students. The new classroom promotes social responsibility through critical social consciousness by asking students to develop social action plans for addressing the concerns they've identified, as they work to change their status (Finlay & Faith, 1987; Greene, 1998).

As students identify a problem to address, they are asked to individually answer the questions, "What do I know about X? What experiences have I had with X? What do I think X is?" Addressing these questions about the problem or issue they've identified helps them tap their prior knowledge, their experiences, beliefs, and stories, thus engaging in Phase 1 of critical social consciousness—self-examination. The self-examination is not intended to be an exhaustive or complete representation, since it will be limited by their range of experiences and understanding of the problem.

Phase 2, negotiation, asks students to work in groups and invites them to explore and question others' experiences, beliefs, and stories through a dialogic process. They address the questions, "What do others think or know about X? What experiences have others had with X? How are my experiences different from, or the same as, others'?" Negotiation helps them to see how others think or what others have experienced that may or may not be different from them.

Phase 3, reflection, deals with understanding the interactive and dynamic nature of events and individuals, as shaped by power, politics, history, culture, and language, for defining the context and meaning of a problem or concern. To assist them in this phase, they answer the questions, "How has X been affected by politics, history, culture, language, and authority? How do these define X? How are the meanings of X different?" Focusing on the problem by examining the forces' impact permits them to develop critical social consciousness.

Phase 4, introspection, leads to the development of emancipatory knowledge through a self transformation which asks them, "What transformation must I make in myself to transform X?" Having personalized the process of problem posing and acknowledged and recognized the need for a personal transformation, they develop collective responsibility as they address the question, "What social transformations are needed to transform X?" In answering the question, they move to effect liberating conditions by taking principled action that will bring about change.

Social transformations don't always begin in the classroom with students. Since the arena for change is often the community, it extends to the community of professionals, and that was certainly the case in the fall of 1989. Having just joined the faculty at the university where I am currently employed, I wrote a grant proposal for training bilingual teachers that was submitted to the Office of Bilingual Education and Minority Language Affairs (OBEMLA). When I was notified that the grant would not be funded, I reworked the proposal and resubmitted it, only to be told, once again, that it would not be funded. This time I decided to inquire with the officer who oversaw that program area, and I was told that since the state did not offer any license or endorsement in bilingual education, OBEMLA could not consider funding the grant. It was suggested that I work on having the state establish an endorsement or license for bilingual teachers before submitting another bilingual teacher training proposal to OBEMLA.

A year had passed since I'd written the first and second grant proposals, and not wanting to lose any additional time, I wrote, in the fall of 1990, to the Commission on Professional Standards in Education, the agency overseeing the establishment of new licenses or endorsements, and requested they consider establishing an endorsement for bilingual education. The phases described earlier (self-examination, negotiation, reflection, and introspection) were the stages our dialogue moved through in establishing an endorsement for bilingual education, taking only 4 years to complete. It shouldn't have taken that long, but the forces mentioned in Phase 3 (power, politics, history, culture, and language) converged to try and keep the endorsement from becoming a reality. The process began with my preparing documentation to support the need for a bilingual education endorsement and moved to negotiation, with their telling me why they didn't think or feel it was necessary or important, in spite of the statistics that revealed a high number of second-language students, and a third of the elementary schools designated as bilingual in, at that time, the 11th-largest school district in the United States. The strongest opposition to the bilingual education endorsement came from the school district, which argued that it was extremely difficult to identify and recruit bilingual teachers; hence, the endorsement would make it impossible to find bilingual teachers. If you're understanding their argument, you're understanding more than I could or did at the time. How could the endorsement make it more difficult, unless they were placing unqualified people in the bilingual classrooms to teach students who were at the greatest risk of educational failure? Why would they do that?

Within the classroom, self and social transformations are not achieved any faster than the social transformation just described. The best the transformative teacher can do is to structure the environment for students to undertake the transformative journey, all the while realizing that the final destination, social action, will most likely occur once the students have left the classroom. The teacher will need to be patient and realize that many students will resist, while others will not understand, because students are so accustomed to a traditional classroom—where the teacher tells them what to do, how to do it, and when to do it—that social responsibility, emancipatory knowledge, and the nature or purpose of self or social transformations will mean little or nothing to them (Darder, 1995; Walsh, 1995). In the traditional classroom, the "why" is not always important to students, since they can accomplish the "what," "how," and "when" without knowing or understanding the "why," while the underlying question of the dialogic process is always "why" (Wallerstein, 1987; Wink & Almanzo, 1995).

CAVEATS

Use of *Hispanic* and *American* and Other Ethnic Terms

One of the transformations, described and weaved throughout the text, dealt with ethnicity, revealed through the use of certain ethnic terms: *Hispanic, Mexican American, Chicana, Anglo, European American,* and *Mexican,* and the absence of the specific expression, *dominant culture.* Since the terms have specific meanings and their use or absence was deliberate, an explanation may help to contextualize their meaning, provide further insights to their use, and assist in understanding the transformation process as it unfolded. Some of the terms were defined in the text, so only those whose meaning and use need clarification will be addressed.

As mentioned earlier, while I always knew I was of Mexican ancestry, throughout my grade school years I identified and called myself an American. As a young child, I would never have referred to myself as a Chicana, because Chicanos were considered militant, radical, disloyal members of society. Not only were they viewed that way by Anglos and other mainstream Americans, but those who called themselves Chicanos were held in disdain by members of my own family. Chicanos were associated with and responsible for the riots and demonstrations in Crystal City, Texas, not actions or activities any loyal, patriotic American would engage in. Chicanos were troublemakers who didn't conform or adhere to traditional American values and ideals.

Gradually, through experiences and interactions with others, I came to see myself as a Mexican American and eventually as a Chicana. The process extended from the early elementary school years to my doctoral studies at the University of Kansas. It was slow, and neither deliberate nor conscious on my part, but nonetheless, the experiences and interactions throughout those years formed the basis for the transformation that would follow.

My transformation into a Mexican American occurred on paper years before I deliberately and freely understood and used the term. Each time I was asked on school records, scholarship applications, employment forms, or other documents to identify my ethnicity, I internalized the ethnic marker others used to label me. But it wasn't merely the paper categorization that facilitated my transformation, any more than checking female in the gender box helped me establish my gender identity. I neither felt the need to tell others that I was Mexican American, nor that I was a female, since both were obvious and easily discerned by my appearance. Ethnicity, however, is different than gender identity, since some of us look like a lot of other people. For example, in Malaysia, Malays thought I was Malay and told me that I was, even when I explained I was an American. In Alabama, I was asked by an African American first grader, "Is you black or is you white?" I use the child's language not to stereotype but to accurately relay the question asked and language used. I was an enigma to him, since I was neither dark enough or light enough to conform to his schema of people. To him, I didn't really look like either. I explained that I was like Chico from *Chico and the Man,* a popular sitcom of the time. He nodded and appeared to understand, since Chico was Hispanic; the "man" was white, and the man's best friend was African American.

The term *Hispanic* is like the term *American,* at least in the United States. It's a comprehensive term used to refer to all the different Spanish-speaking groups that exist in the United States: Mexican American, Puerto Rican American, Cuban American, and so forth. Some prefer the term *Latino,* and, at times, news media journalists and other professionals use the terms interchangeably to minimize offending anyone and be as inclusive as possible. The terms *Hispanic* and *Latino* are generally used as generic terms when referring to all Spanish-speaking groups, but also for referring to any member of a Spanish-speaking group in a general, nonspecific way. In other words, if the speaker doesn't know whether a Spanish-speaking person is Mexican American, Cuban American, or Puerto Rican American, a safe, neutral, and inoffensive term to use in describing him or her is Hispanic or Latino. At the same time, any member of the various Spanish-speaking groups knows that no single group can or should speak for any one of the other groups. To further illustrate the point, a dear and special friend and colleague from another university e-mailed me a joke but prefaced it by saying, "Okay. Here's a Puerto Rican joke my nephew sent me via e-mail. Only a Puerto Rican can tell it because we'd be insulted if anyone else told it." Equally offensive would be to call or refer to Cuban Americans as Mexican Americans or vice versa, since this would ignore the subtle and unique distinctions that members of each group value and recognize. Members of both groups would be highly offended and insulted. Furthermore, the only Spanish-speaking group that is typically called or chooses to refer to itself as Chicano is Mexican Americans. While all the Spanish-speaking groups share the Spanish language, it would be just as inappropriate for Americans to be representative speakers for Canadians, Australians, and Britons, even though they all speak a dialect of English.

I stated that I can't speak for all Hispanics because, truthfully, I can't even speak for all the members of my birth family: my siblings. My older brothers still hold the term *Chicano* in extreme disdain, prefer to call themselves Americans, and one is even a Republican. While we are all members of the same family, speak English and Spanish fluently, express deep and unwavering love and respect for each other, we are as different as the various shades that exist for the color white. If you've ever tried to buy white paint to match the white used on a wall, you know that there is no one true shade of white but different hues: gradations of the same color. The same is true for the color black. While black and white are considered basic, standard colors, to find a perfect match is highly improbable. That is what the members of my family are: gradations of one (family) that permit each to be distinct and unique but nevertheless the same. That is what the family of Spanish-speakers are as well, *igual pero diferente,* equal but different.

Equal but different is the same reason that Anglo was chosen as the ethnic referential term instead of the expression *dominant culture.* Anglo (American) does not connote a superior or elevated status that dominant culture evokes. Anglo is used as a descriptor equal to but different from any other ethnic label. While it is readily acknowledged that historically, politically, linguistically, and culturally, Anglo Americans have maintained and continue to control the cultural capital—"the uneven distribution of wealth and power among racial and social class groups" (Oakes & Lipton, 1999, p. 121)—the use of the term *dominant culture* serves to justify and legitimize the uneven distribution of power and wealth by implying and relegating all other ethnic groups to a nondominant status incapable of sharing the responsibility that comes with power and wealth.

UNRAVELING THE TRANSFORMATION PROCESS

We don't always understand what we see, experience, or feel. Because we are constantly experiencing and thus constructing knowledge, and because knowledge construction is never completed, we may never be able to pinpoint when we developed an understanding or describe how the understanding was achieved. It's not as important to know when or how an understanding was attained but that it was.

In trying to illustrate the transformation process, Oakes and Lipton (1999) used an example of a caterpillar transforming itself into a butterfly. The example concretely illustrates the process but also oversimplifies it. Oakes and Lipton explained that "a butterfly is not simply a larger, quicker, more complex caterpillar; it is a fundamentally different creature" (p. 72). While the example helps explain the butterfly's transformation, it does little to assist in understanding the complex process involved in the transformation of individuals, since people's transformations do not involve a metamorphosis—a change of physical form, structure, or substance. To liken the physical development that occurs automatically in adolescents to a transformation is to discount volition and reduce a person to an *object,* someone that something happens to rather than a *subject,* someone who controls and determines what will happen. Stated differently, the physical transformation of the caterpillar to butterfly occurred whether the caterpillar wanted to become a butterfly or not, much the same as the physical change that occurs automatically for adolescents. Transformations, on the other hand, do not occur automatically but as a result of a desire to change.

The events that set in motion a transformation often occur long before a person decides to make a change. At the same time, while the events present themselves, a person may not recognize or understand them and hence never make a change. Transformations require constant, active, and continuous construction of meaning, accompanied by a cognitive disequilibrium, which leads to and results in a cognitive reorganization. The transformational process can be impeded at any point within the learning cycle. Faulty thinking or old meanings can keep a person from experiencing cognitive disequilibrium and thus never achieving cognitive reorganization.

The process of my transformation is delineated in the text, but what makes it difficult to discern is that it was not a clear linear or sequential unfolding. Transformations seldom are. The phases described in the dialogic process (from the later section, "Facilitating the Connections") are intended and should be viewed as a guide for facilitating transformations. The phases are not meant to be prescriptive, since transformations do not adhere to a recipe progression of successive, orderly steps. The phases attempt to identify and describe a process beginning with the individual through a self-examination, while recognizing that self-examination, at times, begins only after negotiation with others. The reflection phase encourages a deeper understanding of self and others by exploring the impact that politics, history, culture, language, and power have on our thoughts, actions, and reactions. The introspection phase invites others to take principled action as they enter into both personal and social transformations. The phases are arranged to show a progression from self to others, culminating in principled action resulting from personal and social transformations. Throughout the transformation process, a constant interplay between and across the phases will occur as the individuals struggle with reconstructing meaning and discarding flawed or immature thinking.

Transformations are the result of a complex array of events and experiences coming together during a period of self-examination and reflection. But self-examination and reflection alone will not automatically result in a transformation. Connecting and reorganizing the new and the old, along with discarding flawed thinking, are critical. But still, this will not automatically result in a transformation, since a conscious, deliberate intention to change is needed, and the change is still to follow. It was my responsibility to make the connections by examining, reflecting, and reorganizing my understandings. The reorganization entailed discarding old and flawed meanings and replacing them with new schemata and understandings. Once that occurred, it took a conscious decision on my part to change. Change did not occur quickly or easily and is never completed, since learning involves a constant and persistent struggle to understand, adapt, and change again. At times, change occurs as a consequence of recognizing that something is not working, without necessarily knowing why it's not working. Knowing why something is not working is not a precursor to recognizing that change is needed. Adaptations are attempts at changing without having to make a complete change or to struggle with reconstructing understandings and meanings. It should now be evident that transformation is a complex process.

TEACHING AND LEARNING FOSTERING TRANSFORMATIONS

The teacher who embraces and understands the transformative process recognizes, incorporates, and translates several basic learning tenets into daily classroom practices. Simply stated: Learning is active, involves the construction of meaning, reorganizes our thinking, and creates disequilibrium (Oakes & Lipton, 1999). The learning tenets appear so obvious and are so easily understood that they can be overlooked and discounted prematurely by the novice or skeptical teacher. A brief description of each will follow.

The transformative teacher recognizes that learning is an active process that requires the active engagement of the student. When teachers are doing all of the talking or become the transmitters of knowledge, the student is relegated to a role of passive participant in the teaching–learning process. The student must be an active and involved participant in the construction of meaning and knowledge. The transformative teacher recognizes the need for the student's active involvement and establishes a classroom where students are actively learning through engagement with each other and materials, for grappling with old ways of thinking and understanding. Concrete materials are readily available for use and engagement, and the classroom is filled with the students' voices as they create scaffolds for learning within the zone of proximal development.

Creating a zone of proximal development in the classroom permits the students to learn by constructing and reconstructing meaning and understanding. Scaffolds created by the teacher, through group work and active learning, assist the student in the construction of knowledge and meaning by mediating the learning. The transformative teacher recognizes that the student is central in the construction of knowledge and meaning, not the teacher. While the teacher is important to the process, the transformative teacher recognizes and acknowledges the centrality of the student, since the student is ultimately responsible for and must construct the new knowledge.

The construction of knowledge and meaning leads to a reorganization of thinking by the students. By creating a learning environment that forces the student to grapple with inconsistencies or flaws in reasoning, the student is able to reorganize his or her knowledge base. The reorganization of understanding and meaning results not only from acquiring new knowledge and understanding, but also as a consequence of cognitive maturity that permits the student to understand more and in different ways. The transformative teacher understands the limitations in the students' understanding tied to the cognitive developmental process. Activities and instruction are geared to permit the student access to the next level of cognitive understanding, by challenging them within their range of cognitive understanding.

The construction of meaning resulting in the reorganization of thinking often creates disequilibrium, not only for the student but also for the teacher, since the student may not be ready or capable of cognitively understanding. The transformative teacher creates a safe learning environment that permits the student to test old theories in light of new information by matching the activities and learning to the students' level of cognitive development and maturity.

At the same time that students are actively engaged in learning through construction and reconstruction of meanings and knowledge, the transformative teacher incorporates and weaves the phases from critical pedagogy into the teaching–learning process, since these facilitate the students' learning. Teaching and learning within the transformative classroom permits students to grapple with the construction and reorganization of meaning and knowledge, by actively involving them and recognizing their importance in the teaching–learning process.

CONCLUSIONS

When you approach a street that appears to be a dead end, do you trust the conclusion you've drawn, or do you check to see if your initial perception is accurate? How long is it before you realize an error has been made, and how do you respond or react to your error? Do you freely acknowledge the error or hold steadfast to the faulty thinking? When you meet a parent who has little or no formal education, do you equate the lack of education with limited capabilities, further assuming the parent does not value education, or do you address the parent with the same dignity and respect you'd show a medical doctor or a lawyer? Do you recognize how politics, history, and culture influence your perceptions, thoughts, and behavior toward others different from you? When you see a front page newspaper headline that reads, "Spanish Spreads Across Valley," do you respond with anger and disgust, or do you understand the power of language and culture, as used by the media, to get your attention, arouse your ire, and cloud your thinking? Do you recognize the news media's biased, unreflective reporting of information, or do you blindly accept the information as factual and objective? Do you read other sources to determine the accuracy of the information reported, thus recognizing the influence of politics and history reflected in the headline and the article? Do you understand what you see and experience, what you read and hear, and differentiate between naive consciousness and reflective consciousness?

An inherent limitation to a lack of understanding is a narrow range of experiences, be they direct or vicarious. Conclusions drawn based on limited experiences will always reflect marginal understandings. Youth is a time abundant in sparse experiences and thence faulty and incomplete understandings. Do we realize that in our youth, our experiences were incomplete because our experiences were limited? Do we try to understand that youths will always think they know and understand more than they actually do? Do we recognize the influence that events and people have on how we think and what we do, shaped by power, politics, history, language, and culture? Failure to recognize the interactive nature of events and individuals and the forces influencing them is tantamount to seeing a dead end street that does not exist, blocking the transformation from objects to subjects. Reflective consciousness expands our understanding and facilitates that transformation.

We need to understand them all: the experiences, the external societal forces, and the process of transformations, as well as the people, those who think, act, and feel as we do, along with those who don't, whether they are members of our ethnic group or not. The experiences may not always be initially understood, and only with time and through reflection will a pattern emerge, linking the conscious and unconscious acts, allowing us to comprehend the dynamic and interactive nature of events and people as shaped by external societal forces. Biased, prejudiced people can limit not only what we understand but also what we do, since the barriers and obstacles they erect can keep us struggling, instead of developing the understanding that will permit us to be who we are and do what is needed. Only through reflection and introspection can critical social consciousness emerge, leading to self and social transformations that result in principled action. Social transformations can be achieved, but for some, the price is too high, the struggle too long, and the turmoil too painful.

REFERENCES

Anderson, T., & Boyer, M. (Eds.). (1970). *Bilingual schooling in the United States* (1st ed., Vols. 1–2) Washington, DC: U.S. Government Printing Office.

Ayers, W. (1998). Foreword: Popular education: Teaching for social justice. In W. Ayers, J. A. Hunt, & T. Quinn (Eds.), *Teaching for social justice* (pp. xvii–xxv). New York: Teachers College Press.

Bass, D. (1999, September 5). Spanish spreads across valley. *The Las Vegas Review-Journal*, pp. A1, A16, A17.

Collier, V. P. (1992). A synthesis of studies examining long-term language minority student data on academic achievement. *Bilingual Research Journal, 16*(1–2), 187–212.

Corson, D. (1993). *Language, minority education and gender: Linking social justice and power.* Clevedon, England: Multilingual Matters.

Crawford, J. (1992). *Hold your tongue: Bilingualism and the politics of "English Only."* Reading, MA: Addison-Wesley.

Crystal, D. (1992). *An encyclopedic dictionary of language and languages.* Cambridge, MA: Blackwell.

Cummins, J. (1989). *Empowering minority students.* Sacramento, CA: California Association for Bilingual Education.

Cummins, J. (1991). Interdependence of first- and second-language proficiency in bilingual children. In E. Bialystok (Ed.), *Language processing in bilingual children* (pp. 70–89). Cambridge, England: Cambridge University Press.

Cummins, J. (1995). Power and pedagogy in the education of culturally-diverse students. In J. Frederickson (Ed.), *Reclaiming our voices: Bilingual education, critical pedagogy and praxis* (pp. 139–162). Ontario, CA: California Association for Bilingual Education.

Cummins, J. (1996). *Negotiating identities: Education for empowerment in a diverse society.* Los Angeles: California Association for Bilingual Education.

Darder, A. (1995). Bicultural identity and the development of voice: Twin issues in the struggle for cultural and linguistic democracy. In J. Frederickson (Ed.), *Reclaiming our voices: Bilingual education, critical pedagogy and praxis* (pp. 35–51). Ontario, CA: California Association for Bilingual Education.

Diana v. California State Board of Education, No. C-70-37 R.F.P. (N.D. Cal., February 3, 1970).

Elsasser, N., & John-Steiner, V. (1987). An interactionist approach to advancing literacy. In I. Shor (Ed.), *FREIRE for the classroom: A sourcebook for liberatory teaching* (pp. 45–62). Portsmouth, NH: Boynton/Cook.

Finlay, L. S., & Faith, V. (1987). Illiteracy and alienation in American colleges: Is Paulo Freire's pedagogy relevant? In I. Shor (Ed.), *FREIRE for the classroom: A sourcebook for liberatory teaching* (pp. 63–86). Portsmouth, NH: Boynton/Cook.

Gibson, M. A., & Ogbu, J. U. (Eds.). (1991). *Minority status and schooling: A comparative study of immigrant and involuntary minorities.* New York: Garland.

Greene, M. (1998). Introduction: Teaching for social justice. In W. Ayers, J. A. Hunt, & T. Quinn (Eds.), *Teaching for social justice* (pp. xxvii–xlvi). New York: Teachers College Press.

Hollins, E. R. (1996). Culture in school learning, revealing the deep meaning. Mahwah, NJ: Erlbaum.

Lederer, R. (1991). *The miracle of language.* New York: Pocket Books.

Nobel, B. L. (1982). *Linguistics for bilinguals.* Rowley, MA: Newbury House.

Oakes, J., & Lipton, J. (1999). *Teaching to change the world.* Boston: McGraw-Hill.

Ogbu, J. (1978). *Minority education and caste: The American system in cross-cultural perspective.* New York: Academic.

Ortega, P. D. (1972). Schools for Mexican-Americans: Between two cultures. In E. Simmen (Ed.), *Pain and promise: The Chicano today* (pp. 224–233). New York: New American Library.

Reddy, M. (1998). The fourth *r*. In W. Ayers, J. A. Hunt, & T. Quinn (Eds.), *Teaching for social justice* (pp. 169–185). New York: Teachers College Press.

Rodriguez, R. (1982). *Hunger of memory: The education of Richard Rodriguez.* New York: Bantam.

Rios, F. A. (1972). The Mexican in fact, fiction, and folklore. In E. Simmen (Ed.), *Pain and promise: The Chicano today* (pp. 79–93). New York: New American Library.

Shor, I. (1987). Educating the educators: A Freirean approach to the crisis in teacher education. In I. Shor (Ed.), *FREIRE for the classroom: A sourcebook for liberatory teaching* (pp. 7–32). Portsmouth, NH: Boynton/Cook.

Stoddard, E. R. (1973). *Mexican Americans.* New York: Random House.

Thomas, W. P., & Collier, V. O. (1997). *School effectiveness for language minority students.* Washington, DC: National Clearinghouse for Bilingual Education.

Wallerstein, N. (1987). Problem-posing education: Freire's method of transformation. In I. Shor (Ed.), *FREIRE for the classroom: A sourcebook for liberatory teaching* (pp. 33–44). Portsmouth, NH: Boynton/Cook.

Walsh, C. E. (1995). Bilingual education and critical pedagogy: Critical reflections for teachers. In J. Frederickson (Ed.), *Reclaiming our voices: Bilingual education, critical pedagogy and praxis* (pp. 79–98). Ontario, CA: California Association for Bilingual Education.

Wink, J., & Almanzo, M. (1995). Critical pedagogy: A lens through which we see. In J. Frederickson (Ed.), *Reclaiming our voices: Bilingual education, critical pedagogy and praxis* (pp. 210–223). Ontario, CA: California Association for Bilingual Education.

Reflective Activities

PEDAGOGICAL COMPONENTS

Origins of a Transformative Journey

Why were Spanish-speaking students prohibited from speaking Spanish? When were these policies adopted? How long were the policies enforced? In which states did this occur? What was the political climate of the time? Why didn't the Spanish-speaking students question the no-Spanish-speaking rule? "Our experiences are not all the same, but we need to try to understand them all, if we are truly to be tolerant and transformative teachers." How can we understand them all?

Understanding Transformative Journeys

How do others' perceptions of us transform us? How do a teacher's perceptions of students transform them? How was the author trying to be the good American? What does the statement, "The transformative journey takes time, self-examination, and reflection," mean? Why is the transformative journey an individual journey?

The Transformative Teacher

How have power, politics, history, culture, and language influenced education? What is social injustice? What is political incoherence? What is the difference between education and schooling? Why did Mrs. Smith's judgments reveal a naive consciousness? How does literacy in the native language transfer to literacy in

English? What is CALP? How it is different from BICS? What is the significance of the statement, "Did Mrs. Smith also feel that British students were smarter than American students?" Why is the injury exacerbated and the shame felt anew when a monolingual English speaker says to a Hispanic, "You don't speak Spanish, but you're Hispanic. Why don't you speak Spanish?"

Facilitating the Connections

What is a social transformation? What is emancipatory knowledge? Why didn't the state want a bilingual license or endorsement if one third of the elementary schools were designated as bilingual schools? Why were nonbilingual teachers being placed in bilingual classrooms? How could nonbilingual teachers be bilingual teachers? What are some examples of things you can do without understanding why? Why is understanding the "why" of something important? How is "why" essential to the dialogic process?

The writing activity for "Understand Them All" should engage the students in self-examination by answering the questions, What do I know about X? What experiences have I had with X? and What do I think X is? related to a topic or issue from the chapter. Rather than the teacher answering the students' questions or providing additional information about certain topics or issues presented in the chapter, the students are asked to write what they know, think, and have experienced related to the topic or issue they are asking about.

Having written their responses, the students will work in groups and explore and question others' experiences, beliefs, and stories through a dialogic process for exploring, What do others think or know about X? What experiences have others had with X? How are my experiences different from, or the same as, others'?

The readings should be initiated by the students as they attempt to answer, How has X been affected by politics, history, culture, language, and power? How do these define X? How are the meanings of X different? Each student, or a small group of students, can focus on the effect or influence of one of the different forces: power, politics, history, culture, or language, relative to the topic or issue.

Activities for the Classroom

RESEARCH BASE

Preschool and Elementary Students

At the elementary level, activities should be selected that promote social cognition rather than diversity awareness, since even kindergartners are aware of and acknowledge cultural diversity. While students at this age are aware of diversity, they don't always know how to respond to those who they perceive as different from themselves. It should be recalled that preschoolers and elementary age students are egocentric in their thinking and thus will need assistance in learning how to respond to others. In selecting activities, teachers need to consider the students' cognitive development, since the students' cognitive abilities mirror their social cognition and thus their capacity to understand and relate to others.

But the activities are secondary to the example the teacher and school staff set as they interact with students and other adults in the school setting. Elementary age students are in the process of developing and tend to learn by emulating behaviors they see adults model. The most powerful and enduring lessons teachers teach are by example. Teachers who chastise students for name calling but who belittle or ridicule students themselves are teaching by example that domination and control of others are acceptable and appropriate by those in authority. Great care should be given to modeling the behaviors that are desired from students.

Many age-appropriate books can be used for promoting diversity understandings among elementary age students. Preservice teachers should confer with the faculty who teach children's literature for appropriate books and activities that promote diversity understandings. In-service teachers can consult with their school's librarian about age-appropriate books focusing on different diversity issues. The books and activities should be selected based on the diversity understandings the teacher is attempting to nurture. Students learn best when the material is relevant and meaningful to their immediate social cognitive needs and circumstances. To capture the essence of the diversity understandings, the activities should mirror the diversity dilemma the students are grappling with. Students' social cognitive understandings are advanced when the learnings are concrete and authentic. At this level, development of social cognition should be the goal. A review of any child growth and development text will provide a detailed description of social cognition.

Middle and High School Students

Preschoolers tend to be egocentric in their perspective and understanding of others, and while adolescents demonstrate greater intellectual capabilities that permit them not only to empathize with others and to understand others' thoughts, feelings, intentions, and motives, they also tend to exhibit egocentric thinking, although different from that of the preoperational or concrete operational child. In other words, every stage of cognitive development has some form of egocentric thinking associated with it. While preschoolers do not possess the social cognition to empathize, adolescents' egocentrism manifests itself in misattributing their feelings to others. Adolescents' egocentrism is characterized by a preoccupation in thinking about themselves and comparing themselves with others. Their egocentrism leads them to conclude that others feel exactly the same way they do, and at other times that no one knows how they feel.

Elementary

Ask the students how many Spanish words they know. Make a chart of the words the students suggest. Initially list all the words the students suggest, even if some of the words are not Spanish origin words. Decide when the list has enough words to group them into different categories. For example, words like *taco, tamales, tortillas,* and *chile* can be classified as food. *María, José, Juanita, Marcos,* and *Inez* can be labeled students' names or proper nouns. For early primary students (prekindergartners and kindergartners), accept the label "students' names," but for intermediate elementary students, the label "proper nouns" should be encouraged.

Once the classification has been completed, ask the students how they can determine if the words are Spanish origin words or not. If students have problems suggesting possible sources for verification, ask them if the words can be looked up in a dictionary to determine their origin. Intermediate elementary students should be shown how to use a dictionary to determine etymology. For example, the word *taco* will show **[MexSp],** shown in boldface square brackets preceding the definition. Have the students look up the words to determine if they were borrowed from Spanish. Have the students identify the etymology of all the words listed. For instance, if *shampoo* was one of the words on the original list, its origin should be identified as [Hindi].

Have the students make a new chart of words based on their etymology: Spanish words, Hindi words, and so forth. Have them retain the subcategories they initially developed: food, proper nouns, and others. Ask the students what they learned about the origin of commonly used English words. Record their answers. Ask them why they think the English language has borrowed so many words from other languages. Ask them how the borrowed words are like the people of the United States.

Early primary students can also complete this activity by pairing the preliterate students with intermediate students and having the older students look up the words and make a list of the words with their etymologies, while showing and discussing what they are doing with the younger students. Early primary students can be asked what they learned, why the English language has borrowed so many words from other languages, and how the borrowed words are like the people of the United States. The students' answers will reveal their level of understanding and should serve as an instructional guide for the teacher in planning future lessons.

Middle School

Middle school students can be asked how many states have Spanish names. Following the discussion, the students should be asked how they can determine the accuracy of their hypotheses. For students who do not have access to a computer or are computer novices, have them use an encyclopedia to check their answers. Whether they use a computer or encyclopedia, they should also explain how the states' names were chosen. Students should write their answers and be prepared to orally share their findings. Students should be permitted to work in groups, particularly if some of the students are English language learners who would benefit from the literacy scaffolds that their peers could provide.

High School

Why doesn't the United States have an official language? Why didn't the founding fathers adopt English as the official language of the United States? Which language almost became the official language of the United States? Students should be encouraged to hypothesize, check their hypotheses, and present their findings to the class. In answering the questions, the students should be encouraged to explain the influence of power, politics, history, culture, and language on the decision not to have an official language. Why is there a current effort to make English the official language? Have the students determine the influence of power, politics, history, culture, and language behind the current efforts.

WEB SITES

The students are encouraged to use Web browsers, such as Internet Explorer or Netscape, for identifying and accessing Web sites related to a specific topic or issue. They may use Internet search engines, such as Yahoo or Google, for locating topics, authors, or subjects. Educational search engines and databases, such as the ERIC Educational Resources Information Center and the U.S. Department of Education, may also be used.

The National Clearinghouse for Bilingual Education

http://www.ncbe.gwu.edu/index.htm

"The National Clearinghouse for Bilingual Education (NCBE) is funded by the U.S. Department of Education's Office of Bilingual Education and Minority Languages Affairs (OBEMLA) to collect, analyze, and disseminate information relating to the effective education of linguistically and culturally diverse learners in the U.S. NCBE is operated by The George Washington University, Graduate School of Education and Human Development, Institute for Education Policy Studies. As part of the U.S. Department of Education's technical assistance and information network, NCBE works with other service providers to provide access to high quality information to help states and local school districts develop programs and implement strategies for helping all students work towards high academic standards."

TESOL: Teachers of English to Speakers of Other Languages, Inc.

http://www.tesol.org/

"TESOL's mission is to develop the expertise of its members and others involved in teaching English to speakers of other languages to help them foster effective communication in diverse settings while respecting individual's language rights. To this end:

- TESOL links groups worldwide to enhance communication among language specialists.
- TESOL produces high-quality programs, services, and products.
- TESOL articulates and advances standards for professional preparation and employment, continuing education, and student programs.
- TESOL promotes advocacy to further the profession."

Office of Bilingual Education and Minority Languages Affairs

http://www.ed.gov/offices/

"The mission of OBEMLA is to provide limited English proficient students with equal access to equal educational opportunities. Established in 1974 by Congress, the Office of Bilingual Education and Minority Languages Affairs helps school districts meet their responsibility to provide equal education opportunity to limited English proficient children."

National Center of Education Statistics (NCES)

http://nces.ed.gov/index.html

"NCES is the primary federal entity for collecting and analyzing data that are related to education in the United States and other nations. (U.S. Department of Education)

NCES provides data and information services:

- *What's New?:* Provides updates on latest Web applications, recently released publications, and employment and funding opportunities.
- *Electronic Catalog:* Locates most recently released publications and searches for any NCES publications and data products.
- *Students' Classroom:* Special content tailored to a younger crowd.
- *Survey and Program Areas:* Locates information on all NCES surveys and programs—links to products, staff, and survey specific homepages.
- *Encyclopedia of ED Stats:* Browse through and search NCES major statistical compendiums—discover education statistics from all program areas.
- *Global ED Locator:* Locates information on colleges, public school libraries, or private schools in the United States.
- *NCES Fast Facts*
- *Quick Tables and Figures:* This search tool allows the search of all tables and figures published in the inventory of NCES's *Education Statistics Quarterly.*
- *Search NCES:* The comprehensive search engine helps to locate information anywhere on the NCES Web site."

U.S. Department of Education

http://www.ed.gov/

"The U.S. Department of Education offers a range and an ever-growing collection of information about the Department, including: initiatives and priorities, grant opportunities, offices, publications, research and statistics. Special collections of information are offered for parents, teachers, and students. Links are provided to organizations supported by the Department and a state map showing which Department-supported organizations serve different states. Several finding tools may also help site navigation:

- Topics A–Z—an alphabetical index of the best starting points on the Department web site.
- Search—finds resources on the Department site—and on more than 400 other federally supported web sites.
- Site Map—a bird's-eye view of the Department's entire web site."

http://www.ncbe.gwu.edu/index.htm

http://www.tesol.org/

http://www.ed.gov/offices/

http://nces.ed.gov/index.html

Chapter 9

Safe and Growing Out of the Box: Immersion for Social Change

Jean Moule, Oregon State University, Corvallis

Focus Questions

1. What boxes do others put you in? What is comfortable about this perception?

2. What do you gain by growing out of the box?

Being creative involves a willingness to step outside the boxes that we and others have created for ourselves.

—Robert J. Sternberg

My journey to bridge multicultural education theory and classroom practice began in my early personal experience as an African American female and an isolated student of color. My life experiences have resulted in a need to help others understand the nature and effects of prejudice. This has led me to develop creative ways to help preservice teachers and their students emerge from the boxes society has constructed for them.

Such social boxes often lead to a false sense of security while keeping the occupants in the margins. *Margin* is defined as "an edge and the area immediately adjacent to it, border" (Morris, 1985). My experiences as an isolated individual of color and as an instructor working with preservice teachers from European American homogeneous settings have revealed the marginal nature of my circumstances in the larger perspective of the United States of America. The first part of this chapter describes some transformative incidents that have occurred during the course of my life on the margins. My experiences enclose a space that we can use to consider similar issues that we all confront.

I also see my work as providing a margin of safety for others by offering "an allowance beyond what is needed" (Morris, 1985). My goal is to facilitate transformation as individuals emerge from socially constructed boxes to begin to develop independent perspectives on the world. Educating for transformation may require working in the margins to create safe places in which others may change. The second part of this chapter provides an example of transformation through one preservice teacher's efforts to break out of the box. A box can be a confining space or a protecting one; it can be an elevated place from which to view a situation such as a carriage or opera box, or it can describe a predicament (Morris, 1985). Each kind of box appears here.

A Box Metaphor for Racial Identity Development

Before describing my encounters with the boxes society and I, myself, created for me, I would like to propose a box metaphor for racial identity development. I believe this metaphor will help enrich the understanding of my own story, and perhaps help other people understand their own stories.

For the last 5 years I've taught multicultural issues in education. It quickly became apparent to me that this was a process course, not a content course. My students needed to process their own movement through the stages of racial identity if they were going to be culturally competent educators in our pluralistic society. I had studied several theories of racial identity development, particularly Cross (1995) and Helms (1990). I wanted my students to have a much clearer and quicker understanding of the theory, so I proposed a four-level racial identity development scale with very simple terms.

I call stage one "I'm okay; you're okay." This corresponds to the preencounter stage found in many racial identity development theories. The second stage I call "Something is not okay." This corresponds to the encounter stage found in most theories. The third I call "I'm okay; I'm not so sure about you." In this stage I summarize several stages from different theorists, including anger, denial, pseudo-independence, immersion, and emersion. Depending on the group I am working with and their interests, I expand and define this stage using details from various identity development models. A last stage I call "I'm okay; you're okay." This stage is equivalent to the autonomy or independent stage, where people are ready to work for change in a more fully integrated manner.

Different stages may be seen as corresponding to certain positions in or on the box. In the preencounter stage, someone is inside the box. The individual is standing on a level area and does not see beyond the box. People in this position believe all that they see is all that there is, and feel fairly happy and secure about themselves and their perspectives—and their understandings about others.

During the encounter stage, the individual finds her- or himself outside the box examining all sides of the box and perhaps trying to climb up to gain a better view. It is very disconcerting, with little security and little frame of reference because things look different depending on which side of the box the person is viewing or climbing at the moment. It is a confusing time, and it is a time when the effort to continue often doesn't seem like it's worth it. Something is "not okay," but the person hasn't defined this "not okay" yet.

Once someone chooses a place to climb up, for a while the only thing visible is the face of the box that they are climbing. During this time of effort and focus, the individual loses sight of the whole, does not understand another scaling the other side, and thinks, "I'm okay; but I'm not so sure about you." During this stage it is sometimes especially hard to communicate with others who are elsewhere in the process.

Finally, when someone is on top of the box, they are back on a level place again, feeling secure. "I'm okay; you're okay," again summarizes this stage, but the individual now has a higher perspective, a better understanding of the whole, and may be in a position to help those scaling the four sides of the box. From this position, the individual has the advantage of a new perspective and is ready to move out with a little more knowledge and stability. Never mind that there is a bigger box balanced on top of the first within which to begin the process again.

TRANSFORMATIVE INCIDENTS IN MY LIFE

Speaking From Isolation Inside a Box

As I began my journey as a teacher educator, I found myself recalling stories of my childhood. These stories, as harsh as some seem now, encompassed a secure world that I made sense of at the time. I'm not sure it was truly a preencounter, "I'm okay; you're okay" world because I often did not feel "okay" in it. As a child, these events were intensely personal, and I often felt they were my fault when they did not work out. Still, it was my world, it was secure in many ways, and I accepted it.

I believe these stories also became part of my encounter, "Something is not okay," stage as I wrote them down. This happened in retrospect, because as a child, I did not have the skills to understand or move through the process. Others have understood that early stories influence current work. Foster (1993) felt that the stories from her childhood influenced the course of her study. Ellis made this transition in *Evocative Autoethnography: Writing Emotionally About Our Lives* (1997). She started with a formal, citation-laced report, and then moved to a first person, friendly discussion of her data, before eventually creating a piece that began "I was born . . ."

As I began to work with preservice teachers, these stories simply came unbidden to my consciousness, and I wrote them down for the first time. I believe I had an internal need to process this information in a new way before teaching others. I began to reevaluate these experiences in light of my efforts to work more holistically with preservice teachers. The stories became a step in my own understanding of racial identity development in my life before asking others to take a similar journey.

Isolated by Race and Ethnicity
Brown v. Board of Education, 1954. I was 8 years old. My family had quietly moved into an all-white, mostly Jewish neighborhood 4 years earlier. And some people did not want me there. I had been doing in New York City what 7-year-old Linda Brown's parents had wanted her to do in Topeka, Kansas—going to a local school within walking distance, regardless of its racial makeup.

Only recently my father told me about an event that happened during that time. One morning he had gone outside and seen "N___, go back where you came from" scrawled on the outside of the house. Without telling anyone, he had washed it off.

I shudder when I visualize the scene, but it helps me understand why he raised me as he did, with a level of determination that my sister and I would become exemplary citizens. This story helps me understand his need to have us "fit in." Yet the pressure to conform did not work. I experienced being different even as I worked to assimilate. The resultant dissonance separated me even further from my peers.

My mother tells me that she came to pick me up from first grade, and the teacher recounted that I had waited at the door of the classroom and stomped on the toes of my classmates as they exited. My mother speculates that I was being naughty or seeking attention. What spurred my 6-year-old, usually eager-to-please personality to do such a thing, I don't recall. Was I seeking attention (albeit negative) in an environment that frequently ignored me?

I remember the isolation I felt during a Jewish holiday; only two students remained in the entire school. As the sole student in my class at such times, I wondered, "Why isn't the teacher teaching me today? I am here!" I remember having only two "friends," one invited me to her home once, but mostly I was alone. It is only now, as I study preservice teachers in homogeneous classrooms with one or two isolated students of color, that I wonder what meaning I made of my experiences at the time and contemplate the fact that "Something was not okay."

Isolated in Safety

Summer had been a traumatic experience, moving from an East Coast urban area to a West Coast suburb, from a two-parent family to being raised by a single mother, as my parents separated. My previous classroom had been Jewish except for me, and my new school was as culturally diverse as anything Los Angeles could offer.

Miss Thomas was graying and, to a third grader, she seemed elderly. She used strategies that seemed to validate every child in her room. She gave "permanent value" to each of her students.[1] She also understood the concept of "taking the lid off" for students and helping them to stretch, to pursue their own interests.[2] Each day, Miss Thomas wrote a phrase in Spanish in the corner of the blackboard. She read it to us, then had us repeat it. In less than a minute of classroom time, well before the official establishment of bilingual education, she acknowledged her Mexican American students and opened the door to languages for the rest of us.

Miss Thomas's classroom exemplified the proverb, "You could hear a pin drop." She spent most of her time, like a castle sentry behind fortified walls, regarding us from her desk/turret at the back of the room. She was strict and unyielding. Her classroom was safe from any disrespect toward her or between students. Miss Thomas's room was a secure and healthy place for my own emotions in transition and my classmates' toes. I was safe, yet isolated by silence and authority. Wasn't this quiet room yet another box—a box that would continue to ensure my isolation from those around me?

[1]*Permanent value* means considering each child to be of value regardless of behavior. It could be called unconditional love. How teachers develop and express this valuing of students may depend on the teacher's own value system, character, and personal philosophy. Dreikurs (1968) recognized the importance of permanent value. He stated, "The child's realization that he has *permanent value* [italics added] and that his value is recognized by his teacher regardless of what he is doing at the moment or where he may fail. . . . opens the way for an unselfish desire [for the child] to do his best."

[2]Cohen (1991/1992) used the term *taking the lid off* of the labeled boxes in which we may place children to sum up her rules for meeting the learning needs of all students.

Isolated by Assumptions

From junior high I began a love–hate affair with history. My academic Achilles' heel was rote memory history tests. My current test anxiety stems from a poor short-term memory and those impossible bouts with unrelated dates and facts. In the eighth grade I had to attend a summer session to raise my low history grade. We were studying pioneers and the western migration, which interested me. I was devastated, however, when my teacher, a European American female, accused me of plagiarism. I wrote a stirring, creative beginning to my term paper, and she did not believe me when I said I wrote it myself. What was her reason for not believing the work was my own? Was it because she did not trust the cultural divide between herself and me, an African American student? I did not bother finishing the research paper and received another low grade. Her assumptions and her low expectations hampered my interest in writing, as well as in history. I hated the study of history for 20 years, marrying an historian with some misgivings.

Fortunately, at the age of 38, I discovered the rich local history in the towns where I taught. As my students and I explored and learned and researched, history became a delight for me and for them. They won an award and community praise. I won back part of my past. Yet the incident remains as a reminder of the far-reaching effects of one teacher's prejudgment of a student's ability, and . . . I still struggle to write freely.

Making Sense of the Stories

I believe I had done much of the work in racial identity development for my life as a wife, mother, and teacher in a rural community. As I began to examine these stories during my work as a teacher educator, I found new meaning in them, and they initiated a new encounter stage in my growth toward influencing others.

As I examine the stories, I can see other factors related to racial identity development. For instance, in the neighborhood isolation story, I see both my father's and my own denial of a problem—just pretend there is no problem: Erase it, go to school anyway, and proceed as normal. In Miss Thomas's classroom, I probably experienced the calm and false security of a pseudo-independent stage. And, in retrospect, I find myself angry when I consider the history teacher's actions.

Isolated, but Connected to a Way of Knowing

Reading the book *Naming Silenced Lives* (McLaughlin & Tierney, 1993), I began to discern that my early life had been silenced. I was *not* led to reflect. In fact, I believe that my parents encouraged me to abandon all history, relationships, and culture related to my African American heritage in order to assimilate into white middle-class society. I believe this reflects the racism of the times, when assimilation was the easiest way to succeed in "White America." Despite my parents' earnest efforts, I've retained some African American cultural patterns in my actions and speech because of the inevitable transfer of cultural ways of knowing from mother to child. My mother was brought up in the Deep South, in Charleston, South Carolina, and, later, in an exclusively African American rural community of 300 people, where it seemed that everyone was at least a third cousin. Her cultural traditions were evident in how she raised me, and I believe I have some of her speech patterns.

These youthful experiences form the roots of my later thinking and theory about issues of social change, as they do for most individuals. As an adult, I began to reflect on these childhood incidents using a more global understanding of race, intellect, history, and my recent study of racial identity development. I have also come to accept that my perspective transcends my personal lived experience, for society imposes on me perspectives or reactions to perspectives not my own. This difference in perspective is articulated well by Collins (1990):

> All African-American women share the common experience of being Black women in a society that denigrates women of African descent. This commonality of experience suggests that certain characteristic themes will be prominent in a Black women's standpoint. For example, one core theme is a legacy of struggle. . . . The existence of core themes does not mean that African-American women respond to these themes in the same way. . . . For example, although all African-American women encounter racism, social class differences among African-American women influence how racism is experienced. . . . Black women's work and family experiences and grounding in traditional African-American culture suggest that African-American women as a group experience a world different from that of those who are not Black and female. Moreover, these concrete experiences can stimulate a distinctive Black feminist consciousness concerning that . . . reality.   (pp. 22–24)

As I read Collins, I found her words describing my experiences. Through her I began to understand black women's unique perspectives and the "core themes of a black woman's standpoint." She says, "Very different kinds of 'thought' and 'theories' emerge when abstract thought is joined with concrete action" (1990, p. 29). For me, there is little distance between theory and practice, thought and action. Thought is my talk, action is my walk. I try very hard to make them the same. At some point in my formative years, I believe I became disenchanted with the duplicity I saw in society, in politics, even in my father. At this point, I believe I made a choice that, beyond all else, I would try to speak and act with integrity. I am still examining the fact that this decision and Collins's thesis on African American women's standpoint coincide. My easy acceptance of the close connection between her thoughts and my concrete actions is in itself a reflection of this standpoint. This ongoing effort to bring my *walk* closer to my *talk* inevitably leads me to both external and internal conflict, especially in higher education when theory and practice are often separated.

ISOLATED BY INSTITUTIONALIZED RACISM

In this next story, I am again a student in the presence of a European American teacher with an unquestioned assumption—this time about the nature of research. Unlike the others, this story is not dependent solely on my memory and interpretation. A videotape of the event and conversations with those present confirm my memory of it.

One of the hurdles on the way to a doctorate at our university is a library research paper. This paper is designed to ensure competence in analyzing prior research before proceeding with one's own. Our school of education was making the transition from an exclusively quantitative–positivist research expectation, to a standard that includes qualitative–postpositivist–postmodern perspectives. The room was filled with proponents of both sides, and my presentation needed to satisfy both. For my own satisfaction, I had to show the context of my own journey thus far and also add what I thought were relevant details of the studies I had chosen to review, including, for example, the race of the researcher.

Acknowledgment of the author or researcher's perspective and experiences, and the possible impact that they may have on the study, have been crucial in both feminist and ethnic research. Reinharz and Davidman (1992) noted

> I have feminist distrust for research reports that include no statement about the researcher's experience. Reading such reports, I feel that the researcher is hiding from me or does not know how important personal experience is. Such reports seem woefully incomplete and even dishonest.   (p. 263)

Because my context as an isolated individual of color and identifying the race of the researchers in the articles I reviewed were central to my study, I included such factors, leading to a break from tradition in my presentation. The faculty member who had appointed herself the academic gatekeeper wanted to see a more narrow and traditional analysis and presentation. She had difficulty recognizing the importance I placed on the role and background of the researcher as part of the research methodology.

At one point in the videotape of my presentation, I stand with my hands on the table in front, my head hanging down, documenting my frustration in trying to answer the third challenge from this faculty member. I felt that she was questioning not only my analysis, but my very being. Strangers viewing the tape marvel that faculty members are allowed to verbally accost doctoral students in such a manner. Such questioning, if ever appropriate, is usually reserved for the closed part of an oral exam or doctoral defense. At a certain point this probing seemed to cross a line into racism. Let me explain.

This faculty member's insistence on only a Eurocentric perspective may have evidenced institutional bias. Kochman (1981) argued that "White[s] . . . consider an idea authoritative when it has been published. . . . Blacks consider it essential for individuals to have personal positions on issues and assume full responsibility for arguing their validity" (pp. 24–25). I was determined to include my personal position and current life context, while the faculty member wanted only hard objective facts. Reinharz and Davidman (1992) assert that claiming objectivity is itself the biased stance of privileged white males. In her zeal to discredit my inclusion of additional criteria in my work, she was blinded to the strength of my objective analyses and missed my effort to bridge paradigms. Other participants found my standard analyses to be clear and complete.

When I wrote this story, it was evident that it still evokes an emotional and unsettled response in me. I believe this is key to revealing this story as one that occurred during the rocky "I'm okay; I'm not so sure about you" period. I believe that writing this story is part of my own continuing journey to understand the need for bridging between perspectives and understanding racial identity development: "We avoid telling stories that evoke feelings that we do not care to relive" (Schank, 1990, p. 47). I have chosen to relive these stories in the hopes that they will move others. My intent in writing is to tell stories that are remembered as well as to write in a way that reveals new insights, to the reader and to myself. Ideally, you have an ongoing dialogue with the text while reading. Then, you and I both become part of a continuing dialogue that will lead to a fuller understanding of issues raised by this work.

ISOLATED BY MISINFORMATION: A STORY THAT IS *NOT* MINE

I've been asked both to reveal the transformative incidents in my life that led me to work for social justice and to explain how I resisted the "mystifications of media" and other pressures. I began to question certain truths following a formative experience as a college student. This story would also reflect a rebellious stand that acts out, "I'm (we're) okay; but I'm not so sure about you."

It was 1964, and the free speech movement at the University of California, Berkeley, was fomenting. I was a first-year student, both idealistic and naïve. I was also a risk taker. Maybe it was my inability to be present in the history-making marches in the South at the time. Perhaps I was stirred by the rousing rhetoric of the First Amendment. Maybe I was merely seeking a chance to rebel or to express a deeply felt passion. At any rate, I marched, and I stayed to be arrested. Years later, when I became a teacher, this action caused me extra work each licensing period as I explained my arrest. Yet, as a teacher educator, I am glad that I was not afraid to stand up for what I believe is right. But the primary lesson I learned from this experience was a healthy skepticism about the media.

That evening in 1964, Sproul Hall was a risky place to be, especially after the building was locked for the night. My future husband and I were followers, not leaders; yet a series of small events led us to be more noticed than we had planned. We were photographed under a registration table in Sproul Hall, the scene of the action. We were studying. Yet the headline near the photo in *The San Francisco Chronicle* screamed "Headquarters of the Rebels." I learned then the power of labels not self chosen. The larger lesson was still to come.

After our arrest, stories came out in newspapers around the nation. I read few, but my interest was piqued when a *New York Times* appeared among our fellow arrestees, for my father lived in New York. By now we had been released from jail on bail, but I had not decided whether or when to inform my father of my arrest. I wondered what he would make of the story, so I looked over shoulders to get a glimpse. The reader of the newspaper, who I did not know, said, "Who is Jean Golson?" As this is my maiden name, I was suddenly quite interested in reading each detail of my arrest. I also wondered, and I still do, why I, a faceless follower, was chosen out of hundreds to be specifically named by the *Times*. Then, I drank in every detail of the story and realized immediately that the story was not mine. A journalist had merged a standard arrest and my name. Never again would I fully trust the media, even as I became a correspondent myself. From the age of 19 I have taken everything I read, especially in the media, with a grain of salt, for I knew firsthand the falsity in that particular article. This experience was formative: "susceptible of transformation by growth and development," because it is clearly part of my transformation and it explains my immunity to certain brands of media hype.

A BOX OF COLOR

Part of my own transition from observing on the margins to becoming an active agent of change comes from a position, another box, forced on me by others. Students and others in academia tend to assign me, first and foremost, to an African American reference group, although I had not usually defined myself primarily by ethnicity in forging professional and personal relationships. My heritage is part of me, so it was not ignored; it was simply not my primary orientation. I would probably have defined myself by many other adjectives before using my race as a descriptor, unless someone was searching for me in a crowd. Yet, this has changed, because in my role at Oregon State University, my race and the diversity it brings to our setting is very important to others.

EMERGING FROM THE BOX

It is the present. My current journey arises in part from my need to make meaning of these experiences and to use them to help preservice teachers translate multicultural education theory into classroom practice. These upward struggles in understanding have caused me to reach a stage where my main focus is to make a difference in the lives of students.

In the spring of 1996, I was invited to teach a course on multicultural issues in education to 83 incoming preservice teachers. As I began to study the research and literature in this field, I found little that connects the college instruction of preservice teachers to the classroom performance of these students in the area of multicultural education. In the often homogeneous settings of the Pacific Northwest, and especially following the racial incidents on the campus of Oregon State University (OSU) in February 1996,[3] teaching teachers to teach their students to treat others as they would want to be treated seemed a worthy goal.

I am in a unique position: I have access to preservice teachers both during their undergraduate preparation and in their internship placements in a university town setting where 90% of the K–12 student population (Oregon Department of Education, 1998), and 95% of the preservice teachers are European American (Moule, 1997).[4] I was available to the preservice teachers, and vice versa, in the college classroom, for one-on-one discussions and observations.

I have chosen to be a teacher educator in the field of multicultural education. In this role, I am a black female whose life is open to her students and colleagues, and I am willing to risk misunderstanding to further growth in my learning community. I have decided that, regardless of how difficult this may be and how isolated I may feel, I will be as open as possible to others.

This is the work that I do when I am feeling strongly at my autonomy, "I'm okay; you're okay," stage. Considering the filter of my own background and current roles, my focus as I work with students is quite natural. My mission is to provide a margin of safety for the preservice teachers in my care so that they may learn to value and

---

[3]In February 1996, the increasing incidences of verbal and written racial slurs on campus alarmed some people. At this time the African American student population of Oregon State University was about 160 students, or 1.2%. The turning point in campus and community passivity came after students on a dormitory balcony verbally harassed and attempted to urinate on an African American student. This incident resulted in a campus-wide boycott of classes, a march, and a rally. At least 2,000 students and community members participated in these events. The students who accosted the African American student were arrested.

[4]A large research institution of 17,000 students, Oregon State University is located in the city of Corvallis, with a population of about 50,000. The surrounding area is rural. The school district has 7,300 students, and 12.5% of them are identified as minority.

work for social justice. They need safe environments themselves so that they can provide safe and nurturing environments for their students of color and a solid foundation for understanding diversity for all of their students.

Yet, how could I bring a sense of context, of true cultural awareness, to the preservice teachers in my classes and on my advisee list? Preservice teachers' thinking about multicultural issues in education, whether rooted in traditional Eurocentric assumptions (Loewen, 1995), personal history-based beliefs (Holt-Reynolds, 1992), or course work material are the box—the theory—they create and bring with them into the K–12 or college classroom. My frequent experiences as an isolated student of color in K–12 and college classrooms have moved me to plan unique immersion experiences for the preservice teachers under my influence.

I believe I continue to cycle through the "I'm okay; I'm not so sure about you" stage as I vacillate between strong movements and actions to encourage and support faculty and students of color and simply "doing my job" as an assistant professor. The former must be undertaken when I am in a "not so sure about you" phase as it is against the grain of most action in my university, although there is much talk about it. It is as if I see reflected in those around me an "I'm not so sure about you" attitude when I work against the grain. So perhaps movement into the autonomy stage of racial identity development happens for me only when I have more allies where I work and we become collectively more integrated in our thinking and actions and ready to work more positively for social change.

An example of this growth with my allies occurred when a white colleague introduced me to bell hooks's *Teaching to Transgress*. She arranged a time for us to meet over lunch to discuss the book, and during this time chided me for not being more up front in my dissertation about my race and perspective. She seemed to want to know how my perspective was shaped by being black and female. Because of her encouragement, I made efforts to share my viewpoints in writing and in conversation when it seems relevant, and especially when issues are shaped by the intersection of race and gender. Yet I am discouraged. Recently this friend seems dismissive, with a response of, "Oh, we all do that," when I related one of my behaviors that seemed to be a response to my feelings of isolation at the university. I feel that she wants me to move beyond race and gender in my work, yet these are issues that don't go away. If this is the response of a friend and ally, I fear the reaction of those who don't care to explore different perspectives on these issues at all.

I believe my earlier connections and occasional confrontations have helped me to move our unit into a new social justice advocacy role this academic year. We are jointly journaling and examining ourselves as we wholeheartedly undertake this new perspective and stance. I'm finding my contacts with my colleagues more emotional on my part as they press me for responses and answers to their new questions. It is tiring, but good. I told one of my advisees, "It's a phase the faculty is going through."

Helms (1990) described the struggle European Americans have confronting their own transitions through stages of racial identity. Especially among those whose isolation has allowed them the capacity to ignore matters of race, realization and personal reflection are not easy. I care deeply about those in this transition, particularly my students, and have structured my courses and interactions so that I may listen carefully. I include opportunities for privately written or spoken exchanges. I allow considerable choice of material and self-grading to alleviate stress and to help students break through the facade of political correctness. I have found working in pairs, in small groups, and a class listserv valuable as multiple avenues for preservice teachers' reflection and growth. Their journals reflect the importance of these spaces in which to consider such issues.

I have come to anticipate with both dread and pleasure the knotty journey that we all take each quarter I teach this class. When I began working with a new graduate teaching assistant, I was reminded of the difficulty of this work and how much I have grown in order to withstand this regular onslaught. After our first day, Adrian, who is quite experienced as a Chicano in diverse environments but not in the role of college teaching, asked, "Do you find the students . . . resistant?" He has begun to understand the complexities of bringing others to an open understanding of multiple perspectives. For example, a study by Barry and Lechner (1995) on the attitudes of undergraduate elementary education students found that a particular course in multicultural education actually reinforced some biases. Could we avoid that pitfall?

Many of the preservice teachers in the class struggle both with the subject matter and their reactions to having their first African American professor. Add to this my commitment to teach in a constructivist and student-centered manner, that presents a different atmosphere than most university courses, and the barriers to growth and openness grow alarmingly high. Because of my own experiences that lacked fairness and equality I often ask myself: Is this course a safe place in which to learn and grow?[5] Not only is this essential for the growth of the preservice teachers, but it is important to model this atmosphere for their future classrooms. As a researcher observing in classrooms, the foremost question in my mind is whether this classroom is safe for all children, particularly children of color. Asking "Is it safe?" was defined as a central teacher characteristic in the research of Gonsalves-Pinto (1997) and was implied in the work of others (Burbules, 1993; Ellsworth, 1990; Moule, 1991; Nieto, 1994; Noddings, 1997).

As education students moved into intern placements, I noted that the preservice teachers were becoming comfortable in their primary placement and were apt to seek positions working with children they could already identify with. Could I help them enlarge their boundaries and their understanding by encouraging them to experience other ways to interact and other ways of knowing? Could they break out of their set script for behavior?

A script is a set of expectations about what will happen next in a well-understood situation. In many life situations, participants seem to be reading their roles. Scripts lay out what is supposed to happen and how various actions of others are to be interpreted and responded to. Schank (1990) supports the need to have additional experiences and learn various interactional styles to enable people to "feel comfortable and capable of playing [any] role effectively" (p. 8). In a very practical workbook, *Preparing for Student Teaching in a Pluralistic Classroom,* Blair and Jones (1998), working from a study by Michaels (1981), described how teacher–student interactional styles may severely hamper the learning process for a child whose cultural discourse style differs greatly from the teacher's.

---

[5]I would define as *safe* an environment in which the feelings of each individual are considered. I agree with Burbules (1993) and Ellsworth (1990), that sensible and fair rules of participation are not enough to make a classroom feel safe for many students. Burbules explained, "It often will not be enough just to listen; one might have to work to create an environment in which a silenced voice feels the confidence or security to speak" (p. 33).

FACILITATING TRANSFORMATION IN ANOTHER

A Project for Transformation

Perhaps the means to helping our preservice teachers emerge from their boxes and leave their scripts for behavior is not simply through reading and thinking about diversity, but through a rich immersion experience in another culture. Some studies have indicated that just getting to know people of color increases preservice and inservice teachers' classroom ability to work sensitively with children of color in the classroom (Hinchey, 1994; Reed, 1993). Perhaps my own sense of isolation drives me to want to help other people connect. So, how could I get my students to immerse themselves in a different environment?

Once on a quiet afternoon, I read through a request for a proposal for an Eisenhower Higher Education Grant. Thinking of the needs of the preservice teachers I serve, I dreamed of a plan. It was idealistic. It seemed impossible. And then it was funded. Here are excerpts from our project proposal:

> As the proportion and number of Children of Color in the nation's and Oregon's school districts have increased, so has the need for teachers who have multicultural perspectives (U. S. Department of Education, 1992). While it is important to continue to work on increasing the number of Teachers of Color, Oregon's underrepresented and underserved students will continue to be taught by non-minority teachers.
>
> Progress has been made at OSU through courses and strands in courses focusing on multicultural issues, and the installation of an alternate placement requirement. These placements have included socio/economic diversity, as well as ethnic and racial diversity such as at Warm Springs Indian Reservation for Native American populations, the Woodburn area for Latina/Latino populations, and occasionally in Portland for African American populations.
>
> The distance of Oregon State University from these areas of rich cultural diversity makes it difficult for preservice teachers to work with more than a few isolated Children of Color in local schools, many of whom are assimilated into their communities. Immersion in the school culture of a predominantly minority school in Portland would give the preservice teachers a unique perspective, and provide an opportunity for them to experience teaching in a different environment.
>
> The object of this proposal is to strengthen the classroom practices of preservice teachers while increasing support to target populations.
>
> Throughout the project, the project director will be available to assist interns and mentor teachers, to observe, to provide curriculum assistance, and to find staff and material resources.

TURNING THE PAPER TRAIL INTO A TRANSFORMING REALITY

First task, find a school in Portland. I am commonly asked by new acquaintances, "So, are you from Portland?" Oregon's African American population of 1.5% concentrates in Northeast Portland, so I can understand the question. What I cannot understand is the easy acceptance of the racial segregation that has made this so. The point is that everyone expected me, an African American female, to have contacts in Portland. I had none.

To locate a suitable school in which to immerse our preservice teachers, I began as anyone might. I found a list of all the schools in Oregon that included their ethnic makeup and highlighted every school in Portland with a minority population of 80% or more. Next, I located a database that also had the race of the teachers, for I thought it would be best if the preservice teachers had additional mentors of color. Two schools caught my attention. I called one school and talked to both the vice principal and the principal. No, they had recently been "reconstituted" (reassigned everyone and started over) and did not think this was a good year to have guests.

A bit disappointed and not willing to face another no response over the telephone, I decided to find placements through direct, new, personal contacts. I showed up at Martin Luther King, Jr., Elementary School cold. "Is the principal in?" I asked. "No," replied the secretary, Claudia, "Would you like to speak to the vice principal?" "Oh, yes." I waited. To my surprise and relief, I know this woman. She and I had worked together on the talented and gifted educational circuit years before. Her name, Joy, expressed my emotions. I pleaded. I explained. I became excited. The principal returned, and Joy introduced me.

Joseph Malone is the best principal I have ever worked with. One intern describes him like this:

> The principal of King plays a very active role in the culture of this school. He has a very dynamic personality. I have noticed that he often interacts with the students, more than I have seen in many other principals. He makes a concerted effort to connect with the students. I have observed him on the playground, in the halls and at the lunch line . . . He worked the lunch line due to understaffing. He has the respect of the teachers who I have heard acknowledge his flexibility and contribution to the school. I feel the principal of King is a great gift to this school, the students, and the teachers.

I recall his regular stint helping to serve lunch (and calling the children "Doctor") and the difficulty of finding him in his office since he was usually with children and in classrooms. The image I remember most was the day the governor visited with his entourage and a pack of legislators. Many saw him in his role as chief tour guide and facilitator of the visit. I was one of the few who saw him an hour earlier in rubber gloves, checking each restroom for cleanliness. (Many people visiting this school are struck by its polished halls and stately old appearance.)

At our first meeting, Malone explained that he would support the 3-week placement of our interns, but that the mentors would have to be volunteers. There was a staff meeting that day. I held my breath and asked to be allowed to share my vision with the teachers. He agreed.

At the meeting I had only my ideas and my enthusiasm, but I found an ally. Lolita Darby, her gray hair framing her face, her warm voice promising both strength and care, sat on the edge of the crowd. It is a crowd to me, for the school has 800 students and 35 staff members, miles and hues from Corvallis. I am energized. I drink in the diversity, the myriad colors. I feel as if I have returned to the school of my childhood.

Lolita catches the vision. She sees it, feels it, reflects it. She volunteers on the spot. I have envisioned older teachers, particularly teachers of color, passing the torch to a new generation. She buys it, no, she invents it, for I had little idea of what could be. Eleven days later, Lolita and another teacher, Gloria, come to Corvallis to help with a workshop. By the end of that day, Lolita has chosen her two mentees from their application forms.

By the end of the fall quarter, more than two dozen preservice teachers have "walked about" King School. Lolita has a ritual that I have witnessed over and over. A stranger looks in her room. She pauses and introduces the guest by her chosen honorific, Doctor, for me and others, and Miss and Mr. First Name for the interns from Oregon State University. She uses our visit to build a community of respect and to give an audience to the work of the students.

The following excerpts from a press release by Christine Decker of OSU give a more complete picture of these immersion placements:

> A group of 13 Oregon State University master's degree pre-service teachers are heading to a northeast Portland elementary school for three weeks in April. The university pre-service teachers will be working as student teachers in eight classrooms at King Elementary on the best ways to teach math and science to culturally diverse students.
>
> Jean Moule, an instructor in OSU's School of Education, said teachers in the Professional Teacher Education Program hope to improve their ability to establish a culturally just classroom climate—conducive to learning for all pupils—that recognizes the effects of a student's home and community on learning . . .
>
> "The best classrooms focus on the strengths of the children's cultures while teaching skills to succeed in the larger community," she added. Moule said that there are some differences in learning that can be culturally based, "For example, there are some cultures that are more family-oriented, or some that are more respectful of age, or that encourage more hands-on learning than the dominant culture in America, and we need to incorporate this information when we teach."
>
> King Elementary Principal Joseph Malone said he decided to be part of the Alternative Placement and Math/Science Curriculum Development for Pre-service Teachers of Minority Students program because he saw it as a win–win situation. "It was an information and growth opportunity for our teachers, and also a win situation to entice students who wanted to become teachers to know what the school and the classroom is all about," he said . . .
>
> "When these OSU students come out of this program they'll teach science and math better. They're going to know how to treat students as individuals. And, I expect the experience will explode their stereotypes," Moule said.

During the placement in April, Lolita spends long hours giving her two mentees strong, clear words on teaching. Miss Jennifer comes to love the room, the school, and the students so much that she invites her mother to drive 400 miles to visit during the last week. Mr. Charles, a creative and energetic intern overwhelmed with frustration in seeking a teaching license, drops out of the program right before the placement starts. He does this placement anyway and at the end decides to continue his student teaching with Lolita the following year.

TRANSFORMATION OF A PRESERVICE TEACHER

Thirteen preservice teachers were placed at King School. Here is the journey of one of them: Jennifer enters the placement with much thought and a strong desire to connect and learn. Her journals reflect her attitude and reveal details of her growth in understanding and working with a culturally diverse student population. As I share some of her words and reflections, I will often refer to her by the name Mrs. Darby chose, Miss Jennifer or Miss Jen.

In August 1998, Jennifer completed an application for the alternate placement project. She said, "I have grown up in a rural area . . . and I have never been exposed to the city in an educational sense." Jennifer listed her ability to place others' needs ahead of her own as a strength she brought to the project. She added, "I hope to gain the satisfaction of 'connecting' with a child." At the beginning, she recognized her many strengths, such as "dedication, empathy, sincerity, flexibility, and a strong desire to learn and teach," while realizing that "I will make mistakes and will face *many* challenges."

In the first week she reports feeling, "overwhelmed, scared, and apprehensive," although these feelings are primarily connected to her fears about the subject matter she is to teach, rather than the setting. During her first week on-site, Jennifer was able to meet one-on-one with an OSU faculty member whose specialty is mathematics. Lolita also calms her, suggesting she work for the kids and *with* them. Miss Jennifer adds, "Their needs and acceptance far outweigh my own fears. . . . We are all in this together." She is clearly focusing on the children.

As Miss Jen becomes more comfortable with the subject matter, she also continues to bond with the students and becomes immersed in the classroom and culture:

> Each day I am getting more and more attached to the kids and my mentor. . . . They are so willing to share many things about their own personal lives. They are so inviting and compassionate about people. . . . I feel that the culture is very family-oriented and they really watch out for each other. . . . The language and "lingo" is great to hear, sometimes it confuses me, but one way I know that I am included is when they share with me what certain terms and phrases mean. It is one small way that they "invite" me in.

As Miss Jen works with the students, her observations begin to line up with research. At one point I shared the following excerpt from Delpit's book (1995), *Other People's Children,* with the preservice teachers at King:

> Research suggests that children of color value the social aspects of an environment to a greater extent than do "mainstream" children, and tend to put an emphasis on feelings, acceptance, and emotional closeness. Research has also shown that motivation in African-American children from low socioeconomic groups is more influenced by the need for affiliation than for achievement. (p. 140)[6]

Miss Jen observed this herself: "The kids are very overt about helping and do not want to see anyone left behind. I did not notice this in my other placement." After reading the excerpt, Jennifer was surprised that the research reflected her observation. "Wow! This paper hit right on the spot what I have directly observed but have been unable to put in words." Reading this information opened Jennifer's floodgate of reflections, as her experience was validated. Also note that she now referred to the class as "my class":

> I have noted all along that my class is like a family, very social, and very close. They all know something about one another and obviously have "relations" outside the school in their neighborhoods. Lolita also knows many of the parents, grandparents and other extended family of the students. In many cases, she has had the parents as students. . . . Not only is affiliation with friends and family important, but so is the affiliation that these students have with the Lord. They have "been saved" and have asked me if I have been saved also. There is not the fear/stigma/unacceptableness of talking about

---

[6]The study referred to is one by Holliday (1985).

the Lord in my class. It is a subject of great value and of great identity. I have also noticed the strong affiliation with the "fashion" scene and the music world.

Many times, Jennifer learns another interaction style directly from her mentor. Miss Jen has positive things to say about Lolita on almost every page of her journal: "Lolita—what a special lady. I tear up just thinking about not seeing her each day. She has taught me of the compassion and dedication that a teacher should have—she 'WALKS THE TALK' all the way." Miss Jen sees in Lolita what bell hooks (1994) and others call the other mother of the African-American community: "I see her as a very *strong nurturer* and she knows the kids on many different levels. . . . Lolita takes on this amazing nurturer role . . . she reminds me of my grandmother who is very compassionate, loving, and WISE." Miss Jen comes to see the teacher taking on many roles: "counselor, goal-setter, moral figure, mother, disciplinarian." This too, is supported by research quoted by Delpit (1995):

> [African American] students grant teachers a wide latitude of emotions in which to make their expectations and dissatisfactions known. Assertive, aggressive and even angry behavior are all rated acceptable means of communicating one's intentions as long as these emotions are perceived as genuine. If expressions of emotion are too subtle, however, students are likely to misread a teacher's intentions and become disoriented. Responses lacking a sufficient emotional quality are likely to [be] read as non-caring. Totally unacceptable, however, is non-responsiveness. Students expect a response, and failing to get one will generally interpret this behavior as non-concern. From students' perspective the non-responsive teacher demonstrates not only lack of control, but a non-caring attitude as well.   (p. 141–2)[7]

Miss Jen sees this played out in Mrs. Darby's classroom:

> She lets them know when she is happy with them, but she has no hesitations to reveal to them when she is upset. . . . Lolita is brutally honest with the children, which I admire, yet this honesty could be perceived as harsh and very authoritarian. This honesty may not fly in a different setting and with a different culture. However, they know that she cares and respect and *love* her even when she is yelling at them or openly saying that she is mad and disappointed at them. She will raise her voice just as quick and she will soften it and soothe and nurture the children. Control and respect are very important in this environment. She knows that all of her students are very capable and she wants to see all of them succeed in school and in the game of life. I do believe that if Lolita was too soft and non-responsive with the students, they would view it as "non-caring." Pretty crazy! Cultural differences are definitely shining through and this research is very interesting to me. It definitely changes the way I will plan my lessons and how my expectations will have to be stated very *clearly* and followed-up on. By no means could I ever manage the class the way Lolita does, but I have to remember to be strong and firm and to not back down. I tend to be "too nice" sometimes. I am a little nervous about this.

In her earlier journals, Jennifer writes pages labeled "Friendly Teaching Advice from Lolita":

- Do as many hands-on activities as possible with students—only use textbooks as a reference.

---

[7]Research by Foster (1987).

- Be HONEST with the children—do not be afraid to open up from the inside and share yourself with them.
- Be there to *listen*.

Later on, Jennifer internalized these perspectives. Her reflections led to a clear connection between theory and practice that she has made during her journey as she lists specific changes she will make in her work sample lesson plans. I can incorporate this in my work sample by

1. Really mapping out my expectations—put in terms they will understand
2. Think through classroom management
3. *GROUP WORK*
4. Relate lessons to their interest and real-life situations.

An analysis of the achievement of her students as measured on a pre- and postassessment showed that Jennifer succeeded in teaching her subject matter well and effectively. She also engaged the class at a level that matched her mentor teacher in an analysis of time on task for the class.

Jennifer's experience allowed her to pass on a torch, from mentor, to intern, to student. She reported the following exchange with obvious emotion:

> I had one student who stayed after school just to be with me, which was very special to me. She really does not talk much, but when she does, you know she means it. She told me, "I am really going to miss you Miss Jen. Can we keep in touch?" Of course I want to keep in touch with the students. She walked me out to my car and a little girl said, "Hi, Nyesha." She turned to me and said, "I don't even know that little girl." That is when I explained to her that she is a fifth grader and younger kids look up to her at all times. She needs to be a good example for them. She said, "Do you think she looks up to me like I look up to you Miss Jen?" This was one of those moments when I felt needed and it just reinforced my desire to be a teacher. Just knowing that I influenced one young person made the experience even more important!

Jennifer had fulfilled her wish to connect to one student.

Not only did Jennifer find practical applications for her new understanding as well as strong support for her role as a teacher, I believe she developed a deeper understanding of diversity and its role in her life and the lives of those around her. After her return to the Corvallis area, she wrote:

> I miss the diversity, energy, spirit, and overall feeling of MLK. My mom felt it right when she walked in the doors on Friday and she said, "I can understand why you don't want to leave." She said that she did not know what she was expecting but it was nothing compared to actually experiencing what I had been trying to explain to her for three weeks. She said it was one of the neatest places that she has ever visited. I was so glad that she was able to come. Unless you have been there, it is hard to describe to an outsider.

When Jennifer returned to her placement near Corvallis and Oregon State University, she compared her time in Portland with her primary placement:

> My students did not seem very excited to see me. I felt kind of like a stranger, a person that they will need to get to know again. The kids were so quiet and subdued. . . . I

started to cry. . . . It is going to be a hard adjustment for me. . . . I feel like I am a new person. I have learned that I value, respect, and need *diversity*. (Emphasis in original)

Not only did Jennifer experience a transformation in her understanding of cultural differences, she ended her long journal with a telling statement that may speak to the deeper and longer lasting effect of this placement. She said, "I think my kids [in this town] need exposure to this also." I believe Jennifer was changed by her experience and has a new view of the choices ahead. I trust she will often take the road that leads to social justice. Only time will tell how Jennifer will fare in maintaining and sharing her new perspective.

THE NEXT FEW YEARS

I remember the first week back on campus, longing for the warmth and vitality of that particular school. I missed my new colleagues, as well as the children. I, too, had left part of my heart at King School. Meetings seemed particularly irrelevant. I longed to go back. I know that the experience changed me, making me more passionate about arranging such experiences for more of our preservice teachers.

Within a week of our return, I learned that this project had not been funded for the next year. There is an increasing risk to myself, professionally and personally, if this work must continue without additional institutional support for my time. My dilemma is to balance my time-consuming position assignments and my passion to continue this kind of work. Yet, I feel I have no choice. I am compelled to try.

The original writing of this chapter caused me to review the journals of my students. In her last journal entry, Jennifer had written, "Thank you, Jean, for having this vision and making it happen. It will have to continue." As I reread that entry I picked up the phone to make the first of many calls in an effort to keep this option open for our students. Two years after the first placement, we finally received funding to take all 55 of our preservice teachers for an immersion experience in highly diverse school settings; most went to King School.

During that placement, one of our mentor teachers, who was a former student of mine and also a friend of Jennifer's, read this chapter as an extension of her partnership with our interns. She wrote:

> In being a part of this partnership I have witnessed social change. I think that Jen's experience is a perfect example. I think that White teachers go into a school of children of color and think that everything will be the same as their experience in school. I have found this not to be the case. I think that Jen and I both experienced this. When you go into the school there is definitely a different atmosphere. Jen experienced a change in her attitudes and beliefs through this experience. I know that she has taken her experience and used it in her own classroom. I think the social change is the change in attitude you experience through working with the children at King School. I know my thoughts have been challenged by working at King School; it has brought about a change in my way of thinking and how I treat all students. I know this is the same for Jen. . . . I don't think anyone can leave King and not have their attitudes changed.

ONWARD

What place does this chapter have in this project? Writing it has helped me to articulate my passion. Knowing that you may learn and grow energizes me to continue. Senge (1990) said, "The discipline of team learning starts with 'dialogue,' the capacity of members of a team to suspend assumptions and enter into a genuine 'thinking together.' To the Greeks, *dia-logos* meant a free-flowing of meaning through a group, allowing the group to discover insights not attainable individually" (p. 10).

For us, both you and me, to continue to work for transformation, my end of the dialogue must engage you. Ellis (1998) wrote, "A story's 'validity' can be judged by whether it evokes in readers a feeling that the experience described is authentic and lifelike, believable and possible; the story's generalizability can be judged by whether it speaks to readers about their experience" (p. 29). If you have become engaged and reflective on reading my journey, may we in some ways continue this transformative journey together:

> The travelers stopped to rest. They looked back the way they had come. The path seemed longer and more difficult than they had remembered . . . Now that they had the vantage point of the ridge, they saw that what they perceived as a summit had only been the beginning of the foothills. They continued.   (Moule, 1998, p. 169)

REFERENCES

Barry, N. H., & Lechner, J. V. (1995). Preservice teachers' attitudes about and awareness of multicultural teaching and learning. *Teaching and Teacher Education, 11*(2), 149–161.

Blair, T. R., & Jones, D. L. (1998). *Preparing for student teaching in a pluralistic classroom.* Boston: Allyn & Bacon.

Burbules, N. C. (1993). *Dialogue in teaching: Theory and practice.* New York: Teachers College Press.

Cohen, L. M. (1991/1992). A gifted education for all children. *Our Gifted Children, 6,* 22–30.

Collins, P. H. (1990). *Black feminist thought: Knowledge, consciousness, and the politics of empowerment.* Boston: Unwin Hyman.

Cross, W. E. (1995). The psychology of Nigrescence: Revising the Cross model. In J. G. Ponterotto, J. M. Casas, L. A. Suzuki, & C. M. Alexander (Eds.), *Handbook of multicultural counseling* (pp. 93–122). Thousand Oaks, CA: Sage.

Delpit, L. (1995). *Other people's children: Cultural conflict in the classroom.* New York: New Press.

Dreikurs, R. (1968). *Psychology in the classroom* (2nd ed.). New York: Harper & Row.

Ellis, C. (1997). Evocative autoethnography: Writing emotionally about our lives. In W. Tierney & Y. Lincoln (Eds.), *Representation and the text: Reframing the narrative voice.* New York: State University of New York Press. pp. 116–139.

Ellsworth, E. (1990). Why doesn't this feel empowering? Working through the repressive myths of critical pedagogy. *Harvard Educational Review, 59,* 297–324.

Foster, M. (1987). *"It's cookin' now": An ethnographic study of the teaching style of a successful black teacher in a white community college.* Unpublished doctoral dissertation, Harvard University.

Foster, M. (1993). Self-portraits of black teachers: Narratives of individual and collective struggle against racism. In D. McLaughlin & W. G. Tierney (Eds.), *Naming silenced lives: Personal narratives and processes of educational change* (pp. 155–175). New York: Routledge.

Gardner, H. (1999). *The disciplined mind: What all students should understand.* New York: Simon & Schuster.

Gonsalves-Pinto, L. (1997). Voices from the trenches: Students' insights regarding multicultural teaching/learning. *Multicultural Education, 5*(1), 44–48.

Helms, J. E. (Ed.). (1990). *Black and white racial identity: Theory, research, and practice* (Vol. 129). New York: Greenwood.

Hinchey, P. H. (1994). Introducing diversity: We don't have to wait for a program. *Action in Teacher Education, 16*(3), 28–36.

Holliday, B. (1985). Toward a model of teacher–child transactional processes affecting black children's academic achievement. In M. B. Spencer, G. K. Brookins, & W. R. Allen (Eds.), *Beginnings: The social and affective development of Black children* (pp. 117–130). Hillsdale, NJ: Erlbaum.

Holt-Reynolds, D. (1992). Personal history-based beliefs as relevant prior knowledge in course work. *American Educational Research Journal, 29,* 325–349.

hooks, b. (1994). *Teaching to transgress: Education as the practice of freedom.* New York: Routledge.

Kidder, R. M., & Born, P. L. (1998/1999). Resolving ethical dilemmas in the classroom. *Educational Leadership, 56*(4), 38–41.

Kochman, T. (1981). *Black and white styles in conflict.* Chicago: University of Chicago Press.

Loewen, J. W. (1995). *Lies my teacher told me: Everything your American history textbook got wrong.* New York: New Press.

McLaughlin, D., & Tierney, W. G. (1993). *Naming silenced lives: Personal narratives and processes of educational change.* New York: Routledge.

Michaels, S. (1981). "Sharing time": Children's narrative styles and differential access to literacy. *Language in Society, 10,* 423–442.

Morris, W. (Ed.). *American heritage dictionary* (2nd ed.). Boston: Houghton Mifflin.

Moule, J. (1991). Consultant teacher model: A means of providing inservice to regular classroom teachers. *A Different Drummer, 7*(4), 9, 14.

Moule, J. (1997). *Multicultural education: A survey of preservice teachers.* Unpublished manuscript, Oregon State University.

Moule, J. (1998). *My journey with preservice teachers: Reflecting on teacher characteristics that bridge multicultural education theory and classroom practice.* Unpublished doctoral dissertation, Oregon State University.

Nieto, S. (1994). Affirmation, solidarity, and critique: Moving beyond tolerance in multicultural education. *Multicultural Education, 1,* 9–12, 35–38.

Noddings, N. (1997). Accident, awareness, and actualization. In A. Neumann & P. L. Peterson (Eds.), *Learning from our lives: Women, research, and autobiography in education* (pp. 166–182). New York: Teachers College Press.

Oregon Department of Education. (1998). *1997–1998 Summary of organization, students and staff in Oregon public schools* (Report No. SF98-07). Salem, OR: Author.

Reed, D. F. (1993). Multicultural education for preservice students. *Action in Teacher Education, 15*(3), 27–34.

Reinharz, S., & Davidman, L. (1992). *Feminist methods in social research.* New York: Oxford University Press.

Schank, R. C. (1990). *Tell me a story: A new look at real and artificial memory.* New York: Scribner's.

Senge, P. M. (1990). *The fifth discipline: The art and practice of the learning organization.* New York: Doubleday.

U.S. Department of Education, Office of Education Research and Improvement, Center for Educational Statistics. (1992). *Digest of education statistics, 1991.* Washington, DC: Author.

Reflective Writings[8]

Open-ended

The most powerful reflections often come from strong stimuli followed by a set-aside time to write. An open-ended format may work well because the writer is not constrained by form.

Open-ended writing activity: Simply start writing whatever comes to your mind after reading the stories in this chapter. A facilitator may want to collect the unsigned pieces, read the writings, and, in the next session, simply share anony-

---

[8]Ken Winograd, language arts methods teacher at Oregon State University, helped design these questions.

mously any particularly telling selections or common themes. Participants seem to like the anonymity, yet share the experience of learning from each other.

Sentence Completion

On the other end of the continuum, reflective writing can be prompted by very specific starter statements, such as, "The ideas and reflections in this chapter (choose one: concern, excite, confuse, confound, encourage) me because _____."

Reflective Questions
General

What do the ideas and reflections in this chapter remind you of (person, movie, book, personal experience, etc.)?

Personal History

To fully understand who we are as teachers, we have to understand our own histories. Think about your life and an experience you have had with someone who is different than you by the color of their skin or culture. What made this person different from you? Does this person look different, talk differently, dress differently? Was this person more or less advantaged economically? How did these differences make you feel? Were you able to develop a meaningful relationship and friendship? If yes, what facilitated that?

How does your life experience with people who are different than yourself help your work as a teacher of students who are different than you?

In the event that you have had very few experiences with someone different than yourself, what are the implications in that for you as a teacher? What concerns might you have about your capacity to work with students of color, for example?

Racial Identity Development

Where are you in terms of your racial identity development? Explain how you see yourself in terms of the four levels of "I'm okay; you're okay" (preencounter); "Something is not okay" (encounter); "I'm okay; I'm not so sure about you" (anger, denial, etc.); "I'm okay; you're okay" (autonomy).

Are you comfortable where you are currently on the continuum? Where would you like to be on the continuum? Would you like to change or develop further? What can you do to facilitate your development?

Reflective Activities
Racial Identity Development Activity

Use a series of cartoons with racial themes or ones that mirror the stages in some manner. After learning the four "okay" forms of racial identity development, students in pairs or groups of three discuss one of the cartoons, taking turns putting it on an overhead and telling their idea of the racial identity level it represents. This activity allows participants to work at racial identity development one step away from themselves. This work can be personally difficult and threatening, but the distance and humor of the cartoons makes it easier.

Activities for the Classroom

Multicultural, Multi-intelligent—Finding the Gifts in Each

This activity is a great "ice breaker" and may be connected to self-studies on learning styles, a lesson on multiple intelligences, diversity among ethnic groups, and/or general appreciation of others. It helps to "level the playing field" for it recognizes the value in multiple intelligences (Gardner, 1999).

Verbal/linguistic intelligence is the form of intelligence that dominates most Western educational systems. Focus on the other intelligences may help bring us closer to valuing ways of knowing valued by other cultures.

Age group: For third grade and up; may be adapted for lower grades.

Objective: To help each one in the learning community know the unique gifts and abilities of others.

Materials: A self-ranking sheet for each person, large numbers, 1 to 5, placed around room.

Procedure: Each person, including the teacher, selects her own ability in each area. As items are read, people stand by the numbers placed around the room that correspond to their self-ranking.

Hints: You may want to say something like "Be honest about where you go to stand. Sometimes you will stand with a group and sometimes alone. If you are with a group and see someone standing alone, what are some important things to consider about what you say and do to the person standing alone?"

Cautions: Teachers are cautioned to watch for students who do not rank themselves high on any item. This can be partially solved by asking a student what he or she does well. Add that category verbally to the list, and the class members rank themselves on that ability. Another strategy is to move quickly to the next item if a child seems isolated at number one on an item.

Extensions: I have used a simpler form of this ranking for many years and have seen it adapted by teachers for different grade levels and subject areas. For instance, a kindergarten teacher drew pictures of the different abilities. A music teacher added categories like "recognizing a friend's voice on the phone" and "finger snapping." Some teachers became more creative and sensitive to their students and changed the rankings from numbers to three categories. "This is hard for me," "I'm okay at this," and "I'm very good at this," is one example. Another teacher used "Not yet," "So-so," and "Right on." Yet another used "I'm still learning" for the low category.

SELF RANKING IN THE EIGHT INTELLIGENCES

Circle the number that indicates your rating of your ability and/or interest.

	Low				High
Visual/Spatial					
Drawing	1	2	3	4	5
Using maps	1	2	3	4	5
Learns best by observing	1	2	3	4	5
Putting together puzzles	1	2	3	4	5
Bodily/Kinesthetic					
Enjoys physical activity	1	2	3	4	5
Use hands to explain	1	2	3	4	5
Making things by hand	1	2	3	4	5
Learns best by touching	1	2	3	4	5
Musical/Rhythmic					
Dancing	1	2	3	4	5
Singing	1	2	3	4	5
Recognizing voices	1	2	3	4	5
Listening to music	1	2	3	4	5
Verbal/Linguistic					
Speaking two languages	1	2	3	4	5
Writing/writing stories	1	2	3	4	5
Telling stories/speaking	1	2	3	4	5
Reading books	1	2	3	4	5
Logical/Mathematical					
Math	1	2	3	4	5
Asking questions	1	2	3	4	5
Playing checkers or chess	1	2	3	4	5
Giving/following directions	1	2	3	4	5
Interpersonal					
Making new friends	1	2	3	4	5
Working well in groups	1	2	3	4	5
Serving others	1	2	3	4	5
Spending time with family	1	2	3	4	5
Intrapersonal					
Valuing silence	1	2	3	4	5
Keeping a journal	1	2	3	4	5
Know own cultural identity	1	2	3	4	5
Reflecting on new ideas	1	2	3	4	5
Naturalist					
Connecting to nature	1	2	3	4	5
Observe plant behavior	1	2	3	4	5
Caring for pets	1	2	3	4	5
Prefers outdoors to indoors	1	2	3	4	5

Common Values for the Common Good

During the process of learning about and exploring differences, students of all ages may begin to experience chasms between themselves and others, particularly as they move through stages of racial identity development or confront material that brings up intense discussions and surprising reactions. I have used the following strategy to bring some measure of unity while at the same time emphasizing that it is okay to disagree.

I indicate the chalk and the erasers at the blackboard and propose that we work on a list of common values. Anyone may write anything, and anyone may erase anything without comment or reason. Once the chalk dust has stopped flying and the list has remained static for a minute or so, I then ask the students to reflect on how they will model these values among themselves.

This exercise produces a change in climate, even for those whose pet values are erased, as the list of common values is fairly standard for each group of students; this is supported by the work of Kidder and Born (1998/1999). The students then leave the session with a sense of unity. Whatever students' persuasion in multicultural matters, most have, or should develop, personal belief systems that help build democratic principles. Out of these principles come common values, such as honesty, integrity, justice, and compassion.

Age Group: Third grade and up; may be adapted for lower grades by having the teacher write the values on the board. Younger ones may still erase if carefully monitored.

Objective: To help each one in the learning community to know and appreciate their shared values, particularly after a time of difficult reflection.

Materials: Chalk and blackboard, or marker and whiteboard, and eraser.

Procedure: Students are invited to add or erase anything without comment. Teacher ensures respectful, nonjudgmental atmosphere.

FURTHER READING

Tatum, B. D. (1997). "Why are all the black kids sitting together in the cafeteria?": And other conversations about race. New York: Basic Books.

WEB SITES

Web Sites Immersion Project

http://www.osu.orst.edu/dept/soe/programs/license/immersion.html

The Eisenhower Professional Development Grant that supported the immersion experience for Jen and others requires dissemination of information from the recipients. This chapter is one way results from this project have been shared; this Web site is another.

The Implicit Association Test

http:// www.tolerance.org/hidden_bias/index.html

Equality is a birthright in the United States, protected by the Constitution, supported by civil rights laws, and embraced by citizens. Yet not a day passes without reports of unequal treatment of individuals. This discrimination is based on negative stereotypes and prejudice that, according to social psychologists, linger in most of us. Even if we believe in our hearts that we see and treat people as equals, hidden biases may nevertheless influence our actions. A new suite of psychological tests measures unconscious bias. We invite you to take these tests online and reveal to yourself what may be hidden in your psyche. Each test takes about 5 minutes. (This information is from the Web site.)

Parent Teacher Scenario

http://osu.orst.edu/instruct/ed419/anim/index.html

This interactive Web site consists of 24 panels of a teacher and a parent learning to communicate across cultural lines. In each panel you read what they are saying, and as you roll the mouse over their heads, you can see what they are thinking. This scenario was produced at Oregon State University to accompany two of Jean's Web courses. You will need to download Shockwave in order to view this scenario.

Racial and Cultural Harmony in the K–12 Classroom Web Course

To create an account:

1. Go to http://my.oregonstate.edu.
2. Log-in.
3. Preview as guest.
4. Go to course folder.
5. Find education.
6. Scroll to bottom of the education course list and link to pages until you get to ED599 ST/RAC and Cultural Harmony in the K–12 classroom.
7. Click preview button. You may view everything on the course except the discussion board.

This Oregon State University Web course provides an overview of the issues particular to an increasingly racially diverse student population in public schools today. Implications concerning curriculum design, teaching strategies, and parent–teacher–student interactions are considered. The course may be visited anytime and is available for two or three undergraduate or graduate credits each summer. Jean Moule is the course instructor.

http://www.osu.orst.edu/dept/soe/programs/license/immersion.html
http:// www.tolerance.org/hidden_bias/index.html
http://osu.orst.edu/instruct/ed419/anim/index.html

Chapter 10

Immersion and Rebellion: Growing Up and Out of South Carolina

Robin Hasslen, St. Cloud State University, St. Cloud

Focus Questions

1. As we begin to "lose" some aspects of our more ethnocentric natures, what might take their place?

2. Can you recognize yourself at any of the stages of racial identity development and recall any particular experiences which might have guided your journey?

3. What are some ways to assist others (either very young children or college–age individuals) in understanding issues of privilege, equity, and oppression?

EARLY IMPRESSIONS AND LATER IMPLICATIONS

It was a hot day in Columbia, South Carolina, in July of 1964 when two young Black men entered Drake's Restaurant during the noontime rush. A sudden hush fell over the normally bustling atmosphere. It was the summer of my freshman year in college, and I had been hired as a waitress at Drake's. The civil rights legislation had just been enacted, and we at the restaurant had been forewarned about this possibility and the repercussions which would befall us should we serve any of "them." Following my initial surprise at the boldness of these men, I picked up menus and waited on them.

Taking a stand cost me not only a job, but a relationship with a White male who was irate over my actions. As I reflect on that incident over 30 years later, I am able to put it in its proper perspective. It was far from an earth-shattering event, but for me it was the beginning of my journey on the path toward a more just society. At that time in my life, I thought that journey would just be a matter of taking similar stands. Little did I know that my own transformation was far from over.

A product of southern culture, I was raised in segregated schools and had my room cleaned by Black "maids." My education and my peers were blatantly racist. However, in the midst of such an environment stood my mother, a powerful proponent of justice and a woman who acted on her beliefs. She had worked in tenement houses, walked picket lines, and sat at lunch counters alongside Blacks. She picked up strangers on street corners and brought them home, organized the first League of Women Voters in South Carolina and then integrated it. She was not there to urge me on that day at Drake's, but her teaching by example had been strongly instilled in me.

REBELLION

The journey along the path from racist to antiracist has been described as a series of phases that define an individual's transformation. Janet Helms (1990) has outlined some important characteristics which define one's racial identity development through a model of five stages: contact, disintegration, reintegration, pseudo-independence, and autonomy. For Whites, the model assumes a route from the abandonment of the individual's racist identity to the opposition of cultural and institutional racism. While my development follows that outline, I have at times chosen different descriptors. Rebellion became the focus of the initial steps in my journey. Rejection of all that had been part of my experience was undertaken. I joined Students for a Democratic Society in college and demonstrated in Washington and New York. I spent weekends in Philadelphia working with the Quakers. Needing to experience others' existences, I labored several days in the fields of southern New Jersey alongside migrant workers and upon graduation moved into a house I constructed out of a pigpen in eastern Kentucky. I set out to save the world from poverty and injustice. I wrote letters to my mother questioning "man's inhumanity to man" as I looked out over the Kentucky strip mines and read about the Vietnam War. I criticized my mother's acceptance of her wealth and her employment of African American "maids." I met and married a conscientious objector, and as we spoke out against war and racism and welfare, we were exiled from the community.

Another loss? At the time it was devastating to have been forsaken by all of the mountain people we had befriended. In hindsight, it was but another painful part of a greater transformation. We were aliens in a culture unwilling to accept our "good intentions." We fled to Minnesota and rented rooms from a Black couple and began our life as the only Whites in an urban, African American community. Again, I believed our intentions were "noble"; we would show that integration worked because we moved into "their" neighborhood! In the late 1960s, Black power did not include wanna-be Whites. Disillusionment continued to mount for me as I became the target of angry Blacks.

The one satisfaction for me at this time in my life, as it had been during my Kentucky experience, was acquired from my role as teacher. While I became more and more discouraged about changing attitudes of adults, I became increasingly convinced that working with very young children was hopeful. However, in the Kentucky holler as well as in the St. Paul inner city, I was attempting to provide the preschoolers in my care with the curriculum content and pedagogy I deemed appropriate, undeterred by their cultural experiences or needs. After all, I believed in standards driven by my own experiences and my "innate" ability to interact with young children.

REMOVAL

Removal from the political arena followed rebellion on my journey. We joined the "back to the land" movement, bought some land and a one-room tarpaper shack and spent the next few years in isolation, licking our wounds and believing that "they" could fight their own battles. Reflection on those years brings forth feelings of contentment as well as a growing awareness of the privilege we had as Whites to step away from the issues of equity and justice that need not involve us. During those years I directed Head Start programs in several rural counties. Again, I was driven by the need to bring about change, this time in families about whose cultures and lifestyles I knew very little.

REENTRY

Reentry was a long and tortuous process. I furthered my education with master's and doctoral degrees and began teaching in a midwestern university at the same time that the concept of cultural diversity became the focus across the country. Thinking that my past experiences would enable me to help spread the word, I jumped into the "workshops on diversity" circuit. During the course of a month and a half one Fall in the early 1990s, I facilitated five workshops on racism for early childhood professionals.

In the midst of my passion for enlightening others about issues of race, I was unaware of the image I was portraying. It took a colleague's confronting me with perceptions of my peers to begin some serious self-analysis. It seems I had "changed": I had become more serious, more obsessed with racism and my agenda with my students, more cloistered with students and faculty of color and apart from my White colleagues, and less rested and healthy looking. Most of my colleagues' perceptions were realities. From mid-July through the end of October that year I never slept through a night, lost 20 pounds, and directed my energies into my work.

How could I maintain my passion for this work and still operate without cynicism and judgment of others with less "commitment" to an antiracist agenda? Were my experiences and knowledge base about oppression sufficient for the work I was doing? Unfortunately, I was far from where I needed to be in my own transformation from savior to ally. Fortunately, I was speaking most often to Whites about our role in the system. After all, that was *my* vantage point. Feeling that I now was neither accepted by Whites nor people of color, I determined that it was time to step back and do more self-reflection and self-education. I joined an inner-city group of women from diverse backgrounds who were involved in culturally sensitive early childhood education and antiracism.

REEDUCATION

For the next 5 years, my reeducation was full of a growing realization that my understanding of the issues of oppression was grounded more in my passion for equity than in my grasp of the scope of the reality of racism for people of color. While I was not raised to be "color-blind," as is the case for many well-meaning Whites in this country, I *did* believe that we humans just need to interact with basic civility and respect (Banks, 1991). Several painfully humbling, critical incidents within the group of women of color occurred during these times.

At our initial gathering, we 20 or so women shared our life stories. I, of course, related all the wonderful antiracist attempts I had made toward unity, peace, and other causes. The group listened patiently and only years later shared with me how patronizing I had been. When we broke up to eat, the women of color segregated themselves. Being the great equalizer, forever insisting on integration, I took my plate over and asked why they didn't join *us*? They smiled and replied that perhaps I needed to learn how to join *them*! Another non–earth shattering insignificant incident, it was a giant step for me on my journey.

A second incident occurred when I attended a women's writing group in California for a weekend of working and writing together about diversity. By this point in my journey I had become somewhat more humble and slightly more enlightened about the bigger picture of oppression; however, I was still laboring under the impression that the simple answer is respect. During the course of the weekend I interacted with an Asian woman and thought we had become friends. Before I left, she approached me and said she felt the need to tell me that I had offended her. I was flabbergasted! I asked her to recount the incidents—which she did explicitly. One example was that I had commented on how I appreciated her infectious giggle. She perceived that as a stereotypical remark about an ethnic trait. On another occasion, sitting together in a large group for an extended period of time, I put my foot under hers (which didn't reach the floor) and said I would give her a rest. Again my action was perceived to be a statement about her stature.

REFLECTION

As I reflect on all of these incidents, I am aware of their seeming insignificance to others, but for me they were life changing. Certainly, we are all members of the human race (as our "color-blind" parents often remind us), but we are different in numerous ways, and those differences need to be understood and respected. The soul-searching I did following the writing workshop was deep and long lasting. It would not have been appropriate for me to have responded to the Asian woman that I was sorry about my insensitivity. I needed to apologize and say that I appreciated her willingness to inform me of my lack of awareness and that I had learned from her confronting me. It is at times like this that I am reminded of Naomi Wolf's (1995) description of WMWP (well-meaning White people), and I dig deep into myself to attempt to honestly evaluate my racism and its cover-up.

It would be wonderful to say that such occurrences took me all the way to the end of my journey. Unfortunately, the road just continued to stretch on around more bends. After designing and teaching a multicultural education course for five or so years at the university and feeling that it had a powerful impact on students, I learned that a colleague of color in another department had criticized the course. My self-doubts about my ability to facilitate discussions about racism skyrocketed. My immediate reaction was to retreat again. I would not submit myself to such a damaging critique. I would no longer teach that course. After all, what *did* I know? What was my formal training in issues of oppression? Was it even legitimate for me as a White woman to discuss such topics as racism and oppression?

To add to my confusion about my role as a white teacher of multicultural education, I was shortly thereafter forced to swallow more pride. Several racial incidents and hate crimes occurred on campus. My students discussed them daily, often foregoing any preplanned content discourse. The White students desperately wanted to demonstrate support for the people of color who had been targeted in the incidents. A colleague of color and I thought perhaps the wearing of a button would symbolize unity against racism. After much discussion about that in class, it was decided that we distribute black and white buttons which read, "We Are All in This Together." The discussions leading up to that decision were eye-opening for the White students in the class. Rather than just distributing the buttons, students thought that perhaps students of color could possess them and White students would have to ask for them. A Black student responded that obviously not all students of color wanted to be bothered with that. In response, a White woman suggested that the students of color who carried the buttons should wear one, so White students would know whom it was safe to approach. Obviously, that brought forth an angry response from the Black student, who said, "Do you think that when we enter any classroom or dorm on this campus, we have any way of knowing which Whites will accept or reject us?!"

The outcome of the buttons was a powerful leg on my journey. They were not carried by students of color, but rather had to be acquired at deans' offices. They were apparent all over campus, but they were not wholeheartedly accepted. Many students and faculty of color felt the buttons were a cop-out, another way for Whites to superficially and cowardly stand quietly by the sidelines. While I could understand their perspective, I could also understand how large a step that was for White students who had never before in any way taken a stand against racism. Again I retreated. Nothing works. Why can't solutions be simple and actions accepted in good faith? Obviously, I was taking the response to the buttons very personally. Was I still stuck in my ethnocentric state and unable to see or accept others' opinions and attitudes and life experiences out of which those grew? The end of the road was farther away than ever before.

REDEFINING MY ROLE AS A WHITE TEACHER

Fortunately, or at least if we allow it, our personal lives and professional competencies are intertwined. It is in hindsight that I apologize to students who are products of my early years of teaching. Hopefully, learning was a result of their experience, but it was no doubt somewhat painful. The year, 1988, marked the beginning of the requirements of 12 quarter credits of multicultural, minority, and gender studies (MGM) for graduation from our midwestern state university. The objective of the MGM requirement was to "promote respect for human dignity and differences by methods that employ and strengthen the cognitive and critical powers of students by an impartial and critical examination of facts, interpretation of fact, and arguments" (General Education Review Committee, 1987, p. 23).

I enthusiastically welcomed the MGM requirement, and within the Department of Child and Family Studies designed the course, Children in a Changing World. The course syllabus outlined such objectives as: (1) to analyze the impact of societal change on childhood; (2) to learn about family structures, parenting styles, and childhood experience across cultures; and (3) to develop an understanding of various theoretical perspectives on child development. However, the unwritten objectives included the philosophy upon which the class was designed: the challenging of ideas, the exploration of alternative standards and norms, the development of individuals who accept the lifelong task of responsible citizenship, the dispelling of myths, and the empowering of students.

Despite the fact that the course gained a positive reputation among students, it was clear to me that not everyone was experiencing growth. As I experimented with pedagogy and content, I felt the need to ascertain the most effective methods and tools for attaining the desired course outcomes. It became more apparent to me that students were unable to identify with other cultures based on their very limited exposure to diversity. I realized that many students were entering the class with very little understanding of cultures other than their own, a scanty knowledge of either the history or the current state of people of color in this country, and no sense of responsibility for racism or for affecting its change.

The obstacles to the fulfillment of the course's goals are numerous. Resistance from students is constant as they battle previous learning with a growing understanding of oppression, which results in a certain amount of cognitive dissonance for many. Teaching in a traditional discipline from a perspective of critical pedagogy means that I often encounter students who say, "I thought this was supposed to be about children, not racism" (hooks, 1994). I find myself often having to explain the course philosophy, intent, and strategies. An effective method is often to "beat students to the punch" by relating stories of past student experiences so that current students are aware of my expectations. For example, early on in the history of the class I was confronted by a few students complaining that I was "White-bashing" because I talked about racism and would not let them research European cultures. I now share that perspective at the outset of each term, point out my skin color, and encourage them to call me on incidents of "White-bashing" when it is perceived. Part of my transformation has been to accept that perception by students, and out of that has grown my recognition of the power of the developmental approach of the class, which prepares students for discussions of racism in a more objective, less defensive manner.

Students have been some of my best teachers. The university undertook an off-campus teachers of color alternative licensure program in which I agreed, with a great deal of trepidation, to teach. It was one thing to be a White instructor in a classroom with a few students of color of traditional age. It was quite another to undertake "teaching" a class of all nontraditional students of color with years of experiences of oppression. I prepared by reading more and more about children and families of color (to "augment" my White-based course content). I tried to adapt curricular requirements to the different times and resources accessible to the inner-city students, most of whom had families and full-time jobs.

To say that such an undertaking took me around a bend in my journey would be an understatement. I began with my normal routine of somehow letting them know that I was an antiracist racist (i.e., I had to admit my racist position as a privileged White, but I felt I needed to expound on my efforts to confront racism in myself and others). In reflection, I can only imagine the depth of patience with which they heard me out. However, I was the "teacher," and as such was accorded respect. About 3 weeks into the term, I circled the students up and asked for feedback about the course. After their initial hesitation, and their unwillingness to believe there was safety in opening up to me, they began to provide me with insights, at times painful, about everything from course content to expectations. I felt caught in the balance between high expectations, which would assume their competencies, and appropriate requirements based on their busy lives. I facilitated between thinking I needed to identify with them (could I be more African, more Hmong, more Latino?) and accepting that I was indeed an outsider, a White teacher, in their midst. I offered the theory and they, the practice. We shared and exclaimed about unknowns. We researched and examined and applied what we had learned.

Did my students of color learn as much as I? I doubt it. And how would I translate that into classrooms on campus? While there were periods of discomfort and no class was without its anticipatory anxiety on my part, there were great rewards. Never before had I been "Amened" in class. Never before had I been cross-examined nor as equally affirmed. Never had I been among such eager learners with such depths of insight, not only about themselves and society, but about me. I have never expected White students to respond in class with the same intensity. I was never able to experience again similar extremes of classroom dynamics, but I have been able to carry away from those teachers of color a lasting impression of their passion to learn and their lessons about being a teacher.

White students have played their part in my journey as well. Because I have never perceived myself as an intellectual, as one who has hoarded a great wealth of information which can be doled out in consumable amounts to students who obviously know less, I have not had difficulty experiencing us all together as learners within the same classroom. It has become obvious to me, however, that teaching and learning about diversity and oppression have demanded both flexibility and humility on my part.

Despite my years of college teaching, I still consider myself as primarily an early childhood educator. I have attempted through various means, and as often as possible, to maintain some connections to classrooms of young children. When I recently overheard a 4-year-old tell his teacher that he could tell a bad person from a good person because the bad person had a "dark face," I was reminded that we still have much work to do. Since my role in that work impacts young children only through their teachers (my students), I strive to use my journey to assist the preservice teachers on theirs. Mine is a deeply emotional, lived journey; therefore it translates meaningfully to students for whom the textbook definition of racism or the video of oppression in a different context might not be as credible or easy to translate into an early childhood classroom.

CONNECTING OUR JOURNEYS: ETHNIC IDENTIFICATION

As I became more aware of students' resistance to new information, it seemed essential to me that they be able to connect the course content with personal relevance to their own lives and involve their affective as well as cognitive responses and understanding. It has been helpful to think about the metaphor offered by Derman-Sparks and Brunson Phillips (1997), of the artichoke which has to be eaten away from the outside to finally arrive at the core. For many students there has been no experience with "artichokes," no realization that they themselves exist within a culture which has surrounded them with particular meanings, values, and behaviors. As

Maxine Greene (1978) has described the need for "conscientization," or the deepening of the attitude of awareness, it is a goal of mine to assist students in their ability to reflect on their own situationality, and their own historical existence in a world of incongruities and inequities. Greene views learning as "liberation." Many of my students need to free themselves of myths, ignorance, and fear embedded in 18 years of miseducation. As a facilitator of this learning, I want to raise these students' awareness levels and assist them in shedding some of their layers of guilt and taking some responsibility for their own and others' education.

An understanding of others seems to call for a rudimentary connection with students' experiences, and thus the recognition of their own ethnicity seemed an appropriate beginning for students in the MGM course. Thus the initial assignment, the writing of their ethnic autobiography, provides students with the opportunity for introspection and analysis of why and how they have become the people they are. Unfortunately, this autobiography assignment often baffles students, some of whom have never considered their ethnicity as part of their identity and rather perceive themselves as "just American."

For students of color, however, the ethnic autobiography provides a vehicle for them to introduce themselves in a validating way. I recall the day I returned the autobiographies to the students, stopping by the desk of a Black male, putting my arm around his shoulder and whispering, "M., that was the most moving life story I've ever read; what a tribute to your grandmother!" M. had been raised by his grandmother in a southern state and had shared in his paper the wisdom she had bestowed upon him. As I continued toward the front of the room, I turned to see M. picking up his book bag, standing, and walking proudly to settle himself at a table in front (used primarily for group work). From that day on, M. never sat among the rest of the students, but proudly perched on his chair in the front facing the class.

Occasionally biracial students, adopted individuals, or students who have chosen to identify themselves as something other than their ethnicity dictates, struggle through this assignment. A female student whose mother was Vietnamese related in her paper that she had moved away from home so that no one would recognize her ethnicity about which she was ashamed. I encouraged her as a research assignment to gather information about the Vietnamese culture. In time, she was able to uncover a culture hidden from her by her American upbringing and to awaken a sense of pride in her ethnicity.

Although many White students struggle initially with this assignment, they soon begin to recognize its purpose, and through discussions with others, also become aware of the nonuniversality of their upbringing. I often share my own story with students, and my early embarrassment over the Armenian customs, smells, and language I experienced at the home of my grandparents, who with my father had escaped Turkish massacres to come to this country in the early 1900s. Unfortunately, because of my father's horrendous memories, his culture was rarely mentioned in our home. Much to my dismay, I was not very knowledgeable about my ethnicity until I, as an adult, began my own study of Armenian culture. That information has affected who I am and how I feel about myself. I explain to students that they also have a history with which to connect. When such connections are made, the idea of universal cultures, beliefs, and values is replaced by a sense of affirmation of identity and feeling of empowerment which often erases a need to devalue others.

CONTINUING THE JOURNEY: REFLECTIONS ON RACIAL IDENTITY

Having gained some sense of their own ethnic identity, students are asked in the middle of the term to write about their racial identity development, their understanding and acceptance of others, based on the theoretical stage theories. As with the ethnic autobiography assignments, students again display some anxiety about this task. However, I continue to be amazed by the honesty in the students' disclosures about where they are in their development. Because they know that they will not be assessed on their particular place on the journey, they are brutally honest. This gives me the opportunity to respond to questions, comment on growth, and to encourage further strides in their study and interactions. It also provides me with necessary information about "where" they are in their journeys and "why" they may be stuck at particular stages of development.

An initial phase of denial is a developmental level with which all students can identify. They take pride in being "color-blind" and in viewing humanity as similar in all ways. Answers to the issues inherent in racism are simply to "get along" and appreciate this democratic society! They describe their initial 18 years of existence in homogeneous environments and their nonprejudicial unbringings as evidenced in the following excerpt:

> The first step, denial, has definitely been a part of my life. You think that if you don't see color, then there is no problem. You can tell yourself that you don't see color as much as you want to, but everyone sees color. It is always in your mind, whether you'll admit it or not. I've also had the thought, "I'm not prejudiced, but. . . ." run through my mind. Maybe you think that because you talk to some people of a different race that you're not prejudiced, or maybe you think that because you have an open mind, you're not prejudiced. But there's always a "but" in the stage of denial, you just don't recognize that it's there until later on in life. That "but" is what makes you prejudiced!

Often, prior to their college experience, students have not dealt with the responses and feelings typical of a resistance stage. Being unaware of racism or unexposed to people of color kept them from having to defend their own race and beliefs. Suddenly they are forced to confront issues, and the resistance is displayed in numerous ways, often without students' conscious awareness that they *are* actually in this stage. Several students shared that:

> I truly didn't understand (in high school) why I was being blamed for something that happened a long time before I was even born. I was being made to feel terrible over something I didn't even do, and I didn't understand why, so I got angry. I began to place blame on people of color. I felt it was their own fault for the things that happen to them. Stereotypes of blacks that were portrayed in school were that blacks were lazy, stupid, violent and horrible. And I believed these stereotypes because I had never met or personally known a black individual before. I had nothing to counteract those stereotypes, so I believed them and pushed the blame on people of color instead.

I think in some ways it is the people of color who drag on the issues and make big deals about them. I would love to understand and get along with everyone, but at times I feel pushed away. I try to initiate conversation or talk about things I don't understand and I feel put down because "You could not possibly understand because you are not of color." It has become very frustrating, and at times I do want to give up because I'm tired of getting bashed or taken incorrectly. But then I think, if everyone "gave up" nothing would get accomplished. I have to be strong and keep trying because it is so important.

During the stage of confusion, often students are able to identify with less guilt because it acknowledges some awareness and willingness to grow and learn. To a certain extent, they can now place blame on the society which neglected to educate them appropriately. Many students seem to reach this stage during their years of college:

> The reason I believe I am in this stage is because I have come to realize my prejudices and sometimes with my white privilege I just want to go about my life and not worry about things. I know in my heart that that is not a good thing. I am confused as to what part I play in all of it. I can't imagine feeling the way I did, but I still feel awkward around those that are not like me. One thing that is particularly exciting for me to witness is my ability to view things from a different perspective. I can now watch the nightly news critically and evaluate it. I am not ready to move on yet because there is still that need to smile at all those that are not like me. When I came to the university I had never seen a young person of color before, and as I walked through campus I was slightly stunned. I think my body would even tense up when I would walk by a person of color. I'm not really sure why this would happen, but I noticed it. That is when I realized "I am not color blind." I don't think I went through the resistance stage yet; I think I went right to the confusion stage.
>
> Confusion hit me my freshman year of college. "Toto, I don't think we're in Elk River anymore!" I started to wonder why I never knew about other cultures. Who did I have to blame? Was it my parents, my church, or my teachers? Yeah, that's it. None of these people ever helped me discover other cultures, right? So I began to try and learn about these issues myself. I have at least figured out that all these other cultures are important. The more I learn the more I start to feel better about things. On the other hand, the more I learn, I sometimes end up more confused or at least question what I had thought before.

There are very few individuals who perceive themselves in any final stage of racial identity development. However, they, like the following student, discuss their aspirations and commitment to work against racism:

> I now know racism is wrong. I know I have power and privilege, yet I don't do anything to stop the problem. I continue to try to ignore it. This class has helped me because I now speak out a little but only among family and friends. This class has been very hard for me because I have had to look inside myself and see what I am truly made of and how I have developed. I know what words to say, but I don't mean them yet, so I don't take the chance by voicing them. It is very scary but I feel I am working on it.

COMMITTING TO CHANGE

As my personal transformation continues, so also does my comfort level with allowing students more control of their learning. "Engaged pedagogy," as proposed by bel hooks (1994), is a philosophy and teaching strategy I attempt to instill in students. They are valued learners, respected for what they bring to the classroom, affirmed for their stories and well-intentioned attempts to broaden their perspectives. My stories are shared as well in my attempt to set an example of my own humanity. Conversations with students continue beyond the classroom as I agree with hooks's belief that our work is not merely to share information, but to share in the intellectual and spiritual growth of our students.

At the end of every term there remain several students who are still culturally encapsulated (Banks, 1994). During the last few minutes of a final class for the semester, a White female announced to the class that, "This is the worst class I have *ever* taken!" I was speechless. As I attempted to practice what I preached to students, and formulate a nondefensive response, I was "saved" by a Black male who eloquently summarized some lessons of the semester. When class ended I raced to my office and locked the door, assuming of course that I had failed with the entire class. Nevertheless, students knocked on the door and entered in twos and threes wanting to talk about what they had learned. Suddenly the outspoken student was asking to speak with me. She explained that she had grown up in a small rural town and attended a parochial school with seven classmates and been told what to think. This was her first semester at college and in it she had been bombarded in three courses with issues of homophobia, abortion, and racism. She said she did not know *what* to think. I told her I appreciated her candor, and it was fine if she wished to have and raise children in that same setting, but that she owed it to herself and her children to first broaden her perspectives.

None of us must ever stop widening the lens from which we view the world. While there are various theories of ethnic identity development and antiracist identity stages to consider, we each have individual paths which unfortunately do not always continue in a forward direction. For example, I may come to a disagreement with a colleague of color in the college and find myself circling back to an earlier stage of defensiveness, only to awaken at some point and realize that I have already been there. Perhaps if I allowed myself to step out intellectually and leave behind my emotions, I would make better progress. However, I remember being told once by a White antiracist that until I can acknowledge the impact of racism on myself (and other Whites) and experience the resulting pain, I still have miles to travel.

It is not out of pride, but anguish, that I have shared my personal journey with you. Moving from savior to ally, from a state of self-confidence to confusion, from a sense of hurt to an awareness of privilege have been constant battles in a growing identity of myself as a White woman. I attempt to balance my pride in my ethnicity, my Armenian history of devastation and Scottish security with my role as a player in a dominant culture of privilege. Today it is terribly risky to write about my partial transformation, because tomorrow I will read it and shake my head at my place on the journey and wonder how I could have been so naive. I cannot yet see the end of the journey, the "light at the end of the tunnel," but I *can* reflect on the past and thereby summon up the courage to continue.

References

Banks, J. A. (1991). *Teaching strategies for ethnic studies* (5th ed.). Boston: Allyn & Bacon.

Banks, J. A. (1994). *An introduction to multicultural education.* Boston: Allyn & Bacon.

Derman-Sparks, L., & Brunson Phillips, C. (1997). *Teaching/learning anti-racism: A developmental approach.* New York & London: Teachers College Press.

Greene, M. (1978). *Landscapes of learning.* New York & London: Teachers College Press.

Helms, J. (Ed.). (1990). *Black and white racial identity: Theory, research, and practice.* New York: Greenwood.

hooks, b. (1994). *Teaching to transgress: Education as the practice of freedom.* New York & London: Routledge.

St. Cloud State University. (1987). *General education review committee.* St. Cloud, MN: Author.

Wolf, N. (1995). The racism of well-meaning white people. *Glamour, 93*(8), 230–234.

Reflective Questions

Ethnic Autobiography Paper

Students explore their ethnic roots: national, linguistic, religious, and so forth. They complete a worksheet to share with a cooperative group of students from similar ethnic backgrounds. They share some of the ways in which their family life was influenced by their ethnic heritage (family composition, roles, discipline, communication patterns, etc.) to answer the question, *Why* are you who you are? How do your interests, opinions, beliefs, self-concept, and aspirations relate to your ethnic identity? The worksheet is turned in, as well as a two-page paper. Students become aware of similarities within and across cultures, as well as differences. They learn to recognize the importance of ethnicity.

Racial Identity Paper

Using a racial identity stage theory model (for whites and students of color) students write about where they are (and why they are there) in their understanding and attitudes about race, as well as to recognize where they have come from and where they can go from here. Students are encouraged to acknowledge both conscious and unconscious behaviors and sources, and not to burden themselves with guilt. Rather, their understanding allows them to move forward in their journey toward greater cultural sensitivity and understanding.

Bias and Antibias Books

Students evaluate children's books for bias and antibias content, using several sources to assist in the determination. Students bring the books to class and share their findings. They are surprised at the subtle ways of displaying oppression and discrimination.

Think About It

Students in groups are asked to "return to their roots" and share such things as: What is your first childhood memory of people different than you? Do you remember stories in your family, books, or on television that portrayed those people? Students then reflect on adolescence, the workplace, and social interactions, and finally address how they might be racist and antiracist.

Book Buddies

Students are assigned to work one-on-one with an elementary student who is from a different ethnic background. They spend the year in weekly half-hour sessions of relationship building, reading, and game playing. The students keep journals of their experiences. It is an excellent way for White students to gain exposure to students of color in nonthreatening ways.

Activities for the Classroom

(for Early Childhood Students)
Reality-based Learning

Young children need to touch, feel, taste, hear, see, and smell to experience learning—learning which leaves the deepest impact. Exposure to anything or anyone who is different is essential. Children need to feel comfortable in the presence of difference, whether it is from food, people, music, or other sources.

Antibiased/Not Just Diverse

While it is important for children to understand that differences are exciting, it is also essential that they learn from an early age that life is not always about fairness and equity and that they can and must take steps to recognize injustice and work toward a more just society.

Play

Young children learn most constructively and comfortably through play. Teachers should be aware of structuring as often as possible the kinds of play situations that are cooperative rather than competitive, and help children problem-solve and work out dilemmas for each other. Dramatic play props can always add to the promotion of respect for diversity.

FURTHER READING

Cronin, S., Derman-Sparks, L., Henry, S., Olatunji, C., & York, S. (2000). *Future vision, present work: Learning from the culturally relevant anti-bias leadership project.* St. Paul, MN: Redleaf.

King, E. W., Chipman, M., & Cruz-Jansen, M. (1994). *Educating young children in a diverse society.* Needham Heights, MA: Allyn & Bacon.

Nieto, S. (1992). *Affirming diversity: The sociopolitical context of multicultural education.* White Plains, NY: Longman.

Saderman Hall, N. (1999). *Creative resources for the anti-bias classroom.* Albany, NY: Delmar.

York, S. (1992). *Roots and wings: Affirming culture in early childhood programs.* St. Paul, MN: Redleaf.

WEB SITES

http://www.splcenter.org/teachingtolerance/tt-index.html

This site provides articles and archives from *Teaching Tolerance* magazine, classroom resources and activities, and lists of ways to fight hate, with examples from across the country.

http://www.civilrights.org/publications/reports/talking_to_our_children/

This site contains a booklet for parents and children on the discussion of common questions about racism, educational materials about oppression, and lists programs around the country, by state.

http://www.ecewebguide.com/antibias.html

This site has information about antibias curricula, appropriate curricula from *ERIC Digest,* information from the National Association for the Education of Young Children about teaching young children to resist bias, and numerous other links.

http://web.nmsu.edu/~gpeterse/book2.htm

This site provides an extensive bibliography of antibias books for young children, as well as curriculum materials.

Chapter 11

My Personal Journey—In Part

Bruce Romanish, Washington State University, Vancouver

Focus Questions

1. How do your ideologies relate to your childhood environment? How do they relate to democracy?

2. When your unexamined beliefs or ideas are challenged, how can you benefit?

3. What privileges does the author have and how does he use them transformatively?

There is great value in understanding the genesis of our personal philosophies and belief systems, particularly if we choose to enter the noble profession of teaching. And the importance is more pronounced when we realize that schools are socializing agencies that rely upon teachers to carry out this central task. Teachers who are unconscious of the intellectual paths leading to their general worldview become mere clerks for transmitting the agenda of the system and thus the larger social order. This is an unflattering characterization of the nonreflective educator, but one that unfortunately describes too many within the teaching ranks.

In describing my own personal journey, the aspect I want to focus on is not any particular belief or set of beliefs so much as the intellectual barriers to such transformation, intellectual barriers erected for us by the process we term socialization. We are not born to be racists, sexists, homophobes, Christians, democrats, communists, capitalists, or many other belief sets or ideologies. All that we hold to be true is cultivated by a complex series of experiences we attempt to order and make sense of, given our environment. My personal journey is laced with examples of how my own outlooks and beliefs have been dramatically altered, but it is the process of that alteration I believe is key to opening the path to intellectual liberation that is essential if we are going to make this a possibility to our students.

Another important reason I choose this alleyway for the essay is because I'm uncertain how accurate I can be in characterizing the true essence of so many earlier experiences. Time has a way of revising our experiences, or at least our accounts of them. It's one of the reasons I suspect that many people are able to romanticize their childhood; they are at some distance from it and tend not to focus on things unpleasant. So the negatives get squeezed from our vision or get tucked away, leaving more positive memories for the public record. Nonetheless, there are certain features of our beginnings that, not unlike evolutionary explanations of our species, have organic characteristics that give shape to formative experiences. I will be as intellectually honest as I can in terms of what I extracted from these episodes and what I can attribute to them from a distance of many years. Since these pages do not represent my memoirs but rather depict part of my personal journey, I will be sensitive to the limitations of space.

I begin with my family setting which, as with most of us, goes a long way in explaining who I am. Some families, for instance, work very hard at assuring that children grow up to hold the same beliefs, values, and attitudes of the parents. Often this is done in ways that make it doubtful that the children will ever be able to claim they are the true owners of their thoughts and outlooks. This in part helps me see, for instance, why so many young married couples have difficulties with in-laws; there hasn't been the necessary declarations of independence, and the parents proceed as though they are still entitled to determine the direction of their children's lives, as though they ever were entitled.

IN THE BEGINNING

In referencing my origins, I borrow from Cornell West's (1993) dictum that race matters by asserting that class matters as well. In my own case, a blue-collar, working-class, unionized household was the setting. My mother, somewhat before her time, worked both in and outside the home, beginning in the mid-1950s. My dad, born and raised on a very poor and small Pennsylvania farm to Ukrainian immigrant parents, never completed high school but demonstrated keen qualities of mind in learning to be a talented machinist and mechanic. He worked lots of overtime and always held a part-time job in addition. My parents chased their version of the American Dream, but it was a chase that left me ample time on my own during adolescence. In retrospect, one conclusion I reach about how my perspectives changed to be at such variance from my folks is that other forces had access to me in ways that made growth in new directions possible. Not all these forces can be described as wholesome and positive influences, I must admit, but I believe they contributed in some measure to a liberation that was essential to later changes.

With my parents often gone and only a younger sister at home, I managed to spend my fair share of time on the streets in the small city of Easton, Pennsylvania, once I reached my junior high years. Looking back, this had both positive and negative consequences. On the downside, I worked my way out of the top academic track of a large and highly regarded public junior high school. On the plus side, I never memorized all the vice presidents of the United States. But more important, I believe, is that I experienced a sense of independence and freedom at a much earlier age than many of my peers. With family life in considerable disarray, I was left to my own devices to make sense of the world, at least in some matters. I carry that streak of independence and a valuing of freedom with me today and, in the main, I believe it is a good thing.

The working class, just as every other social group, is not a social or political monolith. There are differing ideologies represented within each cultural group. Some working-class individuals are earthy, even vulgar. They may have little appreciation for the value of education and what it can mean in terms of living a full life. They may see it instead in almost purely utilitarian terms: Get an education and you'll get a good job. A good job means not only higher earnings but also less toil, less sweat, and the status and respect that more professional occupations bring. In some measure this is the message I received at home.

In important respects, it is an outlook that reflects the basic purpose for acquiring an education in America today—an essentially vocational one. It is a view corporate America embraces as the aim of education, except for the children of the managing classes and influential educated elites, who value education in very different terms. For them, the goal of college ultimately is to have an employment pay off, but in the process an investment of family resources and student time is spent often in desirable liberal arts studies. Education is to be vocational in some larger sense, but it is to be aesthetic as well, preparing one to live life richly in addition to provide for it economically. The goal, as Susan Ohanian (1999) describes, is not merely to make a living but also to make a life. That, she avers, should be the goal for all our children. So while working-class youngsters are learning about the reality of school to work, those of more privileged backgrounds, Jonathan Kozol (1991) notes, are learning about the relationship of school and power and Harvard or Princeton.

Class differences are evident in current reform efforts, which generally embrace a "school-to-work" ideology. For example, all students are to learn technical writing. Is there any purpose in wondering aloud whom this is intended to benefit? And what becomes of the student's educational opportunity to blossom intellectually, or to become the creator of one's perspectives? They are sacrificed to the demands of the global economy. And while everyone may be required to demonstrate proficiency in technical writing before leaving high school, those who go on to college at least still have a chance to develop their aesthetic capacities and will experience writing as a creative act, one that can provide personal expression. The rest become the worker bees.

THE FEMALE EXAMPLE

Let me cite Exhibit A from a portion of my experience that greatly shaped my attitudes about females. Because I was a boy raised in an era of male dominance, when women were expected to be domestic workers and provide child care while males went into the world and carved out an economic existence, it did not seem unfair to me that I learned early that it would be a good thing to go to college, although this was a message my sister received in only muted terms. We had the same parents, and she is very bright. But I went to college, pursued advanced degrees, and she is a high school graduate.

Why would I question these arrangements? Not a single mother in my neighborhood worked outside the home other than my own. My home was different, and I yearned to have a household as normal as everyone else. Only later did I realize that the notion of "normal" in family life is somewhat a fiction, that in fact most families have their goblins and very often what appears on the outside is dramatically different from the internal reality. And we can never underestimate the impact of social dictates and how we swallow them, unwittingly, and all the baggage they bring with them.

For instance, all my elementary teachers were women, none were young, and only two were married. Elementary teaching, just as nursing and secretarial work, was a career avenue available to women. What these occupations held in common was meager pay in fields that constituted either the caring or serving vocations and, most important, the supervisors, managers and superiors were men. The real power in social, economic, and political realms belonged to men.

By the time I completed college in 1971 I was well on my way to holding an overhauled worldview. I had the very good fortune to be in college during the end of the 1960s and the beginning of the 1970s. In some respects it was like walking through a minefield; there were explosions all around me. Things were happening that I didn't understand and couldn't comprehend—and few others seemed to understand either. In educational terms, I was experiencing cognitive dissonance, trying to hold on to beliefs and ideas I never actually thought very carefully about on the one hand and which were colliding with a new set of outlooks that were disturbing in many respects on the other. I was raised to fear and oppose communism, for instance. I didn't understand much about it and was never asked to read Marx or Lenin as part of my general education to become a teacher, this despite my major in the social sciences. In retrospect, it served as an object lesson for me in understanding how belief systems are forged socially and culturally, and how these belief systems "have" us before we have them. More than any other aspect of my work as an educator, this simple truth marks my approach in terms of the intellectual development of my students. They must be liberated before education can fully begin. Or, to paraphrase Malcolm Forbes, the task of education is to take an empty mind and make it an open mind. The part I disagree with here is that any child ever has an empty mind. But surely one of the fundamental educational challenges is to open minds.

Why is this so important? It matters if and only if we believe in the value of human freedom. What else does freedom mean if not intellectual considerations? We do not want freedom to mean we can run around and crash into each other, or do literally whatever we want without regard for the effects of our actions on others both present and in generations yet unborn. But freedom speaks as well to the conditions necessary in the event people choose to adopt different beliefs. In other words, in order for us to be able to change our minds, we must have a society arranged in ways that invite and make such changes possible. This, in part, defines a free society. Democracy becomes vital in this equation not for its own sake, but for freedom's sake. Democracy is necessary because it is the best way humans have devised to make the fulfillment of human freedom possible. And this again must be seen in intellectual terms, which is why education is so essential in a democracy.

But my sojourn at the close of college was only the beginning. Raised in a traditional American family with standard beliefs about blacks, women, gays, and lesbians, not to mention socialism and atheism, the changes unleashed as a result of the civil rights and women's liberation movements meant I had a lot more to learn. Even though I considered myself a liberal, having volunteered for the McGovern for President campaign in 1972, the challenges to my thinking were only beginning. While I had progressed to a point where I favored an equal rights amendment to the U.S. Constitution, a document I have grown to revere, I had yet to internalize on a deep level the kinds of changes necessary in seeing women as true equals. And by then I had been a teacher for several years.

It came home to me when I was confronted by women, including my wife at the time, who indicted me as a sexist. I was seeing myself as a very progressive guy who subscribed to most of the important liberation movements of the day, yet I was feeling assaulted, fairly regularly, by women who were angry at men and who saw me as part of the problem. My initial response, like so many of my peers, was to engage in denial. I wasn't sexist as I saw it. How could I be sexist? I adored women, at least in my mind. But did I see them genuinely as people entitled to be who they wanted to be? Did I diminish their being when they sought to be equal in ways that threatened me by feeling they were aggressive or male bashers, or worse? When I was confronted with my own sexist attitudes, I determined the problem was not with me, it was with them. Then I became defensive and even angry about what they were claiming—not an uncommon reaction when our way of seeing things is under siege.

The importance of this illustration is that the views and beliefs I held about women were planted in my mind without any expectation that I would examine them, indeed interrogate them, and decide for myself whether they were just, desirable, and, in the end, mine. This process began when I was very young and things were regularly reinforced by the dominant cultural values. Because these outlooks seeped into my mind relatively unnoticed and certainly unexamined, I had little option but to become defensive when confronted with the nasty side of those ideas. Had I adopted the beliefs through a process of careful reflection and thought, I would be more secure in my position. But we must always reserve a residue of doubt in any positions we hold because it is the only way we can shift our views, and that is the only way for genuine personal growth to occur. If our intellectual stance is closed, not only are doorways to change locked shut as a result, we are also unable to live in a state of human freedom.

Another consideration to ponder is the effect socialization has on the way we learn. Not only do we adopt many beliefs we do not truly own, because our task as learners in the process is to acquire beliefs rather than examine their worthiness, over time we become accustomed to relying on authorities and experts, which in turn diminishes our capacity to think critically. Since we don't value thought processes that ask us to be active thinkers, there is a tendency to be irritated by those who do engage in these practices. We become accustomed to thinking in ways that are passive in nature and bestow great authority in the hands of others. Needless to say, this is not a good formula in a democracy.

ANOTHER PART OF THE STORY

My experience as a young teacher education student began a process that dramatically changed my outlook on many fronts and it is a process that continues to this day. Intellectual liberation was a necessary step, but it was supplemented by educational experiences that made new directions possible and available. It has been and remains an exciting prospect. I have had the good fortune of a colleague, mentor, and friend who helped me see so many things in new ways. But each shift in outlook meets less resistance than before because I know that I once believed things in other realms I now see as false. I must hold open the possibility that other mistaken views remain.

The most profound awakening in my later adult years relates to children. My colleague and friend exposed me to the oppression of children and the young in our society early in our relationship, which began in 1982. I now see the silencing, the mistreatment, the assumptions of their evilness, the absence of healthy parent–child relationships, the poverty, and the status of property our society bestows upon the young. If we want to better understand the tragedy of Columbine High School, a deep look into the lives of children would pay many greater dividends than posting religious commandments on schoolroom walls or compelling students to wear uniforms.

By the lives of children, I don't mean the culture of technology and all its manifestations. For the majority of young people, their exposure to and awareness of the dimmer side of our culture does not result in acts of violence toward others. So to blame violence on the media is to take our eye off the ball, as it were. After all, the Nazis cooked people in ovens and murdered millions without ever watching TV or being influenced by Hollywood. But child rearing in mostly two-parent, churchgoing families provided the ingredients upon which the dark social turn was built, because in part children were treated in oppressive ways. Alice Miller's *For Your Own Good* (1990) is a good primer on the subject.

Nothing short of a revolutionary change in our view and treatment of children is in order, a change that parallels the shifts accomplished in our attitudes towards race, gender, sexual orientation, and other human dimensions. Unless we can begin to see children differently, there is little hope that we will begin to treat them differently. I'm not speaking about a romantic notion of children akin to Rousseau's *Emile,* but rather a perspective that insists upon and begins with dignity and respect for every young person in the same way each of us wants that for ourselves. We are living through a social period in American history where a concerted effort is under way to restore us to key aspects of an earlier age. It is an attempt at a conservative restoration masked by a "moral" revolution. I am not merely skeptical of the motives of these groups in our midst—they terrify me. They do not represent the first time right-wing extremists have sought to ride a moral agenda to political power in the modern era. A careful reading of *Mein Kampf* will show how Hitler (1934) cited the obscenity of cinema, proliferation of prostitution, corruption of the young, warnings of broad moral decline, and other factors as the justification for a much-needed new direction for Germany. The rest is now history. And to paraphrase the title of Sinclair Lewis's powerful 1930s novel, "It can happen here."

A PEDAGOGIC CREED

As beginning teachers, it is important to answer questions about the purposes of our work. Why do we proceed as we do? What are the political implications of how we practice our craft and of our beliefs about children and young people? In what ways do we see ourselves building or affecting the future through our interactions with students day-to-day? Answers to these and related questions provide an anchor as we attempt to navigate the complexities of the teaching role in a public school system created in part to serve the interests of a democratic political experiment.

Two concepts always at the center of my educational project are democracy and liberation—democracy as a way of living, liberation as an intellectual direction. Democracy must be lived in the day-to-day if it is to survive and be meaningful in the political realm. I do not say this lightly. Hitler came to power in a free, democratic election not unlike what we experience on our national level. One thing is clear from the German experience: Their education and social arrangements were not designed to prepare the citizenry for life in a free, democratic political system. To the contrary, the primary institutions of socialization were characterized by authoritarian features and paved the way for the rise of Nazi totalitarianism. Educational institutions, more than any other in a society, must be the incubators of democracy. Yet schools, too, must be supported and surrounded by other social and economic agencies that reflect democratic characteristics and purposes. This is especially true for universities and the preparation of future teachers. Since very few public schools qualify as fermentation tanks for democracy, preservice teachers need to begin their democratic sojourns as part of their professional development. An adjunct to the democratic theme is intellectual liberation. This is so vital because there must be a concerted effort to unpack the effects of years of antidemocratic socialization. There is always a tension between the importance of the individual on the one hand and the requirements of community on the other. The community, therefore, must arrange itself in such a way as to safeguard individual rights.

It is fair to say my philosophy of teaching fits within the fold of what is termed social reconstruction. I am reluctant to cast myself under specific labels, however, because when we apply a term to someone we rub dangerously close to reaching a host of unwarranted conclusions. Each of us applies certain connotations to labels, whether it be liberal, conservative, leftist, fundamentalist, reconstructionist, and so forth. The tendency is to assume that others fit our individual conceptions of the labels when in fact there is always a wide range within most categorizations. For instance, I subscribe to the ends that social reconstruction has in view, both politically and economically, yet I increasingly eschew any educational program that sees the young as a means rather than as the ends themselves. Philosophically, I draw considerably from the pragmatist position, but I also have a strong libertarian streak in the Jeffersonian tradition. I mix in a healthy dose of a critical perspective; humanists and I share some basic values, many existentialists connect with me on several levels, and I count myself a feminist.

All this is central to understanding the perspective I operate from when I teach. Before we can be transformative as future teachers, most of us must first be intellectually liberated. In *Wheels in the Head,* Joel Spring (1994) describes the process by which our ways of thinking are often established. When we are taught to adopt and embrace certain cultural beliefs, usually in our youth, it is not only the beliefs that are being implanted, it is also a way of thinking. These can be viewed as "viruses of the mind." Dewey (1916) offered insight into this when he discussed how schools serve to sustain and maintain the established order of things. Part of their mission is to pass on to the next generation not only the knowledge of the age but also morals and standards of conduct that are handed down from the past. An important point from Dewey's *Experience and Education* (1938) is that in order to get the young to accept these ideas and beliefs, they must first be pacified. For them to be accepting, we must first ask them to be quiet, acquiescent, docile, and passive. In this way, the particular ideas and beliefs they are asked to adopt matter little, since their duty is to demonstrate they have internalized them as their own regardless of the ideas themselves. It requires an experience in being silenced, something education too often achieves.

The accomplishment of this educational ideology is that the young learn not to question but to repeat the answers of others. Their education can be viewed as a script written for them by those in authority. In the end, the most devastating effect is the pattern of thought it establishes. It is one that is very difficult to overhaul later in life. This represents Spring's "wheel in the head" because it is the way in which we are able to conceptualize and formulate things intellectually that is most lasting and therefore has the most devastating impact. For many people, both their beliefs and the ways they assemble them change little from their early education. The liberation I reference equates to an awakening or what Maxine Greene (1988) would term consciousness.

Because so many central beliefs are assigned to us culturally, education must be something other than the acquisition of skills and specific sets of knowledge if democracy is to be seriously considered. The school curriculum is not, in the main, for the young; it exists for different purposes, and chief among them is the interests of adult others. In time, a rather remarkable and not so subtle success is achieved, namely, generations equipped with the proper set of ideas needed to sustain the established order and carry it forward. For many, only life-jolting experiences can cause us to thoughtfully examine what once was accepted as truth. Intervening events serve as powerful educators when a person is rocked to the foundation by experiences that don't fit neatly within the framework society provides.

It has long been my thesis that men, to cite a coarse example, have created far more feminists than college departments of women's studies. This is in no way meant to disparage the vital work of these programs and the necessity of their presence within university curricula. It is a profound intervening event when women, who follow their social script regarding who they are and what their relationship should be to men, have it shattered by men who do not play according to the script. Many women have awakened to a reality that is 180 degrees from the one they learned at home, in church, and in school. Unfortunately, deep pain is the catalyst for the transformation through which these women then travel.

My belief is that education needs to be an intervening event that is as profound in its effects as any of the life experiences that shake a person's worldview at its core. We should not expect people to suffer immense pain in order to experience intellectual growth. Life should not be that way. But education can serve as a means of transformation that can in turn spare people at least some of the pain that flows from being intellectually unauthorized.

The transformative teacher is one who believes that teaching can make a difference, and the reconstructionist educator believes that a difference needs to be made. I would say this is an article of faith for teachers who desire to have an impact on learners as well as society. There are many pundits from the right who view the 1960s as a period that marks the beginning of the unraveling of the social mores and fabric that made America great. Yet which groups among us would desire a return to the morality of the 1950s, when women were significantly more oppressed than at present; when African-Americans were treated to separate public facilities in large parts of the nation; when domestic violence was largely ignored because the victims were still viewed as property of men—a condition befalling children to the present day; when a right-wing juggernaut threatened constitutional liberties and basic American freedoms at every turn?

In using the term *education,* I treat it in the spirit of John Goodlad (1997), who notes that it is something that happens in many places, not just schools. He describes education as ubiquitous, happening everywhere all the time. The school is but one of the institutions and agencies engaged in educational activities. To the extent these entities view the young more as means than as ends in themselves, then to that extent are they willing to insert "wheels in the head." The young are left to accept their assignments. Again, it is not the beliefs themselves that are at issue alone here, though many of them deserve scrutiny as well; rather, it is how we come to hold those beliefs and the net effect this has by way of democratic implications.

Dewey's (1938) distinction between experiences that are educative versus miseducative is particularly helpful in my view. We learn things all the time and in all sorts of ways and contexts. But those experiences that enhance growth and make future growth likely are considered educative. Those that are growth arresting or reducing are miseducative. For example, any institution that aims to manipulate the minds of the young is surely teaching them things and they are certainly learning things. But the outcome is intellectually inhibiting and therefore miseducative. The prospects for future intellectual growth are significantly diminished. This is central to Dewey's concept of freedom because it is essentially an intellectual consideration prior to the making of choices or engaging in any forms of action. His formulation stands at odds with popular conceptions of freedom, which hold that freedom is about choices and actions, and if people exercise their freedom in genuine ways—this perspective holds—society will experience chaos and turmoil. In fact, many conservative voices lament the excesses of freedom in the modern period and offer it as the explanation for all forms of social turmoil and negative behavior.

This fundamentally confuses the case, for it leaves society little option but to reject human freedom. To do so rejects human growth and strikes at the heart of what life's purpose and meaning are to be. Denying people authentic freedom reduces them to chattel and little more than economic units. People become valued for their capacities as consumers and ability to perform work, work that is defined and controlled by powerful economic interests. The chief harm politically is not that we must all perform some economic functions; rather, it is that we develop little or no capacity for being self-directed and self-determining. Without this, democracy loses its utility. In an economic ideology of the private there is little need for the public. Without the public, democracy dies of anomie. All this relates to my view of intelligence. In the main, I assume that it is socially constructed. I conclude that the students I've worked with, covering a span of more than a quarter century, have all had innate intelligence of a level that would enable them to succeed in almost any ventures they might choose. The students whose minds seem less nimble or who are largely intellectually disinterested are not so due to some limitation of potential or capacity. Instead, it is a reflection of the miseducative experiences that have gone before and which have served to close off the mind in important respects. Their problem is not that their minds cannot work more effectively, it is that their minds are in need of opening. In a closed mental state, if I can use this term, the learner is by definition not available for new possibilities. The excitement of intellectual challenges does not materialize because the mind has learned to be quiet or, worse, already has the truth by the throat.

The great educational challenge of this century is to prevent young minds from being closed by forces committed to that end, and to liberate those who have fallen prey to this kind of intellectual development. In my own students I have observed something

I believe is relevant here. The students who are most closed in intellectual posture are often the most certain of the answers they hold. Moreover, they are also terrified by discussions related to their deeply held convictions and beliefs. I conclude that this is a reflection of both the ideas and beliefs they have been asked to embrace as well as the process they encountered during it all. It seems apparent to me that their inability to engage in open discourse about differences in perspective grows directly from the way in which they came to hold their outlooks in the first place. In truth, the beliefs they clutch to their breasts so tightly cannot be subjected to scrutiny because they are not beliefs they came to hold on their own. They have not arrived at their positions after a process of careful examination, interrogation, investigation, research, and dialogue with those of other persuasions. So, when faced with a circumstance that calls for us to display our understanding about the beliefs we hold, many become terrified and quite defensive. This defensiveness is a direct reflection of the intellectual insecurity that comes from holding beliefs that have been culturally or otherwise assigned.

REFERENCES

Dewey, J. (1916). *Democracy and education.* New York: Free Press.

Dewey, J. (1938). *Experience and education.* New York: Collier.

Goodlad, J. (1997). *In praise of education.* New York: Teachers College Press.

Greene, M. (1988). *Dialectic of freedom.* New York: Teachers College Press.

Hitler, A. (1934). *Mein Kampf.* Munich, Germany: Eher Nachf.

Kozol, J. (1991). *Savage inequalities: Children in America's schools.* New York: Crown.

Miller, A. (1990). *For your own good.* New York: Noonday.

Ohanian, S. (1999). *One size fits few: The folly of educational standards.* Portsmouth, NH: Heinemann.

Spring, J. (1994). *Wheels in the head.* New York: McGraw-Hill.

West, C. (1993). *Race matters.* Boston: Beacon.

Activities for the Classroom

Let me briefly share two assignments I often use. One is an activity I developed many years ago which makes use of editorials. I use them in different ways in different courses, but in my social and cultural foundations of education classes with undergraduates I use them as a way to invite intellectual openness, to scan the social and political landscape, to obligate critique and reflection, and to give evidence of using one's own voice. I ask students to give "editorials" about burning social issues facing humanity, something in need of our collective attention or in need of amelioration. I ask them to use this as an opportunity to raise the consciousness of their peers about something they believe is important to us as a people either in our society or in global terms. They are obligated to stake out a position rather than simply inform us on the topic. And their perspective needs to be clear; they cannot be firmly planted on the fence.

For many undergraduates, this task is much more difficult than it first appears. If they know or care little about the social currents in their midst, selecting a worthy topic can be quite daunting. Then formulating a position requires that one know something about the subject, thus posing an additional challenge for some. But most of all, the requirement to make our views public is what is most taxing because in that arena our thoughts and ideas can be examined and countered. As long as the student body has some diversity of perspective, the likelihood of which is increased by the presence of a diverse student population, the potential for a rich and robust series of honest conversations about subjects of importance is considerable. All this is a means of having future teachers make connections between what happens in the broader social order and what happens in schools.

It should be apparent that this assignment poses serious challenges for a number of students when we begin. For some, an immediate concern is their nervousness with doing what amounts to public speaking, something that terrifies more than a few in each class. To reduce their anxiety along these lines I incorporate several conditions. One is that they remain in their seats when giving the editorial, which makes them somewhat more relaxed. This is accommodated by the seating arrangement, a large semicircle, designed to give every student a front-row seat in every class, one where they can easily converse as a group. Another is that they can read their editorial in fully prepared text, thus providing further security to the presenter but, as important, it also prompts them to stay within the allotted time by preparing adequately for the presentation. I also underline the need for us to be respectful in the posteditorial conversations, to learn how to differ in ways that advance our understanding rather than attempt to win debating points. But most important is the effort I make to create a forum for the honest exchange of differing perspectives.

An "Intellectual Autobiography"

I use this as a vehicle for tracing the development of the perspectives we each hold about things that matter in life. How did I become a Democrat or Republican, or socialist or fascist? At what point did I conclude this was my outlook? What influences can I identify that gave shape to my views on race, sexuality, religion, and other matters? Can I say, after tracing the origins of these in a way that is as intellectually honest as possible, that I chose these for myself after careful consideration and examination? Or, do I see that to some extent my beliefs were implanted and it's been my task to accommodate them as my own?

This activity can be modified depending upon the grade level of the group and the purpose of the assignment, but the primary aim is to provide a means for reflection as a way to understand the nature of socialization. As someone once said, history "has" us before we "have" it.

Web Sites

http://w3.ed.uiuc.edu/EPS/category.asp

This site, provided by the University of Illinois, addresses philosophy, theory, and education. Many citations include full-length treatments of individuals or works about them.

http://cuip.uchicago.edu/jds/index.htm

The Web site of the John Dewey Society for the Study of Education and Culture provides essential information on John Dewey's ideas and the organization that carries on in his name.

http://www.infed.org/thinkers/et-dewey.htm

The *Encyclopedia of Informal Education* cites John Dewey and is a useful primer on Dewey's ideas and major works.

Chapter 12

The Miseducation, Reeducation, and Transformation of a "White"[1] Male Educator Working for Social Justice

Paul Spies, Metropolitan State University, Minneapolis

Focus Questions

1. How have you been socialized into racism, sexism, heterosexism, and classism?

2. How Eurocentric are you? When do you feel most Eurocentric? When do you feel the least Eurocentric?

3. How have you gone out of your way to learn about other groups' experiences, perspectives, and relationship to you?

When I was teaching African American studies in an ethnically balanced[2] high school north of Chicago, my only European American student in the

---

[1]The term *white* is put in quotes because it is a social construction which I reject and take offense at being used as a descriptive term. *White* subliminally perpetuates racist ideology as something oppositional to *black*. Caucasian is perhaps the only other term commonly used in our society which offends me more because of its implications that there are three races—caucasoid, negroid, and mongoloid. I prefer to acknowledge the biological truth that I am one of more than 6 billion people belonging to the human race *Homo sapiens,* and that my cultural heritage or ethnicity is European American. As a member of the dominant ethnic group in this country, which has for too long and too often defined "the Other" with labels, I will refrain from making commentary regarding what terms should be used for other ethnic groups, and I will use various terms (i.e., black/African-American, Latino/Hispanic) interchangeably.

[2]When I started teaching in Waukegan in 1989, the school population was approximately 30% African-American, 10% Asian-American, 30% European-American, and 30% Latino/a. It is now more than 50% Latino/a, and the European-American population is less than 20%.

elective course moved with her family to another town only a month after school had started. However, Desiree's new school in a predominantly white community had no African American studies classes. When she requested to be enrolled in a similar course at her new school, she was told by her new counselor, "We don't have a need for a class like that at our school because there are no blacks here." Desiree was very upset and spoke to her new principal. I was pleased to read in her letter to me that winter how she had responded to her new counselor's and principal's ignorant attitudes. She told them emphatically, "That's all the more reason why black studies should be required at this school!" Unfortunately, Desiree never got what she demanded, nor what her peers needed.

As a numerical minority in my class of mostly African American students, Desiree had quickly learned as a high school sophomore the critical importance of having a multicultural education, and she tried to educate the educators of her new school. Desiree's experience highlights an unfortunate truth—that thousands of schools around the country still are not doing more to equip their millions of students to work for social justice and appreciate the diversity that defines our humanity.

To be clear, I am not advocating simply an additive approach to multicultural education in predominantly homogeneous schools (Banks, 1999). However, if our schools, regardless of their location and socioeconomic makeup, ignore continuing demographic trends and the rich multicultural history of our nation and world, we are doing privileged, underprivileged, and oppressed youth alike an injustice in our increasingly interdependent global village. We are also planting the seeds for a future in which prejudice and discrimination continue to flourish if the uncivilized system of separate and unequal schooling continues to dominate the public school landscape (Kozol, 1992).

My advocacy of a meaningful multicultural and antiracist education has increased and developed since 1988, when I began my career teaching as a confident but naive 22-year-old until now, as I work to promote social justice among teachers and teachers in training. Like most teachers and students of teaching in our country, however, I am not the product of a multicultural elementary, middle, or high school education. I grew up as the son of educators in a predominantly European-American middle-class suburb of Minneapolis with little exposure to students of color, diverse perspectives, or multicultural content in my classes. In a largely homogeneous community and school, my education was extremely Eurocentric.

While in many respects I received a quality education, I soon came to realize that I was also disempowered by my school experience, because the "real" world I have encountered since high school is much more diverse, interesting, complex, and unjust than I was led to believe as a teenager. As African-American historian Carter G. Woodson wrote so convincingly about the "miseducation of the Negro" (1933/1990), I have come to realize over the past 15 years how miseducated I was as a youth and how I can continue to be misled if I'm not careful and critical. In turn, I have needed to consistently unlearn the subtle forms of racism, sexism, heterosexism, and classism, in which I have been socialized to think throughout my life in and outside of school.

I don't believe in racism, and I try to challenge racism whenever I can. However, as difficult as it is for me to admit and for others who know me to accept, I am a racist. This admission stems from my uncomfortable recognition that I have been and continue to be socialized and privileged by a racist society. In the same line of thought, I must admit to being a sexist, a heterosexist, a classist, and an ableist. As a product of our society in which these and other "isms" have festered for centuries at the expense of people who are not demographically like me, I cannot escape the realities of my environment and its effect on my conscious and subconscious thinking. Hence, much like an alcoholic or other drug addict must first admit to his or her problem, my transformation began and continues when I acknowledge my psychosocial diseases.

As a European American, middle-class, able-bodied and heterosexual male, I have found the need to acknowledge my socially constructed diseases in order to resist them on a daily basis. Thus, it is important to note that as this chapter is being written, it reflects the particular place during a long, nonlinear journey of recovery from the "isms" which I have been explicitly and tacitly socialized to believe in the United States. While I have often realized the cliché that "ignorance is bliss," I have come to learn that being a reflective and transformative educator concerned with justice necessitates personal transformation so that my rhetoric in class matches the realities of how I choose to live my life.

In this chapter, I will first share some critical moments in my journey toward personal and professional transformation, including attempts to resist strong yet subtle societal forces shaping my views of reality. After making record of my miseducation, I will then describe some of my attempts to unlearn and reeducate myself in the process of transformation. This is a personal and professional story of transformation which I take no pride in, but which I am grateful for having begun and for having the opportunity to continue in writing this chapter.[3] The second part will focus on describing how my transformation has impacted my work in various settings as a teacher in public schools.

THE MISEDUCATION OF A "WHITE" YOUTH

In my adult life, I have grown to feel that I was denied part of my humanity,[4] part of what makes me human, as a youth within a Eurocentric environment. While I could never claim this to be a similar level of injustice that oppressed people in the United States and around the world encounter, I do believe I was culturally impoverished. I recognize that I had culture (contrary to the beliefs of many whites), but I didn't have multiculturalism. I was sheltered from diversity and only found out later in life that I had many things in common with people who were considered by society and myself as "the Other" (Banks, 2000).

It is difficult to lay blame on my parents, because they raised me to have empathy and an open mind. Never once did I hear words of bigotry spoken in our home. However, issues of race were also absent. Similarly, I was never explicitly taught to

---

[3]This journey itself is even a privileged one in that it is part of my profession to engage in such reflection. I realize that having sustained time to think, write, and read is afforded to few in this world.

[4]In fact, I believe I was denied a basic human right, according to the United Nations. Article 26, Section 2 of the Universal Declaration of Human Rights (1948) states: "Education shall be directed to the full development of the human personality and to the strengthening of respect for human rights and fundamental freedoms. It shall promote understanding, tolerance, and friendship among all nations, racial or religious groups, and shall further the activities of the United Nations for the maintenance of peace."

hate or feel superior in school, but little in my secondary school education prepared me to live and work within our increasingly multicultural country and increasingly interdependent global village.

In my suburban high school of 1,800 students, there were no known Latina/os and fewer than 10 African Americans. There were approximately 100 students with roots in Southeast Asia, but my school had segregated them in our building. They had all of their English as a second language classes on the top floor of the building, where special education classes were also located. Rarely did majority group students venture to the third floor.[5]

A major reflection of the demographics of our school was the curriculum—it was totally Eurocentric. While my interdisciplinary, team-taught American studies and world studies courses were two of the best I had experienced in high school because they challenged me to think rather than memorize, the curriculum we were taught only represented the humanities from a particular social lens. We did not discuss the varied experiences of different ethnic groups in this country, nor did we study anything dealing with Africa, Asia, Latin America or the Middle East.

A couple of examples illustrate how I was blind to the underlying diversity that was present in my school. I remember playing on the soccer team with a kid named Sarung, who was from Cambodia. I had no idea why his family and others were in the United States or of his struggles in a new country; I also didn't care enough to know or didn't know enough to care. All I knew is that he was one of the best soccer players on the team and that he struggled to speak English. I do shamefully remember being upset but silent whenever an opposing team would say something derogatory to him because of his dark "Asian" appearance. Unfortunately, it wasn't until some years later, in college, that I learned about the genocide attempted by Pol Pot's regime in Cambodia during the late 1970s. I now think it is highly probable that Sarung and his family were refugees who fled in some miraculous way for their lives. It still disturbs me today that I missed a unique opportunity to learn from Sarung, and that my ignorance made me incapable of having any real empathy for his struggles.

In a similar vein, my interactions with my few African American peers were also superficial and limited. Not surprisingly, my knowledge of African-American history and culture was extremely limited. Today I am embarrassed by my memories, triggered by a yearbook picture, of standing in a crowd of white kids around one of my few African-American classmates as he break-danced in the hallway after school to music of Rick James playing from his boom box. I can also remember wanting to sit next to Al at basketball games because I liked hearing "his" music. Besides these disturbing, stereotype-creating experiences, I remember watching *Roots* with millions of other Americans.

Intensely watching *Roots* every evening for a week was definitely an emotional and transformative experience for me as a youth. However, when I was in high school there was no opportunity in my classes to process what we had seen or to learn more about this realm of history. I can remember the television special prompting a debate in my mind for a few years on whether or not learning about slavery was good for combating prejudice. I wondered whether ignoring this horrific past might allow "whites" to see "blacks" as equals in the present rather than descendants of people

---

[5]Today, the school has "dramatically changed" and created challenges for the staff according to members of the community, yet the student of color population is just more than 10%.

who were thought of and treated to be less than human. The point here is not how naive I was as a freshman in high school, but why I was so naive.

Again, my teachers and school were silent regarding multicultural and global history, yet I needed guidance in processing the important docudrama more Americans watched than any other television show in history. If my well-regarded suburban school was attempting to prepare me for the real life I would experience in college and thereafter, it failed. This strong feeling of betrayal and denial eventually developed into a persistent motivation to be a transformative teacher with public school students and teachers.

A MULTIFACETED PROCESS OF REEDUCATION: COLLEGE YEARS AND COMMITMENT TO LIVE FOR JUSTICE

My undergraduate education in and out of the classroom marked the beginning of my journey to being a transformative educator committed to an expanded notion of democracy and social justice. My suburban public school experience had given me the academic tools to be a successful college student; however, I was unprepared for the cultural diversity I encountered (although still limited) at even a small state university in northwestern Minnesota. Moorhead State's limited diversity included a few faculty of color, a few dozen international students, and even fewer U.S. citizens of color, most of whom were recruited to participate in athletic programs.[6]

One of the significant periods in my life—a definite turning point in choosing to live for social justice—occurred while I participated on a national student exchange program at Rutgers University in New Brunswick, New Jersey, during my junior year. Compared to Moorhead State and its small farming community of 40,000 people, attending Rutgers for a year made me feel submersed in a kaleidoscope of cultures. It was my first experience living with persons from different racial and ethnic groups. Living on the same dormitory floor with a variety of African Americans, Asian Americans, Jewish Americans, and Latinos provided numerous opportunities for me to engage in conversations and form relationships which most of us had not previously been fortunate enough to have.

The first semester that I was at Rutgers was a difficult one for many reasons. In a sense, I had experienced both information overload as well as cultural and cognitive dissonance. Sam, my social problems instructor in the sociology department, taught me to ask the question, Why? and to think critically about everything from the war in Nicaragua to the growing class differences in the United States. Everywhere I turned, I began to see problems and injustices in society and the world. As I became more aware of these societal problems, I got more and more depressed about where our country and world were heading.

In the fall of that year, I saw one chance to make a small difference—to vote in the elections that would determine which party controlled the U.S. Senate during the end of Ronald Reagan's second term as president. On the evening of the elections, one of my peers was sitting in the hallway of our dorm painting her fingernails while

[6]Of course not all students of color, especially African Americans, were athletes at Moorhead State, but most were athletes, and there was a tacit assumption, or stereotype, among white students and faculty on campus that "they" were all in sports.

looking at a fashion magazine. She was a friend of one of my neighbors, so I thought I'd ask if she had voted that day. She responded in a confused tone, "What?" It was as if she heard me, but didn't understand what I asked.

Partly perplexed because these elections had been so widely and repeatedly covered in the news for months, I replied, "The elections today, for control of the Senate. Did you vote?" With her blank facial expression and silence, I realized she had no clue what I was talking about. I was stunned and speechless. I went in my room utterly bewildered at her indifference, and I became depressed in thinking that the world would never change for the better as long as even seemingly educated people like her were so self-immersed to be unaware that major elections were taking place.

This encounter with what I characterized as the prototype of self-centered apathy common among Americans kept eating away at my soul and my hope in the future. I got so depressed[7] that I severely struggled to even speak or write a complete sentence. In the event that I would meet and engage in a conversation with someone, I had little idea how I would proceed. My solution to bridging the gulf between terrifying small talk and my global concerns was to wear a conversation piece.

In the mid-1980s, multicolored "friendship bracelets" made out of yarn were popular. I wanted to put a different kind of bracelet with meaning on my wrist, which I had hoped would serve as a catalyst for the kind of serious dialogue I felt needed to occur continually if our society was going to confront injustice. I placed a simple brown rubber band around my right wrist.

Since 1986 I have attempted to wear a rubber band every minute of everyday, and I plan to do so the rest of my life. Throughout my teaching career, at my wedding and birth of my children, in the shower, and at job interviews, a rubber band has been wrapped around my wrist. Because fewer than 10 people have ever asked why I consistently wear a rubber band and given me the chance to share what I think is important in life, I now continue to wear one more as a reminder of important but often conveniently forgotten things and people.

To me, the rubber band is partly symbolic of all the people in the world who are oppressed and exploited. Like those who are the victims of injustice, rubber bands are numerous and often discarded or seen as expendable. They are inexpensive but are often used for many purposes. They can be colorful and powerful, but usually they go unnoticed until they aren't around to do the job assigned. They are more flexible and adaptable than many other things which may be stronger, but if you stretch them too far or use them too much, they will break.

In reminding me of people in the world who are oppressed and less fortunate, wearing a rubber band and looking at it in these metaphoric ways also helps anchor

---

[7]It was not until the spring semester of my year at Rutgers that I pulled out of my near clinical depression, which made me question the purpose of living. Here I need to give credit to my friend Mitch, who joined our dorm floor in January after finishing his second round of chemotherapy to put his leukemia into remission. Mitch and I found comfort and admiration in each other's struggles. I admired Mitch's determination to live life to the fullest each day and go to school for an English and art history double major despite no guarantees to live until graduation (he earned all A's despite being a jock in high school who didn't often care to excel in the classroom). Mitch admired me for what he perceived as my selfless commitment to making the world a better place. We shared a distaste for narcissism and personal pettiness. Even though Mitch passed away almost 2 years later, remembering his zest for appreciating even the simple things in life helps give me perspective when I engage in work for social change.

me and keep me grounded. I believe our past, present, and future are interwoven. It serves as a reminder that the things which I possess and the things which I accomplish are not entirely due to my effort. As a middle-class European American male, I have come to realize that I bear the fruit of a privileged upbringing along with a foundation of privilege that has come in general to European American males for more than 2 centuries. While in many ways my parents, my grandparents, and their parents had to struggle to provide food, clothing, and shelter for their families, my status is the fruit of their labor within a society that allowed them and does allow me the opportunity to advance and fulfill our dreams.

When many liberal European Americans learn about past injustices suffered by people of color at the hands of "whites," they tend to feel a sense of guilt. I felt guilty for a period of time as an undergraduate, but I have come to think, with the help of people of color, that such guilt is self-serving and misguided. I have come to the realization that I can't be judged or feel accountable for the past as a "white male." However, contrary to the beliefs of white supremacists and many conservatives, I must acknowledge my historically rooted privilege and feel a sense of responsibility for addressing and correcting injustices and inequities in our society, which "White males" created and from which we continue to benefit.

Traveling Abroad to Find My Humanity and See My Backyard

Traveling and submersing oneself in another culture for extended periods of time can also broaden one's perspective and serve as another source of reeducation. In the late summer and fall of 1988, I took advantage of the opportunity to spend almost a month in Calcutta, India, followed by almost 4 months in southern Africa as a student teacher. I went to Calcutta with a close friend from college, Partha, who was going home for the first time in several years. As countless other travelers have also witnessed, the millions of people who live in Calcutta suffer from severe overpopulation, pollution, and poverty. However, rather than pass through the city as part of a tour group or as a vagabond, my opportunity to stay with Partha's family in Calcutta allowed me to also experience a genuine hospitality and culture based on strong family ties and a long, rich history.

The following 4 months in the southern African country of Lesotho were somewhat different because I did not know anyone in the capital city of Maseru. I was student teaching in Lesotho through the Student Teaching Abroad program at Moorhead State University because I felt I needed to experience some of the world if I was going to teach about it as a secondary social studies educator. While most student teachers in the program chose placements in western Europe, Australia, or New Zealand, I asked the program director about placements in developing countries. He said he just got a request from a school in Lesotho, and I demonstrated my typical American geographical ignorance by saying, "Where?" He told me, "Go look it up in the library and let me know if you're interested." When I saw in the atlas that Lesotho was a landlocked country in the middle of South Africa, my heart started to race with anticipation. I saw this placement as an opportunity to learn more about racism and do personal research on the effects of apartheid.

While this goal was accomplished during my work and travels in the region, I unexpectedly found that I also learned much about the United States and injustices back home. I learned how limited and biased the U.S. news is regarding the rest of the world. I realized how the forced removal, attempted genocide, and the reservation system inflicted upon indigenous peoples of North America served as a model for the racist settlers and leaders of South Africa. I had known about how the South African government was determined not to let a civil rights movement similar to that in the United States grow among its majority population, but I was struck by how most whites in South Africa live in a totally separate world from blacks.

I was struck by finding how surprisingly easy it was to ride into black townships and feel a sense of being welcomed. I also found it equally easy to accuse white South Africans of conveniently and maliciously ignoring or misinterpreting the harsh realities of neighbors with darker skin. However, after I rode with ease and without fear into the townships bordering Johannesburg and Cape Town, I critically reflected upon my life growing up in a homogeneous suburb. I saw that my community had also conveniently chosen to deny, ignore, and serve as an accomplice to the apartheid and oppression at home. I realized how I had never spent much time, if any, in the "inner cities" of the United States or on any American Indian reservations. Again, southern Africa was a mirror of my country, and I was, as Michael Jackson sings, "the man in the mirror" who needed to "make that change."

REVERSE CULTURE SHOCK AND THE QUEST FOR MORE INFORMATION

While my eyes were opened to the poverty and injustices abroad and at home during my travels through India and southern Africa, my reentry to the United States was more of a culture shock for me than going to these countries. I was appalled at the unnecessary abundance of everything, including waste, ignorance, apathy, and self-centeredness. I was also challenged after realizing that few people, including my family and friends, could relate to my experiences abroad and many held only passing interest in what I encountered. I discovered my mission to be a global educator, and I was going to do my part to change the world. I committed myself to helping inform the perceptions and attitudes of people with whom I live, work, and learn so that the ignorance which leads to prejudice, intolerance, and injustice could be challenged.

At the same time I realized that I needed to learn more about my multicultural country and history in order to engage in my mission of working for justice as a global educator in this country. I got to know members of the Black Student Union and International Student Club at Moorhead State. I tried to listen to the issues that were important to them and act as an ally for their causes. I was one of a few European Americans who attended a pan-African conference so that I could experience an agenda and issues determined solely by African Americans and Africans. I took anthropology and history courses in Native American and Chicano cultures. I started reading books about black history, beginning with Lerone Bennett's (1982) *Before the Mayflower,* and *The Autobiography of Malcolm X* (with Alex Haley, 1964). I sought documentaries on public and cable television about the plight of various ethnic groups. I did some volunteering in Minneapolis during my breaks between academic terms. It was as if my thirst for knowledge once denied was thirst for water in a desert. I began to take serious responsibility for my reeducation, and I sought multiple ways to learn from the voices unfamiliar to me, especially when those voices could be considered uncomfortable for a "white" male to hear.

While I actively sought to continue my reeducation and enhance my empathy, I kept in mind that I had the luxury of coming and going, of turning off or on, of closing or opening. I knew that no matter how much I learned, I could not understand because of the privileges I inherently possess, which are invisible to most whites. Therefore, developing meaningful relationships with persons of color has helped to remind me of my daily privilege of being considered "normal" by the demographic group with power in our society rather than being looked at as "different."

NURTURING PERSONAL RELATIONSHIPS AND TAKING A STAND WHEN IT'S NOT ALWAYS COMFORTABLE

My transformation could not have occurred without developing close relationships with people of color in college and the communities where I've taught. They have been another important factor in my growth as a person and as an educator. Beyond mere acquaintances or casual relationships for convenience or liberal image,[8] we have developed friendships and extended family relationships that have strengthened my commitment to social justice, resistance to racism, and motivation to learn more about their histories and cultures. When I learn more multicultural and global history, I learn more about my friends and myself. Now when I hear, read, or witness prejudice and injustice, I take it personally because I recognize how my friends could be (and are) the objects of such bigotry.

These relationships have given me a sensitivity to challenge conscious and unconscious stereotypical statements with knee-jerk type responses which would not have been possible or comfortable for me to make 10 years ago. For example, there are times when European Americans I know, including family and friends, describe an everyday situation or tell a story in which they only identify race when it is a person of color. When such identification was irrelevant to the situation and their language reflects their construction of the "Other," I find myself making an immediate, reflexive response such as, "What are you trying to say? What did the person's ____ness have to do with this situation?" I usually try to follow up my reactions with an explanation that I'm not encouraging people to be liberal racists who claim to be "color-blind," but that we need to critically think about the implications of when we do and do not identify race.

Another example of developing an instantaneous response to prejudicial comments occurred one Halloween when my wife and I were bringing our once 18-month-old daughter from door to door for treats. As we walked around the block from our house in southwestern Milwaukee, we came to a house where four African-American children dressed in various costumes had just left. After we had said, "Trick or Treat!" and the homeowner gave us some candy, we said thanks and started to walk away. She then said in a negative tone, looking for a receptive ear, "What are they doing in this neighborhood?" I immediately stopped, took the candy out of my daughter's plastic pumpkin, walked back to the woman and tersely said, "We don't

---

[8]I struggled in writing this section because one of the quickest ways to recognize a person blinded by ignorance who claims not to be racist is to hear a defensive retort, such as "I'm not racist, I have black (or any other group) friends." However, not acknowledging the authentic relationships I have had would be unethical and a form of exploitation because I have learned a great deal from these friends.

want candy from anyone with an attitude like that." The woman stood in her doorway stunned, and I was angry that we moved in the neighborhood without learning more about it first.

Like most cities in the United States, Milwaukee has very segregated housing patterns, which we were not fully aware of at the time we moved there from the very diverse town of Waukegan, Illinois. Although we made a conscious decision to live in the city limits rather than a suburb, it seemed as if we were living in a homogeneous suburban community. While we were living in this segregated section of Milwaukee, I noticed something troubling about my own consciousness.

I found myself taking second looks in a curious way at people of color who were in this part of Milwaukee for whatever reason. Although my second or sustained looks were not ones of suspicion or resentment, such as my neighbor expressed on Halloween, I still found myself quietly wondering, "What are they doing here?" In contrast, when I have lived in diverse communities, I only take first rather than second notice of someone just because they were of a different ethnic group than myself.[9] In essence, then, I found myself becoming a product of the suspicion in my homogeneous environment, even though my commitment to antiracism was probably as strong as ever.

Consequently, upon accepting my first college teaching position at St. Cloud State University in central Minnesota, my wife and I decided that I would commute to work 65 miles each way so we could live in an ethnically diverse area of the "Twin Cities." We ended up finding our home in an area we had considered to be a "rough," no-travel zone when we grew up in the suburbs more than a decade earlier. As parents, we didn't want the intolerance that often festers in places where people are segregated to find its destructive way into our minds or the minds of our children.

CONCEPTUALIZING MY PROCESS OF REEDUCATION

In the first part of this chapter, I have described how interpersonal relationships, traveling, and other perhaps more formal efforts at reeducation have brought me an increased awareness of other cultures' strengths rather than deficits, potential rather than failings, and opportunities denied rather than granted. When analyzing my reflections, it seems that I've engaged in a four-front effort (see Figure 12–1) of transformation and reeducation. I believe this multidimensional effort has been and will be consistently required to resist my psycho-social diseases and work sincerely for authentic democracy and social justice.

I believe that exemplary teachers need to critically reflect upon their practice and have a strong understanding of self when working with students. Without critical and often uncomfortable reflection, there is limited awareness of the attitudes, actions, and policies which thwart justice on an individual and institutional level. Whether these attitudes, policies, and actions are conscious or subconscious, explicit or implicit, they affect how we teach and how our students learn. In turn,

---

[9]I just want to make it clear that I am not suggesting that I "don't see color," as many well-meaning but misguided European Americans often claim in attempting to deny their prejudice and state they have an open mind. As Gloria Ladson-Billings (1994) writes, seeing color and culture is both respectful and a necessary process in being a culturally relevant teacher.

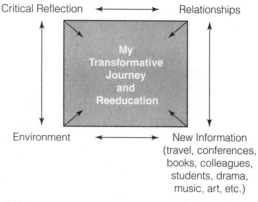

FIGURE 12–1 A model of reeducation.

without relationships, there is the tendency to believe in a concept like equity but not act to achieve it. Without authentic relationships, differences are often depersonalized and different people are seen as "the Other." Furthermore, without an environment that is diverse and respects diversity, stereotypes can go unchecked and opportunities to learn can be limited. Finally, without new information from a variety of sources, perspectives are limited to those gained from one's environment and relationships.

FACILITATING TRANSFORMATION IN AND BEYOND THE CLASSROOM

One of the first lessons I taught in my African American studies classes each semester involved reading and discussing a speech by Malcolm X to youth. In the preface to the speech, the book stated, "Malcolm believed the re-education of Afro-Americans was necessary to build a new mass movement capable of fighting effectively for human rights." Throughout the semester, I tried as their white teacher and fellow learner to make this statement a central theme throughout the course. Moreover, since then I have tried to apply the concept of reeducation for social justice to every class I have taught as a high school social studies teacher and as a teacher educator. I continually seek opportunities for my students to critically reflect on their personal lives while taking a critical look at our past and present society. In the process, we both become students and teachers, and our learning becomes transformative.

In this section, I will give examples of how my personal transformation has impacted my work as a public school teacher for social justice both in and out of the classroom. While the two efforts described later in this section demonstrate how my personal transformation has impacted my deliberate approaches to curriculum and instruction, it is also necessary to mention some examples of how I've tried to stand for social justice on a daily, impromptu basis in my classrooms and schools. These examples are described first because it is important to recognize that being a transformative educator is more than organizing a unit, event, or club; I've learned that it is ongoing and often unplanned.

The following two examples demonstrate reflexive responses to incidences of injustice that I'm not sure I would have undertaken had I not begun my journey of reeducation and transformation. In other words, my journey has given me the power to act reflexively to incidences of injustices by being sensitive enough to readily recognize and respond to them. My ultimate goal becomes turning these incidences into teachable moments for my students.

One of the most prevalent examples of injustice that occurs on a daily basis in schools all across the country is the harassment of some students by others using derogatory language. Too often, teachers become accomplices in the crime and choose to "turn their back" on what they hear or see for a variety of reasons, including fear of confrontation, personal insensitivity, and pressure to "finish" a lesson.

Even though I tried to prevent such harassment from occurring in my classroom by explicitly expecting students from the first day of class to have respect (for self, others, and property) and contribute to a positive classroom environment, my classroom did not exist in a vacuum. Whenever I heard or saw harassment that challenged the safe and positive learning environment that I wanted for each of my students, I acted immediately and in such a way to be instructive not only to the harasser but the whole class. Each situation varied, but I usually stopped the lesson and sternly asked the student into the hallway for a discussion that eventually included the victim and some disclosure with apology to the class. Whenever a student made an offensive homophobic, racist, sexist, or ableist comment during a lesson—whether or not the comment was directed at anyone in particular—I challenged the student's comment in front of the whole class. My approach was to use questions to expose his or her bias and give other students an opportunity to join me in condemning such language. While I could have just quickly responded to such situations with punishment or a short corrective comment like "Don't say that," I tried to respond by creating a learning opportunity for reeducation that sometimes took most of the class period.

Another reflexive response example involved one of my students whose family was the victim of racist graffiti spray painted on their garage during my third year of teaching. My student, "Monique," came to class and was unusually quiet. I waited for an opportunity to discretely ask her what was wrong. She told me what had happened and that the city had told her mother that they had not found the criminals and would not assist her in repainting her garage door. Because I had come to understand that hate crimes are intended to affect not only the immediate victim but a whole community, I was upset that the city responded with such indifference to the crime and my African American student's family. I asked her if we could discuss the situation as a class, and she agreed. During our discussion, she informed us that her mother and grandmother were going to the city council meeting that night to ask for more to be done. I told my class that I was going to go in support, and I encouraged them to come as well.

That evening, Monique's mother approached the microphone during the public comment/question portion of the meeting, only to be told by the mayor in a condescending way, "We're doing all we can, ma'am." I hadn't planned on speaking, but when I observed how she was treated after making a compelling case for the city to take action, I had to approach the council as well. I introduced myself as Monique's teacher and basically repeated the comments of her mother. However, the mayor, who was a white male, became defensive and claimed that racism was not a major problem in the city. After we went back-and-forth a couple times in responding to each other, I was asked to sit down. The next day, a subheading on the front page of the community newspaper read "Mayor Denies Racism," and the article referred to my challenging of the mayor but not to Monique's mother. When talking about the meeting and the article with my class the next day, we discussed how injustice anywhere is a threat to justice everywhere. We also problematized how wrong but real it was for my voice as a white male and teacher to resonate more with the mayor and the newspaper than that of Monique's mother. This experience taught me a number of things, especially the importance of taking public and private stands for social justice as a person of privilege in this society.

Besides these examples of reflexive actions as a transformative teacher, there are also deliberate efforts I've undertaken in and beyond the classroom that serve to describe how my personal transformation has impacted my work. One of the more significant effects that my personal transformation has had on my teaching relates to the style of instruction and learning that I favor in developing my lessons. At the beginning of my career, I thought that I had to know everything and entertain my students in order for them to be interested in the subject I was trying to teach. While I thought my commitments were student centered, I have come to realize that my pedagogy and reflections were teacher centered. Even though I was very concerned about student learning, my reflective questions at the end of each lesson, day, or week emphasized concerns about how students perceived me as their teacher. It was as though I wanted to be one of the most popular teachers in the school while still "making" them learn.

The more I taught, the more I realized the importance of expecting and encouraging students to learn while being a "guide on the side" rather than a "sage on the stage." As my pedagogical emphasis shifted toward student inquiry, expression, and dialogue, many of my students became more engaged and empowered in their learning. We both struggled with this approach because it was not the norm and it is harder work than more traditional, teacher-centered approaches to teaching and learning. However, they did more higher order thinking, they thought more critically than just believing my critical thinking as an instructor, and they took ownership over their learning.

The example I will describe involved students in my team-taught ESL American studies class and my own world history students learning about racism and slavery in their elite suburban school of Highland Park, Illinois. I began planning their units by critically reflecting upon my own experiences as a suburban high school student dealing with these topics without the assistance of my instructors. I decided to start the unit in both courses by asking my students to write on note cards what they thought they knew and what they wanted to know more about in regards to slavery and racism. We also looked at our texts for what information and lack of information existed. In both courses, I showed the docudrama *Roots* over several weeks, during which I expected students to keep a journal of key themes and scenes along with their emotions and questions. It was also important for me to stop the film at various places and discuss what we all heard and saw. In addition, I used clips from the civil rights movement documentary *Eyes on the Prize,* and I had a community activist visit our class as a guest speaker. Finally, students took their questions and formed inquiry projects, which required the use of a variety of sources, not just print media. The final requirement of their project was sharing their findings with the class and having a group discussion.

For many world history students who all had the expectation to attend elite colleges and universities, they told me it was the first time in their school career that they were allowed to think and explore on their own. For them, the experience was transformative. They felt intellectually and emotionally liberated to authentically learn for life rather than for the next test. I observed students honestly confronting their own biases and ignorance, and seeking to be reeducated in response to what they had discovered.

From our in-depth unit on slavery and racism, my ESL American studies students, who came from seven countries, in Latin America, Asia, and Europe, gained fresh insights into U.S. culture and their own immigrant experience. Themes such as "dream to be free," "discrimination," "violent oppression," "courage," and "strong family" emerged from our viewing and discussing *Roots*. My teammate Jody and I facilitated our students' examinations of their own experiences with parallels to the images and stories of the historical docudrama, and the students then developed multimedia presentations about the biographies of various civil and human rights activists in the past and present. Again, the feedback we received from our students at the end of the year was that this unit was a very meaningful and transformative learning experience for them.

In addition to planned efforts to create reeducational opportunities for students in my classes, I have also been involved with student efforts to promote social justice beyond the classroom. During my second year teaching, ironically, a couple months before the Rodney King beating and subsequent riots in Los Angeles, a student came to me concerned about racial prejudice in our high school. She was not a student in any of my classes, but she had friends in my classes and they told her about some of the things we discussed. She was concerned that there was a club for every ethnic group in our school, but not one to bring people together and talk about prejudice. We ended up forming a club called Shades, that had the dual symbolism of "in complete darkness we are all the same" and "respect and appreciate the differences or shades of humanity we all represent" (Jackson, 1989).

We decided to hold our meetings in the hallway after school, much like a 1960s-style sit-in. Students' issues formed our agendas, and I facilitated discussion with provocative questions when needed. In large part, we became a multiracial, multi-ethnic support group, which hadn't existed in the school before. Sometimes we had meetings when tempers flared and when tears were produced from ignorant and insensitive comments. However, because we were basically an open discussion group, our membership and attendance at meetings was always sporadic. We competed for students' attention with other clubs or teams that had definite goals or events to prepare for and participate in.

During the second year of Shades's existence, we decided to take a more activist approach while still keeping a grounding in offering a safe place for dialogue. Over the course of that year and in subsequent years, we marched in the homecoming parade and handed out literature about our organization. We sold buttons, bumper stickers, and T-shirts with social justice messages to promote our ideals and raise funds. We organized a youth conference for 12 area schools, which included 400 students for a day of dialogue about prejudice, discrimination, and social justice. We held an intensive all-night lock-in with lots of food, sports, movies, and discussions for 100 students and teachers, during which we created conditions for dialogue, teamwork, and fellowship. We also organized a protest at a predominantly white upper-middle-class school which made our students, but not their own, go through metal detectors before entering for a tournament basketball game.

Since leaving the school where Shades started, I have learned that several other schools have started their own similar groups, even with the same name. I have also had former students tell me how they have continued their work for social justice in college or their workplace. They have told me that they recall Shades being transformative because it was the first time they felt listened to and that they had the power to make a difference. Student clubs like Shades are not unique, and we were definitely not the first in the country to begin such a group. However, there are still too many high schools and middle schools which don't have a forum for students to discuss and get support for their personal and social concerns regarding prejudice and discrimination. Unfortunately, even fewer opportunities seem to exist for students to form cross-racial relationships while working together for social justice.

SEEKING OPPORTUNITIES FOR PERSONAL AND STRUCTURAL TRANSFORMATION

Based on my own continuous and multipath journey of transformation, I have come to believe that all teachers and teacher educators, especially European Americans, must do all that we can to help expose the cultural assumptions that we and our students possess. We need to continually question, rethink, and refine our cultural and historical ways of looking at the world around us. We need to constantly look for opportunities to be pushed, prodded, slapped, and surprised, so we become encouraged to think and act beyond our "centers" of understanding. This can be difficult personal and professional work, but it needs to happen both individually and in collaboration with others.

I also believe that every school and teacher needs to comprehensively reexamine each policy and course for how they do or don't respect cultural differences and similarities, do or don't treat students equitably, and do or don't promote student empowerment and social justice. The following set of questions are offered (in no particular order of importance) to facilitate such reexamination of courses and school practices and guide an audit of multiculturalism:

1. To what extent do all of our students see themselves in our curriculum? To what extent can our students explore themselves in our curriculum? To what extent do students nonstereotypically explore the diversity of other groups of people other than their own?

2. Do all students and parents have a voice in our school? Are students taught about the importance of living in a democracy without being given the opportunity to experience it?

3. To what extent are issues of racism, power, prejudice, discrimination, sexism, heterosexism, ethnocentrism, nativism, ageism, and ableism discussed throughout the curriculum?

4. Do we really expect all of our students to achieve, or do we make exceptions or excuses because of a student's background? If our school tracks students, does tracking contribute to self-fulfilling prophecies, misplacements, and lower achievement of students of low socioeconomic status?

5. Do we expect our students to assimilate into the mainstream culture of the school, or do we celebrate the rich differences students bring to our school?

6. Is multicultural education just viewed as belonging to the social studies, English, world language, and bilingual curriculum, or is the entire school committed to multiple perspectives and contributions of diverse groups in their respective disciplines?

7. When we teach "other people's children" as author Lisa Delpit (1995) describes, what assumptions and expectations do we hold for these children compared to our own kids or kids from backgrounds more like our own?

8. To what extent do we really understand where our students come from and what their lives are like outside of our classrooms? In what ways do we acknowledge and utilize the talents and knowledge which all students possess, but which may not show in traditional school settings?

9. Do we as a staff recognize that most of us come from privileged backgrounds which create a set of cultural norms, understandings, and biases which may not be readily apparent to us but are apparent to many of our students and their parents from other socioeconomic backgrounds?

Closing Comments

Every school in the nation should infuse meaningful multicultural education in every grade and across all subjects. In my view, meaningful multicultural education is comprehensive, interdisciplinary, ongoing, and transformative. It is local, national, and global in perspective. It is both tragic and triumphant.

Multicultural education should explore both the quest for and denial of the American Dream. It is personal and psychological, social and sociological. It is economic, political, and spiritual. It is music, math, art, history, literature, science, geography, language, sport, and food. Multicultural education should be interesting yet disturbing, and relevant yet rigorous. Its perspective is not limited to the real social constructions and false biological constructions of blacks and whites; it also views the kaleidoscope of Hmong, Filipino, Mexican, Polish, Puerto Rican, Guatemalan, Haitian, Honduran, Japanese, Lebanese, Jewish, Nigerian, Navaho, Lakota, Chinese, and obviously many, many others. It is not just diversity among groups, but diversity within groups as well.

Meaningful multicultural education is a mosaic or kaleidoscope of ideas and people, not a melting pot. Most of all, meaningful multicultural education is not a fad. It is a key to a better future for our students and society. It is essential, and its essence is transformative.

Today's educators, particularly those of European American heritage, need to acknowledge and understand the basic assumptions which underlay our world views. We must also learn to continually think critically about these assumptions, and we must challenge the racist, classist, sexist messages that we and our students receive on a daily basis as members of this society. In essence, we need to reeducate ourselves in many ways, especially by relearning our histories. While the miseducation, reeducation, and transformation I have experienced cannot and should not serve as a model for others, it was the intent of this chapter to describe my journey to date in such a way as to facilitate vicarious experience and critical reflection for you the reader. These two capacities common to members of the human race are essential in our efforts to fight for socioeconomic, political, educational, and environmental justice in this new century.

ACKNOWLEDGMENT

While thanks are due to many unmentioned people who have contributed to my transformation (i.e., friends, teachers, scholars), I would be remiss not to specifically thank my mentor at Moorhead State University and current friend, Andrew Conteh. Before teaching political science at the college level, he served as ambassador to the Soviet Union for his native country of Sierra Leone. As an African who speaks fluent Russian in the small town of Moorhead, Minnesota, it is needless to say that he and his wonderful family have challenged several common stereotypes. Andrew, more than any single individual, has opened my eyes to the world, and I am forever indebted to him as a transformative educator committed to his students and social justice.

REFERENCES

Banks, J. A. (1999). *An introduction to multicultural education* (2nd ed.). Boston: Allyn & Bacon.

Banks, J. A. (2000). The social construction of difference and the quest for educational equality. In R. Brandt (Ed.), *Education in a new era: ASCD yearbook 2000* (pp. 21–45). Alexandria, VA: Association for Supervision and Curriculum Development.

Bennett, L. (1982). *Before the* Mayflower: *A History of black America* (5th ed.) New York: Penguin.

Delpit, L. (1995). *Other people's children: Cultural conflict in the classroom.* New York: New Press.

Jackson, J. (1989). *Rhythm nation 1814* (audio CD). Los Angeles: A & M Records.

Kozol, J. (1992). *Savage inequalities: Children in America's schools* (Rep. ed.). New York: Harper-Perennial.

Ladson-Billings, G. (1994). *The dreamkeepers: Successful teachers of African American children.* San Francisco: Jossey-Bass.

United Nations (1948). Universal declaration of human rights. Retrieved March 6, 2003, from www.un.org/Overview/rights.html

Woodson, C. G. (1990). *The mis-education of the Negro.* Trenton, NJ: Africa World Press. (Original work published 1933)

X, Malcolm, & Haley, A. (1964). *The autobiography of Malcolm X.* New York: Grove.

Activities for the Classroom

- Have students consider how their lives are intertwined and interdependent with people and events around the world. Ask students to create a list of interdependence by starting to look at some things which they own and where these items are made. It is important to not just have students become aware of the extent to which globalization and the world economy have led to interdependence, but also that students have the opportunity to examine the lives of people and nations with whom they are linked. Organizations such as Global Exchange (www.globalexchange.org), Amnesty International (www.amnesty.org), and Free the Children International (www.freethechildren.org) are excellent places to start this critical examination.
- Start a multicultural student club with the explicit purpose of fighting all forms of prejudice and discrimination. Ask for representatives from existing

ethnic or culture-based groups at the school and open the invitation to all students. Consider holding panel discussions, making video documentaries, and having fund-raisers to get your message out. Get members involved in the community and use the community as a resource for information and action. Consider developing a set of beliefs that help define the organization and its purpose.

• Have students interview adults about issues of race and privilege. Students should ask adults about their perceptions of racial, ethnic, religious, and class "boundaries" when they were growing up and how they think things have or haven't changed. Students should analyze interview data by age, race and ethnicity, class, gender, and geography. They could then also examine their lives and the boundaries that they feel exist, and how and why they do or don't cross them. Finally, given the data collected from interviews with adults, have students project the status of current boundaries 25 years from now.

FURTHER READING

Blackside, Inc. (1987–1990). *Eyes on the prize* [8-part series]. Alexandria, VA: PBS Video.

Kivel, P. (1996). *Uprooting racism: How white people can work for racial justice.* Gabriola Island, BC: New Society.

Loewen, J. (1996). *Lies my teacher told me: Everything your American history textbook got wrong.* New York: Touchstone.

McIntosh, P. (1998). White privilege: Unpacking the invisible knapsack. In E. Lee, D. Menkart, & M. Okazawa-Rey (Eds.), *Beyond heroes and holidays: A practical guide to K–12 anti-racist, multicultural education and staff development* (pp. 79–82). Washington, DC: Network of Educators on the Americas.

Takaki, R. (1993). *A different mirror: A history of multicultural America.* New York: Little, Brown.

Tatum, B. (2000). Defining racism: "Can We Talk?" In M. Adams, et al. (Eds.), *Readings for diversity and social justice: An anthology on racism, antisemitism, sexism, heterosexism, ableism and classism* (pp. 79–82). New York: Routledge.

Section IV

The Praxis of Culturally Relevant Teaching

Introduction: Themes Reflecting Critical Thought and Action—Praxis

Paula Bradfield, EDC, Inc., Chicago and Jaime J. Romo, University of San Diego, San Diego

A Zen abbot was interviewing a convert from the United States. Illustrating the difference between Eastern and Western spirituality, the abbot placed two small, apparently identical, legless Japanese dolls in front of the interviewee. However, one doll was weighted in the head and one weighted in the base.

The monk pushed the doll that was weighted in the base; it fell and bounced back up. When he pushed the doll that was weighted at the head, however, it fell and remained on its side.

This story offers us several insights related to transformational teaching. On one hand, it points to the need for us to be grounded in who we are and what we know. Part of this grounding is to apply what we know, our transformational spirit and experiences, in our relationships and to our work with youth.

On the other hand, the story speaks to our unexamined epistemologies or mind-sets that can work against us when we experience dissonance as we interact with diverse students and colleagues (Bradfield-Kreider, 1998; Gay, 1994). The following section typifies themes that have emerged from authors in previous sections—teachers who have questioned their own mind-sets, who have experienced cultural dissonance, who have experienced the pain caused by the actions of misinformed others, and who have begun to face their own demons grounded in their privilege or biases. All, however, continue to struggle in the everyday as advocates for their students.

The authors' stories highlight their intellectual frameworks and integrative practices—praxis (Freire, 1997). Although the stories in this book, and this section in particular are varied, they seem to be guided by the understanding that knowledge itself is political and not neutral, and that schools are a central arena of struggle, resistance, and transformation for both the teacher and the students. They express an appreciation of the forms of tension that open new possibilities of interaction between human beings, and a spirit of challenging the social forces that perpetuate the status quo. They model dialogue as purposeful and transformative, they stimulate creativity, risk taking, doubting, and questioning, and they create and facilitate the conditions for students to find their own voices and participate in transforming their world. Finally, they are all engaged in some form of democratic or culturally relevant pedagogy—teaching and advocating for *all* children (e.g., Chávez Chávez, 1995; Haberman & Post, 1998; Ladson-Billings, 1994, 1995; Nieto, 1999; Oakes & Lipton, 1998; Romo & Salerno, 2000; Zeichner, 1993).

As these advocates take on the additional challenge of systemic transformation, they also embody the expression, *Caminante, no hay camino. El camino se hace al andar.* (Traveler, there is no set road. You make the road by walking).

With this perspective, their stories, as you may have surmised from previous chapters, may seem paradoxical, if not counterintuitive: apparent outsiders who transform systems as insiders; insiders who use the politics of their location to institutionalize respect and honor of those rendered invisible or despised in the status quo. The authors offer us their insights into what helps them to bounce back when the inevitable slips and falls occur along the many paths in their journeys as teachers.

Frank Kazemak, a poet and professor at St. Cloud State University, uses metaphor and prose in "Something That Won't Compute: A Journey of Adult Literacy" as he shares his successes and failures while teaching in Chicago schools. He examines "social justice in small places," through the power and process of literacy. Monica T. Rodriguez, from Columbia College, writes about critical incidents in her experience in alternative schools and the small school movement in Chicago in her work, "Turning Points: A Teacher's Journey." Steven Strull, from the Center for Collaborative Education, addresses his educational reform work in a system of glacial speed. In his chapter, "Small Schools: A Metaphor for Caring," he speaks from the voice of a high school teacher in a reconstituted school in Chicago and his work in school reform. In "Woman Warrior Liberating the Oppressed and the Oppressor: Cultural Relevancy Through Narrative," Chapman University Professor Suzanne SooHoo eloquently narrates her story as an Asian-American woman living and growing in a world dominated by white men; her reflections interrelate identity development, identity politics, and critical pedagogy. Finally, Jaime Romo, assistant professor at the University of San Diego, concludes the section with his reflection on his relationship between recovery, identity development, and advocacy in "Hurting, Healing, Helping: A Pedagogy of Identity, Recovery, and Voice."

REFERENCES

Bradfield-Kreider, P. (1998). Mediated cultural immersion and antiracism: An opportunity for monocultural preservice teachers to begin the dialogue. In C. Grant (Ed.), *1998 National Association of Multicultural Education Conference proceedings* (pp. 117–148). New York: Caddo.

Chávez Chávez, R. (1995). *Multicultural education for the everyday: A renaissance for the recommitted*. Washington, DC: American Association for Colleges of Teacher Education.

Freire, P. (1997). *The pedagogy of hope: Reliving the pedagogy of the oppressed*. New York: Continuum.

Gay, G. (1994). *At the essence of learning: Multicultural education*. Lafayette, IN: Kappa Delta Pi.

Haberman, M., & Post, L. (1998). Teachers for Multicultural Schools: The Power of Selection. *Theory Into Practice, 37*(2), 96–104.

Ladson-Billings, G. (1994). *The dreamkeepers: Successful teachers of African American children*. San Francisco: Jossey-Bass.

Nieto, S. (1999). *The light in their eyes: Creating a multicultural learning community*. New York: Teachers College Press.

Oakes, J., & Martin, L. (1998). *Teaching to change the world*. New York: McGraw-Hill.

Romo, J., & Salerno, C. (2000). *Toward cultural democracy: The journey from knowledge to action in diverse classrooms*. Boston: Houghton-Mifflin.

Zeichner, K. (1993). *Educating teachers for cultural diversity*. East Lansing, MI: National Center for Research on Teacher Learning.

Chapter 13

Something That Won't Compute:
A Journey of Adult Literacy

Francis E. Kazemek, St. Cloud State University, St. Cloud

Focus Questions

1. How does social justice in small places relate to systemic transformation?

2. How do you deal with others'/students' deeper voice, woundedness, struggles, or suffering?

3. What do you see as your road to transformative teaching?

Lord, when shall we be done growing? As long as we have anything more to do, we have done nothing . . . Lord, when shall we be done changing? Ah! it's a long stage, and no inn in sight, and night coming, and the body cold. But with you for a passenger, I am content and can be happy. (Melville, 1967, p. 567)

I remember Marvin,[1] all 5 feet and 70 pounds of him: burnt sienna skin (the other kids often called him Red), black eyes alive with wonder and mischief (oh, how he knew to pull on my particular chain!), and perpetrator of countless classroom disruptions which failed to hide his fear of failure, his fear of being stupid ("I ain't dumb, Mr. K.! I just can't read too good").

I remember Marvin in 1969 and 1970. I had just graduated from the University of Illinois Circle Campus in Chicago with a B.A. in philosophy and English. I intended to pursue an M.A. in English at the University of New Mexico in the near future but decided to take a year off and earn a

---

[1]All names used in this essay, other than my own and those of published authors, are pseudonyms.

little money. The Chicago Public Schools needed teachers in the inner city, and no experience or expertise was required. If you had a college degree and were willing to teach in one of the South or West Side schools, you were hired. I was hired. I found myself suddenly in the midst of a class of fourth graders in the heart of an African American community.

I remember Marvin and his classmates, who quickly realized that I knew absolutely nothing about children, teaching, or classroom management. What I did know something about was literature. The basal readers and other programmed texts I found in the room were inane, so I gathered books from the school and public libraries and tried to build a reading program around them. I didn't know what I was doing, but the kids were tolerant. After all these years I'm not sure if they learned anything about how to read from me; however, I do think they learned that reading can be meaningful and enjoyable.

I remember Marvin, who in fourth grade could read little more than his name and a handful of other words. Reading terrified him, and he fled from it in any way possible. After weeks of utter failure with him, I turned in hopelessness to our fourth-grade team leader: "Linda, I don't know what to do. The kid can't read, and I don't know anything about teaching him how to." She told me to have Marvin tell me a story about something that happened to him and to write it down. Then Marvin and I could read his story together. Finally, we could keep his stories in a folder for future reading.

I remember the first time Marvin and I sat together in a corner while the other kids worked with my help or read independently. I asked him to tell me what he had done after school the day before. I told him I'd write his story down. I remember his apprehension, but then as he got into the story I remember how I had to tell him to slow down—I couldn't write that fast. I remember his smile as I read his long two-page story to him several times. I can still hear him attempting to read along with me the last time.

I remember Marvin and the individualized reading program based on his own dictated stories that he and I pursued for the rest of the year. (I subsequently learned I was doing something called the language experience approach.) It was the one time of the day when Marvin and I found a safe space to engage reading and writing as partners. All of his troublesome behavior was left outside our little corner, and all of my irritation and inadequacy were forgotten. He told me about the joy, love, sorrow, and harshness of his life, and I wrote it all down. I told him about my childhood and its similar joys and sorrows 20 years earlier in a neighborhood not 30 minutes from his by car. I told him one day I'd take him there and show it to him (but I never did).

I remember Marvin at the end of the school year and the relatively small gains we had made together. He couldn't read much, but he could read his own stories—and he did, over and over again. I remember the sense of failure I felt not only over Marvin's reading, but over all of the children's learning as well. "I'm a fraud," I told my future wife. "I got paid, but I didn't teach the kids anything." "You stayed with them for the whole year while all of the other emergency teachers quit," she said. "You like them and treat them with respect. You did your best. That's something," she consoled. "Not enough," I replied.

I remember Marvin and his mom at our last conference of the year. I remember her telling me, "Mr. K., Marvin wants to be like you when he grows up."

In the imagination, we are from henceforth (so long as you read) locked in a fraternal embrace, the classic caress of author and reader. We are one. Whenever I say "I" I mean also "you." And so, together, as one, we shall begin.   (Williams, 1986, p. 178)

Dancing in the Adult Literacy Class

"I wrote a poem," she whispered,
"You know, like you asked us.
It's about my babies,
And how I need more than part time."

"May I see it?"

She opened her blue binder
Covered with stickers of animals—
It must have been one of her kid's—
And slipped from between the worksheets
A single piece of wide-ruled paper.

"It's not too good I think."

Her careful pencil strokes
Swirled in a stiff-legged dance
Of misspellings, missed grammar,
And freedom from punctuation.

I read it silently, and again,
Trying to enter the movement
Of her skipping language.
I asked her to show me
The steps I couldn't follow;
Then I read it aloud, tentatively,
Slowly moving to the rhythms
And motions of her words.

I read it again, sure now
Of all that the poem carried.
And again, this time with her
Joining me in counterpoint,
Maid's fingers tracking each word.

It was in our telling together
That her words reflected the grace
Hidden in the flurry of print:
Lines rose and shone in beauty,
Longing, and a mother's hope:
"I pray for my children,
Going out to school
Coming home from school ..."
On the urban streets of hopelessness.

"That don't sound like me!"
She grinned and shook her head

In bafflement and wonder.
"It sounds like, you know,
Somebody who could really write,
You know, sort of like a poet."

And then we danced it again.

"OK, gang, our twenty minutes are up. Let's go around and all share a little something. Who wants to start?" Jane asked.

No one volunteered, so Jane read a letter that she was writing to the editor of the daily newspaper. It was a wickedly sarcastic response to a letter in which the writer claimed most so-called refugees were immoral welfare seekers, ignorant, criminal, and AIDS-infected burdens on the local, state, and national economy. Jane ended the letter with a quotation from Jesus: " 'I was a stranger, and you took me in.' Obviously, although Mr. Bowles claims to be a Christian, he is really an apostate who rejects the very word of Christ. His congregation should see to him."

They all nodded, laughed, or clapped when Jane finished reading the draft of her letter. Then following their usual procedure of responding to one another's works in progress, they each took a turn telling her one thing they liked about the piece or one thing that would help her improve it. Jane was not allowed to comment or explain. She simply took notes on what they told her. Rennie, a green-card carrying immigrant, said, "You make me proud. You stand up for me as human."

Jane was a tall, plump, and wide-hipped woman in her late 40s. Her garb was always the same: faded jeans, Birkenstock sandals, a brightly flowered cotton blouse from somewhere in Central or South America, and gold-framed John Lennon glasses. Her long chestnut hair flowed to the small of her back, and her freckled face was free of any makeup. The students teased her sometimes and called her a hippie from the 1960s. "You're damn right I am," Jane would say. "And I'm damn proud of it too."

Jane was the instructor of the "regular" adult literacy and GED class at the Covenant School. The "regular" class met four days a week, from Monday through Thursday. If students missed three consecutive meetings, they were dropped from the class. Then they would be able to attend the daily "drop-in" sessions, which were also taught by Jane. The "regular" class was for those students who had the time, inclination, and ability to move ahead quickly.

The class at present was a hodgepodge. There were four people for whom English was a second language; two middle-aged African American sisters who couldn't land decent jobs due to their poor reading and writing abilities; a 70-year-old widow; an ex-con in his 40s who had spent half his life in jails and prisons; and three teens who were making it on their own. The one thing they had in common was that they were all poor.

Jane ran this diverse class with enthusiasm and skill. "We learn by teaching and helping each other," she'd say. "If you want to be some John Wayne–type loner who's going to try and make it on your own, this isn't the place for you." She believed that they would become better readers and writers by actually reading and writing. She was a published poet herself and believed in the power of poetry to help people see the world differently and gain some power over their lives. Her love of poetry had excited the students.

After Jane read her draft letter, the students took turns reading from their pieces. Some read only a sentence. Isabelle, a 16-year-old with sable-black hair and midnight eyes that startled with their fierceness, was the only student to read from a poem. She was smart and witty, and her poems were usually angry or bitter. The poem she read was something she had been working on for a while. The governing image was that of a peasant farmer driving his overworked donkey. She had titled it "Husbands and Wives." The last two lines of the poem were:

> *Ay, Pedro! whose love is a switch in hand!*
> *Ay, Burrita! whose hide bleeds in the sand!*

"In Spanish it should be *burrito,* you know, a little burro," Paco said. "Not *burrita.* *Burro* is a masculine word; there is no female word like *burra.*"

"You don't think I know that?" Isabelle snapped.

"Isabelle," Jane snapped back, "you know the rule about writers not commenting."

"Sure, I do, but, for Chris' sake, Spanish is *my* native language! You think I don't know the difference between *burrita* and *burrito*?"

"Ok. Don, what's your feedback?" Jane asked one of the other teens.

"Well, maybe that's it. I like the poem; it's really wild with hate. But I guess maybe it's too obvious, you know, the title and all, and then saying *burrita,* you know, a female donkey, and calling the farmer Pedro. It just seems too heavy-handed to me."

Isabelle glared at Don and took no notes.

Decoding With Annie

Attack you must
learn how to attack
all these words!
Get them before they get you!

She stared at me:
brown eyes that made me
want to press my forehead
to hers the most solid
thing in the world.

Instead I gave her
vowels and consonants,
told her to split them
with the logic and precise
skill of an executioner:

She placed a finger on her lips
and watched all the VCCV's
and VCV's escape the block,
fleeing forever that kingdom.

We drilled she and I,
close-order, maneuvering
like Marines on a parade field:
sit, see, sock, sun, sand,
about face, and city tripped us
as we passed the reviewing stand.
I forced her to round up families:
without a stutter of conscience

> *I sang as we marched*
> fat, cat, sat, bat, mat,
> *and* pat *into detention camps*
> *and secured them with barbed wire.*
>
> *She cried:*
> *how could we be so cruel!*
> *and while I was sleeping*
> *in the live of the night*
> *she unlocked the gates,*
> *removed the chains,*
> *allowed them to return*
> *to their friends and neighbors.*
>
> *I thrust a* T *into her hand,*
> *she turned it into a ploughshare;*
> *I gave her a* D *as a bow*
> *and a* V *as an arrow,*
> *she brought me cool water in them;*
> *she loosed the corded* S
> *lashed to my wrist*
> *and soothed me with a smile—*
>
> *An EMH smile more lovely*
> *than any sound I had ever heard;*
> *so I threw down my armor,*
> *took her small hand,*
> *and asked her to help me*
> *with the natives make peace.*

When he had free time, George tutored some of the new students at the drop-in center for homeless teens. He was surprised that the ones coming in off the street were getting younger and younger. He worked sometimes with a skinny, sandy-haired girl who called herself Bop. It was summer, and she wore short-shorts and a halter top to cover her flat chest. She was 13 and had needle marks on her arms and cigarette burn scars on the inside of her thighs. She was living in the shelter for women and also participating in its drug rehabilitation program. Her stepfather–pimp came by several times and tried to talk to her; he wanted to take her away. The center's director called the police, and when they arrived he quickly left by a side door.

"Don't ever come back here, you sonofabitch!" she shouted as she chased him out the door.

He knew it was hopeless. He had met several Bops in his literacy work. Like this one, they talked about how good it was to have some older guy taking care of them, loving them, giving them dope to get high. The prostitution was just something they did to please their man.

"Larry ain't so bad," Bop said as they struggled over some GED preparation workbook. "He treats my mom like crap, but that's because she's gotten fat as a old sow. He comes to me for his sugar now. At first I didn't like it, you know, I was too young, I don't know, about eleven. But then I did, you know. He kinda taught me, then introduced me to his friends."

"Yeah."

"I don't know, I guess I just got tired, you know, I'm tired of all that stuff now. You know, I see girls my age going places with their moms, you know, shopping at the mall and stuff, and they seem so happy, laughing and stuff. I see them dressed up real nice, you know, and I wonder why it ain't that way for me. Why I got stuck where I'm at, with the people I'm with, you know."

"Well, things can change. You can be like that some day."

"Naw, I can never be like that. Not in a hundred years."

One morning when George came in, the director was sitting at her desk with her head in her hands.

"What's wrong?"

"That sonofabitch got her," she said angrily with red, swollen eyes. "Bop. I just found out. He came in early this morning and got her to leave with him. I called the child and family services people, and they said they'd get to it. Get to it! They're overwhelmed with cases, said since he's her legal guardian it might take a while."

Two weeks later they read on the sixth page of the daily newspaper that a young prostitute had been found dead of a drug overdose in a rundown motel room. Suicide was suspected, and an investigation was being conducted. The elementary school picture showed a smiling Bop with a missing front tooth. Her real name was Belinda Ann Wilson. Her mother was a homemaker, and her stepfather was unemployed.

On the Job

by Ron

I was offered a job as foreman, but I had to turn the job down because I could not read or spell well.

But I like the job I have done for 30-some years as a crane operator.

Reading Class

by Jeff

I want to feel better and spell better.

I want to better myself and have a better attitude.

I want to read the newspaper and maintenance slips.

I want to learn more words and to read harder books.

I would like to read street signs better.

This condensery, this particular selection, consolidation, and transformation of my life's encounters as a teacher, is emerging and forming itself into a particular shape as I sit at my desk in front of my computer screen and condense. This is the only trade I've ever known: teaching about reading, writing, and literature and then writing about what I learned and how I was transformed in the process. I'm not sure which has had and which continues to have the greater impact on me: the actual transactions with people in public spaces or the writing in solitude. Being by inclination a solitary individual, I must give attention to balance; otherwise, I easily could find myself spinning webs of words that make little connection to anyone but myself.

What does it mean to be a transformative teacher committed to changing the world? Does it mean necessarily engaging the large social issues that threaten daily to overwhelm us? Does it mean manning (or womaning or personing) the ramparts and protesting with picket sign in hand? (I've done that at various times in my life and by nature was always uncomfortable with such public display. Even as I chanted with the rest, "Hey, hey, LBJ, how many babies did you kill today?!" I cynically laughed to myself at such gross simplification: "You! *hypocrite lecteur!—mon sem- blable, —mon frere!*") Does it mean appropriating the language and thought of post- modern theorists and critical pedagogues? (For some perhaps it does, but for me that's a road that I will not take.)

There are various roads to transformative teaching, and mine has always led to small places: individual classrooms, community centers, church basements, senior centers, storefront literacy programs. Small places are often ignored, dismissed, or even ridiculed by some involved in social justice work and transformative teaching. They contend that we must struggle in the broad public spaces where systemic change occurs. They might be correct, but that is one way; it is not my way. Rather, I think of Voltaire's Candide, who says that we must cultivate our garden. I think of Wendell Berry, the Kentucky poet of local places, who admonishes us:

> *So, friends, every day do something*
> *that won't compute. Love the Lord.*
> *Love the world. Work for nothing.*
> *Take all that you have and be poor.*
> *Love someone who does not deserve it.*
> *Denounce the government and embrace*
> *the flag. Hope to live in that free*
> *republic for which it stands.*
> *(Berry, 1985, p. 151)*

Every day do something that won't compute. That's not a bad sentence to have on one's desk or classroom wall. In my efforts at literacy and literature education, it means struggling daily against attempts to turn reading and writing into something that does little *but* compute into something which has little but functional value in the workplace, into something by which individuals can be weighed and measured and found wanting. (*Mene, mene, tekel, upharsin:* the mantra of the "high standards" movement and testing industry.) In my own work as a transformative teacher, it means combatting reductive reading systems and standardized tests with the rich- ness of literature and poetry. Citing myself, it means:

Poetry helps us understand ourselves and our world; it helps us see ourselves and our world in new ways. At the same time, poetry lifts our language. We find ourselves using language in new ways, in ways that are more vivid, more powerful, and more fun. Poetry makes it clear that literacy is not just a set of mechanical skills for read- ing job advertisements or filling out applications.   (Kazemek & Rigg, 1995, p. 4)

Let me describe a current project in which I learn more than teach and am trans- formed more than transform.

———————

Beautiful Women

Women sit or move to and fro, some old, some young,
The young are beautiful—but the old are more beautiful than the young.   (Whitman, 1983, p. 222)

I have been meeting weekly for the last $3^1/_2$ years with a group of elder writers in our local community center. There are 12 to 14 regular members in the group, and over the years another 6 or so have attended sporadically. The elders range in age between 72 and 86. (Two original members, 88 and 92, died almost 2 years ago.) The group calls itself the Senior Class, or as one wag says, "The Almost Dead Poet's Society."

The Senior Class members are all European Americans who have lived their lives on farms or in the small towns of central Minnesota. (Garrison Keillor's Lake Woebegone is not too far distant from our little town!) Their educational backgrounds vary: a few graduated from college, others from high school, and a couple quit school before they completed the eighth grade. Likewise, their life's work varied: A few were farmers; some of the women were homemakers; one was a social worker; another was a mortician; one woman worked in a laundry for 20 years; two were teachers in one-room school houses; and one woman ran her own beauty shop for over 50 years. All of them live on modest incomes.

The elders are independent, active, and enthusiastic about writing in particular and life in general. They suffer from the usual physical infirmities that accompany old age (for example, cataracts, arthritis, heart disease, and prostate cancer), and endure the sorrows that attend upon long lives (for example, the death of a spouse or child, the necessity of selling one's home and moving into a more manageable apartment, the regret of roads not taken or the cruelties done to others, and the daily reminder of one's own mortality). They sometimes are not politically correct in their language or thinking: They refer to African Americans as blacks or colored people; women are often "girls" even though they might be 80 years of age; abortion troubles many of them; several more conservative Christians in the group wrestle with homosexuality as an acceptable lifestyle.

The Senior Class as a group, however, shows me weekly what a small community built upon storytelling, poetry, and mutual concern can be; it demonstrates for me how we can be transformed for the better through our transactions with others. As teachers and learners, we are able to transcend our own particular biases, antipathies, and idiosyncratic pettinesses. We become better than our "everyday" selves through our mutual exploration of issues and ideas and our creation of expressive pieces of writing. Douglas captures the nature of our writing community in his poem, "Senior Class":

> *We write as a group*
> *With feeling and friendship,*
> *Unlike when I was young*
> *And never talked to teachers.*
>
> *We give in fellowship*
> *What we have lived;*
> *We receive from others*
> *Compassion and love.*

The elders, living long themselves, have a respect for life in its infinite forms. They call into question the beliefs and practices that we often never seriously consider as we go about the busyness of our lives. Justice, for both humans and non-humans alike, is not an abstract concept for the Senior Class. It is a specific action. It is for Dan, in his prose piece "The Wasp Nest," looking closely at the "perfect pattern of the comb with each cell identical in mathematical precision and balance" and becoming "suddenly depressed with my power to kill the creatures." Instead, he lets the wasps live in their nest under his shed's eaves. He becomes "respectful of their space" and all into the summer "enjoyed watching the wasps come and go. Somehow I felt a little more like part of their world."

In "What Price Peace?" Dorothy wrote about her son, who was a conscientious objector during the Vietnam War. "How much easier it would have been for him to give in. How much easier to soothe the wrath of the city fathers. But he held to his beliefs. We were proud to call him our son during the Vietnam War." Ardis wrote her poem "Thoughts While Hoeing" during the time that a great portion of the American public was clamoring for the death sentence for Timothy McVeigh. Her last stanza concludes the poem:

> *Nature works so hard to reproduce,*
> *It makes me feel guilty to destroy*
> *The life so generously planted.*
> *Can the jury at the McVeigh trial*
> *Condemn a man to die and feel no guilt?*

When we told stories about outsiders, Geri wrote of her grandfather, who had been abusive to his wife and children; consequently, when "he got old he wandered from one house to another and had no permanent home." As a little girl, Geri alone reached out to the old man: "There was an unspoken bond between us because he felt rejected by everyone but me." Together they would spend hours on the porch telling stories to each other. Similarly, Dan wrote about Steve, a soldier with whom he was stationed during World War II. Steve was Dan's friend, mentor, and a closeted gay. Dan ends his tribute to Steve in the following way: "Whenever I hear jokes or comments about queers, fags, or faggots, I can't connect such terms with my capable, kind, loyal, and lonely friend, Steve."

And when we explored issues of racism, Sarah wrote a long piece, "Carrie," on her mixed-race adopted grandaughter. She says, "Carrie coming into the family taught me a lot about integration. By knowing Carrie I see how unfair racism is." She concludes, "If we are to proclaim ourselves Christian, we must walk the talk, not talk the talk. Above all we must realize that we all are equally God's children."

Most of the members of the Senior Class do not simply "talk the talk"; instead, they "walk the talk." They do what they can to make the world a better place: they visit the local nursing homes on a weekly basis; chauffeur other elders who no longer drive; volunteer at the local food bank; help out at the community center; knit gloves and scarves for needy children; raise money in various ways for the homeless families in our state; read to elementary school children on a regular basis.

One might sneer and dismiss such efforts as those of "do-gooders" who never challenge the larger social-economic system which produces the need for such private endeavors. I don't. Rather, the elders' lives for me are models of social justice emanating naturally from daily interactions with others and from their particular religious convictions. They take quite literally Matthew 25: 35: "For I was an hungered, and ye gave me meat: I was thirsty, and ye gave me drink: I was a stranger, and ye took me in."

> For Dewey, evil was the failure of the imagination to reach beyond itself, the human
> failure to open oneself to a spirit that both chastises one for confidence in one's own
> righteousness and promises the enduring comfort of reciprocal love.
>
> (Delbanco, 1995, p. 175)

Failure of the imagination is what hobbles most attempts to transform education into something more just, humane, and democratic. Educators and policy makers, both progressive and conservative, too often drag around the baggage of unexamined assumptions, cliches, jargon, and self-righteousness shackled to their legs. They never get anywhere. They deal in abstractions and generalizations. (Listen to any dreary debate over educational reform in the U.S. Congress or in any state legislature. Read the mind-numbing prose and Rube Goldbergian graphs and flow charts in many educational research journals.)

Imagination, as John Dewey affirmed (Dewey, 1934), is at the heart of philosophy and progressive thinking. Likewise, as William Carlos Williams exclaimed (Williams, 1988, p. 261), it is the sine qua non of poetry: "it is all/according to the imagination!/Only the imagination/is real! they have imagined it,/therefore it is so." Imagination is also what makes the Senior Class so alive and important to me as a model of social justice in small places. In their storytelling and writing, the elders engage in what Butler (1975) has termed a "life review," that is, a working through of memories in order to deal with unresolved conflicts, ideas, events, and failures in one's life. They often re-vision their pasts, chastise themselves for partial perspectives, and imaginatively envision new ways of acting and being in the world—and all of this as they travel the last years of their lives' journeys. As Ardis concludes in her essay titled "Old Age": "So unlike Montaigne's opinion of old age praising only the past, we strive to praise the present as well as the past."

The Senior Class also praises the present as well as the past through the intergenerational writing it has done with elementary school children. Over the years, a fifth-grade teacher and I have helped bring together the elders and her students for various writing, reading, and sharing activities. These joint creative efforts have allowed both the young and old people to leap imaginatively the chasm of years that separates them. For example, in their biographical sketches of one another, 10-year-old Danielle wrote of 73-year-old Dan's fear in 1945 while "stationed on a very foggy island . . . getting ready to invade Japan." Dan in turn wrote about Danielle and her classmate Katie, and how the three of them "talked about other fears." He wrote that "Katie and Danielle feel that adults should respect children too as children are expected to respect adults."

> If the American left is to revitalize itself, it will have to relearn plain English, return
> to the actual and resistant world, reclaim not only the Enlightenment principles but
> the language of Tom Paine and Orwell for itself—and it will never do that with its
> present encumbrance of theory. (Hughes, 1993, p. 83)

Over the years I have cajoled and admonished students of all ages to be specific in their writing. I repeat again and again my personal mantra from William Carlos Williams (1958, p. 6): "Say it, no ideas but in things." No ideas but in things, in specifics, in the particular events and experiences that comprise our lives. "Don't try to write your life story from beginning to end," I tell the elders in the Senior Class; "rather, write about important events; write particular vignettes."

That's what I've done in this essay: juxtaposed particular events in my life as a teacher (using both first and third person) with the writing of others (both published and unpublished authors). I've used a collage of prose, poetry, and quotations to present a multidimensional portrait of teaching and learning as transformative acts that strive for social justice. If I've been successful (and only each reader of this essay can decide for her- or himself), then readers will have an understanding of where my journey began, where it has taken me up to this point in my life, and where it might lead me in the future.

I'll harangue you, particular reader, whether you are long on your journey as a transformative teacher or whether you are about to set forth, to avoid the seduction of abstractions, cliches, and theoretical generalizations which mistake the map for the territory. I urge you to return to the actual and resistant world, the unique world in which you live and work and in which the unique voices of your students are heard in all their polyphony. Say it: No ideas but in things.

REFERENCES

Berry, W. (1985). Manifesto: The mad farmer liberation front. In *Collected poems 1957–1982* (pp. 151–152). San Francisco: North Point.

Butler, R. N. (1975). *Why survive? Being old in America.* New York: Harper & Row.

Delbanco, A. (1995). *The death of Satan: How Americans have lost the sense of evil.* New York: Farrar, Straus & Giroux.

Dewey, J. (1934). *Art as experience.* New York: Capricorn.

Hughes, R. (1993). *Culture of complaint.* New York: Warner.

Kazemek, F. E., & Rigg, P. (1995). *Enriching our lives: Poetry lessons for adult literacy teachers and tutors.* Newark, DE: International Reading Association.

Melville, H. (1967). Letter to Nathaniel Hawthorne, November 17, 1851. In *Moby-Dick: An authoritative text, reviews, and letters by Melville, analogues and sources, criticism* (pp. 566–568). New York: Norton.

Whitman, W. (1983). Beautiful women. In *Leaves of grass* (p. 222). New York: Bantam. (Original work published 1892)

Williams, W. C. (1958). *Paterson.* New York: New Directions.

Williams, W. C. (1986). Spring and all. In *The collected poems of William Carlos Williams, Volume 1, 1909–1939* (pp. 175–236). New York: New Directions.

Williams, W. C. (1988). The host. In *The collected poems of William Carlos Williams, Volume 2, 1939–1962* (pp. 259–262). New York: New Directions.

Reflective Questions

1. What do you think Marvin's mom meant when she said, "Mr. K., Marvin wants to be like you when he grows up"? What might I have thought at the time?

2. What does the poem "Dancing in the Adult Literacy Class" say about the teacher's role as a "dancer" (sometimes leading and sometimes following) with each individual student?

3. What is the role of poetry in Jane's Covenant School adult literacy class? What sort of impact does it have upon Isabelle? What might it say for *any* classroom and any group of students, preK–12?

4. Politicians of all sorts, both conservatives and liberals, businesspeople, many laypersons, and even some educators argue that we should be concerned only with what takes place in the classroom. They contend that rigorous standards, a common curriculum, and much testing will result in success for all students, regardless of their race or socioeconomic status. How does the story of Bop reflect upon these contentions?

5. Echoing John Dewey, I have maintained that it is a failure of the imagination that hobbles most attempts to transform education into something more just, humane, and democratic. Do you agree with me? Why? Disagree? Why?

Activities for the Classroom

Poetry, as the American poet Donald Hall once observed, is saying the unsayable. There are some things that can be expressed only through poetry. In my past work with homeless teenagers, for example, most of whom dropped out or were pushed out of school, and most of whom rejected any sort of "school work," I found that almost all of them wrote poetry in personal notebooks, diaries, or journals. Poetry reading—and especially poetry writing—in *all* classrooms, preK–12, is real transformative and multicultural education: It allows individuals to explore and express who they are, where they're from, and what they most cherish. Moreover, it helps individuals better understand differences among people.

DAILY POETRY READING

I strongly advocate reading, at the least, a "poem a day" to students in all classes and at all grade levels. It might take a minute or less to open a lesson or begin the day with a poem. Such daily reading will encourage students to bring in their own favorites (which might be popular song lyrics) and will highlight the importance of the personal and expressive in daily school activities. There are thousands of collections of poetry for children and young adults, and I recommend that all teachers read around and find their own favorites to share. As starters, I suggest:

Prelutsky, J. (Ed.). (1983). *The Random House book of poetry for children*. New York: Random House.
This is a fine collection of short poems for the elementary classroom. There is a great deal of language play, humor, and both free and traditional verse.
Janeczko, P. (Ed.). (1985). *Pocket poems: Selected for a journey*. New York: Bradbury.
I recommend this collection of short poems by contemporary poets for the secondary classroom. The topics include meditations on love, war, and the family.

POETRY WRITING

As I have shown in this chapter, poetry writing allows students to say the unsayable. Once again, poetry writing can be a vital part of any classroom, even in content-focused ones. Some of the most interesting poems I've read by students were those "science poems" written by middle schoolers in their science class. There are many valuable resources which can help novices begin to write poetry themselves and to explore poetry writing with their students. Some resources that I especially like are listed under "Further Reading."

FURTHER READING

Alderson, D. (1996). *Talking back to poems: A working guide for the aspiring poet*. Berkeley, CA: Celestial Arts.
This little collection of poems and related writing strategies includes example poems written by students from diverse backgrounds. It is a fine resource for the secondary classroom.

Koch, K. (1970). *Wishes, lies, and dreams: Teaching children how to write poetry*. New York: Random House.

Koch, K. (1973). *Rose, where did you get that red? Teaching great poetry to children*. New York: Random House.

These two books by a major American poet have become "classics" and are a must for anyone interested in exploring poetry with children and young adults.

WEB SITES

http://www.favoritepoem.org/

The Favorite Poem Project features people of all ages (often school kids) from across the United States reading their favorite poems. These are available on the Web site, in video format, and in a book collection. There are many suggestions for classroom use and student and teacher participation in the project.

http://www.kidlink.org/

Kid Link connects students from 143 countries through a wide variety of Web-based activities, including writing and poetry. Its primary purpose is to promote understanding and friendship among young people across the globe. There are many practical curriculum connections for teachers. This is a first-rate site for K–12 students and teachers.

Making Intergenerational Connection

The isolation of people by age is one of the most widely accepted and seldom questioned forms of segregation. Many children and young adults have little contact with old folks and, consequently, have little understanding of them or the rich history and traditions they embody. Intergenerational writing, reading, and oral history projects allow all students to shine, especially those who are often labeled as "special ed" or "nonreaders." My most recent work with adolescent males in a school for troubled youth has involved connecting them with elders in an assisted living center. The mutual trust and friendship that developed among the young and old folks resulted in productive oral history sessions and collections of memoirs, stories, and poems written by the young men.

Connections between students and elders in the community must go beyond the one-time visit to the nursing home or the "grandma in the classroom" sort of thing. Rather, ongoing efforts need to be developed and nourished. Thankfully, there are a variety of resources for teachers who want to make such connections. Some that I have found to be especially useful include:

Brown, C. S. (1988). *Like it was: A complete guide to writing oral history*. New York: Teachers & Writers Collaborative.

This is a fine how-to-do-it book for those with little or no experience with oral history. I highly recommend it.

Kazemek, F. E., Wellik, J., & Bakeberg, C. (2001). About lutefisk and other infamous stories. *Journal of Adolescent & Adult Literacy, 45*, 26–28.

Wigginton, E. (Ed.). (1972). *The foxfire book*. Garden City, NY: Anchor.

The Foxfire Project, which began in rural Appalachia in 1966, is *the* model for linking students to their home communities through oral history and writing. Based upon the philosophical and educational principles of John Dewey, Foxfire promotes intergenerational understanding, cooperation, purposeful educational pursuits, and the celebration of local language, culture, and traditions. There are now 11 Foxfire collections of oral histories and several other student-written books.

http://www.foxfire.org/

The Foxfire Fund Web site provides an introduction to the project, its philosophy, publications, and teacher workshops.

Chapter 14

Turning Points: A Teacher's Journey

Monica T. Rodriguez, Columbia College, Chicago

Focus Questions

1. What is the significance of growing up as a minority in a majority environment as opposed to growing up as a minority in a minority environment?

2. How should a minority teacher interact with minority students?

3. How should teachers be receptive to learning from students' experiences and everyday lives in constructing their lesson plans?

4. What role does racism play in the everyday dynamics of an inner-city classroom?

Once we have understood this much, there is no turning back.

—Mary Daly

Transformation is a deep alteration in the nature of a being. To be transformed is to become something other than what you were before. Many of us can pick out an event or events in our lives that were transformative; others may see a period where they underwent gradual yet significant change. Some people simply consider themselves a work in progress. Although I feel I belong to the last category, I can pinpoint a time of the greatest change for me. It began nearly a decade ago, a time when I spent 4 years teaching in Chicago alternative schools.

My first year was a collision of my naiveté, ignorance, and a few abstract ideas of social justice with the everyday reality of my students' lives. During that year and those following, I struggled to reconcile my personal ideologies of race and class grounded in my previous experiences with my new experiences and those of my students. That first year of teaching was more a year of learning for me; I was a student to many of my students and learned far more than I taught.

It is possible that my lack of any teaching experience contributed to how I approached my first algebra students. I felt confident in my mathematical skills, but I had only taught as a tutor, with no more than one student at a time. This led to my being very unassuming as I walked into the classroom for the first time. In such a drastically new environment, I knew I needed to resist being presumptuous about my students and get to know who they really were. I learned that they would constantly challenge any preconceived notions I had. Over and over again, my assumptions were made painfully clear, assumptions on how they should live, how they should act, and what goals they should have.

One student who aided me in this challenge was Ricardo. Dark, straight hair always hanging in his olive-skinned face, he was a smart young man who kept me on my toes that first year. He was more than capable of doing the level of work my classes demanded and more, but his skepticism and cynicism kept him from trusting anyone who was part of the system, and he certainly did not believe there were any benefits to learning algebra. Far more politically aware than I was, he challenged my assumptions continuously and questioned any statements I made, providing examples from his life as counterarguments. We debated and argued throughout the year, but also came to an understanding, and in time developed a good relationship. Earning his trust was a feat, but eventually he opened himself to learning what I had to teach, and I learned far more from him in return.

Another lesson was at the hand of a class discussion with a group of my math students about the Chicago Police Department's new requirement for all officers to have 2 years of college. I considered it an improvement that might create a more educated police force; perhaps some would be less ignorant and less racist. My students then pointed out to me that it would mean fewer people would be able to obtain jobs as policemen. Later I realized that it also meant fewer people of color would likely obtain those positions which, incidentally, meant there could be more racism in the police force than I felt there already was.

After she got pregnant the third time, staying in school was always in question for Christiana. She attended irregularly and her class work suffered; she had to reapply at one point. It would have been easier for the school personnel to tell Christiana she could not return if she could not focus on school. It certainly would have been easier for her. She persevered, though, and managed to graduate, undoubtedly with great struggle and sacrifice. With three children by the time she was 18, Christiana taught me something important. Although many students respond to previously absent support, there will always be some who will continue down the more difficult path. And they still deserve our support and our efforts—all young people have the right to an education. It is our job to make it available and accessible for them. They may still decide not to accept it, but that does not mean we can give up on the next student.

Comparing my students' lives to my life, it was clear that there were injustices in the education system. Having grown up in a suburb of New York City, I was painfully aware that my experiences were drastically different than my students. Yet, being Puerto Rican, I felt a connection with my pupils, especially those of the same background. It helped to foster a relationship between people with different life experiences, but it also posed questions for me I had never faced. Why had my life played out so differently from those in my classroom? Why was there a gulf between me and these young people, where there could have been great affinity and a strong connection based on our similar heritage? A similar heritage insinuates a similar life experience. But that was not the case.

Teaching and working primarily with students of color, who were for the most part low-income, revealed a trend that was to shift my perception of the entire world. The initial stage was becoming acutely aware of the differences between my upbringing and that of my students. The next was becoming aware of the similarities.

As a Puerto Rican, I had things in common with my students, but at first I felt the differences much more sharply. Those differences were based on class, although I didn't understand that at the time. When a student during my second year of teaching told me, "You're not really Puerto Rican," I was forced to face the differences between us, two Puerto Ricans, which caused her to see me this way. Her explanation was that I "didn't sound Puerto Rican." I had grown up in a white suburb of New York City; she grew up in a Puerto Rican neighborhood in the city of Chicago. For her, part of being Puerto Rican was sounding like those Puerto Ricans she knew. I did not have a Spanish accent in my English, nor did I sound like her when I spoke. I "sounded white," according to her. It took some time to understand that my upbringing in a white neighborhood failed to give me the quality that to her was an integral part of being Puerto Rican: speaking like those from the city. It meant not speaking standard English: That was for white people.

When she first told me this, I felt wronged that a fellow Latina would deny me my heritage. Both my parents had been born in Puerto Rico and immigrated to New York as children. I was born in the Bronx, where they had grown up, but after 4 years my father, a police detective, decided to move us north, out of the city. Along with taking us out of the city, they took us from the people with whom we shared a culture and a language. Moving into a white neighborhood was, to my parents, another effort to give their children all the advantages they did not have when they were young. They wanted us to fit in with white America.

As a result of their good intentions, I grew up seeing myself and the world around me through the white eyes of society more than through my own as a Puerto Rican. When my student told me that I sounded white and therefore was not really Puerto Rican, it was an eye-opening moment. Questions arose: Why did she identify being Puerto Rican with talking like one from the neighborhood, from the inner city? What was her experience that she never met a Puerto Rican who spoke standard English? These led to more questions, such as, Why is it that so many Puerto Ricans are low-income, living in poor areas of the city, and often not finishing high school, much less going on to college? It seemed that the more I learned, the more questions there were. I realize this now to be a true sign of an openness and willingness to learn.

I saw the divide that separated me from my students more clearly after that incident. It made me aware, perhaps for the first time, of the differences in growing up white and as a person of color in this country. Throughout the next three years, working with and teaching Puerto Ricans, as well as other Latinos and African-Americans, my point of view began to shift. Slowly, I started to step away from the Anglo perspective, lift the "veil" that had been pulled over my eyes (DuBois, 1903/1989), and see myself, my colleagues and students, as well as the rest of society from the point of view of my people, of a person of color.

After leaving teaching to pursue my own education, I have slowly come to understand issues of race and class with increasing clarity, with the help of wise friends and insightful writers. DuBois's (1903/1989) concept of the "double-consciousness" resonated deeply with me. Understanding the dynamics of oppression has helped me to better understand my own experiences in relation to others (Bell, 1992; Fine, 1991; Giddings, 1984; hooks, 1991, 1994; Hurtado, 1989; Marable, 1991; McIntosh, 1989; Moraga & Anzaldua, 1983; Morrison, 1992; Sleeter, 1994). I now can see where, when I had personalized conflicts in the past, it was likely a more complicated situation where race and class came into play. Attending nearly all-white schools from kindergarten through college, it would indeed be surprising if I had not experienced problems related to race. In fact, I had, but I did not understand them as such at the time. This prevented me from dealing with situations in a healthier way, understanding that the causes lay in other people's perceptions of me. I can see how I would have become a different person had I had these tools to work with at the time.

But I have them now, as a result of the education my students provided. This education has gone past the point of recognition and understanding to where I can have pride in my heritage and myself. I would never have gained this without my students. This is just one of the ways my students changed me. I also am more aware of how politics, economics, racism, and many other forces work in this country and our world. With this clearer understanding of our society, I have been able to make an informed decision about how I want to spend my life. I have decided to spend it teaching and working with educators and young people.

As a middle-class Puerto Rican woman, I had little concept of how a poor young person of color lived when I entered the classroom for the first time. Almost all I knew of the urban life of disadvantaged youth was what had been fed to me along with the rest of the country through often-skewed media messages. Like many others in our society, I had accepted much of it. My resistance to full indoctrination may have had to do with being able to see my face and those of my family in many of the images used to perpetuate those myths. I believe part of me always knew they were wrong. Perhaps that bit of doubt allowed my conversion to take place. Over the 4 years I spent in the classroom, I came to better understand not only my students' lives, but the reality of the educational system, where it falls short in meeting students' needs and where our energies are best spent in improving our school systems. Most important, I learned about myself as a member of this society and the role I play in it.

After becoming a high school teacher, the teenagers who were targeted by the media as "predator youth" were given faces and stories to go with those images. The flaws in the tales we are constantly fed were revealed to me through the reality sitting in my classroom each day. I saw how various institutions, criminal and juvenile justice, the police, poverty and public aid, and even the institution of education all work to reinforce the cycle of oppression for minority and poor youth in urban America. The contrast of myth and reality and the resulting conflicts wrought in young people's lives moved me to work against the injustice I saw in the educational lives of my students.

Many of my students began as "dropouts," with a scattering of credits and often more than their share of problems, issues, and obstacles that made the road towards graduation look improbable if not impossible. Many finished the year and eventually their high school education more confident in themselves and surer about what they wanted out of life and how they could attain it. While these students were changed by their experience in our school, they changed me as well.

Instead of solely relying on newspapers and the nightly news for my information, I could now turn to those experiencing it firsthand. In my openness to their voices, my students taught me of their life: life in the city, life in the public schools of Chicago, life in poverty. In the span of a year, so many of my misconceptions were shattered, and ignorance was replaced with new understandings—a process that would continue throughout my 4 years as a teacher.

After 4 years in alternative schools, I saw a need for more schools like these, so that young people had somewhere to turn when they were unhappy with or unwelcome in their large, overcrowded school. After learning so much about the challenges facing our youth, educationally as well as socially, and after feeling more aligned with students of color who suffer most from the racially structured institutions in our society, I wanted to work with young people of color and decided I would open a school of my own. The urban setting of Chicago was a perfect place to focus my vision. But there was first more education needed on my part. I left the classroom to enter graduate school.

Since I have been away from the classroom, I have looked for those opportunities to interact with young people. I miss the relationships I had developed with students that allowed me to learn from those whom I taught. It has perhaps highlighted what was special about my teaching experience. I was able to learn from my students what I had not been able to acquire elsewhere. No classroom, no teacher, no book has had the same eye-opening results as working daily with young people who are more honest than adults often dare to be. I have carried their lessons with me as I negotiate the labyrinth of graduate school. The interactions I had with my students provided experiences and lessons I will never forget, and from which "there is no turning back."

A small group of students helped me to see who I am. They showed me the power that education could have in their lives, as well as the role I could play. I went from striving for an architecture career to becoming a teacher, and then a graduate student to attain my Ph.D. in education. I now work with the Small Schools Workshop, which partners with large high schools that want to create smaller schools with a more student-friendly environment. My life has turned from one with a rather individualistic focus to one where I see the bigger picture, aware of the many forces that work in our lives and with a passion to work for educational justice for young people. Working with the Small Schools Workshop, I feel I am doing a small part towards that goal. Helping educators to create smaller, safer, and more intimate environments for their students, I have a hand in promoting and creating some measure of educational justice. But this work is at a distance from the environment where I can interact with, and thus learn from, young people.

To this end, I seek opportunities to work with youth whenever possible. I occasionally work with a small charter high school, assisting a ninth-grade class with a social justice curriculum. When I first arrived in the class, feeling like a first-year teacher once more, I was a bit awkward yet in my element at the same time. It was exciting to work with young minds again. I was rejuvenated, and the youths began teaching me immediately.

My first lesson once again was to not assume. Alberto is a small young man in the ninth grade, with dark hair in a crew cut. He is a quiet student, but when he speaks it always is worth listening. During a small-group discussion on violence and gangs, Alberto was convinced that if an "enemy" killed a fellow gang member, retaliation was necessary. Later, he admitted that this reaction would only continue the cycle of violence. Because of his quiet demeanor, I had pegged this young man as a subdued, meek student. His initial comments surprised me, but I realized they were assumptions and that he could be a gang member himself. After his later conversation, I saw what I had been doing: I was trying to put this young man into a box, to categorize him so I could understand him. I wanted to label him in order to judge him. Seeing him evolve over the course of this class reminded me that all young people are in flux. They are developing and changing constantly, and we need to allow them the space and offer the encouragement to develop in the best way they know.

I now find myself recognized by the students of this small school. The adolescents are energetic and outspoken. They remind me, simply by their presence and demeanor, of the honesty that young people require. If you do not come to them with your true self, you will be held accountable. This is how the lessons are learned. You are forced to be sincere about your motivations, your convictions, and your desires for yourself and for them.

Antonia is another student at this charter school. Dark shoulder-length hair with eyes just a bit darker than her brown skin, Antonia is involved in many aspects of school life. When she asked me if I would have my own class next year, I had to be honest and tell her I didn't know. I could not commit to something on which I was unsure I could follow through. I talked with her about my commitments and also about my desires for the class. I did not completely eliminate the possibility, but I would not create false hope. Either option would have been easier, but I was determined to remain honest with her. In the end, Antonia told me she understood, but that she hoped she would be seeing me back next year.

Young people's enthusiasm can also be demanding for one who has lived and worked among adults for some time; it is much harder to interact with young people. In addition to being honest, you must be attentive, sincere, and indefatigable. These are not requirements for doing the job, that of teacher or other. They are for doing the job well, for being able to connect with young people in a way that will make a difference, both in their lives and yours.

In addition to this work, I am now conducting my own research, working with a small alternative high school to create an ethnography of the school and its members. I listen to conversations, observe classes in session, and speak with teachers and students. I eagerly agreed when asked to teach a workshop on ACT preparation for the school's seniors. At times it was a struggle; I was not at the point I had been when I left the classroom 5 years ago. But I knew to look for those moments when both student and teacher could learn something. The experience was a reminder to remain open-minded and nonjudgmental. These do not always come naturally; they require practice. Having a classroom of students is one way to keep your skills in openness and honesty sharp.

When Gerard, Lisa, and Elizabeth, three seniors in my ACT class, were the only students to show up for the last class, I decided to simply talk with them and perhaps learn more about the school. What I learned was not what I had expected. Instead of telling me how this school had helped them, I heard complaints about the quality of teachers and the curriculum. I found that these students did not feel that the courses were rigorous enough, and they thought some of the teachers were too lenient with the students. I was surprised; everything I had heard about the school led me to believe the opposite. But if I were to remain open to the student voice I had to accept these reports. This was not only for the sake of my research, but also for the relationship between these students and myself. If I discredited or disregarded them in some way, their trust in me would dissolve.

Teaching does not only allow you to affect a child's life. You must be prepared for and accept the changes in your own life that will occur as a result. As an educator, you not only provide opportunities for your students to learn; it is an opportunity for you to learn as well. I discovered much about myself through my students, and I continue to learn, because of the skills they fostered in me. I yearn for a chance to work with students again full-time, to return to the classroom. Instead of having my own group of students, I spend time in other teachers' classrooms, as a part of my research, watching and trying to learn from what I see.

Whether it is collaborating with teachers to divide their large high school into smaller learning communities, teaching youth, or developing my own school, I know I will always work in the field of education, continually striving to bring about equity and justice for young people. Ten years ago, my life was headed in an entirely different direction, but I was faced with a turning point: an encounter with adolescents who inspired an alteration in the nature of my being.

REFERENCES

Anzaldua, G. (Ed.). (1990). *Making face, making soul.* San Francisco: Lute Foundation.

Bell, D. (1992). *Faces at the bottom of the well.* New York: Basic Books.

Daly, M. (1978). *Gynecology: The meta-ethics of radical feminism.* Boston: Beacon.

DuBois, W. E. B. (1989). *The souls of black folk.* New York: Penguin. (Original work published 1903)

Fine, M. (1991). *Framing dropouts: Notes on the politics of an urban public high school.* Albany: State University of New York Press.

Giddings, P. (1984). *When and where I enter: The impact of black women on race and sex in America.* New York: Morrow.

hooks, b. (1991). *Yearning: Race, gender, and cultural politics.* Boston: South End.

hooks, b. (1994). *Teaching to transgress: Education as the practice of freedom.* New York: Routledge.

Hurtado, A. (1989, Summer). Relating to privilege: Seduction and rejection in the subordination of white women and women of color. *Signs: Journal of Women in Culture and Society, 14*(4), 833–855.

Marable, M. (1991). *The crisis of color and democracy.* Monroe, ME: Common Courage.

McIntosh, P. (1989, July/August). White privilege: Unpacking the invisible knapsack. *Peace and Freedom,* 10–12.

Moraga, C., & Anzaldua, G. (Eds.). (1983). *This bridge called my back: Writings by radical women of color.* New York: Kitchen Table: Women of Color.

Morrison, T. (1992). *Playing in the dark: Whiteness and the literary imagination.* New York: Vintage.

Sleeter, C. E. (1994, Spring). A multicultural educator views white racism. *Multicultural Education, 1,* 5–8, 39.

Reflective Questions

1. How do you understand your identity at this time, and how did you come to this point? What influences in your life contributed to your present identity?

2. How can you foster identity development in your students? How can you do this if your students are of different cultural backgrounds than you?

3. What do I need to do to be able to approach teaching as a learning opportunity for myself as well? What are some things I can do in the classroom that will foster an atmosphere of learning for all (both students and teacher)?

The questions following the Power Pairs activity below are also helpful.

Activities for the Classroom

BAFÁ BAFÁ

This activity was created by Simulation Training Systems in Del Mar, California, and was written by Garry Shirts. It divides the class into two groups and essentially creates two cultures, complete with the rules of the culture. The two are isolated from each other while the students learn about their new culture. An observer is sent to the other culture to learn about it and report back. The usual ensuing confusion and misunderstandings about the other unfamiliar culture lead to discussion about how we view people from other cultures. This can be especially useful in a classroom, at any level, where there is a homogeneous group with little experience with diversity.

POWER PAIRS

Students pair up with a classmate of a different ethnicity (gender or other characteristic can also work). They can elaborate on the writing activity or discuss their feelings about their identity. Questions they can use as a guide are: (1) How do you see yourself? and (2) how do you think other people see you? The pair may add other questions, such as: How would you like others to see you? What is it that makes you proud to be who you are? What makes you ashamed or uncomfortable to be that person? The objective here is threefold: (1) to help students reflect on concepts that are usually glossed over, ignored, or are difficult to talk about; (2) to highlight how all people have "ethnicity" or "culture," not only people of color; and (3) to help create a safe environment where feelings and individual voices are not ignored. After one-on-one discussions, pairs convene back into the larger class for whole-group dialogue.

CONFLICT RESOLUTION

Strategies in conflict resolution can be used at any level to raise awareness and understanding. An effective way to conduct this is to create small groups that will perform skits. Skit scenarios will be outlined on index cards that are handed out, chosen at random, or distributed another way. The group first acts out the skit, which presents a conflict of some kind, using violence or some other way of resolving the situation that is not peaceful or respectful. Then, they redo the skit using a more respectful process. This can be used to emphasize various themes or concepts, such as antiviolence and antiracism.

FURTHER READING

Anzaldua, G. (1987). *Borderlands/la frontera: The new mestiza.* San Francisco: Aunt Lute.

Barndt, J. (1991). *Dismantling racism: The continuing challenge to white America.* Minneapolis, MN: Augsburg.

hooks, b. (1981). *Ain't I a woman: Black women and feminism.* Boston: South End.

Fordham, S. (1996). *Blacked out: Dilemmas of race, identity and success at Capital High.* Chicago: University of Chicago Press.

Hurtado, A. (1989). Relating to privilege: Seduction and rejection in the subordination of white women and women of color. *Signs: Journal of Women in Culture and Society, 14*(4), 833–855.

Zinn, H. (1980). *A people's history of the United States.* New York: Harper & Row.

WEB SITES

http://www.splcenter.org/teachingtolerance/tt-index.html

Teaching Tolerance "is a national education project dedicated to helping teachers foster equity, respect and understanding in the classroom and beyond." It publishes the *Teaching Tolerance* magazine twice a year, distributed free to teachers. There are curriculum resources, videos, and posters available, as well as a grant opportunity.

http://eric-web.tc.columbia.edu/

Urban Education Web is a connection to the ERIC Clearinghouse on Urban Education, a collection of scholarly articles on issues related to urban education, urban students, their families, and their educators.

http://www.enc.org/topics/equity/

The Eisenhower National Clearinghouse (ENC) has a large collection of curriculum materials, among other things. Examine the link on equity, which provides essays and reflections by educators, resources, assessment tools, and many scholarly journal articles. The ENC is specifically oriented to improving math and science education.

http://www.leagueofpeacefulschools.ns.ca.

The League of Peaceful Schools is based in Canada and "provides support and recognition to schools that have declared a commitment to creating a safe and peaceful environment for their students."

http://www.prairienet.org/prc/

Progressive Resource/Action Cooperative is an informative listserv with thought-provoking essays as well as updates on local (in Champaign–Urbana) as well as national activities.

http://www.magenta.nl/crosspoint/

A Web site that lists 2,000 organizations, Crosspoint Anti-Racism has a significant number of Web sites linked to organizations that deal with various issues related to racism and human rights in the United States, as well as many other countries.

Chapter 15

Small Schools: A Metaphor for Caring

Steven Strull, Center for Collaborative Education, Boston

Focus Questions

1. How did becoming part of the Small Schools Workshop impact Steven?

2. Trace Steven's growth after he began working with the Small Schools Workshop.

INTRODUCTION

"Beep . . . Hey, Mr. Strull, this is Anetha.[1] Did you hear about Brandon Polk . . . he used to be in our history class and he was killed by the police last night. Also, Taneka had her twins . . . a boy and girl . . . well, I see you're not home, so I'll talk to you later." The next morning I picked up *The Chicago Sun-Times*: "After police shot and killed a suspected drug dealer Wednesday on the South Side—the second fatal police shooting in the same building in just over a month—a longtime department critic expressed concern for officers patrolling the area. In the latest incident, Brandon Polk, 18, allegedly pointed a .40-caliber semiautomatic pistol at a plainclothes officer who was on a team searching for gang members. The shooting occurred about 12:40 a.m. at 4525 S. Federal, with the officer hitting Polk three times, police said" (Main & Lawrence, 2000).

I wish I could say that Brandon's face popped into my head immediately, but the reality is that it took some time for me to remember his image vividly. After a while, I recalled Brandon as a polite young man with a broad smile. We did not have much of a relationship, and I don't remember him as a remarkable student, either good or bad. All I knew now was that he was dead and that he was a victim—a victim of poverty and neighborhood. I also knew that Anetha's reaction troubled me. She spoke of teenage death and

[1]All living former student names have been changed.

motherhood with an affect as ordinary as I might read off a grocery list. These events were and are ordinary occurrences within the context of where I taught high school social studies for several years. Yet, for a Jewish-American man of privilege, they are indeed quite extraordinary.

It has been almost a year and a half since I "graduated" from DuSable High School. I use the term purposefully because after 5 years of teaching social studies at DuSable, and 4 years since I began a journey with Division (homeroom) 914, I was prepared to commence the next portion of my educative journey, as were the students who graduated that evening. Brandon, Anetha, and Taneka are part of my story. Negotiating and accommodating disparate identities and realities is also part of the journey and struggle, as is personal and professional growth. The story I begin here is one of accomplishment, frustration, empathy, growth, and determination. It is not just my story but also the story of the students, in truth the community, of Division 914 at DuSable High School. The remarkable aspect of the story is that, upon reflection, the students I had the pleasure of sharing my time with allowed a community to develop despite some very real obstacles and persistent difficulties—difficulties I had never experienced given my background and identity.

DuSable is a high school in a difficult context, often referred to as the poorest high school in the poorest census tract in the nation. I mention this because we were so often defined by this notion; indeed, we often used this line about being the poorest high school to define ourselves. It was often the first thing Charles Mingo,[2] the school's principal, said when speaking to a group of people. In addition to being the poorest, we were remediated, probated, reconstituted, and, of course, reformed. In fact, we had been reformed by the best, but more about that later.

As I mentioned, the story I want to tell is about Division 914, or at least what was left of 914 when they graduated in June 1999. It is the story of life change and growth—my change and also the students who left 914 different for the experience. *Division* is our way of saying homeroom in Chicago, and in addition to being a social studies teacher, I was the Division teacher for 914 for 4 years. We started in the fall of 1995 at 34 strong; on graduation day, 7 of the original students walked across the stage to receive their diplomas. Of those not present on graduation day, several transferred out of DuSable, several more dropped out of high school altogether, and one was killed in the middle of the street—a victim of the violent reality of living in the inner city. Brandon's recent death now brought the number of dead former students to three—the third having committed suicide in his junior year. The graduation numbers are very consistent with the balance of the school's population; DuSable routinely graduates about 25% of its students—one half the average of the district. My own high school experiences, though, were very different. The only death I can recall was a young woman who died of leukemia, and universal graduation was the expectation. Universal graduation may not have been realized, but it was the articulated norm. By contrast, my experiences at DuSable nagged at my notions of right and wrong, correct and incorrect. As our journey progressed, my students taught me their world and I shared mine—we learned and struggled together.

Despite the frustration and turmoil, though, teaching 914 was an extremely rewarding experience as both a teacher and a learner. Born from the small schools

---

[2]Charles Mingo retired from the Chicago Public Schools in August 1999. He is currently a middle school principal in Gary, Indiana.

initiative in 1995, where self-selected teachers and students formed schools within schools, 914 along with a dozen or so other divisions was going to lead the school toward new academic and life-chance goals for its students. Small schools was *the* reform for DuSable within a sea of options; it was going to make a difference. Small schools, however, was all but forgotten by graduation day 1999, except for a small cadre of faculty and the students to whom the promises were made. Division 914 remembered those promises.

The 1998–1999 school year was the senior year for 914. It was also my senior year, at least metaphorically. Teachers came in and out of DuSable; students were programmed in and out of 914, yet what remained was due in large part to those small school promises. We tried to know each other well, we worked through good times and bad, we supported and nurtured each other, and I think we understood that we were building something—something important, something meaningful: a complex set of relationships. It is often difficult to speak of "we" in a world where there is so much "I," yet the "we" of 914 happened, in very real and significant ways. In addition, 914 allowed real growth, growth of understanding and accommodation and a view into the world of others.

This discussion is the beginning of my reflection of my time at DuSable and what led me, along with students and colleagues, to create a small school. It is also an attempt to frame and discuss the complexities that inform my pedagogical, philosophical, social, and moral purposes. My goal here is not to study 914 as it existed, but rather to query my motivations and explore autobiographically the constructs that inform my asking the larger questions. This is a reflective exercise that probes the meaning of change within the context of teaching and learning. My experiences with the students of 914 have changed me—transformed me into a critical participant in the social construct of our times.

TO TEACH OR NOT TO TEACH

I think part of me had wanted to be a teacher for quite some time before making the decision to return to school and pursue teaching. I refer to my decision to become a teacher as my midlife career change. It was, however, my response to a late-twenty-something career frustration and near personal meltdown that finally persuaded my decision. I was struggling with who I was and where I fit into the postindustrial construct of late 20th-century America.

I have always been good at school. I say "at school" as opposed to "in school" because I find it more accurate. Charles Mingo, DuSable's former principal, often says there is a difference between "holding school" and "teaching school." I was "held" at school for 16 successful years of formal education that I usually referred to with contempt. It was easy and I was good at it; I always felt comfortable at school. It was the contempt, though, that kept me away from teaching; it did not seem that teachers were held in very high esteem and, of course, the ridiculously low salaries did not help matters much.

In February 1993 I finally made the decision. By March, I was enrolled in the master's program at DePaul University, and on a sunny Saturday I hopped on the subway, headed toward my first classroom in 6 years. Notebook in hand, I remember asking myself as I walked toward the subway if I was sure if I knew what I was doing. I was not.

The professor on that Saturday was a former Oakland Public School English teacher. She helped open up the world for me in ways that I did not know existed, and she would eventually become my master's thesis advisor. The first book we read was Ira Shor's *Empowering Education* (1992). Shor's book introduced me to critical literature and the student-centered pedagogy I would try to practice. Prior to that Saturday class, I now realize, my worldview was rather narrow. Always aware, I was comfortable with my constructs and had rarely been challenged. Starting that Saturday, I would have to rethink and reconstruct my world.

My world was and is one of privilege. While not wealthy by American standards, I and just about everyone I ever knew was comfortable. I was raised and attended school in the near north suburbs of Chicago, lived in a traditional nuclear family, and never worried about necessities. We lived the American dream. My grandparents were immigrants, my parents college educated, and I was supposed to continue the ascent toward greater material wealth. This was just how things were done; this was the expectation. Certainly there were people who were less fortunate, but through hard work and initiative the basic construct of the American class system was fluid—one could, indeed should, better oneself through the common institution, the public school. The opportunity was there for all. I was taught this, lived this, from elementary school through high school and even during my noncritical years in college. School provided an opportunity for advancement; it was supposed to provide me with an opportunity for advancement.

And it did. I have come to realize that I function very well in our system of education. It serves me well. I even tend to think it serves many, if not most, well. That's the big lie, or, rather, a truth that disguises other realities and circumstances for many of our children; if the system serves many well, then those it does not serve are the problem. If we continue to blame the children and the children's families who are not served by the system, we can continue to operate the educative system as it has pretty much existed for the last 100 years or so. As we institutionalized much of American life in the late 19th and early 20th centuries, "[s]chools, like other institutions, were supposed to counteract or compensate for indulgent or neglectful families" (Tyack, 1974, p. 72). It seems that where compensation was not possible or the barriers to compensation too great, we have blamed the children for not fitting into the system rather than look toward the system and ask why it does not fit the children. There is, of course, a history of educational policy makers, theorists, and practitioners that have challenged this notion. John Dewey and his contemporaries in the Progressive Education Association, including Harold Rugg and George S. Counts, established complex sets of committees, literature, curricula, and a laboratory school in Dewey's practice to challenge the paradigmatic notion of fitting the child to the school rather than the school to the child (Schubert, 1986). These efforts, though, while reconjured in waves of reform, including Ted Sizer's Horace series (1986, 1992, 1996), seem to have done little to dispel the popular, meritocratic myth (Bell, 1973) toward public schooling.

Therefore, those who are not served by the schooling system are blamed for their inefficiencies rather than celebrated for their uniqueness. In his recent book on the juvenile justice system in Cook County, William Ayers suggests that juvenile court "has become, by all accounts, an unfit parent—unable to see children as full and three-dimensional beings or to solve the problems they bring with them through the doors, incapable of addressing the complicated needs of families" (1997, p. xvi).

We, too, have become unfit parents for many children in public schooling. We can't possibly address the complex web of difficulties that are presented on a daily basis. Yet instead of looking toward and receiving strength and encouragement from the children we serve, we blame and victimize them. We require them to conform to a system and set of principles that has not served them well in the past and wonder in astonishment at their resistance. Eventually, I realized that these were the children I wanted to teach. This brought me to 914—the children of 914.

Deciding to teach these children, though, was a developmental process. When I began to pursue graduate studies in education on that Saturday in March, I assumed I would eventually teach in a place rather similar to where I had learned. I had no other constructs. My view of education was suburban, mostly white, decidedly middle class, and full of nurturing experiences and activities. School, especially high school, was a place of individual assertiveness through collective curricular and extracurricular experiences. It was not especially challenging, yet at times could be extremely competitive. It was safe, clean, and aesthetically pleasing. It was a gateway to college and something with defined boundaries. It had a beginning, an end, and a predictable middle; it was something to be accomplished, and the accomplishment was all but assured.

My construct, however, was very limited. I began to learn that this fuzzy and romantic feeling I held toward my own schooling was not the experience of many children, especially those in the inner city. As I read Shor's book that spring, my construct was beginning to falter at its foundation. The top had not come off; it was the bottom that was beginning to crumble, and I began, for the first time in my life, to begin to ask questions rather than simply supply answers. I also learned that many of my new questions were, if not unanswerable, sufficiently complex enough to require new ways of answering and investigating. I was beginning to develop outside of my comfortable notions of what is and began asking myself what might or ought to be. This was very new to me, at times uncomfortable, but always challenging. I hadn't recalled being challenged to think before—at least not think in school. I was, for the first time, really learning—learning to think, learning to ask, learning to be critical in complex and meaningful ways, and learning to be not so contemptuous. I was growing, developing, learning, and thinking in new and exciting ways; learning and thinking about things in ways that challenged my worldview, my notions about schooling, and my stereotypes about people and the places they lived. It was and continues to be an experience of enlightenment. It was and is a better place to experience life.

DuSable

Toward the end of student teaching in June 1994, I had about a week or so to find a teaching job for the fall. I was planning on leaving town for the summer, and I knew it would be difficult, if not impossible, to job search long distance. Earlier that spring, still clinging to what remained of my suburban fantasy, I sent out what I considered to be the obligatory applications to all the North Shore suburban districts. It was my final attempt to recapture some of the romanticism about teaching I had before my graduate program at DePaul. I realize now how truly conflicted I must have been and how much I needed to learn—learning that eventually emerged through my relationships with my students. I entered teaching because I wanted to do something that mattered; I knew where I thought I could matter most, yet I needed to eliminate the possibility of returning to my own youthful fantasies and romantic misconceptions. Initiating this part of my job search early was a way to exhaust all possibilities before deciding where I wanted to continue to learn and teach. I received not one response from these inquiries. Apparently, first-year white male social studies teachers don't receive jobs in Chicago's North Shore suburbs. The elimination of this possibility afforded me the opportunity to fully explore what would become my real first choice.

I received a tip from the job placement office at DePaul that there was an opening for a social studies teacher at DuSable. I knew nothing about the school and very little about the neighborhood. Prior to my first visit, I probably had only seen the tops of the project buildings from the highway. The neighborhood and the people were strangers to me. All I was told prior to my visit was that DuSable's principal was a "Joe Clarke–type guy" who was involved in some sort of reform efforts. I knew who Joe Clarke was, but at the time knew nothing of the school reform community.

I left the school where I was student teaching around noon midweek and drove the 40 or so miles to DuSable. When I exited the expressway at 55th Street I had no idea where I was. Geographically I knew my exact location, but that was where all familiarity ceased. The school is located about a half mile from the expressway adjacent to a figurative wall of high-rise buildings, the Robert Taylor Homes, the largest public housing complex in the United States. There are commuter and freight train tracks between the expressway and the Robert Taylor Homes that serve to divide the projects from the expressway. That afternoon, though, I was unaware of this significance and reached the school without giving this metaphoric, social, and political fence any thought. As I later learned and as my students continuously reminded me, the buildings themselves take on identities associated with "neighborhood organizations." The two organizations represented in those buildings are the Gangster Disciples and the Black Disciples—"cousin" gangs that resolve conflict with violence, obscene and abject violence.

DuSable High School is a massive prewar factory model school[3] with only one unlocked entrance monitored by a cadre of security. I entered the building and immediately noticed the sticky combination of late spring Chicago humidity and an un-air-conditioned public building. The only other image that remains from that first entrance is the color blue. The lockers at DuSable are painted electric blue and that, combined with the relatively low level of fluorescent lighting, casts a blue hue over the entire main hallway. I walked into the air-conditioned main office, approached the counter separating the public space from the private work space, and asked to speak to the principal.

My intent was to hand the principal my resume and ask for an interview. After a few moments I was asked to come into the inner office to the principal's conference room, where I was introduced to the principal, Mr. Mingo, an assistant principal, and one or two other people. We had a brief and cordial conversation, interrupted by phone calls and short intrusions where someone would ask a question or make a statement. Mr. Mingo would acknowledge and instruct various people with short muffled statements, often implying his intent rather than explicitly stating his directive. After a

---

[3]For a discussion of factory model schools and the effects of scientific management on schooling, see the discussion of Frederick Taylor and Taylorism in Kliebard (1992).

time, I was introduced to the social studies chairperson and asked to return the following day and teach a lesson to a group of students.

Returning the next day as instructed, I taught a short lesson to about eight or nine students. Enthusiasm notwithstanding, I did not make much of an impression on the students. I was a stranger to them, just another white guy making a short visit—sure to return to wherever he came from. The department chair, who sat in on the lesson, liked what she saw, though, and I was asked to once again visit with the principal in his conference room.

I will never forget two things that Mr. Mingo said to me that afternoon. First, he asked me if I knew that DuSable was a black school and, second, that DuSable was part of the Coalition of Essential Schools. I had no idea what either statement meant nor the impact that those two ideas would have on my teaching and learning experiences, though they would both help me define my voice as I began my practice.

Two days after my second meeting at DuSable I completed student teaching. Two days later I left town not knowing where I would be teaching in the fall. I knew I completed a milestone in my life, I was now a credentialed teacher, and that I needed to return to Chicago in the fall to complete my degree. I also knew that I would teach somewhere, substitute if I had to, but that I would teach.

After a series of long-distance calls to the assistant principal at DuSable, I was invited to teach at the school in September 1994. I returned to Chicago toward the end of the summer, made several trips to the Chicago Board of Education, negotiated a cacophony of bureaucracy, and received my number. I mention the number—my assigned teaching position—because without a number one does not get paid in the Chicago Public Schools. Principals are reluctant to give out the number; they seem to be rationed as a commodity, and once I received the number and my employee identification card I finally knew where I would be teaching.

I began my professional teaching career with the enthusiasm one would expect from a beginning teacher. I had big plans. I was going to be the kind of teacher the students could relate to; I was going to construct lessons with the students and try to link curricular material to their lived experiences. I quickly learned, though, that this is a much harder task than had been represented in my teacher education program. The reality of teaching at DuSable became and continued to be a complex web of negotiation and accommodation. As I reflect now, I realize that the learning curve for my students and me was rather steep. I deeply respected them as individuals, yet knew little of their experiences. They usually respected my role, yet had no idea who I was as a teacher or person. Together, we learned from each other and often reflected in astonishment at the differences in our realities.

During my first months of teaching I was enrolled in a first-year teacher induction course at DePaul as part of my degree requirements. The course examined issues of beginning teachers and became a sort of therapy session for me during those early trying times. I was getting to know my students, and they me. I was also beginning the process of socialization in a very new setting. What I experienced surprised and frustrated me. I had many successes and failures and felt as though I was in a constant state of turmoil.

I tried a variety of problem-posing techniques, stating curriculum in the form of questions. I "borrowed" Deborah Meier's habits of mind (Meier, 1995) and spent a long evening converting them to newly purchased card stock paper for display in my classroom. The fifth habit is, "Who cares?" That is, "Why is this important and why should we care about it?" I learned that a disconnect existed between importance and caring for many of my students. I was able to effectively struggle over why a particular nugget of history was important to me, yet often failed to negotiate why students should care about it. I continued by having students write and teach lessons, evaluate each other's work, and sit in and work in "cooperative groups." I demanded and received funding for a new textbook series; the one we had been issued was printed during Richard Nixon's tenure as chief executive—a point not lost on the students. I tried. I tried and tried, but I was alone.

Toward the end of the first 10 weeks of school, I was sitting in my classroom at the end of a long hall on the third floor of the building. It was late afternoon. The school had long since cleared out—even the janitor had come and gone. The sun was low in the sky and for several moments was at just the right angle to bathe the sea of papers before me and enter the uncovered windows such that I could see the dust particles floating in the room. The only sounds were the crumple of papers and my green pen moving from sheet to sheet. It was my first marking period, the first time I would decide what grades to give which student. There was no one to help, no one to ask. What a disservice to the students and their efforts. I was really alone.

REFORM

As discussed earlier, one of the first things Mr. Mingo mentioned to me in our conversations was that DuSable High School was a member of the Coalition of Essential Schools. He said this with pride and pointed toward a poster that listed the nine common principles (Sizer, 1986, 1992, 1996) of the coalition. I was not familiar with the coalition or its principles, but the information on the poster was encouraging.

Begun as an investigation into the American high school, researcher Ted Sizer developed the coalition and its principles in response to the conditions that he found at many high schools during his inquiry (Sizer, 1986). Central to the theme of the nine principles is that teachers and students ought know each other well, teachers should facilitate student work through a coaching metaphor, and high school resources should be reallocated to allow teachers to see fewer students each day. In addition, student work ought to be authentic—related to the students' lives and connected to the larger world. Not dissimilar to Dewey's (1938) notion of relating to the needs and interests of the learner, Sizer provided a fresh outlook from which to view the American high school.

My purpose here is not to provide an overview or analysis of the coalition or Sizer's work. Much has been published over the years, and I have made bibliographic references to the coalition, Sizer's work, and the Annenberg Institute for School Reform, which is a direct descendant of the coalition. What I would like to convey is the importance that education reform work has had on my teaching and learning and how the reform construct has recently caused me to question the direction of my practice.

When I entered teaching, it felt as though I had entered at a moment of real change. Over the next few years, the intensity of that change began to increase. I became involved in a variety of activities, convinced that real change was on the horizon. I went to meetings, attended conferences, wrote curriculum, traveled, and networked with like-minded professionals eager to transfer our ideas to the classroom. I even enrolled in a doctoral program in curriculum design to extend and stretch my capacity, intellect, pedagogy, and practice.

Toward the end of my first year of teaching, I became aware of what I thought to be one of the most exciting educative reform initiatives yet—small schools. The Small Schools Workshop at the University of Illinois at Chicago (UIC) became affiliated with DuSable, and the faculty at DuSable was invited and encouraged to form small schools. I could hardly contain my excitement. We were being offered the chance to actually start a new school—a school where like-minded and self-selected faculty could come together and create a school where curriculum, pedagogy, and assessment would be the province of the learners and teachers in the school. What a chance. It was this chance that created the School of Journalism and Communication, of which Division 914 was a part, along with three other divisions. I was no longer alone.

Four Years Later

I cannot possibly continue my version of the story of 914 in any sort of chronological or comprehensive way in this forum. The breadth and depth of what I have to convey surrounding my small school experience at DuSable will require several volumes. I am able to report, though, that several of us are finding our new situations fresh, challenging, rewarding, and informed by our associations at DuSable.

Anetha and I communicate regularly. After a failed attempt at a small private college, Anetha is attending a large state university in Chicago. She also works full-time and supports herself. Anetha is studying to be a teacher. For as long as I can remember, Anetha has wanted to teach kindergarten.

Nancy and Andrea e-mail and call me regularly. They are both sophomores at a Big Ten university, and although Andrea is home for a semester, she has indicated that she will return to school. The pair are adjusting to college life, studying for exams and writing papers, and remembering with fondness their years at DuSable. Recently, Nancy and Andrea have been articulating their African American identity within the ubiquitous white culture they now find themselves in. Children of segregation, they are experiencing integration by fire and are surprised at the strength and temerity with which they meet their new experiences.

These students, and others with whom I communicate regularly, have become even more familiar in their tone, and I find the connections uplifting. The kids have a need to share their continuing development with me, and I am finding I greatly enjoy being included. We are sharing our lives now beyond the student–teacher relationship and are developing a more mature friendship. As for me, I spend most days in a rather comfortable office at the University of Illinois at Chicago's Small Schools Workshop—the same agency I worked with as a relatively new teacher at DuSable. Fulfilling the commitment I made at DuSable, my graduation was on the same stage as my students. Standing in the auditorium, reading each of their names, I realized I had completed a chapter of my life and my professional development. I will probably not enter a high school as a social studies teacher again.

I have continued my professional development work full-time, and the Small Schools Workshop at UIC is allowing me to explore another role for a midcareer teacher. Teachers teaching teachers can be a powerful construct in school reform, and I believe teachers have opportunities to be reformers, professors, authors, and leaders within the sphere of learning and service.

Traditionally, there has been no real career path for in-service teachers outside of administration. Here at the workshop, we are continually thinking about and rethinking responsibilities of leadership and accountability to schools and students. My role as professional development director allows me to work with teachers and administrators from a wide cross section of educative institutions. Through this work, I am continuously reminded of the powerful analysis Dewey places on needs and interests.

As I settle into my new professional endeavor, I continue to be informed by my experiences at DuSable. The children and teachers continue to nurture and teach me. My suburban fantasy became an urban reality. I found what I was looking for at DuSable, despite the frustrations and bitter disappointments that accompanied the experience.

My time at DuSable was complex, critical, rewarding, frustrating, warm, depressing, crucial, and transformative. I am better for the experience. I know more about who I am and where I fit in; I try to continuously reflect on my experiences through the lenses from which my students viewed me, as difficult and incomplete as that is. I am a better person, learner, and teacher. I read, think, learn, and live a critical life, questioning the status quo and am always wondering what might be. I look for the humanity in the people I associate with; I am slower to be judgmental. I am continually frustrated by the glacial pace of change—societal change, school change, and human change—yet I am tempered by my experiences at DuSable. I understand, indeed, I even see and feel the possibility of change. The children that I had the honor of spending time with day in and day out taught me to focus on my humility, my privilege, my craft, and my future. Together we forged a connection, a community, and a hope. Together, metaphorically and physically, we will continue to develop, enriched by associations and experiences. Division 914 will remain with me always.

REFERENCES

Ayers, W. (1997). *A kind and just parent.* Boston: Beacon.

Bell, D. (1973). *The coming of the post-industrial society.* New York: Basic Books.

Dewey, J. (1938). *Experience and education.* New York: Macmillan.

Kliebard, H. (1992). *Forging the American curriculum.* London: Routledge.

Main, F., & Lawrence, M. (2000, October 26). Cop critic holds tongue after high-rise shooting. *The Chicago Sun Times,* p. 8.

Meier, D. (1995). *The power of their ideas.* Boston: Beacon.

Schubert, W. (1986). *Curriculum: Perspective, paradigm, and possibility.* New York: Macmillan.

Shor, I. (1992). *Empowering education: Critical teaching for social change.* Chicago: University of Chicago Press.

Sizer, T. (1986). *Horace's compromise.* Boston: Houghton Mifflin.

Sizer, T. (1992). *Horace's school.* Boston: Houghton Mifflin.

Sizer, T. (1996). *Horace's hope.* Boston: Houghton Mifflin.

Tyack, D. (1974). *The one best system: A history of American urban education.* Cambridge, MA: Harvard University Press.

Activities for the Classroom

The following tools and techniques (in separate documents) originate from a variety of sources and are used to look at student and teacher work in practiced, meaningful, and critical ways; all inform my practice through my ongoing association with the National School Reform Faculty. These activities are fairly straightforward and relatively easy for teachers and students to engage in, either as colleagues or as learners and teachers. However, sustained engagement with these practices will be enhanced with an experienced facilitator. Please see www.harmonyschool.org for more information on the National School Reform Faculty and for opportunities to share collaborative practices with colleagues from a variety of school reform initiatives. Activities described are the following:

1. Obstacle Resolution Protocol
2. Tuning Protocol
3. Final Word Process
4. Consultancy

Obstacle Resolution Protocol

(This is a variation of the Final Word Process, adapted by Steven Strull.)

Purpose: To resolve an obstacle toward progress of a desired outcome.

Preparation: Each person in the group reflects on *one* obstacle that is keeping them from making progress toward a desired outcome. While there may be many obstacles, this protocol focuses on one at a time. Additional sessions may be scheduled to deal with multiple obstacles. Please work in groups of four with a designated timekeeper/facilitator for each of the four rounds (15 minutes each). For each round:

- The person who starts gets 4 minutes.
- Each person responding gets 3 minutes ($\times$ 3 people = 9 minutes).
- The person who started resolves their obstacle—2 minutes.

Explanation of Procedure for Each Round
1. Begin by designating a facilitator/timekeeper. This role should *not* be filled by the person who will begin the round (and who will resolve their obstacle).
2. One person begins by explaining the obstacle he is facing and any related context. (4 minutes)
3. After this person is finished, each person then comments on the obstacle and offers alternatives for overcoming it. (The premise here is that after all obstacles have been resolved, the underlying goal can be achieved.) Each person in the group has 3 minutes to respond, for a total of 9 minutes.
4. The person who started will then resolve his obstacle. (2 minutes)

Round 2 then begins, with the next person explaining their obstacle. Rounds 2, 3, and 4 follow the same format as Round 1.

Tuning Protocol

(This is adapted from Protocols—Student Work, Annenberg Institute for School Reform.)

The Tuning Protocol was originally developed as a means for the five high schools in the Coalition of Essential School's Exhibitions Project to receive feedback and fine-tune their developing student assessment systems, including exhibitions, portfolios, and design projects. It has since been adapted as a tool for looking collaboratively at both teachers' and students' work and used extensively in the work of the National School Reform Faculty.

Often the presenting teacher begins with a focusing question or area about which he or she would especially welcome feedback, for example, Are you seeing evidence of persuasive writing in the student's work? or Does this lesson accommodate different learning styles? The overarching purpose of a tuning protocol is to give teachers critical feedback on a single aspect of their practice, again either through their work or the work of their students.

Participation in a structured process of professional collaboration like this can be intimidating and anxiety producing, especially for the teacher presenting work. Having a shared set of guidelines or norms helps everybody participate in a manner that is respectful as well as being conducive to helpful feedback.

Guidelines: Be respectful of teacher-presenter(s). By making their work more public, teachers are exposing themselves to kinds of critiques they may not be used to. Inappropriate comments or questions should be reworded or withdrawn.

- Contribute to substantive discussion. Many teachers may be used to blanket praise. Without thoughtful, probing, "cool" questions and comments, they won't benefit from the tuning protocol.
- Be respectful of the facilitator's role, particularly in regard to following the guidelines and keeping time. A tuning protocol that doesn't allow for all parts (presentation, feedback, response, and debriefing) will do a disservice to the teacher-presenters and to the participants.

Schedule for Tuning Protocol
1. *Introduction*—protocol goals, guidelines, and schedule. (5–10 minutes)
2. *Teacher presentation*—context for work, focusing question, group is silent. (10–15 minutes)
3. *Clarifying questions*—this is not the time for warm or cool feedback. (5 minutes maximum)
4. *Examination of work sample*(s) (5–15 minutes)
5. *Pause for reflection*—participants reflect on potential contribution. (2–3 minutes)
6. *Warm and cool feedback*—group shares feedback; presenter is silent. (15 minutes)
7. *Reflection*—presenter speaks to issue(s) deemed appropriate. (10–15 minutes)
8. *Debriefing*—open discussion on the experiences of the group. (10 minutes)

Final Word Process

(This exercise is courtesy of Patricia Averette of the Los Angeles Annenberg Metropolitan Project and Daniel Baron of Harmony School, Bloomington, Indiana.)

Purpose: To expand a group's understanding of a text in a focused way and in a limited amount of time.

Preparation: Each person selects and marks (what is for him or her) one significant quote or section from the text(s).

Please work in groups of four, with a designated timekeeper/facilitator for each of the four rounds (15 minutes each). For each round:

- The person who starts gets 4 minutes.
- Each person responding gets 3 minutes ($\times$ 3 people = 9 minutes).
- The person who started has the "final word"—2 minutes.

Explanation of Procedure for Each Round

1. Begin by designating a facilitator/timekeeper. These roles should *not* be filled by the person who will begin the round (and who has the final word).
2. One person begins by explaining to the group the significance of her or his quote/section from the text(s). (4 minutes)
3. After this person is finished, each person then comments on the same quote/section chosen by the first person in the round. You may choose to respond to what the first person has said, or to speak to the quote or section in any other way that extends the group's understanding of the text. Each person in the group has 3 minutes to respond, for a total of 9 minutes.
4. The person who started then has the final word. (2 minutes)

Round 2 then begins, with the next person explaining to the group the significance of her or his quote/section from the text(s). Rounds 2, 3, and 4 follow the same format as Round 1.

Consultancy

(This is adapted from Protocols—Student Work, Annenberg Institute for School Reform). It was developed as a part of the Coalition of Essential Schools's National Re:Learning Faculty Program, and further adapted and revised as part of the work of the Annenberg Institute's National School Reform Faculty Project, now located at the Harmony Education Center. It is currently used extensively by the National School Reform Faculty.

Time: At least 1 hour

Roles: Presenter, facilitator

1. The presenter gives a quick overview of her or his work. She or he highlights the major issues or problems with which she or he is struggling and frames a question for the consultancy group to consider. The framing of this question, as well as the quality of the presenter's reflections on the work and/or issue being discussed, are key features of this protocol. (10 minutes)
2. The consultancy group asks clarifying questions of the presenter, that is, questions that have brief, factual answers. (5 minutes)
3. The group then asks probing questions of the presenter. These should be worded so that they help the presenter clarify and expand her or his thinking about the issue or questions raised for the consultancy group. The goal here is for the presenter to learn more about the question framed or to do some analysis of the issue presented. The presenter responds to the group's questions, but there is no discussion by the larger group of the presenter's responses. (10–15 minutes)

4. The group then discusses the work and the issues presented. The members answer questions such as: What did we hear? What didn't we hear that we needed to know about? What do we think about the question or issue presented?

   Some groups like to begin the conversation with "warm" feedback—answering questions such as: What are the strengths in this situation or in this student's work? What's the good news here? The group then moves on to "cooler" feedback—answering questions such as: Where are the gaps? What isn't the presenter considering? Where are areas for further improvement or investigation? Sometimes the group will raise questions for the presenter to consider: I wonder what would happen if . . . ? I wonder why . . . ? The presenter is not allowed to speak during this discussion, but instead listens and takes notes. (15 minutes)
5. The presenter then responds to what she or he heard (first in a "fishbowl" if there are several presenters). A whole-group discussion might then take place, depending on the time allotted. (10–15 minutes)
6. The facilitator leads a brief conversation about the group's observations of the process. (5–10 minutes)

Some Tips for Consultancies

Step 1: The success of the consultancy often depends on the quality of the presenter's reflection in Step 1, as well as on the quality and authenticity of the question framed for the consultancy group. However, it is not uncommon for a presenter, at the end of a consultancy, to say, "Now I know what my real question is." That is fine, too. It is sometimes helpful for the presenter to prepare ahead of time a brief written description (1–2 pages) of the issues for the consultancy group to read as part of Step 1.

Steps 2 & 3: Clarifying questions are for the people asking them. They ask the presenter: who, what, where, when, and how. These are not "why" questions. They can be answered quickly and succinctly, often with a phrase or two.

Probing questions are for the people answering them. They ask the presenter "why" (among other things) and are open-ended. They take longer to answer and often require deep thought on the part of the presenter before she or he speaks.

Step 4: When the group talks while the presenter listens, it is helpful for the presenter to pull her or his chair back slightly away from the group. This protocol requires the consultancy group to talk about the presenter in the third person, almost as if she or he is not there. As awkward as this may feel at first, it often opens up a rich conversation. Remember that it is the group's job to offer an analysis of the issue or question presented. It is not necessary to solve the problem or to offer a definitive answer.

It is important for the presenter to listen in a nondefensive manner. Listen for new ideas, perspectives, and approaches. Listen to the group's analysis of your question or issues. Listen for assumptions—both your own and the group's—implicit in the conversation. Don't listen for judgment of you by the group. This is not supposed to be about you, but about a question you have raised. Remember that you asked the group to help you with this question or issue.

Step 5: The point of this time period is not for the presenter to give a "blow-by-blow" response to the group's conversation, nor is it to defend or further explain him- or herself. Rather, this is a time for the presenter to talk about what were, for her or him the most significant comments, ideas, and questions. The presenter can also share any new thoughts or questions she or he had while listening to the consultancy group.

Step 6: Debriefing the process is key. Don't shortchange this step.

FURTHER READING

The following books will give an excellent overview of the current conversations around the possibilities of small schools and their effects on students, teachers, and society:

Ayers, W., Klonsky, M., & Lyon, G. (Eds.). (2000). *The teaching for social justice.* New York: Teachers College Press.

Evans, C., (Ed.). (2000). *Creating new schools: How small schools are changing American education.* New York: Teachers College Press.

Levine, E. (2001). *One kid at a time: Big lessons from a small school.* New York: Teachers College Press.

Meier, D. (1995). *The power of ideas: Lessons for America from a small school in Harlem.* Boston: Beacon Press.

For background on the Coalition of Essential Schools and the condition of American high school, see:

Sizer, T. (1992). *Horace's compromise: The dilemma of the American high school.* Boston: Houghton Mifflin.

Sizer, T. (1996). *Horace's hope: What works for the American high school.* Boston: Houghton Mifflin.

For information on collaborative practice, school change, and the constructs and tools associated with looking at student work, see:

Blythe, T., Allen, D., & Schieffelin-Powell, B. (1999). *Looking together at student work: A comparison guide to assessing student learning.* New York: Teachers College Press.

Evans, R. (1996). *The human side of school change: Reform, resistance, and the real-life problems of innovation.* San Francisco: Jossey-Bass.

Fullen, M. (1982). *The meaning of educational change.* New York: Teachers College, Columbia University.

Newmann, F. M., (Ed.). (1996). *Authentic achievement: Restructuring schools for intellectual quality.* San Francisco: Jossey-Bass.

Senge, P. M., et al. (1994). *The fifth discipline fieldbook: Strategies and tools for building a learning organization.* New York: Currency, Doubleday.

The definitive synoptic curriculum text is:

Schubert, W. (1986). *Curriculum: Perspective, paradigm, and possibility.* New York: Macmillan.

WEB SITES

Small Schools and Collaborative Practice Websites

Annenberg Institute for School Reform:
www.annenberginstitute.org

Bay Area Coalition for Equitable Schools:
www.bayces.org

Big Picture Company:
www.bigpicture.org

Bill and Melinda Gates Foundation:
www.gatesfoundation.org

Center for Collaborative Education and New England Small Schools Network:
www.ccebos.org

Coalition of Essential Schools:
www.essentialschools.org

Looking at Student Work Collaborative:
www.lasw.org

National School Reform Faculty:
www.harmonyschool.org

Small Schools Workshop:
www.smallschoolsworkshop.org

Small Schools Project:
www.smallschoolsproject.org

Chapter 16

Woman Warrior Liberating the Oppressed and the Oppressor: Cultural Relevancy Through Narrative

Suzanne SooHoo, Chapman University, Orange

Focus Questions

1. What can we do to stop student harassment?

2. What conditions promote the "othering" of individuals?

3. How did racism, sexism, homophobia, anti-Semitism, classism, and linguicism become acceptable norms on school campuses?

4. How have we been complicit with these acts of injustice?

5. What responsibility do we have to stop these acts?

6. What acts of courage are we willing to commit to prevent them from happening?

Miss Diversity was the nickname awarded to me by my colleagues for being the only Asian female on tenure track at the university. In 1995, 39% of full-time, tenured faculty in the United States were women. Of this group, 18% were full professors—90% were White, 5% Asian, 3% African American, 2% Latino, and 2% Native American (Glasser, 1999). Am I a token or a trailblazer?

This chapter is about the intersection between my sociocultural identity and my pedagogy. The fundamental assumption is that my social group memberships, both within subordinate and dominant groups, affect the ways I teach. Teaching is defined as: the ways I interact with students, the activities I choose for us to experience, and the academic material I have chosen to infuse into my courses. In the working realities of the classroom, "what I have chosen" for students is negotiated with students and their expressed needs and interests.

It is my hope that this chapter contributes to the void in the literature of Asian woman as social justice educators. I am confident that we must transcend our cultural language of silence so that our voices can be an integral part of shaping a larger social agenda. With other underrepresented groups in solidarity, we need to confront the structures of privilege and oppression.

While I am cognizant of some of the sociocultural dimensions in my teaching, other aspects have yet to be realized. I am also sensitive to the fact that just because one is culturally affiliated does not mean that that person automatically understands multiple forms of human difference. "Culturally sensitive teaching could not be guaranteed by simply being a member of a particular cultural group" (Nieto, 1998). I write so that I may better understand the relationship between my positionality and historical locality and my teaching. And perhaps as I unearth my cultural filter, these cultural markers can provide additional insights on the phenomenon of 'when an Other, become a teacher.'

Central in my inquiry is how the politics of location influence perspective, specifically in three spheres: the study of myself as other, the study of other people of color, and the study of White people of color. *White people of color* is a term I euphemistically coined to mean those individuals who are biologically White but whose ideology is multicultural. They are the White advocates for social justice.

FROM THE EAST

> How far I am from the center has everything to do with the way I see the world.
>
> (Villenas, 1998)

I am forever questioning how far I am from the center of power and influence. Few people understand my indigenous language of silence. I wonder if one has to be Connie Chung in order to be heard: articulate, gregarious, and controversial.

Is my identity self-inscribed, constructed by others, or preordained by a long line of ancestors? Which of the five prevailing stereotypes of Asian women (Chang, 1997) are really me? Which are imposed upon me? Which do I consciously ascribe to?

Am I the quiet, subservient, dutiful daughter who never speaks or makes waves? The one with a tofu worldview, bland and tasteless? Questioning an elder, for her, is a death sentence. Historically, she was the perfect mail order bride, who obediently served her mother-in-law. Asian husbands and fathers have enjoyed the commodities provided by these domesticated females.

Or am I the industrious, androgynous worker? Conceived in the Mao era, she is the hardworking, conscientious, and dispassionate worker. Her efficiency, loyalty, and unquestionable obedience make her a good foot soldier for any government position. In today's world, she would be a good candidate as an emotionally neutral, efficient, reliable accountant.

Economics reinforces this image: "Businesses want docile, subservient workers who will not complain, file grievances, or organize unions. Many businesses purposely seek immigrant workers with limited English skills for this deference. Asians are thought to be loyal, diligent and attentive to detail. They, like other minorities, consistently earn less than whites" (Lee, 2002).

Both the dutiful daughter and industrious worker speak the language of silence. It is the unspoken dialect that communicates more poignantly than words. It is the language of subtle overtures and fortissimo messages, of imperceptible amplification but indisputable clarity. This language, pregnant with meaning, is preferred over what elders describe as pompous, boisterous, clamorous "noise." Silence in this familial context is a language of choice. Out of respect for others, it is understood that one does not speak unless one can improve upon the silence.

Could I be Suzy Wong, the seductress, who uses her porcelain skin and silken hair to influence those around her? She is exotic, provocative, and mysterious; both men and women are seduced by her alluring, feminine grace. Hollywood capitalized on this image, as evidenced by productions such as *Madame Butterfly, South Pacific,* and *Miss Saigon.*

Or am I the "Dragon Lady," the most powerful and cunning of all? She rules her world with an iron fist in a silk glove. This commanding, grand matriarch makes decisions for the entire village. Sharp-tongued and strategic, the Dragon Lady is most often a successful businesswoman.

Popularized by Maxine Hong Kingston, the "Woman Warrior" enters the contemporary scene. She is both a skillful swordswoman and a crusader for social justice who combats oppressive power structures in order to liberate the oppressed. With unbound feet and social consciousness, she carves a path for a new social order that gives voice to the common people.

I am and have been all of these women as daughter, wife, mother, teacher, school principal, and professor. Every facet of Asian womanhood is represented in my genetic tapestry. Much of what I have learned about being an Asian woman has come from my ancestors. Most of what I have become as an Asian American woman has been dependent on white permission.

WESTERN WINDS

At the academy, Western winds infuse my consciousness. Theoretical frames, constructivism, feminism, and critical theory color my ideology. With the same homage paid to my ancestors, I look to theoretical elders: Freire, Kanpol, Darder, Park, hooks, Sleeter, Giroux, Lather, Nieto, and others to bestow wisdom. The writings of critical multiculturalists, feminists, and authors from subordinate groups resonate within my spirit as I try to find my place as an Asian woman warrior, an ever becoming social justice educator among this cast of intellectual giants.

EASTERN INCENSE DANCES WITH WESTERN WINDS

To be in my critical multicultural class for preservice teachers means that you will experience my difference, my cultural identity. The way I view the world and the way I teach are rooted in my sociopolitical location. The decisions I make and the opportunities I present are culturally founded as well as researched based. A question I open each semester with is, How will this class be different from other sections of this course because it is taught by an Asian woman?

"We never even noticed you were Asian," comment some of my non-Asian students. I know that many of them feel uncomfortable publicly recognizing difference. They are afraid that they might be racists. They explain to me that they are color-blind, and I have learned to respond, "I'm so sorry to hear that. How long have you been afflicted with this problem?" (Gaunty-Porter, personal communication). We talk about how their well-intended color-blindness, a seemingly liberal concept, may be objectionable to some people of color. I share with them how people's color-blindness erases me, ignoring my sociocultural heritage.

A few of my students, who have even less exposure to Asian instructors, relegate me to the "forever foreign" syndrome (Howard, 1999, p. 60). That is, the first time they meet me, they wonder what country I'm from and ask, "Do you speak Chinese?" I typically answer with a question, "No, do you?" so that I may open the door to opportunities to discuss mistaken assumptions, stereotypes, social constructions, and English language status.

Model minority misconceptions prompt other predictable commentaries by students each semester. "Why can't they (those other minorities) be like you?" they ask as they give stereotypic examples of assumed math proficiency. These comments are often followed by "I know someone Chinese." I cringe and wonder what the other 1 billion Chinese on the planet think about my representing the whole lot of them. Students begin to understand my sentiments when we talk about questions like: Who benefits by a model minority myth? Who benefits from stratifying a cultural hierarchy among minority groups? What part does the media play in making this myth appear true? Do we commonly mistake personal judgments of other groups of people as accurate descriptions of reality?

I am regularly reminded by my elders and ancestral spiritual advisors (a.k.a. ghosts) that my responses are not becoming of a typical Chinese woman. One shouldn't be so sarcastic, although this is better than being confrontive. Asian women should be accepting, compliant, and produce harmony. Instead of making waves, one should homogenize any differences of opinion by assimilating and making one's self invisible.

I resist. The protective cocoon of assimilation that allowed my immigrant cousins to become ideal Americans confines me. It girdles my desire to participate in this world as an equal and attempts to make me powerless. It requires that I don the "mask of whiteness" (Almojuela, 1999) and submit to the unquestionable acceptance of the dominant culture as pure truth. Instead, I choose to shed the cloak of hegemony and unbutton the coat of sameness, to reveal how the concept of difference can be the source of knowledge and solutions to our problems.

As a society, we affiliate with sameness and avoid differences. We have not been socialized to see difference in a positive light. As early as kindergarten, a teacher points to a row of circles with one triangle and asks children, "Which one is different?" In the same breath, without a second thought, she asks, "Which one does not belong?" Difference has come to mean deviant, and it is "X"ed from the set. Through this seemingly simple instructional task, we inculcate that homogeneity is good, heterogeneity is bad.

OTHERNESS AS TEXT

"Let your life be your teaching"

(Quaker saying quoted by Obear, 2000)

Student narratives of "otherness" challenge the traditional reification of textbooks as the sole sources of knowledge in this course. Otherness is defined as experience(s) in which a person has suffered marginalization, alienation, or oppression. Students are asked to think about an incident, period, or theme in their school lives in which they have experienced "otherness" or have been "othered." They are encouraged to capture these reflections as poetry, autobiographies, letters, or in any style that gives voice to perhaps inaudible life experiences. Students are encouraged to express themselves freely and not be ashamed of their own language or voice, accents, or style (Freire, 1993). Students use various writing styles and consequently address the audience in new ways (hooks, 1999) as they unveil heretofore suppressed themes of alienation. The idea of storytelling narratives is not just about opening up curricular space, but it is about moving "into borderlands crisscrossed within a variety of languages, experiences, and voices," voices and experiences that "will not fit easily into the master narrative of a monolithic culture" (Giroux, 1993, p. 34).

Storytelling is both a way of knowing and an art form. Cognitive insights are derived from the conceptualization via reflection and self-study, and from the often nonlinear presentation of a story. In the narratives of otherness within this book, students were invited to use oral history, poems, dreams, letters, or drawings to tell their stories. They were encouraged to give themselves permission to use any genre that liberated their storytelling voices. Several students used speech patterns and cultural forms indigenous to their communities (e.g., regional dialects and idioms). The opportunity to dismiss academic conventions and express one's authentic voice allowed many narrators to focus more on the experience of the story, ultimately delivering a story that was representative of the creators' soul and spirit.

In this assignment, students are the primary sources of knowledge. The narratives become the center of the curriculum, displacing the sacred textbooks (Freire, 1993); everyday people narrate their lives for collective deconstruction. It takes sensitivity and responsibility in the interpretation of our collective lives as "others."

The assignment can be particularly powerful to traditionally silenced groups because it evokes the production of untold stories. For many students of color, this assignment is often a rare opportunity to (1) publicly pronounce their social and cultural affiliations, (2) publicly confront racism, sexism, ableism, classism, and linguicism (language discrimination, Schnidewind & Davidson, 1998), and (3) work out unresolved conflicts and traumas as a result of prejudice and disenfranchisement. It is a chance to shed an investigatory light on the dark side of human existence. hooks (1999) maintains that these opportunities are uncommon because academia is often less a site for engagement with ideas and more a space of repression, where dissenting voices are easily censored and/or silenced.

Many White students are particularly challenged by this exercise because this is most often the first time they have thought about what it means to be White. Initially, they assumed that only students of color have something to say about otherness. They maintain they are the people of noncolor and therefore have nothing to write. White is the invisible color on the rainbow: the elusive norm, difficult to define.

Students later reason that this paralysis of writing comes from two sources: (1) White students experience greater privilege than students of color and therefore cannot personally relate to the concept of "otherness" and (2) White students are not accustomed to thinking about White identity as a social construct. The concept of Whiteness, according to Howard (1999) is unavailable to the discussion of difference because it remains unframed by White students: "It has been the invisibility (for Whites) of Whiteness that has enabled white Americans to stand as unmarked, normative bodies and social selves. It is a privileged place of racial normativity." This reality is difficult to embrace at early stages of White identity development.

I have learned from my White students that framing Whiteness for the very first time can result in anxiety, shame, guilt, and anger. The discourse on Whiteness can splinter the delicate evolution of the community as we try to bring into focus the concept of White dominance. I am reminded by Audre Lorde (1984) that White dominance is hard to see because it is as American as apple pie.

I am also conscious that I, as an instructor of color, am not the ideal resource for White students during this dissonance. In the past, I have called on White people of color to interact with students at this time. White students receive and process information differently from White people of color. Ideally, these social justice mentors facilitate the multicultural competence of White students by meeting with them separately, providing a safe context to communicate freely, without the fear of judgment for political correctness. When these human resources have not been available, we turned to books like *Promoting Diversity and Social Justice: Educating People From Privileged Groups* by Diane Goodman; *We Can't Teach What We Don't Know: White Teachers, Multiracial Schools,* by Gary Howard; or *Uprooting Racism: How White People Can Work for Racial Justice,* by Paul Kivel. We focus our attention on the relationship between Whiteness and Otherness:

- Is Whiteness the opposite of otherness?
- When are Whites and others both oppressed?
- When are Whites and others both oppressors?

As students examine the social forces of exclusion, they come to realize that White dominance is an oppressive ideological construct that promotes social inequalities and causes great material and psychological harm to both people of color and Whites. White student authors begin to see the social forces of exclusion and oppression as they are applied to them, and subsequently White otherness stories about sexism, classism, anti-Semitism, homophobia, and disabilities surface. Hill (1997) refers to this process as White privilege. That is, White otherness framed by White dominance, Whiteness taking its turn in being framed by itself. Questions that prompt discussion are:

- Are Whites also victims of the media, stereotypes, and bias?
- What are different forms of White otherness?
- Is White oppression of Whites the same as White oppression of people of color?
- How is it different or the same?

IDENTITY DEVELOPMENT THROUGH NARRATIVES

The narrative serves many purposes for both the authors and the listeners, individually and collectively. For individual authors, the process of writing the narrative makes one conscious of identity. Patterns of narratives include stories about colorism, sexism, physical attributes, linguicism, classism, ableism, and heterosexism. Particularly noteworthy are the forms of White otherness identified by White students. Stories are read aloud by student authors to their peers. I analyze them to determine which stories have the potential to act as catalysts to deeper critical discussions. I look for narratives with cultural surprises, new social and cultural information, and information that provokes people to say, "I never knew that." These stories facilitated the critical questioning of history books, texts, the media, and other sources of knowledge by raising the following issues:

- For whom do we educate?
- Why are these stories not publicly acknowledged?
- What epistemologies bar awareness of our sociocultural locations? (SooHoo, in press)
- What reveals latent negative attitudes and expectations of those who are racially, ethnically, and socioeconomically different from ourselves?
- What has potential to raise contradictions, for example, differences in funding of men and women's activities, the preponderance of black and brown males in special education classes?
- What illustrating differences within groups are as great as differences among groups, for example, the English/bilingual debate within Hispanic communities, the influence of different waves of immigration, the difference between assimilation versus acculturation?
- How are Whites framed as both "privileged" and "othered"?
- What forms of otherness exist in an all-white class?
  - Are Whites "othered"?
  - By whom and to what degree?
  - Is there a hierarchy of otherness?
  - What are our multisocial positions as oppressor and oppressed?
  - Who are White people of color? (SooHoo, in press)
- What arouses guilt and action, awakening apathy and complacency?
- What catalyzes moving from a position of indifference to difference, to making a difference?

Narratives provide contextual information about conditions of oppression and reveal identity cornerstones more explicitly. The experiences of people of color are best captured by Cross's (1971, 1978, 1991) five-stage theory of Black identity development. This theory includes preencounter, encounter, immersion/emersion, internalization, and internalization–commitment. A Black person in the preencounter stage, according to Tatum (1998), believes that "White is right" and "Black is wrong" (p. 331). This "mask of Whiteness" (Almojuela, 1999) is similar to the unquestioned assimilation of White norms experienced by immigrants. Triggered by some racial event, the encounter stage is characterized by one's first awareness of one's difference: "There is a realization that race alone, independent of other qualities of the individual, can lead to negative treatment" (Howard, 1999, p. 87).

Immersion/emersion (Parham, 1989) is a reaction to the encounter stage. This stage is characterized by anger toward Whites for Black disenfranchisement, White avoidance, and a strong allegiance to Black culture over White. Internalization begins when this "pro-Black attitude becomes more expansive, open, and less defensive" (Cross, 1971, p. 24). In this stage there is a greater willingness to interact with members of other groups. The fifth stage, internalization–commitment is distinguished by a proactive commitment to work in a broader multicultural context as a way to strengthen Black community. Mature Black identity results from a moral assessment of White dominance and Black responses, which enables Black humanity to flourish without deifying or demonizing others (West, 1993).

While Cross's work details Black identity development, these stages of development are similar for people from other marginalized groups (Howard, 1999). Distinct markers of identity development can be found both in my personal narrative of otherness and in an example of a student's narrative. One can find, among the detailed accounts of ethnic assaults, the reclaiming of ethnic pride, as well as emerging hope for unity within diversity. For most of the students of color in my class, the narrative assignment has been their first opportunity to work out the repressed anger and frustration of their sociopolitical locations. This working through of one's own "otherness" gives students the chance to make visible that which has been denied. The resulting narratives revealed deep emotional wounds incurred typically in childhood that adult students still carry. These wounds are close to the surface. Merely touched, they bleed profusely. Sometimes reading the narratives brings emotional closure to the pain as well as intellectual consciousness.

White identity development, in the works of Helms (1990, 1992, 1994) and Helms and Piper (1994), include six stages, divided into two phases. Phase 1 consists of contact, disintegration, and reintegration. Phase 2 comprises pseudo-independence, immersion/emersion, and autonomy. In Howard's (1999) review of this work, White people in the contact stage do not see themselves as being White but rather as just uncolored people. Some also tell people of color that they are color-blind and do not notice what race a person is. Disintegration occurs when White people acknowledge their whiteness and begin to question what they have been socialized to believe about race. Guilt, shame, and anxiety often accompanies the growing awareness of unfair and unequal treatment to people of color. For some Whites, this guilt turns to fear and anger and results in reintegration and the belief of racial superiority. Reintegration is characterized by a White consciousness that espouses racism as a means of dealing with diversity.

An alternative path to reintegration is pseudo-independence in Phase 2. In this stage, Whites acknowledge White responsibility for racism and attempt to help those people who have suffered from racial inequality. However, this missionary zeal is still informed by white dominance as the White savior saves the lost people of color. Immersion/emersion evolves away from the paternalistic efforts to help others and focuses instead on the changing of one's self and fellow Whites in a positive way. These are the White antiracist allies who work to shape a new White identity. Autonomy, Stage 6, is achieved when Whites draw correlations between racism and other forms of oppression, sexism, classism, and linguicism, and are consistently proactive in the resistance to inequality and dominance. These are the White people of color.

White students, like students of color, enter my course from different stages of identity development. In 45 instructional hours, a multicultural educator can only hope to facilitate educational opportunities for movement from one stage to the next. It depends, of course, on the makeup of one's class. As an instructor of color, within primarily white, upper-middle-class females, I must study and learn from my White students—where they are in their identity development and where they may want to be as aspiring school teachers. In my efforts to raise their consciousness, I am most aware of the delicate relationship we have and how fragile the process is of developing multicultural consciousness. At any moment in my course, there are both students recovering from the indignation of racial constructs and students amplifying heretofore silenced voices. It becomes necessary then to structure activities that bring us together while we explore each other's differences. Working with the assumption that everyone is an "other" and that everyone "others" others (Frederickson, personal communication, 1997), the narratives of otherness elicit diverse voices about something everybody experiences.

OTHERNESS OUT LOUD

Composing a narrative facilitates an awakening of consciousness. Deeper, penetrating meaning comes from listening to other narratives. Each student antes his or her vulnerability, as well as historicity, into the community pool of knowledge. Listeners are eager to listen, tense with anticipation, and respectful of the trust vested in them.

"As a classroom community, our capacity to generate excitement is deeply affected by our interest in one another, in hearing one another's voices, in recognizing one another's presence" (hooks, 1994, p. 8). Even the instructor reads her narrative because "any radical pedagogy must insist that everyone's presence is acknowledged" and "when professors bring narratives of their experiences into classroom discussions it eliminates the possibility that we can function as all knowing, silent interrogators" (hooks, 1994). Collectively, we offer our narratives to the community as an offering of hope and promise for the insights we might gain towards a more just and caring human existence.

Narratives evoke empathy and emotional bonding. They awaken the subjectivity and humanization of otherness, which may have been dulled by the intellectualization of this concept. The emotional energy generated by an empathetic community provides authors with the courage to publicly name experiences of otherness. The naming of these experiences commonly inflames the original pain of oppression, as demonstrated by the author's sadness, anger, and guilt.

In return for this vulnerability comes enlightenment, because to understand one's self is to understand all people (Sapp, 2003). Students empathize with "others" as they come to terms with their own victimization. Some confess guilt at not having spoken up for victims of similar assaults. Others become enraged over the injustices suffered by their fellow students.

Students learn from other students' experiences about issues they have not personally experienced. The power of story links everyone in the room with the pain, humiliation, and injustices suffered by the victims of othering. Through empathy, caring, compassion, and fellowship, the class establishes a sense of solidarity. Henceforth, the classroom is a unique place in the university where difference is accepted and affirmed, and where difference can be discussed, researched, and made public (Nieto, in press).

We conduct a rigorous self-investigation as we struggle to understand the social forces of domination and marginalization. Realizing that these stories could have been stories untold had we not consciously sought them, we ask ourselves, For whom do we educate? Why are these stories not public? What epistemologies bar awareness of our sociocultural locations? We demand to know.

Frustration and anger searches for action as a move towards healing. We ask, What can we do to stop student harassment? What conditions allow this phenomenon to occur year after year, generation after generation? How did racism, sexism, homophobia, and anti-Semitism become acceptable norms on school campuses? How have we been complicit with these acts of injustice? What responsibility do we have to stop these acts? What acts of courage are we willing to commit to?

From this discourse, a community ethic emerges—the right to be different. The community guards this newfound right like a newborn infant. Difference, like democracy, is something we should fight to protect. Difference, seen as strengths rather than weaknesses (Oakes & Lipton, 1999), demonstrates our shift from a modern to a postmodern perspective. Moving from the worldview of an undifferentiated human nature based on universalism, we reach out to that which is different, particular, multiple, and heterogeneous. Our new responsibility is to protect cultural dissimilarity and ensure that nondominant lifestyles are recognized equally, fairly, and justly. We have a duty to protect these lifestyle differences in the same way our political heritage has traditionally protected our right to dissent or protest (Duarte, 1998).

Unity within difference becomes clear as we examine how we are similar to and different from each other. When we name our own "otherness," while naming our complicity in "othering" others, we come to know ourselves as both the oppressed and the oppressors. It is here that a language of possibility unfolds as we attempt to liberate ourselves as both the oppressed and the oppressor (Freire, 1970).

ACTION

> Personal narratives in assorted forms are critical to a counterhegemonic agenda.
>
> (Kanpol, 1994)

Personal narratives, as food for theory making and moral consciousness, give way to practice. With our newfound conviction to end the ongoing victimization of students in schools, future teachers pledged, "Never again, not on my watch, will another child be marginalized or tormented for his or her physical appearance, culture, language, religion, sexual orientation or social class." Shedding the once-comfortable robe of the bystander, teachers armed themselves with individual and collective courage to proactively confront school cultures, practices, structures, and policies that marginalize and disenfranchise youth.

It is not enough to simply understand and deconstruct difference. Students feel compelled to seek ways to challenge forces of domination and structures that reproduce inequality. As a way of marshaling this urgency to act and as a means for students to demonstrate their understanding of critical pedagogy, students engage in social justice projects. These projects take many forms, for example, interviewing advertising executives about stereotypes of women and minorities in the media; writing to Hallmark executives to inform them about the noninclusive holidays which may affect some kids adversely and making suggestions (e.g., Father's Day instead of Parent/Guardian Day); organizing and raising funds for multicultural guest speakers for schools to become culturally conscious (Au, 1993); observing in the classrooms of local teacher–politicians, such as Gloria Mata Dutchman (coauthor of *The Unz Initiative*); to evaluate, firsthand, English-only pedagogy. The purpose of these activities is not to transform those people with different ideologies, but to personally engage individuals and their respective organizations in different truths.

Students are encouraged to expand their sphere of influence (Adams & Marchesani, 1997) within their projects, beyond the personal, that is, to act in arenas beyond their immediate families and friends, and perhaps to educate leadership, communities, and newspapers. This often means that students need to first assess the high or low levels of risks involved in their projects and then stretch beyond their comfort range to initiate action that might make systemic difference.

Simple advocacy is still not enough. Moving from the personal to the public sphere of influence forces students to engage in the politics of social issues. They have to determine what persons or institutions with which to develop a common "platform of possibility" (Kanpol, 1994), that is, where and with whom could they learn? Who might they also influence in the name of social justice? "Change cannot be accomplished by isolated individuals or random acts of critique. Politics is a social enterprise. It requires that persons form communities . . ." (Jay & Graff, 1995).

COMMUNITY OF CRITICAL FRIENDS

It is from this soup of multicultural potential that my own political activism is nourished. Students' narratives of otherness pepper my cultural proclivity of political passivity, resulting in a ravenous appetite for social justice. I can no longer sustain myself by living a life of indifference to difference.

A legacy of both oppression and privilege has shaped one dimension of my life. Critical consciousness and critical friends have shaped another dimension. Fellow social justice educators have generously mentored and accompanied me in my development as a woman warrior. A special thanks to Pat Teft-Cousin, Sonia Nieto, Christine Sleeter, Mara Sapon-Shavin, Lee Ann Bell, Antonia Darder, Paul Heckman, Tom Wilson, and especially, Barry Kanpol. They have broadened my cultural self-awareness and triggered my critical consciousness. They have helped me see my biases, prejudices, and blind spots.

I have come to understand how I have used my current teaching situations to "right the wrongs of the past." That is, when I speak up in name of social justice, it is my way of making up for my past incidents in which I have failed to intervene or stop oppressive situations (Obear, 2000). I know this is what my students and cultural ancestors expect from me.

PERSONAL NARRATIVE

I write this narrative to illuminate the parts of my life which have been pushed to darkness—my place within a White man's world.

I am who I am because of a White man.

Mother divorces my father and marries a White man.
We move from a house above the tunnel near Chinatown to a brick and wrought iron
house in San Francisco's posh Marina district.
The other two Chinese families that live in this area are also part White.
This was the only way Chinese could live in this part of town.

My formative adolescent years are newly rooted in the White part of town, away from
Chinatown's little dark alleys, smells of roast duck and garbage, clicking Cantonese tongues.

Mother has new friends—White friends.
She quickly forgets the language she spoke to her parents with.
She only speaks Cantonese when she swears at the cooks in her restaurants.
Although I am a Chinese-American, I don't speak Chinese.
I understand only a little.
The word behind the hyphen was emphasized more in my household.
Even as she prepares for her death, mother told her daughters,
She didn't want to be buried on the side of the cemetery with all those "Chinamen."
Not until I am an adult do I mourn the loss of my Chinese identity.

I am who I am because of a White man.

When I grow up, I'll be just like him.
He was the best fifth-grade teacher in the world.
We stayed in almost every recess just to hear his stories.
He loved our round faces and almond-shaped eyes.
At the school carnival, we cheered him on as he used chopsticks to pick up marbles from a
bowl of soapy water.
Later he transferred to a school of mostly African American children.
He said they needed him more.
I will never forget him.

I am who I am because of a White man.

I am nine years old when I go to church for the very first time.
The walls are tall and cold.
Frozen marble faces stare at me.
A shiver runs down my arms.
An altar boy lights the candles with formal deliberateness.
I look at the flickering flames, which are the only signs of movement, and like me, they are
struggling for meaning in this cold, holy place.
Everything is white, the pillars, the pews, the altar, the people, and Jesus.

I am who I am because of a White man.

My first boyfriend is the basketball captain, class president and in the honor society.
He teases me and always wants a kiss.
We are "going steady." Everyone in school thinks we're a cute couple, except his White parents.
They say we're too young to go steady.
We ignore them until his mother cries.
She says, "It's nothing personal but he should date White girls."
This is the first time my skin feels dirty, my eyes too small, my hair too black.
I lighten my hair to brown, color my eyes to make them bigger, and cover my arms, but I
am still not white enough.

I am who I am because of a White man.

I am a teacher.
My principal is a White man.
He chooses me over others because I am a UCLA graduate and know how to write
behavioral objectives.
He laughs when my bulletin boards are crooked.
He says it must be because of my slanted eyes.
I am not offended.
He buys us instructional materials, takes us to visit schools and teaches us "the ropes."
Two years later, the teachers and he have a power struggle.
He is angry and feels betrayed.
We are irreverent because we challenged him.
I realize by joining my colleagues, I have challenged an elder.
My ancestral gods will be angry.

I am who I am because of a White male.

I am a school principal.
My supervisor is a White man.
He thinks I'm intelligent, a team player, a change agent.
He flirts with me, reminding me I am female.
He tells me I may not order "pink princess" telephones for my office.
I've stuffed myself into a three-piece suit and also have to remind myself I'm female.
The suit flattens my chest and binds my hips.
I walk and talk different in these clothes.

The women principals work hard.
We organize meetings, create initiatives and follow meticulously district directives.
The male administrators humor us, pat us on our backs (not on our heads), and tell us
we're doing a good job, then leave for their two-hour lunch meetings.
We rebel by not pouring coffee or taking minutes at the next meeting.

I am who I am because of a White man.

Can he lead me through this world of academia?
Does he know how very scared I am; how I second-guess each step of my worthiness?
He is my doctoral advisor.
I don't tell him I have come from a home with no books.
I am embarrassed about my "bookless" pedigree.
It's a secret locked in my heart.
My father was a simple man who shared his wisdom with me by telling me stories and writing me letters.

How does an Asian woman exist in this omnipotent world of scholarship?
My voice seems so small.
I read works by other women and people of color.
I come to realize my personal and acquired knowledge may have a place in this world.
I find out new things, things my advisor doesn't know.

How does an Asian woman teach a White man?

I am who I am because of a White man.

We drink lots of coffee.
With each cup, a new theory.
Feminism, patriarchy, critical theory, spirituality.
He pushes my thinking.
I get lost in his.
He makes me read and write, read and write, read and write.
Then we talk.
I'm starting to find my place in academe.
I am no longer "less than" White.
He is my mentor.

I am who I am because of a White man.

It's my pre-tenure year at the university.
Will I make it or am I merely ethnic window dressing?
I have traversed many boundaries to get here.
While I know it is I who I must not disappoint, I also respect what the community thinks of me.
I want to be a part of shaping this institution's future and not be a temporary houseguest.
My destiny lies in the hands primarily of White men.

I am who I am because of a White man and so are you.

Eastern Inscription

I am who I um because I am an Asian woman.

Grandmother lived with us and took care of me the first five years of my life before she died.
I remember her gray streaked hair, her broad smile, and her frail walk, the crippling results
of early foot binding.
She would soak them in a large tin pan each night.
I would help towel dry her broken feet.
What kind of life did she want for me?

I am who I am because I am an Asian woman.

Thick, hand knitted, itchy sweater-vests worn under dresses were the standard school
uniform imposed on young Chinese girls by their mothers.
Sometimes we would also wear tiger balm on our chests, wrists and temples.
These two practices were aimed at keeping out the mysterious "bad wind" that Chinese
aunties said would give us rheumatism in our old age.

If we had a cold, salted plums and lemon peel were stuffed into our pockets with instructions
to suck but not eat them.
We did as we were told.
This was better than swallowing the one hundred, bitter, black bee bee tea, a proven
Chinese remedy.

When I had my wisdom teeth removed, my father went to the herbalist and brought home
a bag of dirt, nested with twigs, which he carefully boiled in a large pot.
As the silt sank to the bottom, Dad ladled up the bubbling juices from the top into a bowl.
I was made to drink this curious, culinary mud puddle in the interest of fast healing and
unquestioned obedience.

For thirty days after giving birth to each of my children, I was restricted from leaving my
house, my mother-in-law standing guard by the door to ensure this rule was not violated.
Ginger chicken and stewed pigs feet were my daily diet.
Both of these dishes promised quick recovery, shrinking of the uterus, and the prevention of
those, once again "bad winds" from entering my vulnerable body.
The headaches I now suffer occasionally, twenty years later, are the result of my stepping
outside of my house and not obeying this old Chinese superstition.

I am who I am because I am an Asian woman.

My white wedding dress is adorned with nine, heavy, twenty-four-carat gold necklaces.
I wear eight gold and jade bracelets, four on each arm.
Three gold rings have been added to my fingers.
My husband's pockets have been regularly stuffed with little red "lay see" envelopes filled
with money.
Our Chinese families have been very generous in wishing us a good future.
Twenty-eight years later the money is long gone, but the jewelry sits in a safety deposit
box, awaiting the weddings of our children.

One month after our children are born, they too are laden with gold jewelry.
At the customary red egg and ginger party, Chinese aunties and uncles tuck "lay see" under
the pillows of the bassinets.
In return we give each guest a red egg to ensure his or her future fertility.
Our children's baby-sized jewelry sits with our wedding jewelry in the bank security box,
awaiting the births of their children.
I will need to hock the jewelry to pay for the wedding of my son.
My daughter will be "bought" by her future husband's family and we will not be
responsible to pay for the wedding.
That is—if she marries a Chinese.
If she doesn't, who will pay?

The customs and celebrations that have survived three generations have lost their original
meaning through their migration from China, causing confusion and ad hoc Chinese
practices.
The quasi-Chinese customs continue and escape scrutiny because of the "don't-ask-
questions,-it-just-is" discourse between youngers and elders.

I am who I am because I am an Asian woman.

Contemporary Chinese wives must cook, or at least find a book to learn to cook, Chinese food.
Black bean paste, oyster sauce and dried mushrooms are among the staples found in their
pantries.
A wok, a butcher knife, and an electric rice cooker are among the kitchen appliances.
Chinese children become proficient with chopsticks by age three
and can even catch slippery scallops served in porcelain bowls.
My Chinese mother-in-law shows me in her quiet, undemonstrative way how to put
Chinese dishes together, never talking, a silent role model to me.
The contrasts between her and me are sharply defined;
I work hard at "becoming," she works quietly at "being."

I am who I am because I am an Asian woman.

"If you don't speak Chinese, you are not Chinese," jeered my Chinese cousins.
You are what you speak.
You become what you hear.
I am now only "white noise" to them, a translated woman.
I hide my face when someone asks me to speak.

The language I do share with my Chinese cousins is the language of silence.
Walk into any of our relatives' homes and you can hear the loud quiet.
While the vocabulary is speechless, the meaning is profound.
So much is said in our wordless world; our silent way of knowing.

I am who I am because I am an Asian woman.

My public life is Western.
My private life is Eastern.
Sometimes East clashes with West like mah jong tiles.
Sometimes East and West converge in a satisfying stir-fry.
I am a cultural transsexual, always crossing identity borders.

I am who I am because I am the White man.

I am an able bodied, heterosexual, wife and mother,
An English speaking, middle-class professor.
I am both privileged and "othered."
I am both the mentor and the mentee.
I am both the oppressor and the oppressed.
I am a part of "their" oppression and my own.

I am the model minority
"Making it" on the backs of others.
Top of the diversity totem
Pretending to be white
Colonizing "them"; othering "them."

I am who I am because I am both the White man and the Asian woman

the strong, silent woman warrior
Who stretches her unbound feet and boldly crosses borders
Whose influence like burning incense perfumes the air to stir social consciousness.

Brown Is the Color I Am

by Herb Sanchez, Chapman University student

Brown is the color I am.
Brown is not White.
Brown, the color of worn leather.
Brown like the arms of the men who stand at the corner looking for work.
The men my mother does not want me to see.
The men my family never wanted me to be.
Brown is the color of the gardener and the busboy.
Brown, the man who picks up my trash.
Brown, the man working in the lettuce fields.
Brown, the lady hocking flowers off of freeway on-ramps.
Brown is abandoned and pregnant at sixteen.
Brown is no skills and no future.
Brown is minimum wage.
Brown is limited English.

"We will not let you be Brown, my son.
For Brown reminds us of our indigenous past.

Brown is the conquered, not the conquistador.
Brown, our homeland we left behind.
White, the land of opportunity.
White, our dreams.
White, the color of clean hands that never knew work.
White, unstained by Brown (the color of dirt).
White, for whom we pick the fruit.
White, for whom we mow the lawn.

We will not let you be Brown, my son.
For we wish to spare you the pain and degradation of a crushed people.
For we wish you success and respect.
We wish you White.
But I cannot change culture as I would a pair of shoes.
Brown is the color I am.
And Brown is not White.

Brown is the color of shit.
Brown, the color of my hands. My skin. My face.

Brown, the color of shit that my father had to clean out of the bathrooms.
My father, the teacher, coming to America to mop and scrub toilets.
My father who always wished more for his sons.
My father who understood that America sees but two colors.
My father who knew that Brown is not White.
My father who let us know that we were Brown.
My father who taught us the importance of a good education only to discover that
knowledge is not bleach.
Learning does not whiten.

My brother is a lawyer, and I will be a teacher.
But we will forever carry a racial prefix.
The Latino lawyer.
The new Hispanic teacher.
As if to bring into question the merit of our work.
As if to remind me that Brown is not White.
As if to remind me that I am Brown.
Brown like the men who stand at the corner looking for work.
I am they, and they are I.
For together, we are Brown.
We share the White dream.
The dream that we might be counted.
That we might be respected.

For we recognize in ourselves that we are more than the color of our skin.
We are more than minstrels and entertainment.
More than sombreros and Macarena.

We are the product of centuries of mestizaje.
Of crossing and blending.
We are the children born of the mixture of Old World and New.
Spaniard fathers penetrating Aztec wombs.
We are Montezuma and Cortes, both and at once.
Heirs of two great cultures.
We are thinkers and poets.
Doctors and lawyers.
Scientists. Business owners.

Just like you.
Except for my Brownness.
The Brownness that I can no longer escape.
The Brownness that I am.

Brown is the color I am.
Brown is not White.
But Brown is not lesser.
Brown is just darker.
Brown, the color of freshly hewn lumber.
Brown like damp earth.
Brown, the color of coffee or dark chocolate.
Brown, the color of baked bread.
Brown, the first seed that springs forth into the first tree.
Brown, the Earth's first color.
Brown is the color I am.
Brown, the part of me, which I once detested.
Brown, the part of me in which I now rejoice. Brown, the color God gave me.
Brown, the color I am.

What Teachers Don't Know About Being Poor

Christine Clark, Chapman University student

I remember feeling sick to my stomach when, in an education class, I read a passage about "neglect." I read, "If any student is subjected to neglect, it must be reported as abuse." It went on to say that if a child is without food, has low self-esteem, and is often dirty or without grooming and clothes are often torn, that child is neglected. It also stated that these children seldom look their teachers in the eye. I could read no more.

They could have just as easily replaced "poverty" with the word *neglect*. Poverty affects many of our students in ways that are unimaginable to those who have never been bitten by its ugly teeth.

I grew up as the youngest of six. My parents were exhausted, so I raised myself mostly. It was expensive to raise us. My brothers were gigantic and never stopped eating. Also, my father had spinal surgery and could not work for 2 years. Our friends would help us out and sometimes put food on our front porch, like bread and pastries, but that was rare.

My stomach was always empty. When I did manage to get food my brothers would eat my food before I could finish it. I learned to eat fast and to never leave my plate to go to the bathroom during a meal.

Lunch money was a privilege, not a necessity, and if I did pack my lunch it was always a pickle sandwich with mayonnaise. I learned to hide food in the house. I would save any food from school I could get my hands on and keep it in my purse. I loved the days when they served apples, wrapped cookies, and orange juice.

Anyway, grooming was the next issue. Or should I say, "lack of grooming"? I was supposed to keep my hair long for some religious reason—what, I never knew. But I was responsible for my hair, and so dreadlocks became part of me: ratty, ratty hair, and so it was. I didn't care because I had no self-esteem, because when you're a child and you don't have money you don't think you have any value, especially when you hear your parents say that without realizing it. So you really don't care if your hair is brushed or your socks match.

Okay, now what about neglect? Would you report me to authorities? Certainly not—my parents worked two jobs and dealt with guilt on a daily basis. They always thought that they weren't good parents because they couldn't afford what we needed. They felt badly that their youngest daughter had neither a bed nor a birthday party. They never wanted us to feel different, but we did.

My teachers would ask if I would like to go home with them on the weekend. I asked my mother, and she was more happy than I. She needed a break and also wanted me to do well in life. So I went.

And so I would go with anyone who would take me. I moved out young and grew up fast. I met several people who took extreme interest in me and believed in me. They told me to "reach for the stars."

The cycle will not continue. I educated myself and will *not* have more kids than I can give attention to. My brothers and sisters will not have many children either. They struggled with our reality more than I, for most of them tried to kill themselves repeatedly because they just never felt worthy enough. It wasn't enough that we all loved each other. No, they needed more. I will never return to the house I was raised in because it is infested with mice, rats, cockroaches, and fleas.

So, now, as future teachers, maybe you want to know what you can do for students like me? Give them love; they need it. Hug them; compliment them. They eat it up. Look beyond their smelly hair and dirty clothes and do not judge them because, believe me, they have already written themselves off.

REFERENCES

Adams, M., & Marchesani, L. (1997). Multiple issues course overview. In M. Adams, L. A. Bell, & P. Griffin (Eds.), *Teaching for diversity and social justice* (pp. 261–271). New York: Routledge.

Almojuela, C. (1999). *Narratives: Multicultural teaching and the transformative voice.* Seattle, WA: Research Center.

Au, K. (1993). *Literacy instruction in multicultural settings.* New York: Harcourt Brace College.

Chang Bloch, J. (1997). *Rise of the Asian woman.* A paper presented at the World Affairs Council, Irvine, CA.

Cross, J. (1971). The Negro to Black conversion experience: Toward a psychology of Black liberation. *Black World, 20*(9), 13–27.

Cross, J. (1978). Models of psychological nigrescence. *Journal of Black Psychology, 5*(1), 13–31.

Cross, J. (1991). *Shades of black: Diversity in African-American identity.* Philadelphia: Temple University Press.

Duarte, E. (1998). Expanding the borders of liberal democracy. *Multicultural Education, 6*(1), 2–13.

Freire, P. (1970). *Pedagogy of the oppressed.* New York: Continuum.

Freire, P. (1993). *Pedagogy of the city.* New York: Continuum.

Giroux, H. (1993). *Border crossings: Cultural workers and the politics of education.* New York: Routledge.

Glasser, J. (1999). *Shattering the myths: Women in academe.* Baltimore: Johns Hopkins University Press.

Goodman, D. (2001). *Promoting diversity and social justice: Educating people from privileged groups.* Thousand Oaks, CA: Sage.

Harran, M. (2001, January 24). *The role of bystanders.* Workshop for *Facing History and Ourselves,* Pasadena, CA.

Helms, J. F. (Ed.). (1990). *Black and white racial identity: Theory, research, and practice.* Westport, CT: Greenwood.

Helms, J. E. (1992). *Race is a nice thing to have.* Topeka, KS: Content Communications.

Helms, J. E. (1994). Racial identity and "racial" constructs. In E. J. Trickett, R. Watts, & D. Birman (Eds.), *Human diversity* (pp. 285–311). San Francisco: Jossey-Bass.

Helms, J. E., & Piper, R. E. (1994). Implications of racial identity theory for vocational psychology. *Journal of Vocational Behavior, 44,* 124–138.

hooks, b. (1994). *Teaching to transgress: Education as the practice of freedom.* New York: Routledge.

hooks, b. (1999). *Remembered rapture.* New York: Holt.

Howard, G. (1999). *We can't teach what we don't know: White teachers, multiracial schools.* New York: Teachers College Press.

Jay, G., & Graff, G. (1995). A critique of critical pedagogy. In M. Berube & C. Nelson (Eds.), *Higher education under fire.* (pp. 201–213). New York: Routledge.

Kanpol, B. (1994). *Critical pedagogy.* Westport, CT: Bergin & Garvey.

Kivel, P. (1996). *Uprooting racism: How white people can work for racial justice.* Philadelphia: New Society.

Lee, S. (2002). Do Asian American faculty face a glass ceiling in higher education? *American Education Research Journal, 39,* 695–724.

Lorde, A. (1984). *Sister outsider.* Trumansburg, NY: Crossing.

Nieto, S. (1998). From claiming hegemony to sharing space: Creating community in multicultural courses. In R. Chavez-Chavez & J. O'Donnell (Eds.), *Speaking the unpleasant: The politics of (non)engagement in the multicultural education terrain* (pp. 16–31). Albany: State University of New York Press.

Oakes, J., & Lipton, M. (1999). *Teaching to change the world.* Boston: McGraw-Hill.

Obear, K. (May, 2000). *Exploring the phenomenon of triggering events for social justice educators.* Unpublished doctoral dissertation, University of Massachusetts, Amherst.

Parham, T. A. (1989). Cycles of psychological nigrescence. *The Counseling Psychologist, 17,* 187–226.

Sapp, J. (2003). Curriculum of the self. In Chapman University Consortium staff (Ed.), *Essays on urban education: Critical consciousness, collaboration and the self.* Cresskill, NJ: Hampton.

Schniedewind, N., & Davidson, E. (1998). *Open minds to equality.* Needham Heights, MA: Allyn & Bacon.

SooHoo, S. (in press). *Talking leaves: The other side of difference.* Cresskill, NJ: Hampton.

Tatum, B. (1998). *Why are all the black kids sitting together in the cafeteria?* New York: Perseus.

Villenas, S. (1998). *What's diversity got to do with qualitative research?* San Diego, CA: American Educational Research Association.

West, C. (1993). *Race matters.* Boston: Beacon.

Activities for the Classroom

Read books by authors of different genders, sexual orientations, cultures, religions, and physical abilities.

Allende, I. (1982). *The house of the spirits.* New York: Bantam. (Latino)

Anaya, R. (1972). *Bless me.* Ultima, CA: TQS. (Latino)

Angelou, M. (1969). *I know why the caged bird sings.* New York: Bantam. (African American)

Ciscernos, S. (1992). Woman hollering creek and other stories. New York: Vintage Books.

Deford, F. (1983). *Alex: The life of a child.* New York: Viking. (Disability)

Dew, R. *The family heart.* New York: Simon & Schuster. (Sexual orientation)

Diamant, A. (1998). The *red tent.* (Women of the Bible)

Dorris, M. (1989). *The broken cord.* New York: HarperPerennial. (Disability)

Esquivel, L. (1992). *Like water for chocolate.* New York: Doubleday. (Latino)

Flake, S. (1998). *The skin I'm in.* New York: Hyperion. (Special needs, race)

Garcia, C. (1992). *Dreaming in Cuban.* New York: Ballantine. (Latino)

Gonsales, R. (1972). *I am Joaquin.* New York: Bantam. (Mexican)

Griffin, J. (1976). *Black like me.* New York: Signet. (African American)

Hamilton, V. (1985). *The people could fly: American black folktales.* New York: Knopf. (African American)

Hayden, T. (1980). *One child.* New York: Avon. (Autism)

Hayslip, L. L., & Wurts, J. (1989). *When heaven and earth changed places.* New York: Doubleday. (Vietnamese)

Houston, J. W., & Houston, J. (1974). *Farewell to Manzanar.* New York: Bantam. (Japanese)

Huynh, N. Q. (1993). *South wind changing.* New York: Graywold. (Vietnamese)

Kingsleg, J., & Levitz, M. (1994). *Count us in: Growing up with Down's syndrome.* San Diego, CA: Harcourt Brace. (Disability)

Kingston, M. H. (1977). *Woman warrior.* New York: Random House.

Lee, G. (1991). *China boy.* New York: Penguin. (Asian American)

Lewis, S. (1996). *A totally alien life form—Teenagers.* New York: New York Press. (Ageism)

McCall, N. (1994). *Makes me wanna holler.* New York: Random House. (African American)

McCourt, F. (1996). *Angela's ashes.* New York: Scribner's. (Irish, social class)

Morrison, T. (1987). *Beloved.* New York: Signet. (African American)

Morrison, T. (1982). *Tar baby.* New York: Plume. (African American)

Mukherjee, B. (1989). *Jasmine.* New York: Fawcett Crest. (East Indian)

Naylor, G. (1992). *Linden hills.* New York: Penguin. (African American)

Otto, W. (1991). *How to make an American quilt.* New York: Ballantine. (Gender)

Rose, M. (1989). *Lives on the boundary.* New York: Penguin. (Social class)

Sarris, G. (1994). *Grand Avenue.* New York: Penguin. (Native American)

Sasson, J. P. (1992). *Princess: a true story of life behind the veil in Saudi Arabia.* New York: Morrow. (Middle Eastern)

Sleeter, C. & Grant, C. (1989). *Turning on learning: Five approaches for multicultural teaching plans for race, class, gender, and disability.* Columbus: Merrill.

SooHoo, S. (forthcoming). *The other side of difference.* Cresskill, NJ: Hampton.

SooHoo, S. (in press). *Talking leaves: The other side of difference.* Cresskill, NJ: Hampton.

Tan, A. (1991). *The kitchen god's wife.* New York: Putnam. (Asian American)

Tan, A. (1988). The *joy luck club.* New York: Putnam. (Asian American)

Taylor, M. (1981). *Let the circle be unbroken.* New York: Bantam. (African American)

Walker, A. (1982). *Possessing the secret joy.* New York: Pocket Star. (African American)

Wong, J. S. (1950). *Fifth Chinese daughter.* New York: Harper. (Chinese American)

Action research activities from Christine Sleeter's book, *Turning on Learning,* for example, neighborhood walks, stereotyping, and name calling.

Social group membership profile by Pat Griffin in *Teaching for Diversity and Social Justice.*

Social justice projects from the Anti-Defamation League's *No Place for Hate: 101 Ways to Fight Prejudice—A Citizen's Action Guide.*

Videos

(1996). *It's elementary—Talking about gay issues in schools.* Women's Education Media.

(1994). *Color of fear.* Oakland, CA: Stir-Fry Productions.

(1997). *bell hooks: Cultural criticism and transformation.* Northampton, MA: Media Education Foundation.

Journals

Colorlines (electronic journal): http://www.colorlines.com

Multicultural Education (Caddo Gap Press)

Teaching for Tolerance (Southern Poverty League)

FURTHER READING

Heath, S. B. (1983). *Ways with words.* New York: Cambridge University Press.

Darder, A. (1991). *Culture and power in the classroom.* Westport, CT: Bergin & Garvey

Freire, P. (1995). *Pedagogy of the oppressed.* New York: Continuum.

Goodlad, J. (1984). *A place called school.* New York: McGraw-Hill.

Kanpol, B., & McLaren, P. (Eds.). (1995). *Critical multiculturalism: Uncommon voices in a common strug-gle.* Westport, CT: Bergin & Garvey.

Kingston, M. H. (1976). *Woman warrior.* New York: Random House.

Kozol, J. (1991). *Savage inequalities.* New York: Crown.

Lieberman, A. (1992). *Teachers, their world and their work.* New York: Teachers College Press.

Matsuda, M. (1996). *Where is your body? And other essays on race, gender and the law.* Boston: Beacon.

Nieto, S. (1996). *Affirming diversity.* White Plains, NY: Longman.

Oakes, J. (1995). *Keeping track.* New Haven, CT: Yale University Press.

Tan, A. (1989). *The joy luck club.* New York: Putnam.

Wigginton, E. (1985). *Sometimes a shining moment.* Garden City, NY: Anchor Press/Doubleday.

Yung, J. (1995). *Unbound feet.* London: University of California Press.

WEB SITES

Center for the study of White American Culture:
www.euroamerican.org

African American activists and scholars:
www.blackradicalcongress.org

Media Literacy organization:
www.about-face.org

Museum of tolerance:
www.wiesenthal.com

California Coalition for Critical Educators:
www.ccce.net

Anti-Defamation League:
www.adl.org

My personal Web site:
www.chapman.edu/soe/faculty/soohoo/suzi.html

Chapter 17

Hurting, Healing, Helping: A Pedagogy of Identity, Recovery, and Voice

Jaime J. Romo, University of San Diego, San Diego

Focus Questions

1. How do your painful life experiences help you behave as an advocate for all children? How do these experiences make advocacy difficult?

2. Describe the "color of your ideology" that guides your personal and professional development towards advocacy? How does it help you to identify with those who are considered least powerful in society?

3. Who are your allies and colleagues who support your multicultural competency development?

"Where you from?" This is a challenging question that I have heard directed at me or at thousands of other Latinos throughout my life. Although the safest answer, as an adolescent, was "Nowhere," where I'm from has a lot to do with what and why and how I work with teachers to be more multiculturally competent advocates for all children. The following poem, which I recently received from a student, expresses some of the transformational process that my students and I experience in our learning dialogue:

> *Your enthusiasm is magnetic*
> *Your thoughtfulness angelic*
> *Your openness reverent*
> *You care*
>
> *You are as the lighthouse*
> *guiding souls through the darkness*
> *into the warm light*
> *of our own essences*

If only briefly
we chance by your
deep commitment
to the human experience

Then it is enough
for lifetimes of
inspiration and
healing.

While this poem is a humbling affirmation of my experiences, I present it with the knowledge that transformational teaching is related to, yet bigger than, who I am and what I do.[1] Transformational teaching is less about what I do *for* students and more about what I do *with* them. Yet, I am convinced that my experiences of transformational teaching relate directly to my transformational journey as a multiculturally competent advocate for all children, and that my personal multicultural knowledge base, dispositions (attitudes, values, and beliefs), and skills relate to how well I help students move from knowledge to action in their own development.[2]

My experience is that I'm from some very specific and marginalized places and that by working through the difficult process of recovery or healing from my own woundedness, I can also recognize my own privileges and work with them and others to promote justice. I believe that this is what Marianne Williamson means by the words, "Who am I to be brilliant, gorgeous, talented, and fabulous? . . . You are a child of God . . . And as we let our own light shine, we unconsciously give other people permission to do the same."[3]

---

[1] I taught classes for 5 years at National University from 5:30 to 10:00 p.m. in an intensive one-class-per-month format. Most students were working adults.

[2] For a fuller review of the content and philosophy of my teaching related to this course, see Romo & Salerno, 2000, "Towards Cultural Democracy: The Journey from Knowledge to Action in Diverse Classrooms" (Boston: Houghton Mifflin).

[3] *Our deepest fear is not that we are inadequate.*
Our deepest fear is that we are powerful beyond measure.
It is our light, not our darkness, that most frightens us.

We ask ourselves, "Who am I to be brilliant, gorgeous,
talented, and fabulous?"
Actually, who are you not to be?

You are a child of God.
Your playing small doesn't serve the world.
There's nothing enlightened about shrinking so that
other people won't feel insecure around you.

We were born to make manifest the glory of God
that is within us.
It's not just in some of us;
it's in everyone.

And as we let our own light shine, we unconsciously
give other people permission to do the same.
As we are liberated from our own fear,
our presence automatically liberates others.

An excerpt from "A Return to Love," by Marianne Williamson

In the following pages, I utilize various frameworks that have helped me to better understand and promote multicultural competency development in individuals and institutions. The organizer and title of this chapter relates to a recovery perspective. Within these sections, I use the meta-framework of the natural language acquisition process to understand my journey. Part 1, "Hurting," describes my silent (listening) phase. Part 2, "Healing," describes my metaphoric early production—oral proficiency (speaking), early literacy (reading my life), and advanced literacy (reading the world). Part 3, "Helping" (writing), connects these developments to my teaching. Within each section, I relate other personal or organizational frameworks for the reader's own consideration in her or his multidimensional development analysis. While none of these frameworks are monolithic or strictly linear, I find them extremely helpful in working with teachers to develop the skills and "walk the walk" of transforming society through their personal and professional practices.

HURTING: THE SILENT PERIOD

I grew up in Cypress Park, in northeast Los Angeles in the 1960s. In the 1940s, it was a predominantly Italian neighborhood, which gradually became predominantly Mexican and Chicano. The crashes of railroad cars coupling and uncoupling, police helicopters overhead, and occasional gunshots were my lullabies. I crossed daily borders of poverty, violence, and ethnic identity when I left home, entered classrooms, and returned home. The painful process of resolving these cultural border-crossing experiences helps me to not only identify with many young Californians today, but to bring a critical pedagogy and transformative voice to my current work as a teacher educator.

The Census Bureau notes that approximately 13% of children in the United States today live in poverty. Popular wisdom suggests that many more families live one check away from homelessness, like I did. I grew up hungry: physically, emotionally, and materially. Despite my current privileges, I identify with children and families who live in poverty. Such identification is a significant part of the voice I bring to my interpersonal and institutional work. I think that's what the expression, Where you stand on something depends on where you sit means.

Until I left home for college, I lived in one of the duplexes my grandfather built in the 1920s. My parents did not own the small, two-bedroom back house that the six children and two parents shared. Any new Christmas or birthday gift stood out in contrast to the recycled clothes I received from my richer cousins, who had nice clothes, traveled, had a big house on a hill overlooking Dodger Stadium, and had enough to eat. Perhaps my resentment towards them was my way of struggling with some of my family's poverty, due, in part, to the expenses my parents incurred privileging us academically, by sending all six children to the local Catholic elementary school, Divine Saviour.

Mandatory school uniforms were a big yearly September expense for my family, but they did remove any appearance of poverty and thereby reduced some of the shame I felt related to my multifaceted hunger. I remember waking up in the middle of the night and sneaking bits of whatever was in the refrigerator because I was hungry and couldn't sleep. I ate anything, but only enough so the fact that I was reducing what was available for the others might not be noticed.

Once, when I was around 9 years old, I silently crept to the refrigerator. My parents were asleep in the adjoining living room. The only thing I saw was a large jar of carrots, celery, and other vegetables floating in water. I bit into a big carrot slice and stifled a scream. These were spicy vegetables, pickled in a chile seasoned juice. I didn't return to the refrigerator at night after that.

I think it was around fourth or fifth grade that I lied in school and clearly understood the incongruity between my life experience and what was considered normal. We were studying the balanced breakfast, and a nun I don't remember anymore asked me, the perfect student, what I had eaten for breakfast. I hadn't eaten anything, but I had seen enough of *My Three Sons* and *Donna Reed* to know what I should have eaten: "Eggs, bacon, cereal, toast, and orange juice," I announced.

My mother must have known that I was unhappy about how little we had (although I never voiced it). One night, she read me an article from *Life* magazine about a young girl named Theresa Pilgrim, who lived somewhere in the South. Theresa lived in a very poor, rural area under even harsher conditions than we knew. My mother showed me a picture of Theresa and read me the caption about how her parents saved their money and, for her birthday, bought her an orange that she could eat all by herself. How could I complain?

I was awarded a full scholarship and attended a private Jesuit college prep high school across town, where I became painfully aware of my family's poverty vis-à-vis my classmates' wealth. Even television shows reminded me of what my family didn't have. I often felt puzzled at my own resentment of the characters on *Leave It to Beaver* and *The Partridge Family,* whose apparently perfect, secure, White identities mocked my own. They lived in clean, safe neighborhoods, ate beautiful meals in beautiful houses, traveled, and seemed to be happy most of the time.

One reason we did without so many things was that my father, a violent alcoholic, often broke whatever was within reach during his outbursts: televisions, clocks, dishes, stereos. Unlike the family games that I saw TV families play, a family activity we practiced was "hide and seek" when my dad drank. I was the king of being invisible, laying quietly in bed while he drank himself into a stupor at the kitchen table. On many nights, I listened for his footsteps like a backpacker listens for bears through the night. We also had a sick form of dodge ball—that is, sometimes he threw things at those around him. This led us to take frequent trips to the drive-in.

I'm sure that our budget didn't allow for the sudden family trips to the drive-in on those nights when it was just too dangerous to stay home. We generally picked up some food along the way: from Kentucky Fried Chicken or Der Wienerschnitzel or some snacks. Perhaps that's why those who were 12 or older had to fake being asleep or hide under blankets and pillows: so we wouldn't be charged. I was also one of the best pretend sleepers around, making sure that we didn't lose even more of the little money we had left.

Life in the back house was like living in Jurassic Park, and my dad was the unpredictable T-rex. When I turned 13, I moved into the front house of the duplex to help care for my blind grandmother. My grandfather had passed away 4 years earlier, and my older brother had moved out. It was my turn to move a few steps away from home.

The front house was my study sanctuary. I remember one night, however, when I woke to the familiar screaming from the back house. I ran to find my father holding my mother in a chokehold in one arm and waving a large knife at her throat.

I was big enough to attack him, but ended up shouting at him until he released her. The daily degrees of danger varied, but danger was a real and pervasive aspect of my home life.

My neighborhood was dangerous as well. The wars between the CP Boys, Clover, and the Avenues usually took place at night, on nearby blocks. The first case I knew of a daytime drive-by shooting in my neighborhood took the life of my grammar school classmate. He was 15.

Sometimes the violence even carried over to the church property. I must have been just under 10 years old when a normally safe parish fiesta exploded. The crowded schoolyard was lined with food and game booths, and families swarmed the property. "I'm Your Puppet" blared for the 20th time that day from the jukebox in the corner near the snowcone booth. A few feet away from me, someone from another neighborhood must have bumped someone from a Cypress Park clique, and within seconds, a group surrounded the unlucky intruder and kicked and beat him to the ground.

My home and neighborhood life catapulted me into investing myself in school, which was relatively safe. Where else could I put so much effort into something and be consistently and positively recognized? However, without a real voice and being predisposed to trust priests more than my own father, I didn't know how to speak out against being molested by the local priest for many years. My overachievements in school temporarily comforted me against the cost of assimilation that accompanied the layers of abuse. These collective wounds would later show themselves and inform my work as an advocate and activist.

HEALING: SPEAKING (UP FOR) AND READING (MYSELF)

Carl Jung is attributed with saying, "Enlightenment is not imagining figures of light, but making the darkness conscious." Part of my personal and professional literacy development has been in understanding and/or creating critical frameworks: (1) my racial identity development, (2) the dynamic of white privilege in society, and (3) cultural democracy quadrants. My understandings and use of these and other frameworks coincides with my graduate studies, beginning at UCLA. This period of learning also relates to a phase of male identity development that Robert Bly refers to as the Red Knight (see Stage 3, in the next section) and the second Ignatian spiritual developmental stage, "Discipline."

Racial Identity Development

I could have been a poster child for Soliz's (1981) racial identity/biculturalization process. I summarize Soliz's four-stage biculturalization process using modified transactional analysis terminology: (Stage 1) "I'm OK; you're OK"/cultural security; (Stage 2) "I'm not OK; you're OK"/assimilation; (Stage 3) "I'm OK; you're not OK"/ethnocentrism; (Stage 4) "How can we work together?"/biculturalization.

My Stage 1, cultural security, was not only damaged by the effects of poverty, violence, and alcoholism, but was confused by my parents' efforts to blend into the dominant culture. My parents thought that if they spoke only English to my siblings and me, we would do better in school; however, they spoke to one another in

Spanish. Under those circumstances, I developed a very limited and frustrating ability to communicate in Spanish with my grandparents, uncles, and aunts—I could understand many conversations but couldn't participate in them.

My Stages 1 and 2 were a strange searching experience. I internalized that life in *Father Knows Best, My Three Sons,* and *Donna Reed* was normal and that I was not. I wasn't like television people, and I wasn't like the first two people who called me a "Chicano-ese" as they staggered drunkenly by in a park. I wasn't like Speedy Gonzalez or Frito Bandito, my Latino media icons. I somehow knew what I was not, but not who I was.

At some point, I figured that my little hope of living differently than what I was used to lay in being the best dominant culture member I could be. I went across town to Loyola High School, a Jesuit College prep school, and then to Stanford University. I survived in primarily wealthy, dominant-culture environments, told ethnic jokes to fit in, and felt uncomfortable around ethnic or militant Latinos. I was probably what many would have considered the "model minority," although I knew that I was often pretending to be someone I wasn't and denying being someone I was.

I fit a classic racial identity/biculturalization pattern of assimilation (Stage 2) up until my second year at St. John's Seminary, where I was preparing for priesthood. Feeling a void, a psycho-spiritual disconnection to my Latino heritage, I went to the jungles of Chiapas, Mexico, as a field experience placement for the summer of 1984. I felt at home as never before. For the first time in my life, if someone called my name, two other Jaime's turned around with me. I was immersed in *comunidades de base,*[4] liberation theology, vibrant jungles, a celebration of relational living (as opposed to rugged individualism), and Spanish and Mayan dialects.

I saw the exploitation and genocide of native peoples from Guatemala and Chiapas, Mexico. I breathed the poverty that they experienced at the hands of their own governments, and I began to understand the dynamics of capitalism, greed, and exploitation and how it related to racism and labor exploitation north as well as south of "the border." I walked through the Aztec and Mayan ruins, where Hernan Cortes and generations of others had killed communities and destroyed temples, and I felt the sadness and rage of my indigenous heritage, and my violated childhood surge through me. I returned to Los Angeles, emotionally rejecting my elite educational affiliation, and immersed myself in Central American and southern Californian political struggles and race relations with the National Conference of Community and Justice (NCCJ)[5] and Brotherhood, Sisterhood, USA, a human relations summer camp for high school students. This personally integrative work marked my departure from a vocation of church service to public service through education.

One vintage Stage 3 moment came after a year of teaching at Adams Junior High, an inner-city school with a large Mexican- and Central-American immigrant population in the Los Angeles Unified School District. I had a conversation with my sister's *nino* (godfather), Eddie Sams, who was a regional superintendent in the district. He said, "Jaime, I've known you your whole life. You're going to want to

---

[4]Base communities are informal collectives where groups support one another and collaborate to solve community problems, ranging from economic, health care, and educational concerns to religious leadership.

[5]In 1996, the NCCJ changed its name from the National Conference of Christians and Jews to its current name, representing a shift from its institutionalized ethnocentrism to societal interdependence. This weeklong camp continues to engage high school students throughout the country in an intense and transformative workshop centered around antibias living skills.

have a bigger impact than just working in the classroom. Why don't you think about getting your master's degree and becoming an administrator? You could do a lot of good that way." "Eddie," I responded. "I don't want to be a part of the system; I want to tear the system down."

I began two significant relationships at that time that had the most significant impact on my personal and professional development. I met and married my spiritual partner, Philomena, who is White. In our more than 17 years together, we have helped one another stretch and mature spiritually and as mentors and allies for others. This relationship marked the beginning of Bly's "White Knight" period, and a turn towards partnership and "Compassion," the third of the Ignatian spiritual developmental stages.

My other spiritual partner, Ken (also White), was a fellow teacher-warrior and advocate for justice. He was a kind of alter ego who became more identified with activism and unconventional living as I tried to infiltrate educational institutions as a kind of stealth educator, waging peace while wearing a tie and going to graduate school. His untimely death during the summer of 1995 while hiking Mt. Adams, in Washington, left me reeling in the tension of my alignment with conventional living and my commitment to social justice. My choices, experiences, and values clarification (raising a family, completing my M.Ed., wearing conventional ties, becoming a middle school and high school administrator, completing my doctorate, and teaching teachers) are all powerfully wrapped up in those relationships. Philomena and Ken honored my revolutionary Stage 3 spirit and helped me to see, understand, and collaborate with the color of a person's ideology more than the color of a person's skin.

In my first placement as an assistant principal in a poor, predominantly Latino middle school, my heritage and educational critique were valued by my supervisors and community members. In my second assistant principalship (in a suburban, primarily dominant culture high school), I struggled to maintain the spirit of changing the school culture to better serve all students and concurrently manifest a professional style that would match the dominant culture powerbrokers in order to gain their trust.

The last few years, in particular, have been filled with personal and professional epiphanies: embracing both dominant and so-called minority cultures, living more as a partner than as a boss, extending my identification with both cultural sides of myself, and promoting cultural democracy and a pedagogy of revolution through partnerships. This fusion has led me to new personal and professional ground, empowering me to echo Michel Foucault:

> It seems to me that the real political task in a society such as ours is to criticize the workings of institutions which appear to be both neutral and independent; to criticize them in such a manner that the political violence which has always exercised itself obscurely through them will be unmasked, so that one can fight them.   (in Elders, 1974, p. 171)

My educational achievements are not reflected in the general population of Latinos and many others who are outsiders to most educational efforts and organizations. Because I personally and professionally identify with these outsiders, I take the following statement from a recent San Diego Latino Summit 2000 report to heart:

> Schools have a dismal track record in providing Latino/Chicano and low-income youth with the necessary skills to have access to the world of work. Over 40% of our

Latino/Chicano youth drop out of school, while another 30% receive a high school diploma with academic deficiencies that make them underskilled and underemployed. Of the remaining 30%, only 15% enter college, and about 5% eventually receive a B.A. degree.

(Ochoa, 2000)

HEALING: SPEAKING (UP FOR OTHERS) AND READING (THE WORLD)
The Dynamic of White Privilege in Society

How do these statistics occur? Paulo Freire (1985) would say that, because of privilege, dominant culture members actually resist change toward equity. Privilege, therefore, is the gatekeeper of consciousness, which underlies inequity and the implicit hostility in symbolic violence. Richard Delgado (1995) extends Freire's discussion of privilege and suggests that in our dominant culture, those who experience privilege are metaphorically infected with a White supremacist consciousness. As a result, even liberal, privileged, social reformers or educators cannot effectively move beyond self-serving and inequitable de jure (e.g., political referenda) and de facto social structures (Darder, 1994; Smith, 1990; Scheurich, 1993).

In my home state, Propositions 163 (mandating English as the official language), 187 (reducing immigrant's rights), 209 (attacking affirmative action), and 227 (eliminating bilingual education) were passed handily. Perhaps these processes reflect Albert Einstein's words, "Few people are capable of expressing with equanimity, opinions which differ from the prejudices of their social environment. Most people are even incapable of forming such opinions." I agree with Giroux (1992), who challenges this notion of a self-reflective limitation and urges his fellow White, middle-class educators to recognize their own "politics of . . . location" and to address issues of racism, sexism, and class hegemony.

Philomena and Ken proved to me that it is possible and necessary for dominant culture members to advocate effectively for equity once they recognize their own privilege. Freire (1985) explains what I have seen: that members of the dominant culture can only truly understand and reform a system by hearing from those who are oppressed by the system.

I regularly experience the negative effects of White privilege (even though I know I have many privileges regarding health, ability, age, education, and gender). Sheriffs have stopped me when jogging in my own neighborhood. I am checked regularly by the Immigration and Naturalization Service agents on trains and at border patrol checkpoints. I am often treated as a clerk or gas station attendant, regardless of my formal dress.

Recently, I bought and lost a book of stamps at my local post office. As I retraced my steps a couple of times, searching the premises, a post office patron met me at the door, pointed to the lettering above the doorway and loudly enunciated, "Post office." I actually laughed and thanked him, instead of challenging him or leaving in a fury. I knew that this was probably a more polite, albeit patronizing, version of the old question, "Where are you from?" That simple misunderstanding articulated a white privilege corollary, toxic politeness, at work: "You're not from here. You're Latino. You must be a migrant worker who doesn't understand where you are."

I was first validated regarding the existence of white privilege on professional levels 9 years ago, during my final assistant principal interview with then superintendent of Sweetwater Union High School District, Tony Trujillo. He surprised me when he asked, "What are you going to say to the teacher who says, 'The reason you got this job is because you are Latino and the superintendent is Latino?' " We engaged in a role play, discussing my qualifications. He then said to me, "Are you willing to work longer hours than everybody else, work harder and do a better job than anyone else? If you are, then the job is yours."

I was surprised, not by his questions, but by his openness regarding his Latino experience in the context of White privilege. His comments resonated with my own experiences of having felt welcomed and supported as a special member, a kind of outlier, of a minority group. On the other hand, I have often felt alienated, invisible, avoided, or targeted as an unwelcome outsider.

I experienced these as a bilingual education teacher in the Los Angeles United School District (1985–1988), as a bilingual education teacher in Vista USD (1988–1990), as an assistant principal and summer school principal at National City Middle School (1990–1993), but most negatively as an assistant principal at Vista High School (1993–1995). As an assistant principal at Vista, my principal found it meaningful to share his concern that various parents called to say that they thought I had organized the student walkouts surrounding the passage of Proposition 187.

The more I share my experiences, particularly with other educators of color, the more I hear common experiences, feelings, and struggles for equity and justice. Three quotes from my dissertation study set the backdrop of how important it is for me to promote societal transformation toward social justice and cultural democracy.[6]

> Most [teachers] don't even understand their prejudices. The best intentioned don't understand. And then there are some who are just very subtle about what they do. They subtly undermine kids—and you can confront those individuals and so on, but they will eyeball you and say, "I've been here before you; I'll be here after you." It's a very insidious, very difficult system to change. (principal, suburban high school)

> I recall having a conversation with [the superintendent] about the very issue of ethnic diversity in terms of their administrative staff and in terms of their teaching staff. He was very plain and very up-front about it. He said to me in an interview situation—it was a Western Association of Schools and Colleges (WASC) report. He said, "We brought on some ethnic, some minority administrators and what they did then is they began to bring some others that look like them. And we had to put a kibosh on that because in _____, we're very conservative; we have a very conservative attitude." And what that said to me is "We wanted to preserve the status quo. We wanted to maintain a balance between the ethnic population and the majority population—and that percentage was going to be small." And so they directed their administrators to stop doing that—which is a baffling admission. I mean, it's an incredible admission (*laugh*) from a superintendent that they were going to maintain the status quo in terms of the minority population ratio and they had been very direct in maintaining this attitude. (principal, suburban middle school)

In other words, some of the subtle practices of racism and exclusion are recognizable. More often, however, the subtle practices of racism and exclusion primarily

---

[6]See *Voices Against Discrimination and Exclusion: Latino School Leaders' Narratives for Change,* Unpublished doctoral dissertation, University of San Diego School of Education, 1998.

1	2
Hostile towards those perceived as outsiders. Explicit exclusion and monocultural external/embedded traits, which are reinforced at individual, group, and institutional levels, yielding status quo regarding power and the industrial paradigm.	Less overtly hostile than Quadrant 1: exclusion via second-generation discrimination. Individual representatives of "minority" groups (disconnected from group) report pioneer experience. Monocultural identity/values are reflected implicitly via individual/group reinforcement, the industrial paradigm, and the status quo.
4	**3**
Local cultural pluralism/democracy exists as a result of transformational organizational change at individual, group, and institutional levels. The culture reflects postindustrial (both/and vs. either/or and partnership vs. power-over) values. Schools embody transformational, social action–oriented curriculum and instruction.	Apparently welcoming on the surface (e. g., affirmative action may be in place). Diversity practiced primarily as contributions/additive approach. Symbolic difference. Cultural responsiveness primarily realized as awareness and sensitivity, yielding incremental reform and symbolic inclusion of those perceived as different from the dominant group.

FIGURE 17–1   Cultural democracy grid.

feel like passive hostility by community members and staff who may feel threatened or slighted by cultural responsiveness to students and parents:

> And I don't care what people tell you, you have some segments of the county here that may talk a good game about minorities and what they do for minority kids, "children of color." But, deep in their hearts, they're hoping that they'll go away.
>
> (superintendent, large school district)

Cultural Democracy Quadrants

As I review my own personal and professional development, I see some patterns, which help me to better understand my experiences and which help me to mentor others who wish to be efficacious in their teacher education programs. I have experienced social and institutionalized educational contexts (i.e., organizational cultures), which range from outwardly hostile to supportive, primarily focused on my race and ethnicity (Romo & Salerno, 2000). I describe these social and educational landscapes (read in a clockwise pattern) as shown in Figure 17–1.[7]

An example of Quadrant 1 might be an exclusive club, whether by race, class, gender, or another characteristic. While a current racial extremist (e.g., Tom Metzger, director of the White Aryan Resistance) and such supporters or followers offer examples of the beliefs and behaviors of individuals in Quadrant 1, institutionalized examples are more difficult to find.

Quadrant 2 is closely related to the above group. Its characteristics are more subtle and more prevalent in society today. As a student recently commented on his beginning perspective:

---

[7]Katz (1989) describes a wonderful chart regarding organizational diversification, which I wish to acknowledge as an influence on my own work.

It would be hard to convince someone from any culture that blue has been mistaken for green since the inception of the color concept. People would probably resist any effort to correct the problem, deeming it arbitrary to societal function. Individuals would most likely have internalized color codes to such a depth that it would be nearly impossible to convince them that change is a necessity. I have learned that it is possible for caring, sensitive, non-racist people to have values so ingrained into their heads that they are blinded to the many inequities that exist in society for different cultures. And unfortunately, these "good" people can perpetuate societal inequities just as often as "bad" people via complacency.

It is in this context that informal and systemic exclusion and discrimination practices abound under the mystique of unexamined values and beliefs, including meritocracy and individualism. It is in this context that "minority" students and adults experience low representation, support, and success in various roles, previously the de facto domain of European-American dominant culture members.

Quadrant 3 relates to an organization in which well-meaning individuals may be described as armchair liberals. In other words, people may talk about culture or value culture in general without having personally internalized the knowledge base, attitudes, values, beliefs, and skills of other groups. In the words of a student:

> Although I have ventured from my cell via site governance team, after-school basketball, and a multitude of district and national programs (including AVID, Triton, CLAD, GATE, NCEE, and a master's degree), I find that I continually return to my cell upon completion and miss the big picture. I attribute this to the fact that all these programs, barring after-school basketball, attempt to teach you about culture without firsthand experience. . . . It is one thing to be aware of the various cultures that exist, but it is another to be an advocate for these cultures.

Finally, Quadrant 4 looks, sounds, and feels like a pluralistic organization. Its membership is not only diverse (including race, gender, and socioeconomic-status representation), but the individual's, informal group's, and institutional practices explicitly promote all students' inclusion and success. At this point, Quadrant 4 may occur at the individual or group level, but it is still a theoretical construct at most institutional levels.[8]

HELPING: WRITING

Because of the hostility towards so many students who are perceived as outsiders, I see my work as promoting cultural democracy through developing antiracist, multiculturally competent teacher advocates for all children. Sometimes I imagine teaching teachers to be like being an emergency room physician, whose educational, political, and interpersonal emergencies most often relate to privilege and racism. Other times, the following story describes teaching teachers.

Years ago, a tightrope walker thrilled a crowd by crossing Niagara Falls on a tightrope. Upon his return to safety, everyone cheered. "Do you think I can cross again, this time pushing a wheelbarrow?" he asked. "Yes!" the people cheered. With

---

[8]See Romo and Salerno (2000) for a discussion of current cultural democracy and Quadrant 4 applications.

that, the acrobat lifted a wheelbarrow to the wire and crossed again. The spectators were amazed. "Do you think I can cross again with a person *in* the wheelbarrow?" "Yes!" they shouted again. "Who will volunteer?" the tightrope walker asked.

As you might guess, no one volunteered. This story illustrates the difference between belief and faith, between intellectual knowledge and practice, and, most particular to this chapter, between knowing about multicultural competency and acting upon that knowledge as a multiculturally competent advocate for all children (MCCAFAC). What does this phrase, *multiculturally competent advocate for all children,* mean, and how does it relate to transformational teaching?

Imagine the scene from the film *The Substitute,* a horrible Rambo-goes-to-teach movie. The substitute enters a large, urban, crowded, graffitied high school classroom. Students are everywhere, dancing to loud music, playing cards, some carrying on in intimate conversation. The substitute interrupts the various behaviors and attempts to begin class. As he writes his name on the board, a student throws an empty soda can and hits him in the back. In the following moments, the substitute begins to take roll and students respond with mocking remarks and obscenities.

I assert that a multiculturally competent advocate for all children must have a level of personal and professional mastery to effectively respond to and transform that kind of scenario into a community of excellent learners. I loosely refer to a person at this teaching level as an educational black belt. This distinction calls for particular knowledge, attitudes, values, beliefs, and performance levels required to respond powerfully and effectively to the scene I described.

I agree with the expression, We don't see the world as it is; we see it as we are. Because of my life experiences, I approach the task of helping students advance in their own MCCAFAC development as an accelerated (multicultural competency) language acquisition process. The first vignette, taken from my teaching journal, illustrates one way I encourage my students to listen to and talk about their own and others' knowledge bases, attitudes, values, beliefs, and skills.

This particular entrance is intended to place the students in the center of a discussion on teacher expectations, stereotypes, perception, and beliefs. I dress in jeans, a Pendleton, and political T-shirt and solicit students' first thoughts and feelings towards my appearance. At the break, I shave, put on a suit and tie, and return to class and discuss perceptions and teacher expectations, as they relate to student achievement. The following narrative describes some of the thoughts I have prior to beginning a class in this manner:

> 4:30:   I've already hidden my change of clothes in the unused restroom, checked with the center assistant about being late, explained to him or her that I'd clean up later if I missed some whiskers at the break, put most handouts, overheads, and videos in the room (in a closet or in some lesser noticed corner).

> 5:15:   Get some water, eat a Tiger Milk bar.

> 5:20:   Walk, no pace. What will they think about me—again? I spend time praying, reassuring myself that the cost of making myself vulnerable to an unknown group and knowing that some will immediately feel defensive, tricked, and possibly resentful is worth the insight and metaphors and direct learning the students will gain.

> 5:30:   Wait a few minutes longer. Put on my Pendleton—maybe shades. Wait till the latecomers get into class and join the rest of the group, wondering if the teacher will

show—after all, they paid enough. "The least the university could do was get some-one there on time." The lateness eats away at me, who wants to model everything, including promptness, that I want my students to develop.

I walk into the classroom silently, take off my shades, put down the cardboard box I've placed a few handouts in, and still silently begin to write on the board:

> Age
> Educational background
> Hobbies
> Other job
> Why here?

I turn and scan the room, stone-facedly making eye contact with each student. Do they think I'm mad because I'm not smiling? I'm actually praying, blessing all of us for the intensive month we'll spend together. "I'd like you to fill in the answers to these questions," I say slowly, with as little California accent as possible, "about *me*."

The dance begins.[9]

I describe high-level advocates (Quadrant 4) as individuals who publicly act as allies or institutional change agents, demonstrating many multicultural competency knowledge base, attitudes, values, beliefs, and skills. A high-level advocate is recog-nized as a mentor for others and acts as a cultural broker between groups to pro-mote institutional cultural democracy.

I locate medium-level MCCAFACs (Quadrant 3) as individuals who are inter-nalizing/developing multicultural competency and applying their competency knowledge base, attitudes, values, beliefs, and skills in individual settings. Medium-level MCCAFACs work informally or interpersonally to transform individual and group-level exclusionary or discriminatory practices. A medium-level MCCAFAC's primary institutionalized domain is in applying culturally democratic curricular and instructional strategies in his or her classroom. I contend that teachers need to op-erate at least as medium-level advocates in order to truly promote equity and democracy, and consequently be educational transformation agents.

I believe that low-level advocates (Quadrant 2) are interested in helping others and are primarily developing their own awareness or sensitivity regarding themselves and others in the context of diversity issues. At this level, she or he may not consciously condone or participate in exclusionary or discriminatory discussions or activities. However, neither will she or he intervene to interrupt such dynamics or activities.

A future teacher manifesting low-level resistance to equity and inclusion (Quadrants 1 & 2) might unwittingly represent the tension reflected in the urban superintendent's quote about many educators. Individuals in this quadrant may defend various dominant culture values and beliefs in a way that justifies (albeit with some apparent sincerity regarding fairness) privilege, exclusion, and/or in-equity. A belief in meritocracy and individualism tends to correlate to individuals who cannot seem to see personal, informal group, or institutional expressions of exclusion or discrimination.

A future teacher manifesting medium- to high-level resistance to equity and inclusion (Quadrant 1) might behave more like the teachers quoted earlier by the

---

[9]I elicited and analyzed formal student feedback from a recent class and from students I had taught 6 months prior, related to my teaching strategies and students' advocacy development. Our discussions led to the benchmarks included in this chapter.

	1	2	3	4	5	6	7	8	9
High advocates			1		3			Student	Presentations
Med advocates	1	8	13	9	15	17	12		
Low advocates	5	11	12	20	12	12	17		
Low resistors	24	8	1	1					
Med resistors									
High resistors	1	1							
Total	31	28	27	30	30	29	29		

FIGURE 17–2 Class meeting student record.

Fraga, Meier, and England (1986) describe second-generation discrimination, wherein students of color are suspended and placed in special education classes in highly disproportionate numbers, in the context of an apparently open and fair school setting. Stanton-Salazar (1997) outlines the importance of academic gatekeepers and their identification with students as a significant aspect of student achievement.

suburban high school principal or the teachers from the school that "will not listen" to a person perceived as an outsider. As I am conscious of my experiences with these kinds of hostile educators, I am motivated to be a transformative teacher of teachers.

Regarding my last class opening, I interpreted one of 31 students' comments as related to a medium-level advocate (Quadrant 3), 5 as related to a low-level advocate (Quadrant 2), 24 as related to a low-level resistor (Quadrants 1 & 2), and 4 as related to high-level resistors (Quadrant 1). Medium-level advocates can apply the exercise to him- or herself and to the immediate circle of influence. Low-level advocate comments registered an expansion of personal experiences or awareness, albeit sometimes registered in the third person. Low-resistance students did not acknowledge a personal application and/or remained focused on the activity or instructor. The medium- and high-resistance students were bluntly critical.

Figure 17–2, based on daily student written feedback, shows the overall shift in awareness, sensitivity, personal application of course materials, and advocacy skill development over the nine class meetings.

The figure supports my experience that the first third of the course builds student awareness and sensitivity by providing cognitive dissonance and support through a safe learning environment. My approach is to, in a constructivist manner, expose and transform their diversity fear: false expectations appearing real. Students from prior classes as far back as 3 years have reported that this opening was very effective in galvanizing their learning and transformation process.

My second example reflects my (multicultural competency) language acquisition bias of giving students frameworks or models (literacy development) regarding personal development, particularly about racism, and encouraging them to apply these to themselves. Here is how many students described their work with McIntosh (1989), Tatum (1992), and other developmental frameworks I provide (Romo & Salerno, 2000):

Student 1: Reflecting on the impact of this class and its related readings on my perspective, I have found that I was living in the belief that discrimination seldom occurs and was only visible in high profile scenarios. Now, I look back to instances in my past where I feel I was a victim of prejudice and discrimination but not aware of the fact at the time. I believe that I permitted those transgressions because I was probably in what is called Stage 1 of the biculturalization process. Basically, I was hesitant to believe there was a conflict between my race/culture and the dominant white culture. I used to think that I belonged in Stage 4 (total integration), but since the model of the biculturalization process is not linear and all of this new information has changed my perception of social equality, I find myself crossing over between Stage 3 (advocate for home culture) and Stage 4.

Student 2: Right now I am empathizing with the student who told you not to take it personally, but that he hated you. I know it is not you I am arguing with in my head. . . . I don't want to deal with it right now; my plate is full. "Why should you be so special that you get to choose when you want to deal with race when we have to deal with it everyday on the bus, in the workplace, everywhere in our lives," rebuffs the voice in my head.

Student 3: It has been hard for me to open up and dig deep within myself and be reminded of painful situations. I feel at this point I am in the Immersion stage. This class has raised my awareness of how little I really know about the history and struggles of Mexican-Americans. I crave more knowledge.

Student 4: I am a member of the white privilege; I never thought about myself that way. I have never thought that I was treated a different way because of my sex or the color of my skin. This, I think, is exactly her message. We are conditioned to think this way. After reading this article, I have come to realize that it doesn't matter how I view myself or my experiences. What matters is that we *do* live in a society dominated by whites and that I am a member of the dominant culture. I think that it is so hard for whites to accept the concept of white privilege because we would have to give up the "myth of meritocracy," that people get ahead because of what they do and not for who they are (or, more specifically, what color they are).

As a gardening analogy goes, if my class opening was like tilling intellectual soil, this aspect of my teaching relates to mixing the newly opened intellectual soil with nutrients. The students tend to initially report frustration and a sense of cognitive dissonance with the material. As the students begin to develop their ability to see their feelings and develop consciousness in perspective, they also report a sense of liberation and empowerment:

Student 5: As McIntosh points out, not all of the white privileges are necessarily bad, but that we should strive to make them universal for all people regardless of color. True democracy, meritocracy, equal access to housing, jobs, education, and respect would be a start. As a white person of the dominant culture, I have a responsibility to be aware of white privileges, to bring up the issue of white privilege to other white people, to strive to eradicate the aspects of white privilege that denigrate other cultures, and to promote aspects that help everyone have access to the advantages afforded members of the dominant white society.

Student 6: Using the grid on multicultural competency readiness and where I would fit, I see myself coming out of Quadrant 2 and progressing to Quadrant 4. I was raised on the idea of assimilation, so it will take a lot of unlearning to be a complete bicultural competent educator, as shown in Quadrant 4. This is something I will work on as a teacher.

In conclusion, my journey towards wholeness, literacy, Bly's "Black Knight" and Ignatian "Transcendence" is no less complex or difficult than my students' journeys. As a Latino raised in poverty, violence, abuse, and shame, I identify with those who are currently seen as outsiders to our educational institutions. As a highly educated, English-speaking, middle-class male, I use my privileges to influence organizational transformation through developing actively antiracist and antiexclusionary teachers. I believe that these teaching candidates' efforts in their particular school communities, combined with any number of external pressures related to improved character development, international economic competition, or academic performance, will till the soil and nurture the seeds of organizational transformation and cultural democracy.[10]

Inasmuch as cultural democracy is a societal good, personal bi- or multicultural competency[11] is an individual good. Indeed, I assert that to aspire to less promotes the implosion of our democratic ideal and the return to some of the worst examples of our collective inhumanity. I have discussed my interpretations of transformative teaching. I challenge those who assert that, for various reasons, we cannot change society, institutionally or individually. I do not question whether transformative teaching can really happen in K–12 or higher education, or in an intensive month-long format with well-intended and resistant students. I question how we can tolerate less. Meanwhile, I am grateful for the opportunity to serve as a mentor for teachers, who in turn continue my own development as a multiculturally competent advocate for all children.

Sigo pensando America,	I keep thinking America
que vamos a encontrarte,	that we will surely find you,
ese es nuestro destino,	this is our destiny
nuestra necesidad,	and our necessity,
Si el sueno de uno,	If the dream of one,
es el sueno de todos	can be the dream of many
romper las cadenas	to break the chains
y echarnos andar	and begin the work,
Entonces tengamos confianza	then we shall have confidence
que America es nuestra casa.	that America is our home.
(Ruben Blades, in Darder, 1995)	

[10]Cultural democracy is the institutional support for all cultural voices to be heard and integrated within the changing culture and history of the institution. Such a transformation includes the redistribution of material and nonmaterial benefits within the academy, as well as the transformation of ideological tenets, which systematically marginalize the participation of people of color, women, gays and lesbians, and the working class (Darder, 1994, p. 821).

[11]Bicultural competency is the ability to advocate for, speak as a member of, and be accepted as a member of two cultural groups. This comes after developing awareness, sensitivity, and internalized appreciation for both groups.

REFERENCES

Acuna, R. (1988). *Occupied America: A history of Chicanos* (3rd ed.). New York: Harper & Row.

Chomsky, N., & Foucault, M. (1974). Human nature: Justice versus power. In F. Elders (Ed.), *Reflexive water: The basic concerns of mankind.* (pp. 134–197). London: Souvenir.

Clandinin, D. J., Davies, A., Hogan, P., & Kennard, B. (Eds.). (1993). *Learning to teach, teaching to learn: Stories of collaboration in teacher education.* New York: Teachers College Press.

Darder, A. (1994, Spring). Institutional research as a tool for cultural democracy. *New Directions for Institutional Research, 81,* 21–34.

Darder, A. (1995). *Buscando America: The contribution of critical Latino educators to the academic development and empowerment of Latino students in the U.S.* Albany: State University of New York Press.

Delgado, R. (1995). *The Rodrigo chronicles: Conversations about America and race.* New York: New York University Press.

Fraga, L. R., Meier, K. J., & England, R. E. (1986). Hispanic Americans and educational policy: Limits to equal access. *The Journal of Politics, 48,* 850–876.

Freire, P. (1985). *A pedagogy of the oppressed.* New York: Continuum.

Giroux, H. A. (1992). *Border crossings: Cultural workers and the politics of education.* New York: Routledge, Chapman & Hall.

Holstein, J. A., & Gubrium, J. F. (1994). Phenomenology, ethnomethodology, and interpretive practice. In N. Denzin & S. Lincoln (Eds.), *Handbook of qualitative research* (pp. 262–272). Thousand Oaks, CA: Sage.

Katz, J. (1989). The challenge of diversity. In C. Woolbright (Ed.), Valuing diversity on campus: A multicultural approach. *College Unions at Work Monograph Series, 11,* 1–21. Bloomington, IN: Association of College Unions–International.

McIntosh, P. (1990, Winter). Unpacking the knapsack of white privilege. *Peace and Freedom, 49*(2), 31–35.

Ochoa, A. M. (2002, October). *Latino Summit Educational Achievement Report.* Paper presented at the San Diego County Office of Education for Latino Advisory Council, San Diego, CA.

Romo, J., & Salerno, C. (2000). Towards cultural democracy: The journey from knowledge to action in diverse classrooms. Boston: Houghton Mifflin.

Scheurich, J. J. (1993, November). Toward a white discourse on white racism. *Educational Researcher, 22* (8), 5–10.

Smith, K. (1990). Notes from the epistemological corner: The role of projection in the creation of social science. *Journal of Applied Behavioral Science, 26,* 119–127.

Solis, A. (1981). Theory of biculturality. *Calmecac de Aztlan en Los, 2,* 36–41.

Stanton-Salazar, R. D. (1997, Spring). A social capital framework for understanding the socialization of racial minority children and youths. *Harvard Educational Review, 67*(1), 1–41.

Tatum, B. D. (1992). Talking about race, learning about racism: The application of racial identity development theory in the classroom. *Harvard Educational Review, 62*(1), 1–24.

Classroom Activities

The following questions will help to clarify many of the blatant and hidden privileges that affect students in our classrooms and that affected us as we grew up. This activity is most effective when completed with a group. Because some of the questions are very personal, I suggest that you complete this assignment with people you feel comfortable with. I do not suggest that you have students participate in this activity, unless you have tried it first and have a high level of trust, respect, and confidentiality in your classroom and are willing to deal with the follow-up discussions.

The activity itself may only take 10 to 15 minutes. The discussion afterwards may take 15 to 30 minutes. It is helpful for each participant to take a similar-sized step in order to compare outcomes. Thanks to Dr. Al McLeod, California State University at Fresno, for developing this activity.

Read these directions even if you do not follow them:

1. Select a place (a large room or an open space outdoors) where you and the other participants can concentrate on your thoughts and feelings as you silently take steps forward and backwards.
2. Read the directions out loud.
3. Pause after you read each descriptor to allow all participants to move and observe where others are in the activity.
4. Discuss the initial responses to the activity from the spots where each participant ends up (e.g., How was this activity for you to participate in?). Follow some guided discussion protocol (no interruptions, cross-talk, etc.). After some initial discussion about personal insights as well as insights into students in schools, allow a few minutes for participants to talk individually with a person with whom they need to follow up in conversation.

This is primarily an activity for your personal awareness, sensitivity, insight, and advocacy development. When you report about this activity through the discussion thread, you should focus on your personal application of any insights that came up for you as a result of it.

A. If you believe you've ever been discriminated against because of your gender, take one step back. Answer the same question, substituting:

- Because of your race or ethnic group
- Because of your religion
- Because you were perceived as coming from a lower social class
- Because of your sexual orientation (optional).

B. If you believe you've ever been favored or given special treatment because of your gender, take one step forward. Answer the same question, substituting:

- Because of your race or ethnic group
- Because of your religion
- Because you were perceived as coming from a lower social class
- Because of your sexual orientation (optional).

C. If you've ever wished you were a different gender, take one step back. Answer the same question with the other categories in A and B.

D. Take one step forward if you were raised in a home with both parents present most of the time. Use the same direction for the following questions:

- If you believed your parents had a good marriage
- If you had older siblings who inspired you in important positive ways
- If you had no more than two siblings
- If your mother had a college degree
- If your father had a college degree
- If one or more of your siblings had a college degree

- If your home had 100 or more books in it
- If you regularly saw someone reading
- If someone regularly read to you or told you stories
- If you took several trips with your parents as a child
- If you could have good talks about most anything with your parents
- If you were reading fairly well prior to first grade
- If you felt like you were accepted, liked, and given support in the early years of school
- If you went to a private school
- If you did well in school
- If you had several good friends in school.

E. Take one step backward if while growing up:

- You felt like your family was generally not liked in your neighborhood in which you grew up
- You felt your home or neighborhood was dangerous in some way
- You witnessed violence in your home or neighborhood
- You ever heard gunshots in your home or neighborhood
- One or both of your parents abused alcohol
- One or both of your parents abused illegal drugs
- You saw or believed drugs were being sold and used in your neighborhood
- You believed or knew that someone in your home was sexually promiscuous or had affairs
- You perceived that quite a few people around you were "losers"
- You experienced a death in your family before you were 12 years of age
- Your family always seemed on the edge of not having enough food to eat
- You were frequently ashamed because your clothes were old, hand-me-downs, or out of style
- You witnessed a lot of people not keeping their commitments to each other and/or to their jobs
- Someone you knew well was sent to prison
- You feared you might be sent to prison before you grew up
- There were gangs in your neighborhood
- You felt some pressure to join a gang
- You felt that life was generally harsh and unfair.

Conclusion: Encourage people to look at each other silently and reflectively for a minute or so, making their own sense and meaning out of what they see. Then ask for insights and experiences individuals had while participating in the activity. Finally, explore what the activity and insights have to do with our students, and us as teachers.

Note: This current version of the privilege walk is appropriate for college students or preservice teachers. For K–12 students, I encourage the reader to adapt the questions to meet the developmental levels of your students and particular purposes for your classroom.

WEB SITES

University of Southern California Center for Multicultural/Multilingual research:
http://www-bcf.usc.edu/~cmmr/News.html

Teaching Tolerance (Southern Poverty Law Center):
http://www.splcenter.org/teachingtolerance/tt-index.html

Multicultural Pavilion:
http://curry.edschool.virginia.edu/curry/centers/multicultural/arts/songs.html

Teaching 9-11-01:
http://www.teaching9-11.org

Teachers for Social Justice:
http://www.teachers4socialjustice.org

California Consortium of Critical Educators:
http://www.ccce.net

Nike Wages and Social Justice Education:
http://www.nikewages.org/menupage.html

 *Afterword*

Struggles for Recognition and Redistribution

Patrick Shannon, Pennsylvania State University, University Park

Reading the chapters of *Reclaiming Democracy* is like sitting around with friends swapping stories. Here's my contribution.

One of my most vivid memories of youth is a championship boxing match between Muhammad Ali and Ernie Terrell that my father and I watched one Saturday afternoon on *Wide World of Sports*. It was early in Ali's championship years, before he refused to fight in the Vietnam War, but after he had knocked out Sonny Liston, who took a dive. Terrell was enormous, skilled, and brave enough to have taunted Ali before the fight by refusing to call him by his new Muslim name. Terrell referred to his opponent as Cassius Clay—Ali's given name, but one he then associated with slavery. As I remember, it was only a short time before Ali began to pummel Terrell. He wouldn't knock Terrell out though, and my father dismissed Ali as "a light puncher"—thinking he couldn't finish Terrell off. It was clear, however, that Ali was keeping Terrell on his feet with punches as he repeatedly asked Terrell, "What's my name?" And in retrospect it wasn't just Terrell who was being asked forcefully to recognize Ali's new name. Rather, it was my father, me, and all of America being told to acknowledge that the old order was being challenged by new sets of ideas, goals, and people.

Ali's performance clearly presented his sociological imagination. That term, coined by C. Wright Mills (1959), suggests an ability to create imaginative reconstructions of larger social forces that affect our lives. Ali's efforts to reclaim this power to name oneself and the world indicate that this practice is not just for sociologists. Rather, anyone might employ sociological imagination in order to explore problems that beset her or him. In our living room, then, it seemed to be a bout between two men in which each attempted to beat the other senseless and both employed psychology to upset the other.

Now the match seems more a metaphoric struggle between two publics: one demanding that the other recognize its existence in the world and the other clinging to the status quo. Within the context of sociological imagination, the controversy over Ali's name was no longer a personal problem but, rather, a public struggle over recognition. Sociological imagination seems a remarkable catalyst for social change, because

> Without this sociological skill, people are left with the belief that the troubles in their lives are their own doing, or perhaps, the result of some abstract fate, but in either case, they feel that these are matters with respect to which they should and do, feel guilty. The sociological imagination refers to the ability of some to learn—often with good luck or coaching or perhaps formal schooling—to realize that, just as often, one's personal troubles are in fact public issues.   (Lemert, 1998, p. 12)

The contributors to this book demonstrate sociological imagination as they relate their stories in ways that enable readers to see that their trials and tribulations, while personal, are not private or isolated. Rather, they see similarities among the troubles which they or their students face. Moreover, the contributors attribute these problems to structural barriers embedded in social institutions, social policies, and social discourse. At times, they relate how people internalize the logic of these barriers, causing them to neglect their sociological imaginations and to work against themselves. The editors of the book have grouped the chapters for readers to help readers see the similarities, the public nature of the troubles, and the possibilities for productive social action. The editors call this transformative teaching, in which the sociological imagination is aroused, the complexities of difference are explored, and plans for democratic action can be made.

THE COMPLEXITIES OF DIFFERENCE

All contributors recognize the failed attempts at democracy in the 20th century. Self-labeled democratic nations have been unsuccessful in securing universal participation in civic life. In the United States, only half of those eligible to vote do so in national elections; many individuals and groups feel alienated from civic life, even at a local level, and wealth subverts efforts to engage the alienated. Collectivist attempts to overcome the limits of liberal democracy, often through single-party systems, have been unable to protect individual rights of freedom as they tried to construct societies to ensure the universal rights of freedom from want. Perhaps these failures are predictable, given the inabilities of these societies to take up the issue of diversity productively: "What we share and what makes us fellow citizens in a liberal democratic regime is not a substantive idea of the good, but a set of political principles specific to such a tradition, the principles of freedom and equality for all" (Mouffee, 1993, p. 65).

Although conservatives, liberals, and even collectivists claim their positions to be founded on principles of freedom and equality, their respective visions of the good forces them to promote differing definitions of freedom and equality, and to demand consensus about visions and definitions on their terms alone. To the contrary, the contributors to this book suggest that democratic politics require difference among people, cultures, visions, and actions as they advocate for their interpretations and their preferred social or collective identities:

> It is the tension between consensus—on the values [freedom and equality]—and disssensus—on the interpretation—that makes possible the agonistic dynamics of plurist democracy. This is why its survival depends on the possibility of forming collective political identities around clearly differentiated positions and the choice among real alternatives.
>
> (Mouffee, 1995, p. 107)

As the contributors explain, many people in America reject the identities that traditional U.S. ideologies afford them. The Ali–Terrell bout portrays this metaphorically. Conservatives reject Ali's right to name himself and instead offer him a fixed identity with limited opportunities to articulate his life choices or to choose among those available. These limits deter interest in participating in civic life, because consciously or unconsciously, we understand the limits on our freedom and the absence of equality on these conditions. Of course, this alienation leaves traditions and power relations unchanged and little challenged. Liberals might encourage Ali to call himself whatever he likes, just as long as he does his naming within unaltered social, economic, and political structures. Despite the outward appearances of difference (a more humane basis to those structures), the consequences of liberalism are much the same as conservatism, with more cultural freedom possible:

> The liberal version of multiculturalism is premised on a one-sidedly, positive understanding of difference. It celebrates difference uncritically while failing to interrogate its relation to inequality. Like American pluralism, the tradition from which it descends, it proceeds—contrary to fact—as if United States society contained no class divisions or other deep-seated structural injustices, as if its political-economy were basically just, as if constituent groups were socially equal. Thus, it treats difference as pertaining exclusively to culture. The result is to divorce questions of difference from material inequality, power differentials among groups, and systemic relations of dominance and subordination.
>
> (Fraser, 1996, p. 206)

For democracy to work, individuals must recognize that their identities are multiple and fluid. Ali is a slave, Muslim, champion, conscientious objector, American patriot, world citizen, self-promoter, and selfless volunteer. In fact, we are all members of many social groups that influence our thoughts, actions, and values in substantial ways, and we vary our hierarchical arrangements of those memberships according to circumstances and intentions. Beyond that recognition, citizens must learn to use this power to force clear articulations of positions by forming coalitions to enact their shared concerns. Democracy, then, hinges on the development of individual identities that are committed to the values of freedom and equality and active participation in civic life. These are the identities the contributors describe in each chapter. Although these descriptions are not fully specified, they seem to share three elements: reflexive agency, the will to act, and the ability to make room for the adversary.

Reflexive agency invites citizens to evaluate the world in terms of their intentions and values, and at the same time to evaluate those intentions and to reflect upon those values. In this way, citizens take inventory of their identities, values, motives, and actions, investigate the sources of those parts of themselves, and make choices about which ones they hope to enhance and which they hope to diminish.

The will to act, which for many has been diverted from public life to matters of consumption, must be redirected through individuals' sociological imagination. As individuals become aware of the political possibilities of their multiple and fluid identities and the real opportunities to form larger, more effective coalitions for accomplishing goals shared across social groups, the will to act in civic life increases. Reflexive agency ensures that coalitions will not become fixed power blocks, as basic and secondary assumptions for action are consistently scrutinized.

Because those identities are not fixed and future intersections of values cannot be predetermined, citizens begin to recognize the need to respect the positions of their adversaries—not to the point of agreement, of course, but enough to recognize commitment to the shared principles of freedom and equality. The limits on this respect are set by individuals' and groups' commitment to those principles. Anyone rejecting freedom and equality outright stands outside the democratic process and, therefore, becomes the legitimate object of democratic scorn: "Adversaries will fight about the interpretation and the ranking of values, but their common allegiance to the values that constitute the liberal democratic form of life creates a bond of solidarity that expresses their belonging to the common we" (Moufee, 1995, p. 107).

PLANS FOR DEMOCRATIC ACTION

During our lifetimes, the voices represented in these chapters have been louder or softer, but they have been ever present. They have negotiated laws and policies to protect against social and political discrimination, although as the contributors attest, these laws and policies have been often poorly enforced for the last 25 years. When my father and I watched Ali give notice that things were to change, we lived in the midst of shared relative economic prosperity that had not been seen before, nor has it been seen since. The poverty level was below 10% and falling, and more Americans seemed willing to consider both freedom and equality. The majority of voters at that time had experienced the Great Depression and believed that governments should be ultimately responsible for the welfare of their citizens. The remission of the need for the struggle for the redistribution of wealth during the 1960s afforded social space in which struggles for recognition (those recounted in this book) could occupy a central position in progressive politics.

Now the poverty level is 16% nationally and rising, with the official poverty line for family income drawn woefully low. Within the tyranny of global capitalism, more and more U.S. workers are downsized to much less secure economic positions. The gap between rich and poor is widening to the greatest distance in our history. Ten percent of U.S. citizens own two thirds of the nation's wealth. Income levels of poor, working-class, and nearly all middle-class families have declined steadily since 1973, and this drop would be more steep if not for women entering the workforce in great numbers.

At the turn of the last century, a similar economic reality was as readily apparent, with at least one important difference. In the 1890s, the social and economic trajectory for the nation's have-nots was positive because capitalists needed better-educated workers to fill the factories. Now, we are experiencing a downward turn to the prospects for nearly one third of U.S. citizens, who have been rendered unnecessary to business because of technology. Our current governments have employed a politics of subtraction, reducing the braces of federal and state safety nets when our need is greatest. The competition is fierce for jobs that pay a living wage—not for lack of skilled workers, but for lack of good jobs—and there is little help from government if you lose that competition.

Positioned to see fellow citizens as threats to their families' security, many in the United States fail to use any sociological imagination and learn to fear all others who can be characterized as not like them. Perversely, the economic and social structures that create and feed on this anxiety contribute directly to the extraordinary accumulation of wealth among the rich. Downsizing and benefit concessions by labor often translate into gains in a company's stock value.

This economic vulnerability has caused many to become less attuned to struggles for recognition. The end of affirmative action, the demonization of single mothers, black men, and immigrants, and the English-only movements suggest that the influences of these struggles are less direct than they once were. As Robert Putnam (2000) explained in his book *Bowling Alone: America's Declining Social Capital,* fewer U.S. citizens venture into civic life beyond writing a check for membership in the Sierra Club, the National Organization of Women, or the world's largest association, the American Association of Retired People.

With insecurity about fundamental human needs, U.S. citizens seem less likely to associate with and attend to the needs of others. As a nation, we seem less willing to even hear others' voices as they hang from fences in Wyoming, are dragged by trucks in Texas, are sodomized with broom handles in New York City police stations, and are beaten and raped at home or on the street. Our capacities for empathetic understanding are nearly swallowed whole by our economic insecurities. Without strong advocates among the media and government for the growing numbers of poor, and members of what former secretary of labor Robert Reich called the "anxious class," the prospects for freedom and equality within the United States seems bleak. The contributors to this book demonstrate for readers that these issues cannot be easily separated from our daily work in schools.

There have been changes in the conceptualization and practices of schooling during the last 50 years, and we should celebrate the political victories—where the literary canon has been expanded, where cultural differences are sought and examined, where boundaries among teachers, students, and community members are blurred in order to balance commitments to freedom and equality. However, the recent movements toward federal and state governmental control of curriculum and assessment, and even instruction in some places, are steps backward. As those who propose and pursue those controls seek to instantiate their definitions of freedom and equality for all, they work from traditional political ideological positions that cannot deal productively with difference or inequality.

Reflecting upon our positions in these "reforms" while reading the chapters of this book, we discover that these traditional ideologies do not determine our identities as teachers completely. As the contributors to this volume report, they do not lock us, and we are not locked, in fixed positions. We can still use our sociological imaginations within the structures set in the past and present. We might begin by asking ourselves how these ideologies have influenced us, which elements we value and which we no longer value, and what other possibilities are available to us. Our multiple group memberships offer us the possibility of challenging our current positions and creating new alliances and allegiances. We can choose to engage in civic life through our teaching, recognizing ongoing issues of recognition of difference and reemerging struggles of redistribution of economic and cultural wealth as central to our efforts. Through our work, we can provide new spaces and new capacities for all U.S. citizens to produce less violent equivalents to Ali's declarative question, "What's my name?" in order to bring struggles for recognition and redistribution together.

Transformative teachers should struggle to define and develop ways in which schooling can provide service to democratic projects that seek to extend freedom and equality into more aspects of our lives without privileging one too greatly over the other. Those efforts require us to engage in the identification and maintenance of structures that help individuals (re)construct democratic identities of reflexive agency, the will to act, and respect for adversaries and differences. The public nature of transformative teachers' politics—and they could be more public and open—creates spaces in which we can make visible both the limits of current ideologies that attempt to close the open narratives of democracy and the differences heard in civil rights, and student and feminist movements, which accompanied Ali's question. Once these limits are visible, we must be prepared to push against them until we have transformed the structures of schooling in ways directed by our sociological imaginations. The contributors to this book ask you to roll up your sleeves and push.

REFERENCES

Fraser, N. (1996). Equality, difference, and radical democracy. In D. Trend (Ed.), *Radical democracy* (pp. 197–208). New York: Routledge.

Lemert, C. (1998). *Social things.* Boulder, CO: Rowman & Littlefield.

Mills, C. W. (1959). *The sociological imagination.* New York: Oxford University Press.

Mouffee, C. (1993). *The return to the political.* New York: Verso.

Mouffee, C. (1995). Politics, democratic action, and solidarity. *Inquiry, 38,* 99–108.

Putnam, R. (2000). *Bowling alone: America's declining social capital.* New York: Simon & Schuster.